Land of Strangers

LAND
OF
STRANGERS

The Civilizing Project in Qing Central Asia

ERIC SCHLUESSEL

COLUMBIA UNIVERSITY PRESS *NEW YORK*

Columbia University Press
Publishers Since 1893
New York   Chichester, West Sussex
cup.columbia.edu
Copyright © 2020 Columbia University Press
All rights reserved
Library of Congress Cataloging-in-Publication Data
Names: Schluessel, Eric, author.
Title: Land of strangers : the civilizing project in Qing Central Asia / Eric Schluessel.
Description: New York : Columbia University Press, 2020. | Includes bibliographical
references and index.
Identifiers: LCCN 2020010173 (print) | LCCN 2020010174 (ebook) | ISBN 9780231197540
(hardcover) | ISBN 9780231197557 (paperback) | ISBN 9780231552226 (ebook)
Subjects: LCSH: Xinjiang Uygur Zizhiqu (China)—History. | Xinjiang Uygur Zizhiqu
(China)—Ethnic relations. | Xinjiang Uygur Zizhiqu (China)—Politics and government. |
Uighur (Turkic people)—History. | China—Colonies—China—Xinjiang Uygur Zizhiqu. |
Asia, Central—Relations—China. | China—Relations—Asia, Central. |
China—History—Qing dynasty, 1644–1912.
Classification: LCC DS793.S62 .S35 2020 (print) | LCC DS793.S62 (ebook) | DDC 951/.6035—dc23
LC record available at https://lccn.loc.gov/2020010173
LC ebook record available at https://lccn.loc.gov/2020010174

Columbia University Press books are printed on permanent and durable acid-free paper.
Printed in the United States of America
Cover design: Milenda Nan Ok Lee
Cover image: Bilingual Chaghatay-Chinese document, dated 1928.
Photo by author.

To Gwendolyn, who revels in the marginalia

Contents

CONTENTS

Acknowledgments

To my colleagues who have disappeared, or are imprisoned, or silenced: I wish that I could name you here and celebrate your scholarship. I hope that someday you will read this book, and that, when you do, it pleases you. You nurtured me—you were patient when I was headstrong, subtle when I was brash. You taught me diligence, dedication, and commitment to historical and scientific truth. Thank you for welcoming me in.

Thank you to Gwendolyn Collaço, without whom none of this is worth it. You push me to be better—as a scholar and as a person—and to seek out moments of joy. Thank you for your perspicacious eye and quick mind, and for insisting that I take breaks.

This book is the product of many years of other people's kindness. Members of the original dissertation committee tolerated the mounds of paper that I occasionally wadded up and lobbed haphazardly in their directions. Thank you to Mark Elliott for taking me on as a student, pushing me to consider the position and impact of scholarly work, and insisting on philological rigor. You were there for me during some of the hardest times in this process, and I will never forget it. Thank you to Michael Szonyi, who showed me how to build an argument that might withstand his vigorous questioning, fielded endless queries about puzzling through local archives, and modeled a joyful and humane professionalism. Ildikó Bellér-Hann was present in this work from its very conception. Her insightful methodological and empirical critiques enriched the argument greatly, ensuring that it remained grounded in ethnography and textual scholarship while engaging wisely with theory. William Alford, who is a profoundly benevolent individual, saw the value in this work's underlying project and encouraged me to pursue a more disciplined comparison. From the age before Harvard, the humid days of Indiana, I must thank Gardner Bovingdon, who taught me Xinjiang history and politics but, just as importantly, let me play in the great sandbox of social theory. Much of this book is a working-out of questions that I began to ask because of Gardner. Devin DeWeese not only taught me Chaghatay and all sorts of things about Naqshbandīs but was kind enough to read a draft of chapter 6 all of fourteen years after I first walked into his classroom. It has been a great pleasure to reconnect with Christopher Atwood, who understands what kind of book this is. Many other established scholars have given their time and effort to support my mad caper, among them Pär Cassel, Cemal Kafadar, Ablet Kamalov, James Millward, Carla Nappi, Ahmed Ragab, David J. Roxburgh, Birgit Schlyter, Jun Sugawara, Donald Sutton, Onuma Takahiro, and Qiu Yuanyuan. Yet special thanks surely go to Wheeler Thackston, on whose sofa I learned not only to puzzle through a text in Chaghatay, but to grasp it. I hope sincerely to pay their generosity forward.

There is no creativity without a community, and I am fortunate to be part of a generous one. So many hours of intellectual ferment were spent in the company of other true believers in this quixotic enterprise, not least among them Gregory Afinogenov, Katherine Alexander, Elise Anderson, Sarah Bramao-Ramos, David Brophy, Darren Byler, Belle Cheves, Sakura Christmas, Brian Cwiek, Maura Dykstra, Devin Fitzgerald, Joshua Freeman, Billy French, Kelly Hammond, Justin Jacobs, Macabe Keliher, Nicholas Kontovas, Ben Levey, Eve McGlynn, Aysima Mirsultan, Anne-Sophie Pratte, David Porter, Max Oidtmann, Guldana Salimjan, Rune Steenberg, David Stroup, Hannah Theaker, Rian Thum, Wei-chieh Tsai, Noriko Unno, Nicholas Walmsley, and Xin Wen. Special thanks to Mira Xenia Schwerda, who volunteered to read this shambles of a book the weekend before it was due. Many of us met under a purposefully vague rallying cry—"New Directions"—and the promise of snacks, or else because of our questionable decision to study Inner Asian history and culture. We seem repeatedly to demonstrate the power of community, of generosity and collegiality, to raise all of us up and help us achieve the "impossible"—which is precisely how some originally characterized the concept of this book. Thank you for reading the drafty chapters that emerged over the years, but thank you also, as times have grown darker, for standing up for what you know to be right. That is the kind of scholarly community I want to be part of.

Friends and colleagues at the University of Montana in the Departments of History and Political Science and beyond lent time and patience to this project. Thank you especially to Claire Arcenas, Abhishek Chatterjee, Brad Clough, John Eglin, Robert Greene, Tobin Miller-Shearer, and Jody Pavilack for understanding. Thank you to the core members of the Montana East Asia Workshop, or MEAW: Brian Dowdle, Maggie Greene, and Rob Tuck. I am glad that we value one another as scholars and as human beings. Time spent with you—over Rob's unfairly good cooking, Brian's backyard dinners, or fleeing into the mountains to meet Maggie halfway—has meant the world to me. Much of the thinking behind this book played out in conversation with my students at Montana as we tracked patterns of change across the broad sweep of Chinese history, talked through Neo-Confucian philosophy, or critiqued theories of nationalism. If you read this, please understand that it is a singular privilege to know you and work with you. Take a moment to look east along the Clark Fork River, into the space between the mountains, and consider the mystery.

The final draft of this book was completed during research leave under a Mellon Fellowship at the Institute for Advanced Study, where conversations with Nicola di Cosmo, Karl Gerth, and Lydia Liu especially influenced its composition. Research and writing have been paid for in various ways by numerous grants and fellowships: a Fellowship for Assistant Professors from the Andrew W. Mellon Foundation; research and workshop grants from the American Council of Learned Societies and Henry Luce Foundation; a Social Science Research Council International Dissertation Research Fellowship; a faculty development grant from the Department of History at the University of Montana; a Yamaguchi Fund grant from the Mansfield Center at the University of Montana; a one-month residence at the Yuelu Academy at Hunan University; traveling fellowships from Harvard University, the Weatherhead Center for International Affairs, the Fairbank Center for Chinese Studies, and the Asia Center; and a fellowship from the National Endowment for the Humanities dedicated to translating the *Tārīkh-i Ḥamīdī*. The last few weeks of writing were spent as a scholar-in-residence at the Manchester China Institute.

Thank you to Caelyn Cobb and Monique Briones at Columbia University Press, who ushered this book to print with the utmost speed and professionalism. Two anonymous readers enriched the text by providing two radically different perspectives on it. I take full responsibility for any errors that remain and ask others to take them up as prompts for further research.

Thank you, finally, to my father Richard Schluessel, my mother Cynthia Conti, and my brother Edmund Schluessel, who taught me to care, to work hard, and to remain true to my principles. This has been such a long journey, and I am glad that you are here to share it. Of course, I would be remiss not to acknowledge the singular contributions of Ş. and P., our household agents of chaos.

The sources for this work are ragged—they are jagged scratches on mouse-eaten scraps of rustic paper that smell like sheep and death. No neatly sorted case files greet the historian of Turpan. An individual document might be torn in half, intentionally or through some human error, and tucked in the fold of another according to some obscure logic. Stories begin, or end, or pick up in the middle of the action, and the historian is lucky to find a whole narrative packaged and waiting. Even then, half of the story may be a deception. Such is life: a collage of letters cut off halfway through, with lines on every color of paper intersecting at odd angles, and it is beautiful. Thank you all for sharing this cloak of rags with me. May others pull at the threads until everything comes undone again.

A Note on Conventions

This book works between several languages and traditions, some of which may be obscure to the reader.

Chinese reign dates and Hijri dates have both been converted to their equivalents in the Gregorian calendar. Most of this story takes place during the Tongzhi (1861–75, abbreviated in this book's endnotes as "TZ"), Guangxu (1875–1908, or "GX"), and Xuantong (1908–11, or "XT") reigns, and in the years 1280–1330 of the Hijri. It continues in the era of the Republic of China (Minguo, or "MG").

Women in Qing documents were frequently identified only by their surname, followed by the word *shi*. "Wei *shi*," then, is roughly equivalent to "Ms. Wei" or "the woman Wei."

Age as recorded in Chinese sources is reckoned in *sui*. A person is one *sui* old at the moment of birth, and consequently may be one or two years older in Western "years old" than they would be in *sui*.

Yamen was the term used for the office of any Qing official. Terminology for Qing ranks and titles in general follows that provided by Brunnert and Hagelstrom, which although somewhat antiquated is comprehensive enough to include the terms of local administration and reflects a certain understanding of the Qing government around the time this story took place.[1] In the late Qing, Turpan was a "directly administered prefecture" (*zhili ting*), and its highest official a "first-class subprefect." I therefore refer to him as "the prefect." Under the Turpan prefect was the subordinate office of the Pichan "subdistrict magistrate" (*xunjian*). In 1902, Pichan was elevated to the level of a "county" (*xian*), forming Shanshan County, and the subdistrict magistrate was made a full county magistrate. After the Xinhai Revolution of 1911 and the fall of the Qing, Turpan was made a county equal to Shanshan, and its prefect a magistrate.

Turpan was located in one of four administrative units called "circuits" (*dao*), each led by an "intendant" (*daotai*). Turpan was in the Zhendi Circuit of Xinjiang province, and the others were the Aksu, Kashgar, and Ili-Tarbaghatai Circuits. Those intendants reported to a provincial government in the capital of Dihua (modern Ürümchi) headed by a governor (*xunfu*). The governor's immediate subordinates included a financial commissioner (*buzhengshi*) and a judicial commissioner (*anchashi*).

I have chosen to present names and words in the various languages in this book in ways that readers will hopefully not find alienating. Chinese is transliterated according to the Pinyin system. For Arabic, Persian, and Chaghatay I use a modified version of the system of the *International Journal of Middle Eastern Studies*; for Manchu, Möllendorff; and Japanese, Hepburn. Diacritics have been minimized as much as possible.

As minority people in China know well, using Chinese to render long names that include sounds not encountered in Mandarin often yields even longer and unwieldier results. This was true in late-Qing Xinjiang as well, where the Turkic and Islamic names that we encounter in Chinese in the archive sometimes barely resemble what people called themselves. Helpfully, I have found documents in the Turpan archive that present Turco-Islamic names and their Chinese equivalents side by side, providing a relatively systematic understanding of how Turkic speech sounds were rendered into Chinese. On that basis, I present the most likely Turko-Islamic name, if it can be deciphered, alongside its Chinese transliteration in the first instance, for example, "Rawżallah (Ruozangle)." I follow a similar system for place names, in which case I favor the name as it was rendered in Chaghatay over that used in Chinese.

Introduction

AT THE END of the nineteenth century, a group of elite men from China gained control over a Muslim-majority region of Central Asia and attempted to transform it according to their own vision of an ideal Confucian society. This book describes the ramifications of this project for ordinary people. It argues that this effort to transform Muslims into Confucians shaped the social relationships between people who participated in different religious traditions and who spoke different languages. Instead of the assimilation that this civilizing project's engineers intended, it produced estrangement, as the project simultaneously intensified the inequalities and everyday violence that typified the new era, imbued them with new meanings, and provided a powerful new language with which to navigate them. People used its ideology and institutions to police new social boundaries and articulate communal identities in ways that both resisted Chinese domination and were shaped by it. New or reimagined myths of common descent redefined the boundaries of the Muslim community.[1]

The setting of this history of sociocultural change and the everyday is a place that history-writing and the popular consciousness understand mainly through grand political narratives: Xinjiang.[2] Xinjiang, or East Turkestan, is a region that is culturally, linguistically, and historically tied to the societies and states of Central Asia. As of the turn of the last century, the majority of its people spoke and wrote in Turkic languages and practiced a form of Sunni Islam heavily influenced by Sufism. Yet these

"Turkic Muslim" people had come under the control of a China-based state, the Qing empire (1644–1911).[3] While Qing territory later defined the boundaries of the modern Chinese nation-state, the empire was ruled not by ethnically Chinese (Han) people, but by a Manchu royal house with Inner Asian origins. In 1759, this multiethnic empire conquered Xinjiang and appended it to the realm as one of several distinct territories kept separate from "China proper" and ruled through local institutions and aristocrats, much as Mongolia was. A military governor ensured the territory's security, but by and large, local Turkic Muslims ruled on behalf of the Qing and within the bounds of Islamic law. The mid-nineteenth century, however, saw a series of wars break out across the Qing, and the empire lost control of nearly a third of its territory. Xinjiang's people rebelled in 1864, and a series of Islamic states emerged in the vacuum formed by the withdrawal of Qing power.

In 1877, the empire returned, but in a new form: The Xiang Army, which was founded in 1853 in the province of Hunan, had fought and defeated many of the empire's internal enemies, and now it reached Xinjiang on a mission of reconquest.[4] However, the Xiang Army was led by a group of Confucian intellectuals whose philosophy demanded that they bring order to China by imposing what they understood to be the foundation of a harmonious society: the patriarchal Confucian family. Therefore, their goal was not to restore the old regime of indirect rule, but instead to assimilate the Muslim people of Xinjiang and thus ensure their homeland's perpetual inclusion within the Chinese cultural and political ecumene. They attempted to do so by transforming the Muslim family and seeding Muslim society with their own elite norms through education and resettlement. A special legal regime elevated their scriptural idea of the Confucian "rites" (*li*) above even the codified law of the empire. Ultimately, the Xiang Army's goal was to re-create Xinjiang not as a territory, but as a province like its own Hunan or any other in China proper. While that goal was formally achieved in 1884, when Xinjiang province was declared, the Xiang Army's civilizing project persisted nearly until the fall of the Qing empire in 1911 as they continued to struggle to establish control and assimilate the Muslims.

Many ironies resulted. Chief among them was that, instead of attaching Xinjiang and its people forever to China, the project provided a means to articulate a sense of ethnicity that both opposed Chinese power and appropriated it. Put differently, the experience of a historically specific form of domination shaped the discourses and practices of self-definition that emerged among the dominated people. This was in part because people used the resources and language of the dominating power to articulate and resolve their own claims and grievances, but also because the form and ideology of domination quickly became naturalized. Much as French West African or British Indian subjects turned their colonizers' claims of citizenship and respect for human dignity against their exploitation, so did Turkic Muslims in Xinjiang learn to manipulate the ideology and institutions of the civilizing project to advance their own interests as imperial subjects.[5] However, scholarship on colonial discourses of identity reminds us to attend to the role that class plays in articulating anticolonial positions on the part of a dominated community: it is usually those members of the colonized group who have learned successfully to manipulate the discourses of the colonizer who then claim to speak on behalf of the whole group. This book shows how relatively powerful Turkic Muslim people used the resources of the state to police boundaries within what they were coming to see as their own community, to purge the internal Others whom the civilizing project created. New articulations of identity emerged from new inequalities and forms of violence. At the same time, the relationship between the Muslim periphery and the imperial metropole came to seem natural, as though events in Xinjiang were intimately bound to the history of China itself.

Xinjiang is today known for an ongoing and seemingly intractable conflict between the Turkic Muslim Uyghur people who comprise the region's majority and a Chinese Communist Party and state attempting to eliminate their language and culture. The conflict is often analyzed as emerging from a set of conflicting nationalist imperatives:[6] Uyghur nationalism, which predates the Party-state's control of the region, claims Xinjiang as a homeland for the Uyghur people. While the Party-state formally recognizes the Uyghur claim to cultural autonomy, which is enshrined in the modern Chinese constitution, Chinese nationalism's own demand for cultural homogeneity within the borders of the state now takes precedence over legal protections for the Uyghur minority, leading to resentment. The characteristics and origins of Uyghur nationalism have therefore become the

Leitmotif of scholarship on Xinjiang. It would be tempting to draw a straight line from the everyday negotiations of communal boundaries in late-Qing Xinjiang, as described in this book, to contemporary conflicts.

However, the genealogy of Uyghur ethnonational identity is complex. Classically, scholars have emphasized the elite, intellectual, or political dimensions of Uyghur nationalism and attributed its articulation to the coincidence of transnational Turkic nationalism and the ethnicizing regimes of Soviet, later Chinese Communist, government. Such a perspective gives the impression that ethnic identities were magicked into existence in the 1930s. More recently, Uyghur nationalism's roots have been located instead in the complicated transnational environment of Central Asia and its intersection with subtler forms of religious and linguistic differentiation in the Qing realm. None of these analyses is necessarily exclusive of the others.[7] However, I think it is clear that certain strands of this genealogy tend to obscure the others, in particular romantic Uyghur nationalisms, which articulate the appealing idea that Uyghur-ness is an ancient spirit unfolding in time, or a pure line of Turkic development diverted from its natural path by Chinese domination.[8] The formulaic Stalinism of the Chinese Party-state's official histories of "ethnic formation" (*minzu xingcheng*) dresses up a similar story in pseudoscientific clothing, although a romantic narrative frequently shows through.[9]

Regardless of the path they take, tracing the genealogy of Uyghur ethnonational identity inexorably leads scholars back to the period examined in this book, which has nevertheless remained underexplored: the late Qing.[10] Several books have detailed the history of provincial Xinjiang in terms of its elite politics, the policies advanced by the regional government, and the intellectual backgrounds of its rulers. The high-level approach is valuable, but it rarely analyzes the period of Xiang Army domination from 1877 to roughly 1907 in more than schematic terms.[11] Recent works on the history of modern Xinjiang tend to begin at least two decades after the reconquest, at the time when a financial crisis forced the Xiang Army ruling community to consider creative plans to generate revenue that followed the resource-maximization imperatives typical of modern states.[12] Perhaps the fact that the late Qing was temporally within the scope of the global modern has directed scholars to seek the roots of modern phenomena. However, as this book shows, the Xinjiang government before 1907 reflected the priorities and techniques of traditional imperial provincial

[4]

administration more than it did the modern state. Indeed, the peculiar social formation that sustained Hunanese dominance also preserved Xinjiang as an outpost of conservative reformism that, by the last years of the Qing, already appeared to be a fossil. It was not a nationalizing regime, in contrast to the Soviet and Chinese governments that held sway in Xinjiang from 1934 onward. And yet, something took place in this apparently "premodern" setting such that a new sense of groupness emerged, the articulation of a Muslim self in ethnic terms against similarly ethnicized Others.

The present book contributes to the understanding of identity in Xinjiang by illuminating its processual, negotiated, everyday nature as it was during this period. That is, it is concerned with "identification," how people understand, articulate, and act on or perform belonging.[13] It explores that ongoing process in the context of everyday conflict in one part of Xinjiang, Turpan. At the end of the Qing, Turpan was a directly administered prefecture (*zhili ting*) within the provincial system. The prefecture's surviving archive tells thousands of stories that, when read through the politics of translation and representation, illuminate how people negotiated relationships and resolved conflicts in a multilingual, multiconfessional society.[14] In that society, a Chinese-speaking, non-Muslim minority dominated a Turkic-speaking Muslim majority, but there were many gradations in the hierarchy of power. Class was as significant as language or religion, although the conflicts of everyday life when articulated in the language of the civilizing project produced a discourse of belonging that scholars today would recognize as ethnicity.

On the whole, the civilizing project and its effects resemble those that have historically characterized specific forms of Euro-American colonialism, and so comparative colonial history guides the analysis herein. However, "colonialism" has been invoked with regard to the Qing empire many times, and often with differing meanings, connotations, and assumptions, so it is necessary to state precisely what I mean by it.[15] "Colonialism" here is defined as a system of domination aimed at territorial acquisition through sociopolitical reorganization.[16] It is interconnected with "imperialism," a process in which people from one region of the world dominate those from another for the primary purpose of resource extraction or territorial security but intervene less directly in social development, for example by ruling through a local aristocracy. I thus distinguish colonialism as a form of domination aimed at assimilating the people of the dominated territory from imperialism as a form of primarily economic domination that maintains control of plural constituencies through diverse vocabularies of rule. Generally speaking, a transition from plural imperialism to assimilatory colonialism often occurs as a reaction to a crisis of imperial control, and the Qing empire in the mid-nineteenth century was in precisely such a precarious position.

In broad comparative terms, we may see the Xiang Army as agents of that change in conceptions of sovereignty, as its leaders sought an expansion of "normal" institutions into the previously separate borderlands. Generally speaking, expanding empires tend to refrain from mediating between multiple legal and political systems, but instead maintain boundaries between them. Over time, slowed expansion or other reductions in the rate of resource acquisition, as well as the tendency of peripheral peoples to learn to make use of the institutions of the state, combine to encourage homogenization. Local elites, in Xinjiang's case the Turkic Muslim *begs*, are replaced with functionaries from the metropolitan order, here Chinese magistrates. That homogenization is based on a claim to universality but takes a colonial Other as its object. The Xiang Army's efforts in Xinjiang comprised just such a "civilizing project," an effort on the part of a dominant group to impart their norms and institutions to a subordinate group, by force if necessary.[17] Despite the closeness of the British and Russian empires, and the incursions of Euro-American imperialists along the Chinese coast, this civilizing project was of Chinese origin. It had its intellectual and institutional roots in a specific community of Confucian thought centered on the city of Changsha in the province of Hunan, and the leaders of the Xiang Army were part of this community. This book demonstrates how colonialism emerges in a non-Euro-American context.

However, my primary goal is not to produce some grand typological statement, but to use the comparison productively as a grounds for discourse and exploration:[18] If we accept the proposition that the domination of Xinjiang and its people was in some way "colonial," what do we learn? In this case, thinking of Xinjiang as colonial turns my methodological emphasis to the tensions and anxieties that domination through sociopolitical reorganization engenders among its subjects. Whether a colonial power imposes a certain political order, creates a system of economic exploitation, or reconfigures structures of gender and sexuality, it is the production of difference that enables it to do so and that registers its deeper effects.[19] Difference is not a mere intellectual puzzle, or simply a tool of power—as this study shows, it is an ongoing process of identification that relates to formal categories in complex ways. As much has been revealed by scholars of imperial culture and the institutions of knowledge in South China and Taiwan, whose works are a central influence on this book.[20] Scholarship on global frontiers equally informs this study of the Chinese Northwest. There is no single analogy for Xinjiang, but there are neverthe-less many parallels, and exploring them will reveal a largely unexplored "history from below," as presented in the words of ordinary people—however mediated—instead of the minority of powerholders. By regarding imperialism and colonialism as sociocultural processes, we can extend the field of discourse and comparison between expansive states and the societ-ies at their margins.

Within the field of Chinese history, this book represents an effort to bring the methodologies of historical anthropology familiar from studies of South China to bear on the questions posed by the "New Qing History." The New Qing History is an amorphous and expansive field, the chief intervention of which is the illumination of peripheral voices of various kinds. In the minds of most observers, however, this subfield is primarily concerned with ethnic difference in the context of Qing empire. Scholars of the New Qing History have shown, for example, how Tibetan religious lead-ers and Mongol aristocrats related to the Qing court, and earlier seminal works address the production of ethnicity through Qing institutions.[21] Generally speaking, each of the empire's constituencies saw a different face of Qing power that was relevant and legitimate in their own context. Yet Xinjiang has remained somewhat of a mystery in this regard: while Mon-gols and Tibetans might have seen the emperor as a warrior khan or an incarnate bodhisattva, the Qing appeared to have no Muslim guise. The question remains open as to how the Qing's Turkic Muslim subjects under-stood the empire. I argue that an idea of the Qing emerged not from careful imperial propaganda, but rather in the process of routine encounters with Chinese power in the last decades of the empire.

Yet all of these representations of self, empire, and the relationship between subject and sovereign only become clear when we read across the local archive and place it into dialogue with the Turkic-language manu-script tradition. Scholarship on Xinjiang's modern history has often relied on Chinese-language sources produced at the highest levels of government, which tell us little about how policies played out on the ground. Meanwhile, another branch of research focuses on manuscript sources in Chaghatay, the Turkic literary language used in Central Asia into the 1950s. Although these latter sources illuminate rich worlds of piety, economy, and everyday life, they say relatively little about the experience of Chinese rule. The Turpan archive, however, was formed in a multilingual context through the accumulation of records of conflict between, for the most part, ordinary people.[22] Although only a minority of the documents in the archive are purely in Chaghatay, while the majority are in Chinese, almost all are nonetheless products of translation. This book reveals the politics of Turkic-Chinese translation in late-Qing Xinjiang and brings that politics to bear on its reading of sources across and beyond that archive, showing how concepts from within the spaces defined by Chinese power nevertheless colonized the discourses beyond them.[23]

By reading the archive critically, as a site of negotiation and competition, I seek to emphasize the agency of ordinary people over that of high-level officials. "Ordinary people" in this case simply indicates those who held no office and whose activities were largely meant to remain quiet, beyond the sight of the administration. These included farmers, artisans, merchants, prostitutes, dervishes, and butchers, among a whole host of people who were in no position to circumvent the judicial system. At its core, this book is a study of "everyday politics": "the debates, conflicts, decisions, and cooperation among individuals, groups, and organizations regarding the control, allocation, and use of resources and the values and ideas underlying those activities."[24] Everyday politics is the quiet, subtle, and gradual adjustment and contestation of norms and institutions. This book is about how people engaged in that kind of mundane politics, how they resisted power, and how they appropriated it for themselves. Their conflicts could be about very mundane things such as land inheritance, and nevertheless reflect grander questions of import to contemporary scholars, such as the definition of ethnicity. Certain issues are raised frequently in the archive, the disposal of the dead, forced marriage, and the punishment of sex workers among them. Although we cannot have direct access to the discourses and practices surrounding such points of tension as they manifested in the everyday, they are reflected dimly in the corners of the archive.

Let us turn now to the details of the case, focusing on how people in Turpan themselves described their place in history and geography. First, I will locate Turpan in the history of the uprisings that preceded the study at hand. Then we will consider how people described Turpan's location in Xinjiang and its post-uprisings society. Both point to a sense that this was a "broken" place, a shattered society of estranged people.

Prelude: After the World Shattered

The so-called "Muslim uprisings" began in 1862, not in Xinjiang, but in the neighboring Muslim-majority regions of Northwest China.[25] Longstanding grievances on the part of local Muslims, including Chinese violations of Muslim sacred spaces and overtaxation, intersected with a set of ongoing feuds within the communities of Chinese-speaking Muslims, or Hui. Two years later, in June 1864, rumors spread that the military governor of Xinjiang had ordered the preemptive slaughter of Hui people, in order to prevent the rebellion from coming to the borderland. Instead, that rumor prompted Hui military officers and religious leaders to attack Qing garrisons and Chinese merchants. Just then, the ongoing rebellions in China proper closed the lines of communication with Beijing, and the people of Xinjiang found themselves in a vacuum of power. The initial violence against "Chinese" (*Khiṭāy*) people—which included Manchu-speakers and other non-Muslims—soon broke into a struggle among Muslims, as leaders of different Sufi lineages, former Qing commanders, and other claimants to power stood poised to plunder, conquer, and demonstrate their own ability to establish a legitimate Islamic state.[26] By the end of the year, a dozen factions had built competing power bases across the region. In the words of one man, "the world shattered."[27]

The lines drawn in this conflict were fluid and open to interpretation.[28] Economic factors played a role in the rebellion, as did opportunism, but so did the ability of Sufi leaders to mobilize their adherents and others who desired an Islamic state. Their followings tended to correspond roughly to differences in language, as Chinese-speakers related to trends in Islamic piety among Hui in China proper, while Turkic-speakers' orientation around certain texts and shrine pilgrimage connected them more to Central and South Asia. Nevertheless, alliances across boundaries of linguistic and sectarian difference were as frequent as enmities. That is, while "holy war" (*ghazāt*) came to characterize the rebellion, the object of holy war could be ambiguous, as it could be turned against internal or external enemies.

As much is illustrated by the history of the rebellions in Turpan. On August 17, 1864, a Sufi leader named Maʿṣūm Khan Khwaja led the uprising there and directed a series of attacks on Chinese settlements.[29] He was soon joined by forces from the Sufi leaders, or *khwājas*, of the nearby oasis of Kucha, who were then in an alliance with Hui military officers from the old garrison town of Ürümchi. Together they besieged the Chinese garrison and community at Turpan for nine months. In March 1865, after a typically long and bleak winter, they offered the besieged Chinese an escort back to China in exchange for their surrender. Instead, when the Chinese opened the gates, the Muslims let them travel some distance from the city, and then slaughtered them. Those that remained were enslaved. Soon, as the allied rebel forces attempted to expand their territory eastward, a local *khwāja* group based in the town of Lükchün attempted to seize power. The Hui specifically were victimized, as the Lükchün forces burned hundreds of Hui homes to the ground in an attempt to antagonize the Ürümchi commanders, perhaps in retaliation for the Ürümchi forces' enslavement of Turkic Muslims in Qumul (Hami).[30] The Ürümchi commanders' retaliation was swift and devastating, but remnants of the Lükchün faction eventually rose to supremacy in Turpan and expelled the Kucha *khwājas*. Sufis fought Sufis, against and alongside Hui.

Later in 1865, the officer Yaʿqūb Beg (1820–77) arrived in Kashgar from the Khanate of Khoqand, and soon both the battle lines and the discourse of conflict changed. The violence began to be represented as a conflict between bounded communities of people that were identified primarily by language and place of origin, albeit coded in religious terms. As the chroniclers of this period represented it, the primary group of antagonists had been the Chinese-speaking non-Muslims. That these "Chinese" in fact included Manchu-speaking people was lost in recollection—they were nevertheless obvious idolaters and infidels, and their "idol-temples" (Chaghatay *butkhāna*) burned all the same. Yet, as the Chinese fled, died, or converted, and through the conflicts that gradually emerged between Chinese-speaking and Turkic-speaking Muslims, Turkic Muslim writers came to construe the Hui as the enemy. After all, while the Khoqandis and Yaʿqūb Beg originally appeared as outsiders, they nevertheless spoke a language very close to that of East Turkestan, were culturally similar, and despite their integration of Hui and converted Chinese into the state could claim to undertake holy war on behalf of the "Muslim" (*Musulmān*) people. That claim was especially important, as Yaʿqūb Beg had initially come to Kashgar with orders to establish Khoqandi influence there by installing and supporting a Sufi as its leader. However, Yaʿqūb Beg had betrayed the Sufi, while Khoqand fell to Russian conquest, and now depended on his military prowess and identity as a holy warrior for legitimacy.

The Turkic Muslim chroniclers of this period and after accordingly referred to themselves as *Musulmān*, literally meaning "Muslim," while excluding the Hui (Chaghatay *Dūngān*) from this category. Therefore, I use the term *Musulmān* throughout this book to indicate Turkic-speaking Muslims.[31] (Specifically, it indicates those Turkic Muslims who identified with oasis agriculture and life, as distinct from Kazakhs or Kyrgyz, who despite being Turkic-speaking Muslims were depicted as living strictly by herding in the mountains.) Today, most of these *Musulmān*s would retrospectively be labeled Uyghur, according to modern ethnonational categories. *Musulmān*, however, retains the label's historically specific ambiguity, with its religious denotation, linguistic connotations, and implicit rejection of other Muslims despite its superficial inclusivity. The story in this book unfolds in a world before the hegemony of the nation-state, and it is appropriate to use the categories that were active in it. Moreover, as Rogers Brubaker argues, language and religion resemble ethnicity but are not equivalent to it.[32] Rather, these are all "embodied identifications," ways of acting and performing group belonging. These more fluid, performative, or situational identifications became increasingly naturalized through the late Qing by emerging discourses of common descent, and the violence of the uprisings was an important catalyst for that naturalization.

Yaʿqūb Beg's state rose to supremacy, sweeping the factions before it, Musulman and Hui alike. When his armies reached Turpan in 1870, they visited yet more violence upon Hui people.[33] They approached from the west and the town of Toqsun, killing nearly all of the Hui soldiers stationed there. At the gates of Turpan proper, they met and defeated "several thousand" more. Forces from Ürümchi attempted to trap Yaʿqūb Beg's soldiers in a pincer movement but failed. Lükchün fell, and the Kashgar army executed those they took prisoner. Turpan was under siege again, but now it was full of anxious Hui, rather than Chinese, people. For nine months, Yaʿqūb Beg's armies besieged the city and bombarded it with cannon fire. Hui hid in the lodges of

Sufi orders until finally some chose to sue for peace. Mullah Mūsa Sayrāmī (1836–1917), the celebrated historian from Kucha, later recorded how Yaʿqūb Beg visited "tyranny" (ẓulm) against the Hui in his campaigns by massacring innocent Muslims, Chinese-speakers and sectarians though they might have been. However, another chronicler who was an eyewitness to Turpan and a loyal officer in Yaʿqūb Beg's army produced a different account.[34] This writer, ʿAshūr Akhund, characterizes Yaʿqūb Beg as an instrument of God's justice (ʿadālah). He describes the Hui emissary sent to negotiate peace as a treacherous Sufi who distracted the officers while a Hui army prepared for a sneak attack. After the battle, a victorious Yaʿqūb Beg forced the Hui to sell their own belongings to pay for food, and then marched thousands of them toward Kashgar and into slavery. Such, ʿAshūr Ākhūnd asserts, are the wages of sin—what Hui people deserved for being "apostates."

These two writers, Mullah Mūsa Sayrāmī and ʿAshūr Akhund, were part of a flood of historical writing that emerged as Muslims reflected on their own identities and place in history and the world.[35] They also represent two positions on difference that were in tension during the uprisings and after. While the lines of conflict were drawn rhetorically between Muslims and non-Muslims, in fact the violence was frequently between Chinese-speakers and non-Chinese-speakers. Sayrāmī presents Yaʿqūb Beg's violence against Hui as tyranny, while ʿAshūr claims it was justice. A contemporary, the poet Muḥammad Gharīb Shāhyārī, similarly poses a distinction between Musulmans like himself and "non-Muslims" (nā-Musulmān) who have betrayed the faith, namely, the Chinese-speaking Muslims of Ürümchi.[36] The nature of Hui people's alleged sin was obscure, but as we will see, it could later be ascribed to their mythical origins as people between China and the Muslim world. To Gharīb, Yaʿqūb Beg's destruction of the Hui was therefore a means to mend this "broken" (buzuq) land, to purge the internal threat within the Muslim community and make it whole again.

While Musulmans characterized their land as shattered or broken, none of them would see it mended in the way that they hoped. In August 1876, the Xiang Army marched across North Xinjiang, putting Yaʿqūb Beg's forces to flight.[37] In May 1877, as Yaʿqūb Beg strategized from his palace in Kucha, he died suddenly. The cause of death, in retrospect, was a stroke, but Musulman authors began pointing fingers, trying to identify some reason why the Islamic state fell: Sayrāmī, for his part, interpreted Yaʿqūb Beg's sudden passing as a consequence of the same wrath (ghaẓab) that had led him to massacre innocent Hui.[38] Pro–Ya'qūb Beg chroniclers insisted that he had been poisoned, perhaps by a Hui commander who had visited a Chinese idol temple and "drank filth in the imperial manner" (*Khaqan rasmichä ān ichti*), violating Muslim dietary rules, before pledging oaths to the Chinese.[39] Others suspected a former Qing official who had served many masters, Niyāz Beg (d. 1879), of switching sides once again and conspiring with the Xiang Army to betray Ya'qūb Beg.[40]

In the ensuing chaos, Ya'qūb Beg's sons turned against each other, while his armies fell back. In Sayrāmī's words, "The people's patience was exhausted . . . so they turned their faces to the Court of the Creator, their eyes brimming with tears, and wished for the Emperor of China, their cries and pleas growing ever louder."[41] For better or worse, their prayers were answered.

It was the morning of April 27, 1877, when the Xiang Army arrived in Turpan. The army moved quickly, east to west across the valley, and its swift march set people in motion. At this moment, we could identify three of them, all of whom were traveling in different directions: Abū 'l-Mahdī, a young Musulman man, was running for the hills with his brothers. They hoped to avoid the violence entirely. Instead, they wandered in hunger for several years, unable to survive easily in the new social order. A common soldier named Yang Bencheng, a Chinese speaker and non-Muslim, marched with the army. He soon settled in the same town that Abū 'l-Mahdī fled, and there he tried and failed to remake himself on the frontier. Wei *shi*, a Hui woman, was a refugee—she fled the same army westward in search of freedom for herself and her family. Yet Wei *shi* found only bondage and captivity.

Turpan fell with hardly a fight, and a new era of reconstruction began, an era marked by subtler kinds of violence. Over the next thirty years, a new kind of Chinese power transformed the lives of the people of Turpan and of Xinjiang. We will revisit Yang Bencheng, Wei *shi*, and Abū 'l-Mahdī later in this book. However, understanding the arcs of their lives will require us first to illuminate a set of historical processes that transformed Xinjiang's society and culture.

Turpan, the "Land of Strangers"

Fourteen years later, on July 24, 1891, a Russian ethnologist visiting Turpan sat down with a man named Majīd Akhund and asked him to describe his homeland.[42] In response, Majīd counted off the "Six Cities," one by one, beginning with the most distant. These Six Cities (*altä shahar*) by traditional reckoning comprised the land of the Muslims, although some counted seven, or even eight.[43] Majīd described them by their popular nicknames. Far to the west was Kashgar, "land of saints," where those who first brought Islam to this land were buried. Yarkand, "land of masters," was known for its Sufi orders. Khotan, "land of martyrs," was the last to hold out against any invasion—including the Chinese reconquest. Moving to the north, Aksu was the "land of holy warriors," and its neighbor Kucha the "land of God's helpers." (See maps 0.1 and 0.2.)

Finally, Majīd came to his home: Turpan, the "land of strangers" (*gharībāna Ṭurpān*). "There is no river in Turpan," he explained. "There is not much land, nor water, but there are many shrines. Consequently, there are many strangers there. By 'strangers,'" he clarified, "I mean 'wanderers.'" The terms he used—"stranger" (*gharīb*) and "wanderer" (*musāfir*)—according to his own explanation indicated travelers, refugees, pilgrims, and vagabonds drifting in wretched isolation. These words described Turpan's two faces well: Pilgrims came from Kashgar and beyond to visit the Cave of the Seven Sleepers, a holy shrine believed to be the place where a

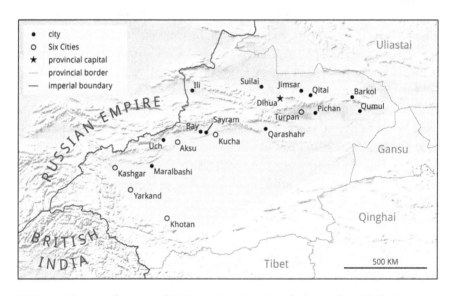

MAP 0.1 Major settlements of Xinjiang circa 1900. Map by Evangeline McGlynn. Location data from CHGIS.

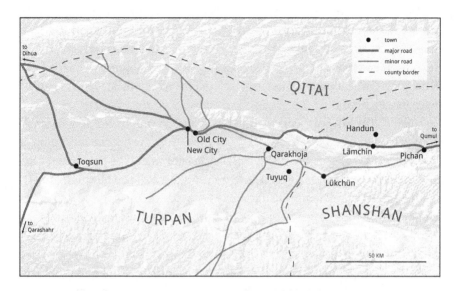

MAP 0.2 Towns of Turpan. Based on a map in *Tulufan zhiliting xiangtuzhi* in XTZG. Map by Evangeline McGlynn.

group of believers had taken refuge from a tyrannical ruler and slept for centuries under God's protection.[44] Others drifted through, many of them migrant laborers or merchants on their way to or from China. Many more survived as day laborers. Turpan had no great river, and the weather could be devastatingly hot in the summer, and so agriculture and the livelihoods of farm laborers depended on mountain runoff. Every spring, water tumbled down from the mountains and into tunnels dug deep underground to protect it from evaporation in the sun's rays. That water fed Turpan's famed vineyards and the small farms that clustered around the tunnels. Life was precarious, but tenacious.

There is another sense in which Turpan is *gharībāna*, "solitary." One could travel through the rest of the Six Cities without crossing mountains, as they formed a semicircle of oases around the expanse of desert in the heart of Southern Xinjiang. Turpan, however, was separated from the rest: to get there from Kucha, one would need to take a long journey eastward across the territory of a non-Muslim Torghut Mongol prince.[45] Then one would cross the "Desert Mountains" (*Chöl Tagh*) and descend into the second-deepest geological depression in the world. As traditional wisdom had it in Kucha, the road to Turpan was a desperate one.[46] To make it a habit meant permanent separation from one's family—according to one saying, for long enough that a man's wife could divorce him *in absentia*. The characterization is somewhat hyperbolic, but it speaks to the sense of Turpan as a subregion that was simultaneously isolated from and intimately connected with its neighbors.

Indeed, Turpan was well traveled as it lay on one of the few passable routes from China proper. As the crow flies, Turpan was not far from the Qing garrison town at Ürümchi, which was later made the provincial capital and renamed Dihua. From there one could travel to the small, mostly Chinese trading settlements that dotted the North. This fact made Turpan a critical juncture between North and South, and between China and Central Asia. However, to travel to Dihua and beyond required traversing the mountain pass at Dawanchin. The Turpan Depression was thus a channel, but also an impediment, a choke point in the movement of goods, people, and ideas. Turpan's geographical betweenness makes it interesting for this study as a place where people who spoke different languages and practiced different religions encountered each other frequently. The archive makes it clear that, even as Turpan recovered from the reconquest, Chinese, Hui, and Musulmans were living in the same courtyards, suing each other for the rights to property, and as we will see, sharing homes and beds as well.

Yet Turpan was no multicultural utopia. As of 1877, the valley had a population of roughly forty thousand, and it rose only to seventy thousand or so by 1900 as people returned, settled, and reproduced.[47] The Xiang Army that went beyond the Pass consisted of some sixty thousand soldiers, perhaps half of whom stayed in Turpan for a year or more. While the army was meant to sustain itself by farming, this was not possible in much of Xinjiang, and particularly difficult in Turpan. They therefore relied on mostly Tianjinese merchants to supply them with grain from China proper and Russia. Grain prices remained high for a few years, but gradually fell once officials implemented the system of granaries and price regulations familiar from China proper.[48] Grain prices appear to have stabilized by 1893, when the province had to lower its own prices to match those on the market.[49] In the meantime, however, the scarcity and expense of food forced people to seek alternate means of survival. Chinese-speaking merchants and former soldiers, while not rich, tended to be much wealthier than

Turkic-speaking Muslims and possess greater access to the power of the state. Those Musulmans who were not bilingual found themselves excluded from key sectors of the new economy, as well as from the provincial politico-juridical system of administration, led by Chinese-speakers, which was imposed on their homeland. Hui often stepped in as intermediaries and helped Chinese people secure economic dominance over Musulmans. Predatory merchants and lenders, usually Chinese, held Musulman farmers and laborers in debt. Demobilized Xiang Army soldiers purchased desperate Musulman women as wives to serve them and bear them children.

A Musulman who could adapt to Chinese settler culture and engage with the provincial government was therefore at a great advantage in this environment, and the civilizing project established institutions of education that provided access to language skills to some people. Yet the Chinese-speaking Musulman interpreters who emerged from these schools were also regarded with suspicion, although less so than the Musulman women who had intimate relationships with Chinese men, who were ostracized from the community. Musulman writers came to label these transgressors of boundaries *Chantou*. *Chantou* is a Chinese word meaning "wrapped head," which Chinese officials and settlers alike used to refer to Turkic-speaking Muslims. In Musulman discourse, a *Chantou* person occupied an unthinkable place within the dyads of religion and language through which Musulmans and Chinese alike were coming to understand Xinjiang society: Chinese-speaking non-Muslims (Chinese or Han), Chinese-speaking Muslims (Hui), and Turkic-speaking Muslims (Musulmans) were now joined by Turkic-speaking people who appeared to have become non-Muslims. Where the Xiang Army intended for Turkic Muslims to assimilate linguistically and culturally, becoming Chinese-speaking non-Muslims, the civilizing project instead fostered the *Chantou*, who became the internal Other against whom Musulmans articulated and policed firmer communal boundaries.

Here again the comparison with Euro-American colonialisms suggests avenues for exploring the history of groupness beyond the search for the nation-state.[50] In French West Africa, a citizen of the Republic who was nevertheless denied their rights on account of race could use the ideology of colonization, the European claim to civilize, to extract certain concessions from the reluctant colonizer. Throughout this book, Musulman subjects make claims on the basis of their imperial subjecthood, as it could be articulated under the civilizing project, through careful acts of representation. The provincial administration's language of belonging was powerful. A person could gain power by invoking the discourse of imperial subjecthood and Confucian patriarchy—or become a subject of power when made to speak in that same language. Consequently, people inverted the civilizing project by using its discourses to police communal boundaries and punish transgressions. Those transgressions themselves were intimately related to the problem of economic inequality, the dispossession of Musulmans from their land and property through debt, and the objectification of Musulman bodies. I therefore seek to demonstrate in this book that groupness in late-Qing Xinjiang arose first from a sort of estrangement—alienation from the self, from society, and seemingly from one's place in history and the cosmos[51]—and second from the naturalization of that estrangement through the mobilization of discourses about self, subjecthood, and history.

Those discourses about self emerged from an entanglement of elite anxieties about class with culturalist ideas of difference in a particular intellectual and social context in China proper, specifically in the province of Hunan during and after the civil wars of the mid-nineteenth century. The Taiping War (1850–64) was a crucible for a new kind of politics, as elites formed new modern armies rooted in local social institutions and identities. Among them was the Xiang Army, whose leadership was intimately connected to the specific Neo-Confucian philosophies expounded at the Yuelu Academy in the provincial capital of Changsha. The Xiang Army not only was credited with the defeat of the Qing empire's internal enemies but also was also a chief agent of postbellum "reconstruction" (shanhou).[52] Reconstruction was a project not simply of physical rebuilding, but of social and moral rectification predicated on the idea that China was in chaos because its people had strayed from the orthodox behaviors of the past. These new leaders were particularly suspicious of lower-class men's potential for violence and the sexual mores of lower-class women, both of which they attempted to control. Later, when the Xiang Army marched northwest toward Xinjiang, its leaders were already primed with ideas about Muslims as people on the edge of civilization, similar to the uneducated men and women whom they sought to save in China proper. The beliefs surrounding difference and civilization that motivated the Xiang Army's members, and that they used to comprehend what they faced in Xinjiang, combined an intellectual program that emerged in the academy with a popular sense of millennial disaster and the need for conservative Neo-Confucian revival. China's reconstruction, from the coast of the South China Sea to Kashgar on the threshold of the Pamirs, was thus a process in which new elites attempted a transformation of the empire and its people. The sociocultural legacy of reconstruction in China proper, not unlike that of American Reconstruction (1863–77), continued to shape lives, memories, and identities long after. Just as Chinese elites saw the so-called "Muslim uprisings" (1862–77) of the Northwest and Xinjiang as part and parcel of the same disorder that brought about the Taiping war, so did Xinjiang's reconstruction follow the methods they had established in China proper. However, the Xiang Army's techniques of moral rectification, originally directed across horizontal boundaries of class, articulated with linguistic and religious difference in ways that reified vertical boundaries between groups.[53]

In this sense, *Land of Strangers* seeks to disentangle certain established ideas about ethnonational identity and the borderlands that have been posed at a more abstract level of analysis, while connecting ethnicity and groupness instead to everyday processes of negotiation that were nevertheless connected to the broader reimagining of the community. This is a subtle distinction, but important for how we understand the late Qing: The Xiang Army and the Hunanese intellectual community that constituted and surrounded it have been characterized as key actors in the creation of a protonational Chinese identity.[54] To be clear, it would be a mistake to characterize the Xiang Army in Xinjiang as straightforwardly "national"— rather, their articulations of identity and project of transformation belonged more to the discourse of Chineseness, or elite Confucian identity, that some scholars call "civilizational." These modes of discourse were and remain in tension in modern China,[55] and late-Qing Xinjiang shows one way that this tension was realized in practice. Civilizational discourses on the level of policy and ideology informed recognizably ethnonational modes of identification on the level of popular practice.

On Naming

I must therefore ask the reader to bear in mind that all of the labels used in this book were under negotiation. The lines of estrangement were unstable, as terms gained new social meanings while shedding others. The implicit meaning of "Musulman" in 1860 was, I would argue, different from what it meant in 1900, and the same was true of "Hui" and "Chinese." However, the fact that the relationships between words and their referents was under constant negotiation poses certain problems for writing history, especially when people shifted between categories, often out of a researcher's sight. We might consider the case of Muḥammad Naʿīm, *alias* Lin Shengtian. Muḥammad Naʿīm was, depending on the context, a Hui merchant, a local Musulman leader, or a representative of the British Raj from India.[56] In another guise, he could easily have been considered a non-Muslim Chinese. All depended on his self-presentation and ability to take advantage of imperial interests. Therefore, this book is careful to use the labels that people gave themselves and others, and to focus on the relational dimensions of naming, rather than seeking stable identities.

This is to say nothing of the multiple terms for groups of people used in different languages. Take for example the term *Hui* used in English and Chinese to designate "Chinese-speaking Muslims"—although it was once used in Chinese to indicate "Muslims" in general, and now refers to an ethnic group within China's formal classification and institutionalization of ethnicities, as of 1877 in Xinjiang, in Chinese documents, it usually referred to Chinese-speaking Muslims. In Chaghatay, meanwhile, writers called such people *Dūngān*. All of these labels therefore pointed not to a fixed object in the world, but to the same contested concept—"Hui" was not an ethnicity so much as a shifting position in a field of relationships. The same is true of "Chinese" or, in late-Qing documents, *Han*. Chaghatay texts referred to *Khiṭāy*, and although the term long before derived from a geographical and ethnic label for the Khitans of North China, it clearly refers in this period to a shifting position of "Chinese." For that matter, Chinese-speaking non-Muslims were frequently labeled simply "commoner" (*min*), indicating their perceived status as normative imperial subjects. To refer separately to *Khiṭāy*-ness and Chineseness and Han-ness, or Hui-ness and *Dūngān*-ness, as separate concepts would introduce a false distinction. There were myriad ways of construing Chineseness and Hui-ness that were in negotiation across languages.

We may say the same about "Musulman-ness," rendered in Chaghatay as *Musulmānchiliq*, in contrast to *Chantou*-ness, or *Chantoluq*. "Musulman-ness" was defined in part positively, through a set of practices and characteristics, but it was most mobilized in dyadic relationships over and against Hui-ness and Chineseness, forming a relational triad. *Chantou* was an explicitly translingual term: in Chinese, it pointed to the position of "Turkic Muslim," but in Chaghatay, to a Turkic Muslim becoming apostate. Nevertheless, we later find people adopting this seemingly derisive label for themselves and their own community. This relationship was part of an ongoing process of distinction, and it is to that process that we must attend.

This book is also inevitably bound up in a politics of naming, and simply referring to the region in question by name implies a political stance. So far, I have called this place "Xinjiang" because that is the name by which most people know it. However, to many Uyghurs and other Turkic Muslims, the name "Xinjiang" is laden with the weight of colonial oppression. "Xinjiang," after all, means "new frontier," and to call it as such means identifying it primarily as China's borderland. Instead, "East Turkestan" has become many Uyghurs' preferred toponym. The term has advantages: it captures the geographical distinctiveness of the region simultaneously with its interconnection with the "West Turkestan" of Central Asia. The Chinese Party-state, of course, opposes the term on the grounds that using it promotes ethnonational separatism.

In this book, I use both terms, *Xinjiang* and *East Turkestan*, but not quite interchangeably. This is because, first, the distinct administrative structure and territorial boundaries that have made up "Xinjiang" in the eyes of China-based states, along with the popular and official imaginations of that place, were historically significant. The creation and maintenance of a thing called "Xinjiang" had a profound impact on the lives of people in the place discussed in this book. Therefore, when I refer to "Xinjiang," I mean Xinjiang as an assemblage of ideas and practices—a governmental apparatus extending over a certain territory, and the ways that people thought about it—and a process of destruction and creation. Xinjiang is the top-down formation of this place, its reterritorialization as a Chinese space.[57] Moreover, writers in Chaghatay frequently used this name, rendered *Shīng Jāng*, to label the region, particularly when referring to Chinese administration and geography. In contrast, I use "East Turkestan" to emphasize a Turkic Muslim perspective, an envisioning and constitution of this place from the ground up. "East Turkestan" points to the practices that were often invisible to the provincial government, yet bound people together in a territorial formation that was overlapping with but not equivalent to the

Chinese administration. The dissonance between "Xinjiang" and "East Turkestan" is near the heart of this story.

Moreover, I am obliged in this book to speak about "Islam" and "Confucianism," neither of which in its social and cultural contexts was or is a single, stable thing. I defer to the historical actors encountered in this book on their own definitions of themselves and their traditions. In the context of East Turkestan, "Islam" generally indicated Sunni Islam following the Hanafi *madhhab*, combined with a number of practices that tend to be associated more with Shia Islam, but centered on hagiolatry and hagiography, pilgrimage to the shrines of Islamic saints, and engagement with their sacred biographies. "Confucianism" similarly pointed to a set of intellectual traditions and ritual practices that were based on teachings set down in scripture, beginning with Confucius. Scholars today would identify the kind of Confucianism active in Xinjiang as Neo-Confucianism, which both purported to rediscover the ideals of the classic Confucian thinkers and provided a set of rules of life that became hegemonic in the late imperial period. Of course, adherents of either would simply describe their own practice as "Islam" or "Confucianism" (*Ru*), or in even more essential terms. This is a book not about defining what Islam is or was, or what Confucianism is or was, but about exploring the fluidity of people's identifications with either one.

The Structure of the Book

This book is effectively in three parts: part 1, consisting of chapters 1 and 2, is a history of the social, intellectual, and political origins and activities of the reconstruction government. Chapters 3 and 4 explore the sociocultural effects of the Xiang Army's policies and their implementation, showing how the institutions of assimilation instead reified boundaries between groups. Chapters 5 and 6 illuminate the changes that followed in historical imaginations and concepts of difference in Chinese and Islamic discourses.

Chapter 1 presents the sociophilosophical origins of a civilizing project that sought to ameliorate difference but instead reified it. I argue that the Xiang Army's policies in Xinjiang originated in the thought of the so-called "statecraft" (*jingshi*) community of activists in Changsha, Hunan, in the early nineteenth century. Their ideology was shaped in turn by the community's experiences during and after the Taiping war. Because members of this community led the reconquest and reconstruction of Xinjiang and China's Northwest, they had the opportunity, means, and motives to enact their conservative reformist policies on a culturally non-Chinese population. The central goal was sociomoral transformation based on an interpretation of the notion of "rites" or "ritual" (*li*), beginning with the pattern of familial relationships.

Chapter 2 continues that narrative to retell the story of Xinjiang's political history in the late Qing through the Xiang Army–dominated government's applications of *jingshi* solutions to emerging crises. I argue that the government construed and treated Xinjiang as a zone of exception, and that the nature of the exception changed along with the community as it reproduced itself over time. Each challenge elicited an ineffective policy response that created new institutional structures but did not secure control of them, allowing Musulman and Hui subjects to take advantage of the state's low capacity and penetration. Eventually, with the intervention of the Beijing court, Xinjiang's *jingshi* regime gave way to an explicitly colonialist approach that was still hampered by a lack of functioning institutions.

Chapter 3 moves more deeply into the Turpan archive and introduces skilled manipulators of cultural and linguistic difference, the interpreters (Chinese *tongshi*, Chaghatay *tongchi*). The Xiang Army intended to seed Muslim society with Confucian values, as they interpreted them, by training a generation of young Musulman men in Chinese language and the Classics. Instead, I argue, this project of "transformation-through-education" (*jiaohua*) created a class of bifluent intermediaries who manipulated the state to their own ends. The interpreters became indispensable: Chinese magistrates were almost totally incapable of operating in an environment that was so culturally and linguistically different from their places of origin, and they struggled to locate loyal intermediaries. The interpreters became not moral patriarchs, but functionaries, and some even climbed the ladder higher. The interpreters' success caused resentment among Musulmans, who depended on them for communication with Chinese authorities. That resentment was reflected in a distinct social persona that emerged in Musulman discourse, painting the *tongchi* as a suspicious, divisive figure and a kind of Chantou.

Chapter 4 turns to the other side of the civilizing project's gendered effects. The Xiang Army, in its efforts to transform the Muslim family, forcibly resettled women into new marriages and promoted Chinese family norms, particularly through the cult of widow chastity. I argue that the civilizing project's cultural and sexual violence intersected with economic inequalities between Chinese soldiers, Hui merchants, and ordinary Musulmans, and so encouraged both trafficking in women and its ideological justification. The exchange of one's own and others' domestic, sexual, and reproductive labor was a strategy for survival during a time of upheaval, and one that adapted preexisting customs in East Turkestan, but it was also a vector of conflict between communities. Chinese and Musulman elites both used the institutions of the civilizing project to police communal boundaries by punishing women who crossed them. Women's sexuality, the control of which was critical to the maintenance of patriarchy, became central to an emerging metaphor of descent used to define the Musulman community.

Chapter 5 concerns the politics of collective memory in the wake of war. I argue that the Muslim uprisings and reconquest were experienced across communities as historical trauma. Chinese-language and Chaghatay-language texts, ranging from depositions to poems to chronicles, figure 1864 and the events that followed as a "disaster," "tribulation," or "shattering," a time when an imagined peaceful age was lost forever. The ruins of war and human remains—and just as significantly, the absence thereof—became powerful sites for discourses of loss and recovery, through which people articulated new collective grievances and identities centered on common descent.

Chapter 6 shifts more fully into the Chaghatay-language manuscript tradition and the politics of Islamic history-writing. I argue that changes in the narrative of the origins of the world's peoples and the arrival of Islam in China reflected the specific concerns of Musulmans under Xiang Army rule in the wake of conflict. That is, mythohistorical texts were rewritten in ways that naturalized the imperial order as it was imagined to have existed before the Muslim uprisings. In history-writing, the emperor of China became a just ruler in the Perso-Islamic mode and protector of the Shariah. Through the discourse of a lost golden age and the struggle to recover it, Muslim writers refigured the relationship between peoples and sovereign as one of lost family. Musulmans' internal Others—boundary-crossing women and interpreters—became signs of a shattered and unjust world, intermediaries where none had existed or been necessary before.

ONE

The Chinese Law

The Origins of the Civilizing Project

ON JULY 22, 1879, Ney Elias (1844–97) was in Yarkand on a mission of reconnaissance for the British Raj. Elias opined in a report to his superiors that the Chinese occupation, although "exceedingly capricious, meddlesome, and devoid of principle," at least from the perspective of this career British agent, was "decidedly not a bloody rule, not even a cruel one."[1] Nevertheless, Elias observed some strange interactions that to him echoed British rule in India. The lowest of Chinese soldiers, he observed, "rides down the Mussulman or lashes him with his whip if he finds him in the way in the street; he addresses him by inferior pronouns in conversation, or swaggers into his house or Yamen and appropriates the most honourable seat without a word of remonstrance." That is, the rule of the Chinese over Musulmans appeared arbitrary, and Elias noted with concern that these abuses resembled those of which Indians accused the British. Moreover, Elias explained, such arbitrariness was cloaked in the mantle of law. One specific practice stood out: women who covered their faces "are liable to have the veil torn from their faces by the first Chinese soldier who happens to pass, with the remark that the custom is not in accordance with the Chinese 'li.'"

This *li*, this simple but enigmatic syllable, haunted the Musulman understanding of the Chinese state in the late Qing precisely because it indicated a set of ideas and practices at the core of the Xiang Army's civilizing project. This chapter establishes the intellectual and social context of that project by exploring the meanings that *li* took on over the course of its evolution. In the Neo-Confucian philosophy that the army's leaders had studied, *li* 禮 pointed to the "rites," the complex of normative social relations and ritual practices that changed human beings and the cosmos for the better. This concept was articulated as part of a theory of civilizational change. Yet it also gained a popular meaning as a kind of essential Chineseness defined over and against the Qing's internal enemies in the mid-nineteenth century. To Musulman observers, *li* therefore appeared to stand for a law-like system derived from scripture that specifically concerned matters of family, ritual, and teaching—a Chinese Shariah.

This chapter traces the genealogy of the Xiang Army's project back to the philosophical and political milieu of the Ming-Qing transition, in which there emerged an antilegal, moralistic stance alongside a vision, rooted in the Classics, of China as civilization and territory. Over the next two centuries, that position gained institutional support and substance as a scholarly community in Hunan developed those ideas into the main stream of so-called "statecraft" (*jingshi*) thought.[2] We will see how the army's plans for Xinjiang grew out of a specific alignment of interests and ideas within *jingshi* thought, particularly with regard to Muslims, family, and law. Those ideas crystallized in the ideological statements of Zuo Zongtang (1812–85), the architect of Xinjiang's reconstruction. Zuo's theories changed in the course of practice, and the Xiang Army's management of Muslims in Shaanxi and Gansu shaped the leadership's ideas about civilization.

There is a historiographical tendency to frame Zuo's activities and those of his compatriots in terms of China's modernization and the emergence of nationalism.[3] After all, Zuo himself was responsible for a number of innovations in the Qing empire's military infrastructure. His activities on the whole seem "modern" in the sense of introducing new technologies to maximize resource extraction, as in Gansu, where he expanded mining operations and established, among other facilities, an arsenal and a woolen mill. The view from just beyond the Great Wall, however, looks very different. In Xinjiang, Zuo's technological interventions were focused on making the region economically independent and capable of supporting an ideal agricultural society that would foster good family morality.[4] Indeed, to Musulmans, provincial reconstruction looked less like modernization and nationalism, and more like a religious civilizing project. We will therefore begin with the insights of Musulman observers, whose depictions of *li* reveal often-overlooked aspects of Xiang Army ideology.

Law Without Law: The Mystery of Li

Western observer of various backgrounds who learned about *li* in Xinjiang through Musulman interlocutors all characterized it as a form of "law."[5] Even the linguist Denison Ross translated the word *li* as "law," despite having written beside it in his own hand the Chinese character for "rites." Orthodox Confucians would object to such a characterization, as would Denison's Sinological contemporaries. After all, Confucius himself contrasted codified law, which repels people from goodness through punishment, with the rites, which subtly bring people to do good by developing their sense of right and wrong.[6] Indeed, the concept of the "rites" is so ubiquitous and central to Confucian thought as to be almost unnoticeable in the Chinese context, and it has taken on a broad spectrum of meanings over time, which could be rendered in English as anything from "propriety" to "comportment" to "politeness."[7] For the late Qing, Angela Zito's definition of *li* is apt: "ways of being human that are considered necessary to the workings of the cosmos as well as its embedded social order, including everything from how to dress to how to venerate ancestors."[8] *Li* united cosmic principle with practical behavior by means of rules that were considered critical to the maintenance of a good and ordered society. Nevertheless, the ways in which the Xiang Army attempted to inculcate the Musulmans with *li* revealed a side of *li* that normative philosophy obscures, its law-like quality: its articulation of a set of abstract categories and restrictions on behavior that demanded imposition on the chaotic reality of life through systematic sanctions.[9]

Early in the army's occupation, all Muslims were made to bow to a certain placard, draped with white silk, that was placed at regular intervals along the highway. This placard was a public display of the Kangxi emperor's proclamation (*Shengyu shiliu tiao*) from 1670, which Zuo Zongtang ordered in 1877 to be distributed across the region, just as he had in Gansu.[10] The proclamation was to be posted along every major road and on the walls of every city, and read aloud in every school and by every village headman.

This text blends exhortations that superficially enforce the authority of codified law with those that speak to a more fundamental set of Confucian values: "bring peace to the village factions to put an end to lawsuits"; "expand schools to bring about scholarly study"; "explain the law to admonish the ignorant and stubborn"; "illuminate good manners to deepen good customs"; "end false accusations to bring about the good"; and so on. In fact, what the Kangxi edict projects is the foundational Confucian belief that, in a well-ordered and moral society, law is unnecessary and even harmful.[11] The Chaghatay translation of the edict, however, was presented as the essence of an untranslated syllable, *li*, pointing to an otherwise undefined, abstract concept to which Musulmans were nonetheless required to attend.

The experience of the enforcement of *li* demonstrated that this concept was bound up with normative Chinese behaviors. To return to Elias's observation, the *li* that the Xiang Army enforced had no obvious connection to the Qing Code, the extensive collection of statues and substatutes that specified infractions and punishments. In Kashgar, the practical enforcement of *li* meant that soldiers tore the veils from Muslim women's faces and otherwise imposed an arbitrary regime of Chinese superiority over Muslim subjects. None of the behaviors that Elias described was commanded by any known order from the Xiang Army leadership, nor were they to be found among the myriad statutes of the Qing Code. However, they demonstrate how ordinary soldiers interpreted their dominion over the Muslims as one of forcing Muslims to respect implicit and explicit norms and rules of behavior. It appeared that whatever a Chinese person believed to be "proper" was implicitly also *li*. We might call this "Sino-normativity": a sociopolitical stance that promotes an explicit or commonsensical idea of essential Chineseness, even as that idea is under negotiation.[12]

Li found further articulation in one of the Xiang Army's first publications in Xinjiang, a translation of a moral primer written in Anhui in 1869.[13] This primer was meant to explicate the Kangxi edict and illustrate its moral principles through parables excerpted from the popular *Twenty-Four Filial Exemplars* (*Ershisi xiao*). Those parables in turn were shown to be manifested in selected, nonconsecutive statutes and substatutes from the Qing Code focused on family relations. In Chinese, the effect was to demonstrate that fundamental moral principles derived from the rites found expression in codified law. The original Chinese text that had become the *Book of Li* was a particular favorite of the Xiang Army community, which promoted its usage among commoners in Hunan, where it joined other Confucian revivalist texts in promoting an austere new morality focused on family and salvation.[14]

When the text was translated into Chaghatay, however, several things changed about its presentation: First, the translators redacted sections of the primer in order to focus the text even more narrowly on family values. Second, in the Chaghatay version, the alternation between genres becomes totally unclear, as stories and statutes blend into one. The intermingling of narrative and code is enforced by the clunky, ungrammatical translation, as the translator attempted to shoehorn Chaghatay words into the conventions of Literary Chinese writing and the peculiar syntax of the legal code. Naturally a Musulman reader or listener unfamiliar with the intricacies of the Qing Code would take it to be a single text, an inscrutable scripture. Indeed, the title was rendered as *Lī kitābi*, which simply meant *Book of Li*, leaving the meaning of this critical syllable obscure.

When Qurbān ʿAlī Khālidī (1846–1913), the perceptive and prolific scholar who was then the chief Islamic judge of Tarbaghatai, was asked about the meaning of *li*, he replied that *li* both divided people into distinct classes and specified corporal and carceral punishments for various infractions.[15] In other words, it was law-like, as demonstrated by the new government's clear emphasis on morality based on scripture and willingness to enforce it through violence. Khālidī was not alone in this understanding. His contemporary and interlocutor Mullah Mūsa Sayrāmī expanded on such observations through a more thoroughgoing comparison of *li* with Shariah, through which he lent textual evidence in support of a popular understanding. He presents *li* as the rules (*qāʿida*) of the new regime of the Xiang Army, in contrast to the regulations of the Lifanyuan, the Qing office that managed the empire's nonprovincial territories in Xinjiang, Mongolia, Manchuria, and Tibet.[16] The Lifanyuan belonged to the imperial past, while *li* marked the provincial present.[17] The Lifanyuan is depicted as a rational source of justice, as it provides both an institutional mechanism for common people to seek justice against officials who wrong them and a consistent set of rules through which the emperor disburses that justice. *Li*, in contrast, appears in Sayrāmī's text as a set of moral rules for life akin to the Shariah.[18] It is presented as a system of paternalistic care, the norms that bind the actions of Chinese officials, as well as a moral force equivalent to the Shariah.[19]

Sayrāmī attempts to demonstrate as much through his account of ancient Chinese history, in which he recounts that "the Chinese people say that they believe in the Shariah of Lū Wāng."[20] He refers to Lü Wang (Jiang Ziya, fl. 11 c. BCE), who played a key role in founding the Western Zhou dynasty (1047–772 BCE), considered the golden age and model for all dynasties that followed. From this perspective, Lü Wang's ancient Chinese Shariah is a corrupted revelation, a system of rules and categories that is Shariah-like in its basis in flawed scripture.[21] Sayrāmī expands upon this comparison by demonstrating through genealogy that the legendary figures of the ancient Chinese past were likewise those who were said to have lived after the Flood in Islamic history. Ethnographic evidence supports the idea that others considered *li* to be akin to Shariah.[22] Such a characterization, in the context of Islamic legends of the origins of peoples and of sacred knowledge, poses Chinese law as an earlier revelation that preceded that of Muḥammad, perhaps a corruption of Mosaic law.

The comparison of *li* and Shariah invites us to leave Eurocentric conceptions of "law" aside and consider how a Muslim intellectual steeped in Central Asian traditions would have seen the Qing state and its late-Qing mutation. To be clear, Shariah is not precisely "law" in the normative Continental or Anglo-American sense.[23] Rather, we may understand it to be "God's will on Earth" as discerned through scripture—this can be many things, among them a vehicle to the greater understanding of divine Truth, as well as a guide to living according to God's wishes. In the hands of a judge (*qāżi*) or an expert in jurisprudence (*mufti*), it is certainly a means to establish and enforce abstract and general categories upon the messiness of life. Yet Shariah can also be contrasted with other law-like systems operating alongside it: In those places where Muslims have lived under non-Muslim rule, particularly in Asia after the Mongol conquests, Shariah came to be distinguished from dynastic law.[24] Dynastic law or sultanic law, often called *qānūn*, generally consisted of royal decrees and might include a formal legal code, and while dynastic law notionally needed to be in accordance with Shariah, the friction between the systems was widely acknowledged. According to Sayrāmī's analogy, if the regulations of the Lifanyuan constituted the codified law of the Qing empire by which the emperor could produce rational justice, then *li* was akin to the Shariah within the Chinese context. Indeed, in Sayrāmī's account, the Lifanyuan regulations are called *qānūn*, while the *li* comprises "rules" (*qāʿida*), reflecting a classical distinction between the two systems. Sayrāmī suggests that, whereas the earlier Qing regime possessed the ordinary tension between Shariah and *qānūn*, the new Qing regime instead posed a competition between Shariah and a corrupted revelation.

We will see throughout the following chapters that Sayrāmī's analogy was perceptive, as the Xiang Army suspended the Qing Code in favor of enforcing their interpretation of the rites as an alternative law-like system. Precisely such a concept of *li* underlay the Xiang Army's civilizing mission, their renewed belief in the Confucian elite's responsibility to transmit their norms and institutions to others.[25] While Confucians had arguably possessed this drive for as long as there had been Confucianism, for the Xiang Army, these practices and beliefs now took on a new urgency, as it was posed as the chief means to restore the primacy of a Chinese civilization that these Confucians felt to be facing an existential threat, not just from without, but from within. This mission was directed not only toward the uneducated, the poor, and those members of the family whom elite men considered subordinate to the patriarch, but also outwardly, beyond the geographical boundaries of Chinese civilization.

The Intellectual Origins of the Civilizing Mission

The Xiang Army's emphasis on *li* and the necessity of sociomoral transformation prior to other forms of development was hardly innovative in itself. Although many self-described Confucians helped create the authoritarian ideologies of imperial China, the idea that ordering the world began with the individual and the family, "the basic building block of local society," and not with the emperor, had long been central to Confucian thought.[26] Yet the specific form of ideology that the Xiang Army applied in Xinjiang arose from the debates of the late Ming (1368–1644/1683). The disorder and tyranny that literati perceived then and during the violent Ming-Qing transition that followed, and the solutions they advanced for the ills of their time, directly informed developments in the nineteenth century. In the following pages, we will outline those influences that were most significant for the Xiang Army's rule of Xinjiang.

The relevance of late Ming thought to the efforts of China's conservative reformers to save the empire in the nineteenth century is well documented.

Ming military writings profoundly influenced the organization of the Xiang Army, particularly through an emphasis on strong interpersonal relationships between members of units and the need for militias to maintain local roots.[27] At the same time, the militia organizations themselves reflected institutional continuities that had survived the Ming-Qing transition. The revival of local militias and their transformation into the new armies that won the Qing civil wars, including the Xiang Army, are thus often depicted as a triumph of a uniquely Chinese tradition of "practical" thought over the ossified institutions of the Manchu court. This apparent practicality is considered a hallmark of the so-called "statecraft" (jingshi) school of thought, in which the Xiang Army's leadership was deeply engaged. Some elements persisted through educational institutions, while others were revived through the study of texts dating to the Ming-Qing transition. Those ideas lent jingshi thought a set of core beliefs that were not "practical" in the sense of "practical learning" (shixue), which the movement also emphasized. Here we will focus on those ideas that provided the jingshi community with a sense of mission—a mission to "order the world," as we may more literally translate jingshi—and of their own role as literati in that quest.

The late Ming witnessed renewed philosophical debates about the nature of law, the need for education, and the role of Confucian scholars in ordering the world. Dominant currents of Confucian thought held that one could perform correct action and discover metaphysical truth through nature and contemplation alone, but many blamed this idea for the rise of tyrannical emperors and corrupt ministers. At the same time, many thinkers concluded that the Ming was founded on a grasping autocracy masked by an increasingly complicated legal code. Finally, the visible dominance of corrupt eunuchs at the Ming court prompted literati to join reformist factions based at academies, among them the Donglin Academy, whose partisans sought to restore the moral authority of scholars and the tradition they upheld. When the Manchu Qing invaded the Ming, however, many Donglin reformists and their intellectual kin found themselves in a difficult position: having been rejected by the corrupt Ming court, they now fought against the Qing invaders, as well. It seemed as though no monarch could bring peace to all-under-Heaven, and that this responsibility lay instead in the hands of educated men.

Two scholars, Huang Zongxi (1610–95) and Wang Fuzhi (1619–92), stand out in this period for their systematization of the anti-statist, moralistic ideas that such reformists generally held, and that influenced the *jingshi* group and Xiang Army leadership later on.[28] Modern scholarship, however, has often misconstrued Huang and Wang's central claims, particularly by placing them in a genealogy of "protonationalist" thought. This is due in part to nationalist intellectuals' own appropriation of Huang and Wang's writings at the turn of the twentieth century, but also to an unfortunate tendency on the part of Western scholars searching for the origins of nationalism to accept those claims. Others in Mainland China and Taiwan have projected proto-Marxist or protoliberal interpretations into their writings.[29] Therefore, in order to demonstrate the significance of Ming-Qing thought for the Xiang Army's ideology, it is necessary to clear away a mound of assumptions about these thinkers and the ideas they synthesized. If, as Stephen Platt argues, Zuo Zongtang's connection with Wang Fuzhi's writings was critical to his ideological development and that of his comrades, it is necessary to understand how Zuo might have read him, not how Zuo's modern admirers hoped he would have.[30]

A textually grounded reading of Huang reveals a figure that a modern observer would consider conservative, even reactionary, and certainly elitist. Huang and his contemporaries explicitly articulated the need for educated men such as themselves to regain control of government, not only by asserting themselves as the equals of kings instead of their servants, but through education. Confucian reformists at this time believed that, in the golden age of the Western Zhou, schooling had been universal, and the potential for sagehood open to all. If such a system were in place in the present day, they reasoned, literati could control both the curriculum and the process by which bureaucrats were selected. Sociopolitical change would therefore be driven not by the emperor above, or by discontented farmers below, but by the figure who mediated between state and society, the scholar-bureaucrat.

Scholar-bureaucrats had the legitimate authority to lead from the middle, Huang and his colleagues reasoned, because they understood the rites.[31] To Huang, there had been no genuine "law" (*fa*) in China since the Zhou because avaricious princes had used government to their own advantage, spun ever more elaborate legal codes to compensate for the resulting corruption, and so perverted the very concept of law. These "unlawful laws" (*fei fa zhi fa*) brought about chaos and social disturbance. Conversely, looser laws—"law without laws" (*wu fa zhi fa*)—permitted people to realize the principle of law underlying the text of the code.[32] His work shows that the educated man's responsibility is to awaken people to the fundamental truth that informs both Confucian sociomoral ideology and the imperial legal code. It is akin to the intent of the *Book of Li*, which asserts that this fundamental truth is embodied in the relationships between members of the family, prior to those between rulers and subjects.[33]

Wang Fuzhi, our second representative thinker, looms large in the historiography of modern China and of Hunan in particular. Wang was a scholar from Hengyang, Hunan, who became involved in reformism on the eve of the Qing conquest.[34] Like many others, he focused his critique on corrupt officials and received his inspiration from the Donglin movement. Later, when the Ming court was retreating southward under assault from the Qing, Wang led a short-lived guerrilla war against the invaders. Scholars have made much of Wang's resistance to the Manchus, and the romantic image of a lone literatus standing against the tide of barbarism later captured the imaginations of turn-of-the-century nationalists, who traced the origins of their own anti-Manchuism back to Wang Fuzhi. The interpretation of Wang Fuzhi as a "protonationalist" has some grounding in his work, as certain passages in his *Yellow Book* (*Huang shu*, 1656) have clear anti-Manchu messages, including justifications of dominating a barbarian Other. Indeed, while some of Wang's works were later included in the official Qing compilation of approved and important books (*Si ku quan shu*), the *Yellow Book* was excluded and instead circulated mainly in manuscript form, allegedly for its anti-Manchuism.

However, Wang's primary contribution to Chinese thought in his own time and in the early nineteenth century was not protonationalism, nor should we characterize his work in such presentist terms.[35] The attribution of nationalism or racialism to Wang is based on a highly selective reading of his otherwise extensive corpus of work, and one that emphasizes individual words over their philosophical and even rhetorical contexts. Certainly, in the *Yellow Book*, Wang here and there describes the world in terms of "kinds" (*lei*).[36] However, by "kinds" he explicitly means scholars, who are tasked with instructing ordinary people in the maintenance of the rites. Commoners (*min*), constituting a second "kind," are responsible in turn for ordering material things. At one point, the people of China (*Huaxia*) are termed a "clan" (*zu*). While the word *zu* implies a metaphor of ancestry, we ought to consider its interpretation according to Wang's probable source,

Lü Pu (fl. 1346). To Lü, the clan as an extended family unit is a natural phenomenon, and all within it share a common substance (*qi*). However, the clan is primarily a ritual construction, not a biological one. Through ritual, one may be transformed into a part of this clan, not just socially, but in one's substance.[37] In the same vein, Wang explains that this *Huaxia* is the realization of a transhistorical essence he calls the "Central Yellow" (*Huang Zhong*).[38] People maintain this Central Yellow by practicing the rites, the performance of which shapes the substance of people and the world. Therefore, the analysis presented in the *Yellow Book* as a whole is fairly orthodox: social stability is the responsibility of educated men, who must enforce norms through the rites. What, then, was so subversive about Wang, and so appealing to his Hunanese readers?

Wang argued that rites and substance are mutually constitutive, or rather exist in a historical dialectic, and therefore the boundaries of the Chinese essence can grow and contract. Moreover, his writings express a sense of mission resulting from the Ming-Qing transition. He describes at length how North China was originally the seat of civilization because of Northerners' observance of ritual norms. However, Wang argues, as Northerners failed to practice the rites, while Southerners learned them, the center of civilization slipped away from the North and into the South, specifically into his native Hunan. During the Mongol conquests, this land of "former outsiders" (*qian yi*) became an "oasis of culture" (*wen jiao zhi sou*). Wang feared that the Qing conquest would mean a final retreat of the civilizational center into the provinces further south. Ultimately, Wang warns, total domination by Northern outsiders might return China to the state of "primal chaos" (*hundun*) that reigned before civilization. In short, Wang Fuzhi argues that human beings change through the process of civilization or decivilization. The boundaries of civilization depend in turn on the practice of the rites—one could retake the North by enforcing them there.

Therefore, if Wang Fuzhi's writings express a political program, and one that influenced Zuo Zongtang, then it is one fundamentally in accord with the Donglin movement's values and the principles of Neo-Confucianism.[39] Yet there is "a religious tone to his sense of history, a sense of ultimacy achieved once upon a time" in his depiction of the idealized past and the possibility of reviving it through spreading universal truths, even to the point of transforming barbarians with ritual.[40] Many have cited Wang's call to "Occupy their territory and thereby substitute for their customs the virtue of our letters and teachings, as well as confiscate their property and thereby increase our own people's provisions" as a sign of violent protonationalism—but even this statement he framed in terms of those outsiders' (*yi*) failure to practice the rites.[41] Because the distinction between Chinese and outsiders could be collapsed into the distinction between the "gentleman" (*junzi*) and the "petty man" (*xiaoren*), and because the rule of petty men posed an existential threat to the essential rites, it became the gentleman's burden, as it were, to rectify the morals not only of the lower-class Other but of the external Other.

Huang Zongxi and Wang Fuzhi did not secure widespread influence in their own time. Instead, the intellectual milieu they represented lost currency in the halls of government for some decades before its slow revival from the mid-eighteenth century onward. To summarize those Ming-Qing sensibilities that were carried down this narrow stream to the nineteenth century, they included the following beliefs: that peace and order are best achieved not through law, but through teaching; that this teaching must be managed by moral men; that government is the province of the educated, whom the monarch ought to recognize as peers; and that people can be brought into the Confucian ecumene through good ritual, or be lost by failing to practice it. Most intriguingly, Huang and Wang's writings advance a vision of civilization, law, and geography, according to which the laws imposed by the Manchu outsiders in the North would need to be suspended in favor of the rites if those places were to be brought into the Chinese ecumene—and this is precisely what the Xiang Army did in Xinjiang. Such beliefs are not incompatible with "protonationalism," but they do not define it either. Sino-normativity was not an explicit ideology of ethnic superiority, but instead informed a metaphysical discourse and an ideology of rule. As we will see, the Xiang Army's project, insofar as it conformed to these basic beliefs, was an attempt not to turn "Uyghurs into Chinese," but rather to effect a change of creed: "Muslims into Confucians."[42]

The Social Origins of the Xiang Army Community and Ideology

Huang Zongxi and Wang Fuzhi were among those Ming-Qing thinkers whose influence on nineteenth-century reformism was both canonized in the formal collection of *jingshi* writings and institutionalized in the academy that formed the nucleus of the *jingshi* community. Anglophone history remembers the *jingshi* writers as scholars of "statecraft" and participants in a broader practical, technically minded, and reformist but conservative turn in Confucian thought and imperial policy. However, few scholars have taken into account the depth of their conservatism and the vision of the ideal world that it implied. Mary Wright aptly characterized the elite manifestation of this phenomenon as "Chinese conservatism" rooted in preserving a set of abstract social norms that were more central to the project than the technological innovations that served their preservation.[43] That is, when late-Qing reformers famously sought to use Western methods to protect a Chinese essence, their concept of that essence resembled Wang Fuzhi's Central Yellow more than it did any racial ideal. This mission to bring popular social practice into line with elite norms, which was suffused with zeal and a sense of historical purpose, coincided with the rise of a new popular moralism and was intimately tied to a "network of messianic alumni" centered on the Yuelu Academy in Changsha, Hunan.[44] As Tobie Meyer-Fong puts it, "revivalist forms of Confucianism" and "a religious vision of the dynastic order" emerged as answers to the challenge of the Taiping. We can understand the civilizing project in Xinjiang as part of those answers.

The Yuelu Academy dates back to 976 CE, but for the purposes of our discussion, we may begin with its revival in the mid-eighteenth century as a center of *jingshi* study.[45] One key figure in the revival was Chen Hongmou (1696–1771), a scholar of Hunanese origin whose own work in government reflected a dedication to education for all aimed at reviving the age of universal sagehood. He founded schools for non-Chinese-speaking people in Yunnan and for the lower class in Jiangxi, which he called "charitable schools" (*yishu* or *yixue*), cast "dwelling together as a family" (*jujia*) itself as a vital moral act, and produced a manual for the proper conduct of family ritual. Chen's writings called for settling wandering men into domestic units, which both civilized their members through the performance of the rites and enabled neighbors to police one another at the grassroots. Such ideas were institutionalized in the Yuelu Academy, which Chen endowed in part because of Changsha's tradition of conservative scholarship.

In 1829, the Yuelu Academy became the site of Wang Fuzhi's revival at the hands of what Wang Jiping terms the "Xiang Army group" or "clique"

(*Xiangjun jituan*).[46] That is, the leadership of the Xiang Army came from a tightknit network of men who taught or studied at the Yuelu and those related to them. The nucleus of this network included many of the most famous names of late-Qing history, who also read Wang closely and formed relationships around reading his work: Wei Yuan (1794–1856), Zeng Guofan (1811–72), Hu Linyi (1812–61), Guo Songtao (1818–91), and of course Zuo Zongtang, among others. These students and teachers undertook the compilation of *The Treasures of Chu*, a collection of regional scholarship celebrating the contributions of Hunanese scholars. Wang Fuzhi, among many others, was placed on a trajectory of local scholarly exemplars from the self-sacrificing official Qu Yuan (ca. 340–278 BCE) through the revivalists of the Qing. Years later, in 1862, Zeng Guofan used his position to initiate the publication of Wang Fuzhi's collected works at a printing house Zeng had established to rebuild Chinese culture in the wake of the Taiping war, demonstrating Wang's continued significance to this group.[47] Indeed, Wang became known as the quintessential philosopher of the Xiang Army and of the Hunanese conservative reform movement. The same period saw the compilation of the canonical collection of *jingshi* writings in 1827, which featured essays by Huang Zongxi, Chen Hongmou, and others, some of whose work specifically influenced the Xiang Army's efforts in the Northwest. Meanwhile, the location of the academy in the Qing's South was significant: there the boundaries between Chinese settlers and non-Chinese-speaking autochthones were porous, and as Hunan itself was a kind of borderland, it lent itself to *jingshi* scholars as a site of social experimentation. Many of the essays in the compilation and in its published continuations therefore reflect the problems of governing those whose beliefs and language did not conform to Chinese norms.

Around the same time, a crisis turned the *jingshi* scholars' attention away from the open South and toward the bounded, non-Chinese space of the North, where institutional differences and the official closure of most of Mongolia, Manchuria, and Turkestan to Chinese settlement prevented the sort of gradual transformation through education that Chen had tried to effect in the South.[48] The Jahāngīr crisis of 1826, which threatened Qing sovereignty over East Turkestan, spurred the court in Beijing to solicit new ideas on frontier policy.[49] Proposals from established officials included further restricting Chinese settlement, as they believed that uncultured Chinese and non-Chinese would simply corrupt each other further, as well as measures to make frontier garrisons more self-sufficient. Imperial ortho-doxy favored separation and security. Scholars in Changsha, in contrast, developed a curiosity about these "Western Regions" that spurred a new imagination of Xinjiang both as an idyllic realm of shepherd life and as a more or less empty territory that might serve as a solution to many of the empire's problems. For one, during the Qing's long period of stability, the population had boomed, leading to an increase in so-called "bare sticks" (*guanggun*), unmarried common men, who they feared would disrupt the social order by roving the countryside as bandits instead of settling down and raising children. *Jingshi* scholars proposed large-scale colonization of Xinjiang as a solution to the bare stick issue. Their plans reflected Chen Hongmou's idea that underclass Chinese and uncivilized non-Chinese could have a mutually civilizing effect if settled in normative family units. James Millward identifies in this generation of the *jingshi* school a new "expan-sionism" as exemplified by Wei Yuan: "To call in Chinese people (*Hua min*) and turn this rich loam into China proper [literally, 'the inner lands,' *neidi*] would greatly ease the exercise of our authority and greatly increase our profit."[50]

In 1833, in the midst of this debate, a young Zuo Zongtang imagined the transformation of Xinjiang.[51] He held that the system of indirect rule was untenable, as the military administration under the Ili general (*Yili jiangjun*) that was meant to keep Qing borders secure required generous financial support from China proper. Instead, Zuo argued to remake Xinjiang as a province. His proposal echoed the *jingshi* ideal: if the institutions of good government in China proper were established, then stability and self-sufficiency would naturally follow. Yet those institutions depended on a systematic transformation of the population into morally upright people who would intuitively understand the rites, eventually weaning local soci-ety off of formal law entirely. Some years later, in 1841, Zuo's reading of Wang Fuzhi's work on the rites provided him with a theoretical grounding for such a project: "The difference between China and the barbarians is that the Chinese have benevolence," which was brought about through the rites.[52]

The Yuelu Academy group began to transform into the Xiang Army lead-ership in the late 1840s, when Hunan experienced a series of popular upris-ings that prompted members of this circle to organize militias (*tuanlian*).[53] This process of militarization had its roots in traditional China, but crises accelerated militia formation and placed it more firmly into the hands of the educated gentry, rather than of the local government. This development effectively gave local elites a legitimate force of arms with which to organize and discipline their communities. In 1853, following the entry of Taiping forces into Hunan, several gentry-led militias combined into a single fighting force under Zeng Guofan's leadership, the Xiang Army. Zuo Zongtang became one commander among many. However, their purpose was to combat the Taiping not simply as an existential threat to the Qing empire, but as an existential threat to the fundamental principles that constituted Chineseness: the rites. The Taiping, as a Christian millennialist movement, were not ordinary rebels, who often sought justice within the bounds of Confucian discourse—instead, they sought to replace Chinese ways with foreign beliefs and literati authority with that of their own messianic leader. The Taiping war was not only a civil war, but a religious conflict over ways of life and claims to truth, and one that the Manchu Qing seemed unable to prosecute effectively. The Xiang Army therefore sought to create a society in which authority shifted into the hands of moral patriarchs as appropriate guardians of orthodoxy. This process of re-creating the shattered society of China in the wake of the Taiping war was called "reconstruction," or in Chinese shanhou.[54] Shanhou did not simply indicate the physical reconstruction of the landscape, but the meritorious act of re-creating society according to Neo-Confucian ideals.

Therefore, the project of transforming commoners into Confucians was not confined to the Muslim Northwest but was part of a broader conservative revival in the post-Taiping era that sought to rectify popular morality and thus save the world from its apparent slide into chaos.[55] A chief tool of that effort was exhortative morality literature, much of which was performed orally, that focused again on the importance of the rites as the central means to save oneself and the world. The Xiang Army remained invested in the production and distribution of this literature throughout the Taiping period and well into the reconstruction of Xinjiang, including their publication of the Chaghatay translation of the moral primer known as the Book of Li.[56]

In this light, the Xiang Army's actions in the Northwest, which were also termed shanhou, can be understood as extensions of their experiences and programs during the Taiping war. The complex of practices and ideas that were crystallized in the Xiang Army by the end of the Taiping war in 1864 included the strategic suspension of law in favor of an essentialized notion of morality, the inculcation of that morality through print literature, and the belief that both were the responsibility of educated men. Deeper still, the *jingshi* canon, to which Xiang Army leaders now added their own contributions, advanced the idea that civilization could and should be brought to uneducated Others through schooling.

Zuo Zongtang and the Reconstruction of the Muslim Northwest

The *jingshi* program evolved mainly in the social and political terrain of South China, within the bounds of the provincial system's civil administration and with the assumption of a shared culture, but against the familiar strangeness of the culturally non-Chinese peoples of the South. Certain institutions and symbols provided a common morphology and vocabulary of power, a conduit for negotiations between Chinese officials, elites, and commoners, as well as a gradual means to integrate culturally different people.[57] The Xiang Army's occupation of the Muslim-majority provinces of Shaanxi and Gansu, however, presented conflicts between the *jingshi* program, the *jingshi* imagination of Muslims, and the practical problems of administration. In those regions, the encounter with a Hui majority—with people who were linguistically similar to Chinese people and participated in many of the same institutions yet remained separate—shaped the specific approach that this group later took to Xinjiang.

Most histories of the Xiang Army end with the departure of Zeng Guofan from its leadership in 1864 following the victory over the Taiping.[58] In fact, although the army grew smaller, the central clique maintained, renewed, and strengthened its boundedness and the centrality of its common rituals and ideology as it marched out of Hunan under Zuo Zongtang. There is some confusion about nomenclature: officially, Zuo's fighting force, constituted in 1866, was the Chu Army (*Chujun*). Later on, it was regularly called the Xiang Army (*Xiangjun*), just as Zeng's force had been. I use "Xiang Army" because the vast majority of the primary sources concerning the army use that name exclusively, from the depositions of demobilized soldiers who settled in Xinjiang to elite accounts of the army's history. The core group of Zuo loyalists, later termed the "Old Xiang Army" (*lao Xiangjun*), then had its own trajectory of intellectual and institutional development in the Northwest. Indeed, modern historians of the Xiang Army place the Northwest and Xinjiang campaigns in the army's "middle period," following the Taiping defeat but preceding its role in the Sino-French War (1884–85).[59]

This middle period began with the assignment to suppress the ongoing Nian uprising in North China. In September 1866, Zuo was appointed governor-general of Shaanxi and Gansu and soon arrived in Xi'an with a revived fighting force made up of Xiang Army veterans from Zuo's immediate networks and those they recruited.[60] This new Xiang Army was truly a community centered on Zuo himself. Zuo prioritized the defeat of the Nian, which was accomplished in 1868, and then turned his army to the Northwest. By 1873, the Qing armies had fought all the way to Jiayuguan, where a fortress marked the transition from China proper into the Inner Asian territories beyond.

In Shaanxi and Gansu, the Hunanese *jingshi* project became increasingly independent of the central authority of the Qing empire. Even though the court rejected some of Zuo Zongtang's *jingshi*-based plans, he and the Xiang Army implemented them nonetheless.[61] In a pair of memorials in 1867 and 1868, Zuo laid out his understanding of the causes of unrest in the region and their solutions: the lack of a Confucian gentry, he wrote, meant that militias had been poorly organized and unable to combat the uprising or command the respect of local people. In the future, a native military force on the model of the Xiang Army, formed from militias but trained and equipped with modern weapons and methods, would be necessary. They were to be under the command of local gentry, the emergence of which required education, and that meant establishing schools. Immediately after the Gansu campaign ended, Zuo had a printing house in Hubei produce woodblock editions of the Classics and basic textbooks. These were distributed to a series of institutions across Shaanxi and Gansu that Zuo called "charitable schools."[62] In this plan and its terminology we see again an echo of Chen Hongmou, who used the same name for his popular schools, appropriating the idea of charity for the goal of "transformation through education" (*jiaohua*).

That concept of transformation by teaching, which was as old as the *Book of Rites*, remained central to Xiang Army articulations of policy toward Muslims throughout their occupation of the Northwest and Xinjiang. To

Zuo, the difference between Chinese-speaking Muslims and sinophone Confucians was "not a difference of nature, but a difference of teaching" (*fei xing zhi yi, jiao zhi yi ye*).[63] Zuo argued that the "people of Arabia" were not uncivilized by birth, but because they had learned Islam, itself a "teaching" (*jiao*) analogous but inferior to Confucianism. One antecedent for Zuo's plan is Lu Yao's (1723–85) "On Enlightening the Muslims," collected in the first compilation of *jingshi* writings.[64] In line with the *jingshi* critique of codified law, Lu criticizes the Qianlong-era (1735–96/99) legal distinction between ordinary subjects and Muslims (Hui) as an impediment to the integration of Muslims into the moral order. Instead, Lu proposes a solution that begins with organizing the Hui into the *baojia* mutual-security system. The purpose of *baojia* was to discipline communities so that families (*jia*) organized into larger units (*bao*) learned to police one another, eliminating the state's need to do so. Next was to establish "charitable schools" in order to enlighten the Muslims, who would study the Classics. Both measures reflected his contemporary Chen Hongmou's plans to assimilate the non-Chinese peoples of the South.

The next step of Lu Yao's plan was to transform the Muslim family, the fundamental unit of *baojia*. Note Lu's use of language: he refers to the marriage customs common to Chinese as the customs of "commoners" (*min*), not as pertaining to a group coded explicitly in terms of ethnicity. This superficially neutral language masks an elite Sino-normativity. Lu Yao wrote:

> The Hui people's marriage practices should all be unified with those of the commoners. We find that the Hui people entered China over a millennium ago. However, marriage between men and women has not yet become like that which is common in China. As a result, the people of China despise how the outsiders (*yi*) disdain to associate with them. Hui people have likewise come to possess a self-segregating mindset. So, they look askance on our China and do not desire to marry. . . . They simply stick stubbornly to their teachings.

Lu recommended incentivizing Hui marriages to "commoners" with material rewards and placards honoring the new families. Integration into a family, as Lü Pu had once argued, would transform the Muslims' "substance" (*qi*), so that the children of these homes would possess "Chinese ways" (*Hua feng*). Zuo later used precisely the same language for his own plan to organize, educate, and transform the families of Xinjiang Muslims: "Assimilate them to our Chinese ways" (*tong wo Hua feng*).[65]

Zuo's model for the practical moral transformation of Gansu was the Xiang Army veteran Tao Mo (1835–1902), later governor of Xinjiang but at the time only a county magistrate.[66] Tao vigorously promoted a model of marriage rooted in the *jingshi* reading of the *Book of Rites*. In order to induce a popular educational transformation beyond the classroom, Zuo also introduced the "village compact" (*xiangyue*) system familiar from China proper, according to which proclamations would regularly be read out to local subjects by carefully selected readers. (In both Xinjiang and Gansu, these readers themselves came to be called *xiangyue*, which is translated as "village headman.") Leadership could thus distribute sociomoral lessons down to the village level through hierarchical oral transmission. The compact system had its roots in the thought of Zhu Xi (1130–1200) and other Southern Song Neo-Confucians, who advanced it as a voluntarist, organic alternative to centralized government. Like the "charitable schools," Zuo appropriated the village compact instead as a top-down means to transform society. This exact same system was later used in Xinjiang's reconstruction.

Zuo's conflicted approach to Muslims and Islam solidified during the Gansu campaign. Zuo probably would not have succeeding in retaking Gansu without Dong Fuxiang (1839–1908), a rebel leader who switched sides. Although Dong himself was not a Muslim, he brought perhaps forty thousand mostly Hui soldiers into the Xiang Army–led force.[67] Meanwhile, as Zuo's soldiers established military farms, he proposed the large-scale removal of Muslims from the central road through the Gansu Corridor.[68] The court in Beijing twice rebuffed him: "Muslims," they reminded Zuo, "live in their own place. . . . How can they lack natural goodness?" Zuo was instructed to differentiate not between Chinese and Hui, but only between "the good and the bad." Imperial rescripts presented a message of imperial universalism, which many Muslims took up in Xinjiang in the years that followed: everyone was equally a subject of the Qing emperor, or at the very least, both Hui and Chinese were expected to live under the provincial "counties-and-prefectures" (*junxian*) system of hierarchical administration. Zuo was aware of the history of Muslim service in government, but he held that his proposal responded appropriately to the on-the-ground realities of the Northwest:

> The way to deal with the Muslims is not like the way we dealt with the Taiping and Nian. . . . They have accumulated deep enmities with the Chinese. Their marriage customs differ, their temperaments differ, and when they see each other, murderous intent immediately arises, which is very difficult to get under control. Moreover, their races (*zhongzu*) are distantly separated, so they differ even in appearance. . . . Furthermore, I fear that Chinese subjects' reactions will redouble the enmity.

Despite resistance from Beijing, Zuo implemented his plan. The Xiang Army granted Hui and other Muslims plots of barren land far from the main road through Gansu and organized them into the *baojia* system, as Lu Yao had proposed.[69]

Muslims' segregation from Chinese in theory ought to have prevented their assimilation, producing the opposite of Zuo's ultimate goal. In part, Zuo sought to prevent a repetition of violence between groups that had so recently been at war.[70] A further explanation lies in Zuo's understanding of Islam: he was fearful of the New Teaching (*Xin jiao* or *Jahriyya*), which he regarded as a "heterodox teaching" (*xiejiao*) akin to the White Lotus in China proper, while he saw the Old Teaching (*Lao jiao* or *Khufiyya*) as Islamic "orthodoxy" (*zhengjiao*). Zuo explained that this Old Teaching, having come via the Hui scholar Liu Zhi (ca. 1660–ca. 1739), was actually "similar to Confucianism" (*si Ru*). The Xiang Army thus set about promulgating regulations for mosques, establishing examinations for the civil service that favored Old Teaching adherents, and otherwise finding ways to define and promote Islam as they preferred it to be.

The Xiang Army's project of reconstruction had begun, in the Taiping context, as the moral reordering of China alongside its physical rebuilding. Fears of "bare sticks" and other putatively disorderly lower-class elements motivated the promulgation of conservative moralism and, as we will see in the next chapter, deployment of exceptional violence. In the Northwest, the Xiang Army learned to divide and rule—to identify good and bad forms of Islam, enforce those definitions, and use them to encourage gradual assimilation. This became part of reconstruction as well, and relied once again on the Xiang Army's ability to act with great independence from Beijing. That shift from vertical relations of class difference to horizontal relations of religious difference, however, signaled the emergence of a recognizable "civilizing project" based on the effort to assimilate a peripheral people to the assumed norms of those at the core.[71] This politics of differ-ence later guided the army's approach to Xinjiang, where Turkic-speaking Muslims, despite their greater cultural difference from Chinese, were nev-ertheless regarded as more docile or easily assimilable than Hui, whom offi-cials still considered sources of violence and disruption.

*　　*　　*

Imperialism is not only a set of institutions and processes; it is culture and ideology.[72] The Xiang Army's emergence and its reconquest and rule of the Northwest produced its own ideological formation, a set of narratives, sym-bols, and theories that legitimized and explained their project. This forma-tion in turn had a specific genealogy rooted in the *jingshi* community of Changsha, Hunan, and in the popular Confucian revival in the Taiping and post-Taiping era. In this sense, Xinjiang's reconstruction was very much part of the Xiang Army's reconstruction of China proper, and it partook of many of the same ideas and techniques. Nevertheless, the encounter with religious difference in the Northwest placed aggressive assimilation at the center of reconstruction. This was justified and enabled by both the army's high degree of de facto independence from the empire and its ideological motivation to order the world.

The civilizing project's ideology and the manner of its actualization invite comparisons with empires elsewhere. A civilizing mission is gener-ally an emergent property of imperialism, not a primary motivator for imperialist enterprise. Once an dominant power finds itself in the position of managing a subject people, its agents articulate an ideology of "enlight-enment" that justifies economic exploitation instead as a means for "civi-lized people" to protect and uplift the "savage."[73] Nineteenth-century Europeans based such civilizing missions on a newly discovered faith in pedagogy, "a belief that truths, one recognized as such, had only to be learned and applied." That is, Europeans came to assert that their own assumed norms were not only universal, but self-evidently true, never mind that those norms were constantly shifting. Instead, it was through interaction with the colonized Other that varieties of Europeans, in spite of their significant differences in class, customs, and languages, articulated more essentialized ethnonational identities. To put it differently, I recog-nize in Zuo Zongtang's thought the "forked tongue" of colonialism: the desire for an Other that is "almost the same, but not quite."[74] As we will see in the following chapters, while that position was articulated by a distinctly Hunanese group of actors, it nevertheless helped Chinese-speaking non-Muslims of various origins claim a common identity, one that associated them with the civilizing project and against Musulmans. Through Zuo's approach to Muslims in the Northwest, the elite's approach to an internal Other—the unenlightened masses who needed guidance and education—was transposed onto the external or peripheral Other, effecting a tension between the demand for similarity and the insistence on difference that played on lines of both religion and class.

It is unsurprising that the civilizing mission was also a justification for adventurism as the performance of sovereign control over territory. As the army remained in Gansu, a debate emerged at the Qing court as officials considered whether or not to reconquer Xinjiang.[75] Many were skeptical of Xinjiang's value, particularly that of its vast and arid South, and advocated instead for a stronger response to the foreign incursions on the empire's long coast and deeper into its heart. In 1874, Zuo Zongtang famously countered that the reconquest of Xinjiang was vital to the security of the empire as a bulwark against Russia as that empire rose to the west. Moreover, he cast the abandonment of Xinjiang as a failure of filial duty—failing to recover that territory was failing to respect the achievements of imperial ancestors. Zuo won the debate and in 1875 was appointed the imperial commissioner for Xinjiang military affairs, making him the first Chinese official to hold a position previously held by Manchus or Mongols. The change heralded the oncoming conversion of Xinjiang from an Inner Asian territory into a Chinese province at the hands of the Xiang Army.

TWO

Xinjiang as Exception

The Transformation of the Civilizing Project

ZHOU JINGTANG'S LIFE was supposed to go so differently. Zhou was born in Ningxiang County in Hunan, fifteen hundred miles from where he now stood at the gates of Jiayuguan in western Gansu.[1] This place, famed as "the Pass," marked the traditional boundary between China proper and the Inner Asian frontier, and generations of exiles had written of their trepidation at approaching it.[2] Zhou was no exile, but an educated man who wrote poetry under a style name, Jiajian. That fact alone set him apart from the masses of soldiers who had also arrived in Gansu with the Xiang Army. Zhou would have regarded them as "bare sticks" (*guanggun*)—untamed and violent men who constituted the army's strength and, in their leaders' eyes, its greatest liability. The rank-and-file were meant to support families back home with their wages, and monthly lectures on the army's moral code kept them in line.[3] Zhou Jingtang, however, had been recognized and promoted several times for his service as a clerk during the wars across China. Now that the army had received its orders to march into Xinjiang, he anticipated an appointment as an assistant magistrate in the new provincial administration.[4] Ordinary soldiers would also cross "beyond the Pass" in search of a better life, farming or trading, but Zhou could envision a career of service.

That vision faded soon. Zhou remained in Gansu for a while in frustration, unable to secure an official position. In 1880, he traveled into Xinjiang in search of advancement and found himself in Kucha, where a number of people from his home county had settled. Some old veterans were serving in the garrison. Zhou befriended the Ningxiang man Yang Xiuqing, an army captain who now guarded the city's North Gate, as well as a number of Chinese who ran stalls at the market. Home was now even farther away, but success seemed closer at hand. Xinjiang, after all, was known as "Little Hunan" (*xiao Hunan*), where speaking Beijing-style Mandarin was far less important than knowing his native Hunanese dialect. Zhou would be among his own people.[5]

Yet Zhou Jingtang's renewed optimism came crashing down two years later on the day he received a letter from home. It informed him that his family remained poor—unlike the rank-and-file soldiers, Zhou had failed to support them. Now his mother was ill and coming to the end of her life. Zhou's duty was to return to Ningxiang—now half of Asia away—but he could never afford the journey. So instead he drank. That night, by lanternlight, Zhou stupefied himself on liquor. He wandered into the butcher shop, where his friend Butcher Tan boiled some tea, hoping to clear Zhou's mind and stave off the worst of the inevitable hangover. As Tan's back was turned, however, Zhou seized the carving knife from the butcher's block and wandered down the road to Yang Xiuqing's post. According to the official record, Yang was in the midst of writing a report when Zhou burst in, weeping and screaming incoherently. Yang tried to calm his friend. Everything went red and black.

The next morning, as Yang lay dying, Zhou awoke in a jail cell, bereft of memory but covered in blood. In the ensuing investigation, questions emerged about how to handle the murder. Zhou's crime was heinous, as it had deprived Yang's own aging mother of her only son, and special rules governing such crimes now allowed the province greater latitude to punish those who destroyed families, tearing the moral fabric that the Xiang Army was trying so diligently to weave. If he were an ordinary person, he would have been sentenced directly to strangulation. However, Zhou also held an official rank—the right to an official position, if not the position itself—and was therefore technically immune to capital punishment. The province ultimately decided to expel Zhou from Xinjiang, not to his home in verdant Hunan, but into exile in the freezing forests and windswept steppe of Manchuria.

Zhou Jingtang's story sits at the convergence of several interrelated phenomena: Xiang Army leaders and soldiers alike perceived Xinjiang as a land of opportunity. That perception, along with special rules that made the region's bureaucracy a nearly inescapable closed system, encouraged its majority-Hunanese members to settle and stay, making Xinjiang a "little Hunan." This administration continued to govern the region in the *jingshi* mode for three decades. As new generations of Hunanese officials entered the provincial bureaucracy, and the administration faced mounting crises of governance, the social and political dynamics of policymaking and implementation changed. By looking more closely at the social dynamics of this dominant group, we can better understand how Zuo Zongtang's influence persisted in Xinjiang even without his presence. This chapter will establish the boundaries of the Hunanese period in Xinjiang, from 1877 to 1915, where 1904 marked the turning point in this group's fall from power.[6]

Whereas the previous chapter outlined the means of Xinjiang's assimilation, this chapter tracks shifts in the conception of Xinjiang as an exceptional space within a zone of Chinese or Qing sovereignty across generations of officials. A certain tradition of critical legal studies, and of colonial legal studies in particular, observes that every legal system contains an "exception," a case in which the normative system is suspended.[7] In colonial empires and their successor states, the exception is realized in geography, as a zone putatively undergoing a state of crisis in which special violent measures must be taken to protect or promote the essential norms of law and bring order to chaos. The enactment of that violence is a performance of sovereignty. If every political and legal system contains an exception, then delineating the exception will therefore illuminate the whole, casting light on the realities of power as well as the norms that powerholders desire to promote. In late-Qing Xinjiang, examining the shifting discourses and practices of exception shows how the region was a distinctly Hunanese project undertaken within the Qing empire, but against it. The end of Hunanese dominance at the top of the provincial government signaled another radical shift toward explicit colonialism, the new politics of exception of which cast the Xiang Army project into relief.

Zuo's Heirs and the Disaster of Provincehood

While most histories emphasize the role of Zuo Zongtang in shaping policy in the Reconstruction period, Zuo actually only entered the territory of Xinjiang once. Real authority resided in the hands of Liu Jintang (1844–94), who was joined by his childhood friend Luo Changhu (ca. 1847–83).[8] Liu was perhaps the most striking example of the importance of Zuo's patronage for determining one's career trajectory, as he became the first governor of Xinjiang despite possessing little administrative experience, apart from a few years as the intendant of Xining, and despite the fact that he did not attempt to take the official examinations. His main qualification was being the nephew of Zuo's trusted commander Liu Songshan (1833–70), upon whose death Jintang was granted his uncle's command. About Luo less is known, save that he had Zuo's attention from an early age. Liu and Luo grew up in the same village, campaigned across China together, and retook the Tarim Basin in concert. Luo achieved the rank of brigade commander, and Zuo favored him for his intelligence and bravery, especially after Luo volunteered to lead a march beyond the Pass during a snowy winter. Later on, Liu, suffering from an old foot injury received during a mudslide in Gansu, sent Luo to command the assault on Opal, a town near Kashgar, in his stead. The two conducted a running conversation about policy throughout and beyond the campaign.

Liu Jintang was effectively in power for fifteen years, as he was the first official in charge of the reconstruction government and then governor through 1891. His second-in-command, the financial commissioner, was Wei Guangtao (1837–1915), a Xiang Army commander from Shaoyang and the nephew of the *jingshi* writer Wei Yuan. Wei Guangtao composed the unofficial history of the Northwest campaigns and considered it his duty to follow Zuo's program closely, as he did during three years as acting governor (1888–91).[9] The next governor (1892–95) was Tao Mo, who had been Zuo's model official for the moral rectification of central Gansu. His successor, Rao Yingqi of Hubei (1837–1903, in office 1895–1902), was Zuo's secretary during the Northwestern campaign.[10] Next was Pan Xiaosu (in office 1902–05), a Changshanese who had served in the Xiang Army since 1861 and participated in the reconquest. Thus a single cohort of collocal men with a common ideology and experience held formal political power in the provincial capital of Dihua for the first twenty-eight years after the reconquest. The same was true of the highest provincial officials below the governor: nearly all of the financial commissioners, their staffs, and the judicial commissioners (the third-highest provincial official) were from the Changsha area. This was a community united by ideology, native place, common experience, and family, and one that maintained its consciousness of its Hunanese origins.

The early governors held closely to Zuo's vision in theory, if not entirely in practice.[11] Their work remained doggedly focused on sociomoral rectification as the Xiang Army group had envisioned it in post-Taiping China proper. Liu was at the head of a provisional government that consisted of a network of Reconstruction and Pacification Agencies (*fuji shanhou ju*) headed by army officers, the organization of which mirrored the planned provincial administration. The Agencies repeated the experiments of Gansu: they resettled Hui, Chinese, and Musulmans on farms, where they were meant to live in ideal nuclear families, sometimes with spouses that the agencies chose for them. Resettled people received farming implements, seed, and livestock in the hopes that they would "reclaim" land—either genuinely fallow fields or unworkable steppe and desert. Ultimately, the goal of resettlement was to create a stable, peaceful society by placing demobilized soldiers and Muslim women into marriages.

Meanwhile, the Agencies established at least two hundred "charitable schools" across the region with the goal of educating Musulman boys in the Chinese language and the Classics.[12] Zuo hoped to create a class of linguistically and culturally bifluent intermediaries who would act as conduits for Confucian ideas into Musulman society. His argument was twofold: First, he stated, there was a nearly insurmountable distance between Musulman subjects and the officials who were meant to play a pastoral role in their lives. Qing magistrates, as "father-and-mother officials" (*fumuguan*), were meant to guide their flocks toward moral behavior in order to maintain a peaceful society. For Zuo, this meant making the Musulmans "assimilate to our Chinese ways" (*tong wo Hua feng*). *Jingshi* thought held that magistrates were fundamental to establishing the trust and respect of local people, and Zuo by this time was already emphasizing the need for local officials to resolve disputes in a consistent and satisfactory manner so as to secure that good will.[13]

As the deadline in 1884 for provincehood drew nearer, however, the leadership became aware that local government was not remotely prepared for the transition, as Xiang Army veterans did not necessarily make good administrators. One, Yang Peiyuan (d. 1879), had been promoted to the rank of assistant magistrate for his service in the army. In 1877, Yang was appointed the acting subdistrict magistrate of Pichan, a small town some ways off the main road east of Turpan and later the seat of Shanshan County.[14] Things went badly for him. One of his servants attempted to extort money from local Musulmans. Yang attempted to resolve the resulting dispute but botched the mediation, owing in part to his total lack of language skills. As a result, Yang reported, whenever he went out on the streets, the Musulmans would gather around and laugh at him. Clearly, he had swiftly lost their respect. Yang was unable to do his duty and formally asked to be removed from office, but the Turpan prefect denied him. Three months later, Yang hanged himself in his office. It was not until two months after that, when an officer came through on inspection, that the higher administration even learned of Yang Peiyuan's death. In the eyes of the provincial government, government itself had failed both at the local and at the regional level through the inability of the magistrate to communicate with and guide his charges.

Reports such as these trickled in from frustrated magistrates all over Xinjiang. Liu, panicked, sent memorials to Beijing gently requesting to be relieved of his duties; after all, he had only been an army officer and never expected to become at the age of thirty-three the governor of a vast and troublesome province.[15] He was, by his own account, "without learning or skill" (bu xue wu shu). Liu's appointment to direct reconstruction, he wrote, was meant to be temporary, "no more than an expedient act under special circumstances. In all matters, I was only to try to bring Zuo Zongtang's plans to realization, and after things had settled down, I would hand over the position." The court refused—nonsense, they replied, it appeared that reconstruction was almost complete. That attitude alone showed a certain naïveté on the part of Zuo Zongtang and of the Qing court: Xinjiang was meant to become a province, and its people ready for Chinese-style civil government, seven years after its reconquest. In Zuo's view, that would be sufficient time to establish the social institutions and cultural dispositions (or "customs," fengsu) necessary to support a stable province, and even to make Xinjiang a self-supporting agricultural society. Xinjiang, in Zuo's vision, was not ready for technological modernization, and certainly not for the construction of a modern arsenal like those he had established in Gansu. A moral agricultural society needed to develop first.

Liu tried to resign again in 1882, arguing that Xinjiang was not prepared to be made its own province. Before 1864, gradual Chinese settlement had led to the establishment of a few counties and prefectures in what was now Northern Xinjiang. These had remained under the authority of Gansu, while the rest of Xinjiang was governed through the military administration in Ili and local officials. Gansu in turn was administered by a governor under the governor-general in Shaanxi. Zuo's original plan would effectively turn Xinjiang into two separate provinces by stationing a governor-general for Xinjiang in Dihua, and then a governor for Southern Xinjiang in Aksu.[16] Liu proposed instead, along with the Shaanxi-Gansu governor-general Tan Zhonglin (1822–1905, from Changsha), making Xinjiang an appendage of Gansu, as Taiwan was to Fujian province, and keeping it under the Shaanxi governor-general. Liu proposed putting the governor's office in Lanzhou, so that Xinjiang would be ruled from a distance. That way, he wrote, his own position would be eliminated, and he could finally return home to treat his debilitating foot injury. Ultimately, Liu was forced to remain in Dihua and become the governor, but Xinjiang constituted a single province, alongside Gansu and under the Shaanxi-Gansu governor-general, as he had suggested.

Then Luo Changhu died of illness while in Aksu in 1883. Liu Jintang sent a request to Beijing to establish a shrine in his memory and used the opportunity to suggest once again that Xinjiang policy was misguided.[17] He quoted a discussion he and Luo had held earlier that year, suggesting that decades more would need to pass before agriculture and the gradual spread of Confucian ideals allowed "talent" (*cai*) to emerge among the Musulmans and ready them for participation in the institutions of provincehood. Liu's memorial was an obvious attempt to ventriloquize his dead friend in support of a political goal. The court rejected Liu's request for a shrine and ignored the suggestion that provincehood needed to be delayed.

Nevertheless, Liu's words proved prophetic. While Xinjiang province was officially founded on schedule in 1884, it was a confused and disorganized affair that in some places took several years.[18] Local government was not prepared to handle the final abolition of the system of local Musulman officials, called *begs*, that had operated before 1864 and still remained largely intact. There were no household registrations, and thus no records to be used for taxation, and none of the new magistrates could speak the Musulmans' Turkic language or read Chaghatay. At first, it was unclear who exactly fell under the jurisdiction of the provincial system, and who under that of the rump Ili military administration or some other authority.[19] Without the begs to serve as intermediaries, even routine tasks became fraught with complications.

Therefore, the history of late-Qing Xinjiang is not in fact the history of the region's assimilation into the Chinese political system so much as its construction as an exception within it. Liu's proposals pointed to a paradox: in order for Musulmans to become included in the Chinese ecumene, they needed to be both separated from it, yet suspended in a state of becoming Chinese. Zuo Zongtang's policies in Gansu had pointed to the same contradiction of normalization, in which the key to effecting sameness was recognizing gradations of difference and segregating space accordingly. In Xinjiang, as generations of officials struggled to achieve the goals of the civilizing project, they worked within the *jingshi* paradigm to find ways to manage difference while still working toward assimilation. In the following pages, we will delineate how a discourse of Musulman Otherness served to legitimize Xinjiang's construction as a zone of exception in several different ways: as a space wherein the ordinary rules of the judicial process did not apply, and likewise of the bureaucracy; as a familiar kind of frontier; and then at the end of the Qing as an explicitly colonial territory.

Xinjiang as an Exceptional Administration

The distinctiveness of Xinjiang was used to justify a set of "flexible" (*biantong*) policies that only applied within the province. Characterizing a policy as "flexible" suggested that it was a temporary measure and, as *jingshi* preferred, an adaptation to local circumstances. Xinjiang was thus governed in part by the "Xinjiang Flexibility Plan" (*Xinjiang biantong zhangcheng*), a special set of rules for the region codified not in formal law, but in a series of palace memorials, by the request of the governor and with the approval of the court. These "flexible" policies included a set of measures that kept personnel circulating within the Northwest, and Xinjiang in particular, in violation of the long-established "rule of avoidance."[20] Imperial regulations intended to prevent corruption and the emergence of entrenched communities of interest prevented officials from serving in their home counties or in any place for more than a few years. In the Northwest, however, the abrogation of this rule meant that members of the Xiang Army community usually spent entire careers in this province's administration. The whole Northwest attained a high degree of autonomy and developed its own largely closed governing community. Personnel records, when considered in the aggregate, show that the entrenchment of the Hunanese network within Xinjiang's civil government began to take shape years before the

march beyond the Pass and then reproduced itself across four generations.[21] Those generational distinctions map onto differences in policies
and practices and the relationship of Xinjiang's government with the imperial court.

It will help the reader to be familiar with the geography of the Changsha
area as it relates to the Xiang Army. In the nineteenth century, the city of
Changsha itself was divided into two counties (*xian*), Changsha and Shanhua, which together composed the nucleus of Changsha prefecture (*fu*).
Several counties within Changsha prefecture and the adjacent Yuezhou
prefecture provided the bulk of Xiang Army officers, while a handful came
from farther afield, including nearby areas of Hubei and Anhui provinces.
Changsha city was home to several institutions that were central to the
Xiang Army community's formation: the Yuelu Academy, across the river
from Changsha city, and the Chengnan Academy just outside its south gate
were the cradle of the army's leadership.

At the base of Changsha's city walls, we would also find the temple of
Dingxiang Wang, the unassuming city god (*chenghuang*) of Shanhua County
who was credited with saving the city from the Taiping assault and thus
became the common object of worship of the Xiang Army's soldiers. They
carried that patron deity's image on campaign from one end of China to the
other, until finally Dingxiang Wang came to settle in Xinjiang along with
the veterans who maintained his temples.[22] As late as 1885, the leadership
of Xinjiang maintained an affection for Dingxiang Wang. That year,
Xinjiang-based Hunanese published a pamphlet at the Baoshan tang printing house in Hunan that was explicitly meant to popularize the Confucian
revival and celebrate Hunanese identity. Not coincidentally, the printing
house was run by a Xiang Army veteran who had returned from Xinjiang,
the anti-Christian activist Zhou Han.[23] The pamphlet lists the "chief masters" (*shoushi*) of the Baoshan tang by their home counties in Hunan—and
every single one was part of the Xinjiang administration, including magistrates, prefects, intendants, and a future governor.

Those chief masters were part of the first generation of officials who
came beyond the Pass with Liu Jintang. They were Xiang Army veterans
from the Taiping era, or else Hunanese who had been recruited during the
Gansu reconstruction. At that time, the army was already led by a small
cohort of men from the same place who were all around the same age, born
either in the 1810s like Zuo or in the 1830s, and who had fought the Taiping

and Nian.[24] These leaders in turn recruited almost exclusively from the core areas of Northern Hunan around Changsha, particularly from their own hometowns fifteen hundred miles away, mobilizing personal connections through family, villages, and schools to maintain the collocal integrity of a Hunanese fighting force far from home. Zuo personally requested recruits not from his immediate surroundings, but from Yongding and Ningxiang Counties. Often brothers or cousins joined together, and so did fathers and sons. The brothers Wang Tingxiang (b. 1840) and Wang Tingzan (b. 1845) of Xiangyin, for example, both joined the army in Gansu and later finished their careers in Xinjiang, while Huang Guangda (ca. 1845–1901) replaced his father Huang Wanyou as commander when he died in battle in 1870, much as Liu Jintang took up his uncle Songshan's role.

In Gansu, after the rebel leader Dong Fuxiang switched sides and joined forces with Zuo, the Muslim leader Ma Zhan'ao followed, and between Dong and Ma, the size of the army nearly doubled.[25] These forces proved to be critical in the occupation of Gansu and reconquest of Xinjiang. However, Dong and Ma's officers did not enter the province's civil bureaucracy later on, as Xiang Army officers did, but were assigned to garrisons. By 1877, the Xiang Army thus comprised two bodies of people: one was a nucleus of Hunanese collocals who shared ideology, worship, and often family ties, as well as the common experience of fighting across the empire. These Hunanese had already begun to reproduce their community by recruiting from their home counties. The other body was made up of Muslims from Gansu who had joined the Qing only when the failure of the Muslim uprisings of the Northwest seemed inevitable. After 1877, most garrison soldiers were still Hui, or at least came from Gansu. The same was true of the Hunanese officials' known servants, concubines, and clerks. Zuo's policies for the control of Muslims in Gansu had come to depend on the complicity of a body of loyal, armed locals, "good" Muslims who held what Zuo considered to be orthodox beliefs.

During the occupation of Gansu, Xiang Army officers began to secure positions in the civil bureaucracy of Xinjiang, even though the region was not yet under Qing control, and the imperial court had not yet approved the campaign of reconquest. Moreover, very few of their number possessed the formal qualifications necessary to take up an official post as of their departure from Hunan. Of the officials who took up posts in the Xinjiang government in 1877, only one had achieved the highest degree in the imperial examinations, the *jinshi*.[26] Another held the second-highest *juren* degree.[27] They were in the company of a very small number of third-level *xiucai* degree holders, while the bulk of the individuals gaining offices in the future provincial government were simply army officers who purchased their degrees or received them as rewards for battlefield performance. Office purchase was not unusual in the Qing, but these Xiang Army officers mainly acquired theirs through the patronage of their commanders.

Several provincial officials in 1877 were members of Manchu banners whose degrees qualified them for work in translation, something of which most Xiang Army officers were incapable. These bannermen were functionaries in Zuo's army, translation clerks whose work recommended them for civil service later on. To give one example, Hanzhabu (b. 1842) was a Manchu of the Bordered White Banner, a cavalryman who passed the translation exam and was appointed to a scribal post in Gansu prior to the Muslim uprisings.[28] Hanzhabu's heroics in 1862 earned him a promotion and eventually an assignment to Zuo's revived army as it marched into the Northwest. Zuo's early approval kept Hanzhabu in Xinjiang for the rest of his career as he rose to a county-level position of his own.

The second generation of provincial officials was also recruited from Hunan in the first few years after the reconquest, 1878–81. They universally purchased their ranks and moved directly from a county associated with the Xiang Army.[29] They were followed by a third generation, recruited 1884–90, most of whom had been in the army but were transferred directly from Gansu. The 1890s and early 1900s saw little recruitment from the outside—only a handful of new county-level officials arrived in Xinjiang, and most of those were also Xiang Army veterans.

Because of the special regulations governing appointments in Xinjiang, it was very difficult for officials to leave the province. When an office opened up in Northern Xinjiang, a replacement would be found according to the "Gansu Flexibility Plan" (*Gansu biantong zhangcheng*), one of the direct predecessors of Xinjiang's own "flexibility plan."[30] Qualified officeholders who had followed the army into the Northwest could be retained in Gansu or Xinjiang by order of the governor. Liu Jintang and his successors used this rule extensively—a new arrival would have the usual one-year trial period, and then he would enter the cohort of Xinjiang magistrates-in-waiting. According to the Gansu plan, for all open appointments, personnel were to be selected from officials already employed in similar positions within the province. This meant that a magistrate somewhere in Xinjiang would be moved elsewhere in Xinjiang, and often within the same circuit. As for the South, and for all newly established offices, the "Jilin Flexibility Plan" (*Jilin biantong zhangcheng*) was employed. That plan recruited personnel who did not yet hold an office into the province, after which they would be reappointed according to the Gansu plan. In theory, this system would bring in talented people from outside, but in reality, it perpetuated existing networks of patronage.

At the same time, the system of battlefield promotions that advanced many careers under Zuo Zongtang continued well into the provincial era. Officials in Xinjiang were constantly being promoted for their actual or alleged participation in military actions and reconstruction projects. For example, Chen Mingyu (b. 1830, Ningxiang) entered the Xiang Army in 1854.[31] He began as a stipendiary (*linsheng*), which is to say that he did well on the examinations and attained the rank of licentiate (*xiucai*), though he found no employment in civil office. Twelve battlefield promotions raised him directly through the civilian ranks until by the conquest of Xinjiang he was qualified for a position as a circuit intendant. Despite Chen's lack of experience in any bureaucratic post, he was immediately appointed to important offices and spent several years as the intendant of Aksu. Members of the second and third generations, who generally purchased their degrees, also benefited from the blanket promotions given to their fellows, even though they were often not even present for the action in question.

If we consider Hunan, Hubei, Anhui, and Jiangsu to be the greater geographical homeland of the Xiang Army community, then 71 percent of the 381 officials with known places of birth from 1877 to 1911 shared a common regional origin. Hunan accounts for 58 percent. Changsha prefecture alone provided 45 percent, while the largest number of officials came from Xiangyin County, where Zuo Zongtang himself was born and raised. (See maps 2.1 and 2.2.) Entrenchment was apparent at every level of government, from the governor's office to the yamens of the county magistrates. Xinjiang was divided into four "circuits" (*dao*), each with its own intendant who reported to the provincial capital: Kashgar, Aksu, Ili-Tarbaghatai, and Zhendi Circuits. Each holder of these offices from the reconquest to the fall of the Qing was a member of the Xiang Army clique, including the Kashgar intendant Yuan Hongyou (b. 1841), who was the son of the former Kashgar

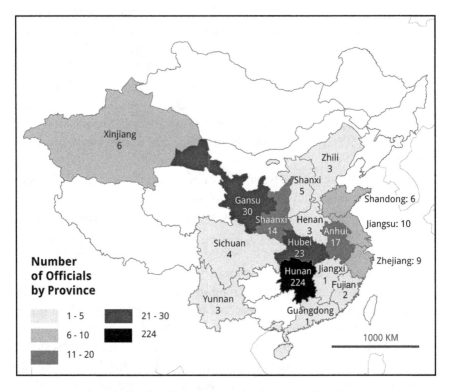

MAP 2.1 Number of officials of known origin by province of birth. Based on collected archival documents from the First Historical Archives in Beijing and the National Palace Museum in Taipei. Map by Evangeline McGlynn. Provincial boundaries from CHGIS.

intendant, Yuan Yaoling (d. 1889).[32] Meanwhile, the Xiang Army leaders had betrothed or promised their children to each other during the occupation of Gansu, and in the mid-1890s, they began to marry and settle in Xinjiang.[33] The family relationships that had characterized succession within Zuo's army also typified the provincial administration, and occasionally fathers and sons, or brothers-in-law, even occupied positions in the same circuit.

The Xinjiang administration was a transposition of the Xiang Army community that had formed in the vicinity of Changsha before and during the Taiping war. Wang Jiping characterizes this community as a social formation with its own internal dynamics and ability to reproduce itself,

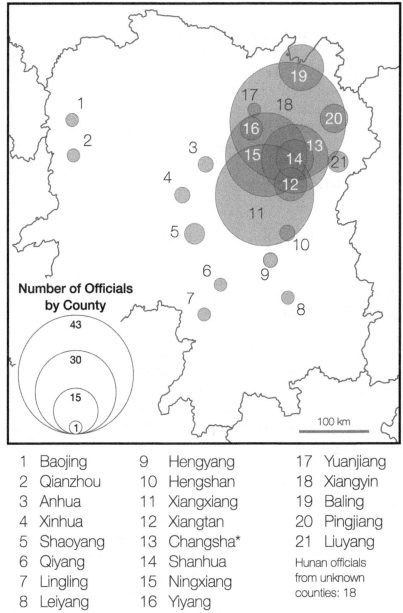

100 km

1 Baojing	9 Hengyang	17 Yuanjiang
2 Qianzhou	10 Hengshan	18 Xiangyin
3 Anhua	11 Xiangxiang	19 Baling
4 Xinhua	12 Xiangtan	20 Pingjiang
5 Shaoyang	13 Changsha*	21 Liuyang
6 Qiyang	14 Shanhua	Hunan officials
7 Lingling	15 Ningxiang	from unknown
8 Leiyang	16 Yiyang	counties: 18

* The centers of Changsha and Shanhua counties are adjacent within Changsha prefecture.

MAP 2.2 Places of origin for Xinjiang officials from Hunan. Based on collected archival documents from the First Historical Archives in Beijing and the National Palace Museum in Taipei. Map by Evangeline McGlynn. County location data and provincial boundaries from CHGIS.

including common practices of worship, familial ties, and connections between teachers and students. A subset of this group moved gradually into the Northwest through the campaigns against the Nian and the Muslims but maintained its intimate connection with home through constant recruitment from its leaders' places of origin. In Xinjiang, the same community's social dynamics persisted, although recruitment from the homeland was eventually replaced with reproduction through family. As Xinjiang became "little Hunan," the distance of the Xinjiang Hunanese from their home grew greater.

Xinjiang as a Zone of Legal Exception

Xinjiang in the late Qing comprised a peculiar space: It was now officially within the system of routine legal procedures and statutory laws and punishments that applied in the provinces, and yet it was simultaneously excepted from them. The Xiang Army ostensibly reconstructed the region in order to assimilate its people through persuasion, but its leadership argued that those people remained dangerous and therefore required harsh punishment. Xinjiang therefore became a zone of legal exception, a paradoxical space in which policies meant to aid the greater penetration of state institutions relied on the devolution of power and legitimate violence to local agents.[34] This paradoxical situation seems counterintuitive, even bizarre, and certainly insidiously violent, and yet it typifies colonial legal regimes.

The chief technique of this legal regime—and the one that sent Zhou Jing-tang into exile—was "execution on the spot" (*jiudi zhengfa*), the authority of provincial officials to authorize capital punishment without the approval of the emperor. "Execution on the spot" involved the suspension of Qing law and the transfer of the power over life and death into the hands of local actors in the service of protecting the rites (*li*), that complex of behaviors at the heart of the army's civilizing project. However, the practice has its origins in the Qing emperors' strategic suspension of the law, first in the early wars of conquest, and then in cases of the urgent need to punish violence, including during rebellions and in borderland areas where a murder might erupt into a feud.[35] Normally, in any case that might result in capital punishment, there was a statutory process of review according to which the emperor had to approve every execution. However, through the mid-nineteenth century, a military officer could occasionally be permitted to perform executions through a process called "requesting the kingly command to execute immediately" (*gongqing wangming jixing zhengfa*). This practice was applied with greater frequency in the Inner Asian borderlands, and it eventually became codified: people who had death sentences commuted to exile and escaped either along the way or from their penal farms were to be executed immediately without review. Because Xinjiang was such a common site of exile, some thinkers associated "executing immediately" (*jixing zhengfa*) with the region.

One of those thinkers was Lin Zexu (1785–1850), the commissioner who had destroyed British opium on the Canton docks and so sparked off the First Opium War (1839–42).[36] Lin had requested permission for the immediate execution of his British prisoners, but instead received the punishment of exile to Xinjiang for what the Qing court considered his disruptive and impudent act. In 1848, Zuo Zongtang met Lin, who now presented himself as an expert on Xinjiang. Lin's influence on Zuo's agricultural scheme is well documented—Lin was fascinated with *karez*, the underground water channels of Turpan, and both saw the potential to irrigate the desert through the art of water management. Yet he also introduced Zuo to what he now called "execution on the spot" (*jiudi zhengfa*), which Lin claimed was not an imperial technique, but rather an expedient measure devised by local officials in Xinjiang in order to save government time and resources.[37] That same year, Lin successfully secured imperial permission to implement this technique in Yunnan as a means to punish local rebels. It was meant to be a temporary measure with a five-year limit.

Execution on the spot soon became one of the Xiang Army's main techniques of government, as it realized in practice *jingshi* theories about minimal government while transferring power over life and death into the hands of the self-declared protectors of civilization. Wherever the Xiang Army pushed back the Taiping, Zeng Guofan implemented a regime of sociomoral rectification over and against imperial law.[38] In 1853, Zeng took up Lin's "execution on the spot" as a means to conduct battlefield executions of people who were notionally Qing subjects during a time of crisis. Zeng and several other provincial governors in his clique simultaneously requested blanket permission to delegate execution to lower-level actors, including gentry. The suspension of ordinary judicial procedure permitted the imposition of rules intended to protect and promote normative family relationships as specified by the rites. Although the initial order for execution on the spot concerned "bandits" (*zei*) and groups of violent men, and so was clearly meant to combat the Taiping, its extension in Hunan and adjacent provinces specified punishments for sexual impropriety, wife-selling, and human trafficking in the name of social stability. Execution on the spot persisted long after the state of crisis was over.

Execution on the spot illustrates an important characteristic of the *jingshi* party's policies: they were often "practical" in the sense that they curtailed the involvement of the central government in economy and society, which technically reduced the state's logistical and financial burdens. However, their fundamental purpose was the ordering of society. In China proper, "execution on the spot" usually went through three stages: early on, it was used to prosecute a civil war, as evidenced by high numbers of mass executions; later, although violence became less general, it gave local officials special authority to punish bandits, looters, and slavers; and only in its final stage did this emergency measure become a normalized part of the politico-juridical system. As Weiting Guo points out, provincial governors' expressed concerns with the potential violence of "roving braves" (*youyong*) long after the end of the war took advantage of officials' own prejudices against the poor and uprooted men who had filled their armies.[39] Even after the war had ended, the same special measures were still applied in particular zones to certain kinds of subjects in the name of stability.

The same was true of Gansu, where "execution on the spot" was also enacted under the Gansu Flexibility Plan.[40] In 1899, long after the war had ended, the governor of Gansu continued to claim that execution on the spot was necessary so that officials could spend less time and energy on adjudicating capital cases and more on civilizing the Muslims. After all, the governor argued, while execution on the spot did not conform to the letter of the law, it grasped, even protected, the essence of the law. The Muslim-majority Northwest was thus constructed as an exception within imperial space and law: Gansu was a province and therefore part of the normal politico-juridical system, but its inhabitants' violent tendencies, it was claimed, necessitated a special regime of punishment. Where execution on the spot had been used in China proper to punish immoral lower-class people, now in the Northwest it was directed at putatively heterodox and dangerous Muslims.

In Xinjiang, it is not clear that execution on the spot was ever used as a battlefield measure—instead, it was a routine technique from the beginning.[41] Xinjiang's governors argued to Beijing time and again that the region was still in a state of chaos and violence, and that the Musulmans were forever on the precipice of rebellion. Nevertheless, the province's own data challenge their assertions: Where execution on the spot was applied during the Taiping war, it accounted for hundreds of executions each season, but all of Xinjiang from 1877 to 1911 only reported an average of twelve capital crimes every year, half of which resulted in execution on the spot. Moreover, while the provincial administration claimed that execution on the spot was a means to manage the Musulmans, violent crime was reported at a vastly higher rate in areas of Chinese settlement in the North, where legal and social institutions were weaker. By contrast, the Musulman-majority South was comparatively very peaceful, probably because of the presence of Islamic legal authorities and established mechanisms for dispute resolution.[42] Finally, Liu Jintang and his successors argued to the court that prosecuting capital crimes was too time-consuming, given the need to report the details of the case to the province, which in turn would seek approval from Beijing. In fact, communications between the provincial capital at Dihua and any given locality were not particularly slow: even before the Muslim uprisings, it took about forty-seven days for a memorial to reach Beijing from Ili on the other end of the empire.[43] Records of capital punishment by statute from Xinjiang after 1877 show that the time between a murder being reported and the imperially approved execution was about eight months. To compare it with a central Chinese province, that was not much slower than cases from Hubei in the same period, which could take as much as a year to process.[44] That delay was shortened after the introduction of the telegraph, despite which execution on the spot continued to be invoked at the same rate until the end of the Qing.

The frequency and geographical distribution of execution on the spot lead us to question its purposes further. Several cases prosecuted through routine procedure took well beyond the statutory time limits to close, which suggests that haste was not really a concern. The technique accounted for over half of all capital punishments in Xinjiang, across the entire region, regardless of distance from the capital. Moreover, capital crimes in the same locale might be punished with execution either "on the spot" or following a report to Beijing. What then accounted for the choice between exceptional or routine punishment?

One case from Turpan in 1899 reveals the politics and ideology behind such a decision.[45] A Hui man named Li Fu was characterized in the archive as a "bare stick": a man of no fixed abode, no familial connections, and no employable skills. One day Li murdered a Musulman—or Hui, depending on the document—over some buns. In this respect, the Li Fu case resembles dozens of others, in which people murdered each other out of hunger and poverty. However, his Muslim victim, a man named Yūnus, was the only son of an elderly couple, who were now deprived of their son's support as well as the continuation of their family line. In contrast, Li Fu was no family man, but a migrant laborer who had come from Xining in search of work on both sides of the Tianshan Mountains, in this case taking up an unskilled job packaging tobacco. It took under a week for the Turpan prefect to recommend execution on the spot, so that Li Fu could be made an example to the other migrants. That a drifter could prevent a filial son from completing his duties to his parents, he argued, could not be countenanced, as it harmed the rites. The governor approved, and Li Fu was beheaded publicly less than two months after his crime. The execution was reported to Beijing later on.

Li Fu's case is instructive: examining execution on the spot in the aggregate shows that it was applied disproportionately to "bare sticks" and to those whose crimes disrupted familial relationships. In other words, it was a means to enforce the cohesion of the family, in accordance with *jingshi* principles. It therefore covered a range of crimes against the ideal social fabric: the kidnapping and rape of a young girl; a woman murdering her husband under her lover's influence, or out of jealousy over his new second wife; a boy killing his grandfather during an argument; deaths resulting from conflicts between countless migrant laborers; as well as occasional prosecutions of the roving bandit gangs for which the measure was nominally intended.[46] Perhaps most strikingly, a destitute man in Khotan, in the midst of a freezing winter, exhumed a corpse and stole its clothing in order to keep warm.[47] He was hanged for graverobbing, executed as swiftly as if he had murdered his mother. Individuals in 282 cases were reported to have been executed, or else given a lighter sentence such as exile or imprisonment, under this measure.

Indeed, execution on the spot did not always result in capital punishment. Instead, the procedure also empowered the governor to first sentence someone to death, and then issue a stay of execution. This power of mercy was also the formal domain of the Qing sovereign, and the ritual provision thereof had for centuries been a means to reintegrate the condemned into the imperial order.[48] Its usurpation by local actors in service of the rites surely informed Mullah Mūsa Sayrāmī's depiction of the shift from a Qing-centered codified law to a kind of scriptural Chinese Shariah. Indeed, his continuator, Ghulām Muḥammad Khan, specifically names the failure to report executions to Beijing as a sign of Xinjiang's administration's inde-pendence from the emperor.[49] Sayrāmī and Ghulām were perceptive: not only had the ideology and institutions governing Xinjiang changed, so had the techniques, and while most provincial functions such as taxation func-tioned poorly, the state was quite capable of enacting violence.

Xinjiang was therefore "exceptional" in the way that much of the terri-tory the Xiang Army held during and after the Taiping War was excep-tional. Execution on the spot in the form discussed here was a product of the actualization of *jingshi* ideas in the Taiping era. It had been applied in Hunan, among other provinces, as well as Gansu and Xinjiang. It progressed in most places from the punishment of "roving bandits," or rather enemy combatants in a civil war, to the punishment of human trafficking, wife-selling, and other infractions against the deeper moral principles believed to undergird Qing law. Yet it was in Xinjiang that this exceptional punish-ment became a routine and persistent technique of politics, a strategic means to achieve a specific social and moral goal over the long term, rather than a means to manage exceptional violence in the short term. Where in China proper this technique was legitimized by claims about roving men, in Xinjiang those same concerns were projected instead onto Muslims.

A Southern Province in the Northwest

Punishment of roving men provided one model for officials' treatment of the Musulmans, but managing difference in Southwest China offered another. Hunanese literati were after all familiar with the diverse non-Chinese peo-ples of Hunan and the broader South, whom they identified collectively as *Miao* and *Man*. These peoples lived within the provincial system, as Musul-mans did after 1877, and the canonical collection of *jingshi* writings offered extensive advice on how to govern them alongside Chinese.[50]

Fu Nai (1758–1811), who was a magistrate during the Miao Uprising of 1795–1806, provided salient advice: "If one desires a lasting peace, the only way is to alter their customs and habits, settle their families, and order their minds. Only then may we 'grasp' the Miao and govern them."[51] Fu's allusion to the *Great Learning* connected a strategy of cultural assimilation to this text, which formed heart of Neo-Confucian learning. He went on to provide a thoroughly Confucian explanation for the intractability of the Miao: the greed and expropriations of merchants and petty officials led to a profusion of lawsuits, he argued, and thus drove the Miao away from local government. Instead, Fu proposed, stations ought to be set up to regulate commerce between Chinese and Miao, to separate them in preparation for slow assimilation. The latter would be effected first through regular lectures on morality, and then the recruitment of the most talented young Miao men into academies. "The Miao will teach the Miao . . . so the rites will prevail, while the wickedness fades, and there will be no difference between Miao and Chinese." The resonances of Fu Nai's essay with Lu Yao's discussion of the Muslims are clear: Both authors proposed a structured erosion of boundaries leading to the transformation of customs. In comparative colonial terms, Fu articulated once again the essence of a civilizing mission, the effort to show the Other the self-evident truth of the dominant group's ideology and thus bring them to desire assimilation.[52] As the Hunanese defined what they wanted these Others to be, they of course advanced an ideal vision of themselves.

Such a Southern model prevailed several times under this first generation of Hunanese rulers, not least of all in Zuo Zongtang's system of schools. A series of policy crises and the policies articulated to address them showed the particular influence of the "Miao borderland" (*Miaojiang*) experience in Xinjiang. Each crisis related to the general problem of debt and revenue, and the relationship of the province and its subjects to merchants. Xinjiang's trade networks were dominated by a new merchant community from the town of Yangliuqing in Tianjin, on China's distant coast.[53] A great famine had coincided with the Xiang Army's march through Central China, and many Tianjinese chose to leave home and "follow the great army" (*gan da ying*) as traders to supply the soldiers. The story of their subsequent migration is still celebrated today in Yangliuqing and in Xinjiang. The Yangliuqing merchants were the largest group, but they were not alone—sizable groups of traders from Shaanxi, Shanxi,

Guangdong, and elsewhere maintained native-place associations that linked them with homelands in China proper. While these networks were nominally focused on trade in goods, the historical record demonstrates that moneylending, especially to farmers, formed a sizable part of their activities, and that debt was a significant source of their income. Just as such merchants could be found across China, so could the consequent problems of widespread indebtedness.

One crisis emerged in 1889 in Turpan, and provincial officials construed it as symptomatic of a widespread debt problem. That year, a Chinese village headman and a merchant brought a farmer named ʿAbdurraḥīm and several other Musulmans before the magistrate and accused them of failing to repay their loans.[54] ʿAbdurraḥīm and his fellow defendants contested that the interest on those loans was unreasonably high, and that it would be impossible to repay them in cotton or cash. The magistrate chose to enforce the loan contract, however, and sent them home to Yarghol (Yanghai) with an order to repay their debt. ʿAbdurraḥīm and his fellows, like indebted Musulmans all across the province, then took matters into their own hands and attempted to burgle a different Chinese merchant.[55] The many archival cases of burglaries gone wrong show that Chinese merchants were tempting targets, as they often lived in isolated houses in Musulman-majority areas and held significant amounts of cash, while Chinese officials had difficulty identifying suspects. ʿAbdurraḥīm's plan failed, though, and his party of seventeen farmers fled into the wilderness for a year. Early in the winter of 1891, they emerged again in a dawn raid on Lükchün, where they broke into the arsenal and stole guns and horses, and then rode for Yarghol. There they killed thirty-six Chinese, including the merchant who had initially taken ʿAbdurraḥīm to court, and burned down their houses. It took a month for the authorities to capture ʿAbdurraḥīm and his followers, most of whom were put to death immediately under "execution on the spot."

Provincial officials questioned why the uprising had broken out in the first place. Their suspicions were raised early on: While the magistrate's runners were still pursuing ʿAbdurraḥīm's party, a group of Chinese merchants from the area sent a petition to the magistrate that blamed corrupt yamen staff for the outbreak of violence. That claim did not ring true to officials, who noted the rebels' involvement in the previous year's debt dispute. Instead, the subsequent investigation pinned responsibility squarely on illicit collaboration between Chinese merchants and the local magistrate himself, who was stripped of his position.

In a memorial to Beijing, Tao Mo proposed extensive new restrictions on Chinese merchants' lending to Musulmans.[56] The Musulmans, he argued, were simple and pliable people unaccustomed to usury, which after all is prohibited by Islam: "The Chantou only plans for present convenience. He does not pay attention to future problems." Tao, following Fu Nai, made an analogy between the Musulmans and the Miao. (Of course, his characterization of the Miao was also based on common stereotypes of peripheral peoples.)[57] As of the end of the Miao Uprising, it was prohibited for Chinese to lend money to Miao chiefs, he argued, and it would be wise to grant all Musulmans the same status. While the court in Beijing did not approve of granting a new legal status to Musulmans, the provincial government implemented a program to clear Musulmans' debt and prohibit future lending. However, financial difficulties soon made it difficult to implement such a policy.

This conscious placement of Xinjiang into a Southern mold meant that the region did not cease being a borderland—rather, it became a different kind of borderland. This was formally true in the sense that Musulmans were no longer under the jurisdiction of the Lifanyuan, but instead became subjects within the provincial system. Moreover, it meant moving from one mode of exclusion and inclusion to another, from a pluralistic mode of government into an emphatically assimilationist one in which standards were set not by the center, but by the priorities and experiences of the Hunanese ruling community.

Reform Within the Jingshi Group

A fiscal and political crisis precipitated by a combination of imperial and local factors led the provincial government not to undermine merchant power, but instead to rely on it. The Hunanese in Xinjiang by the 1890s were deeply entrenched in the provincial bureaucracy. So much quickly became apparent to Governor Tao Mo. Tao, from Jiangsu, was never quite as central to the Xiang Army clique as his Hunanese predecessors, despite Zuo's patronage.[58] By the time Tao came into office in 1892, he had spent over a decade in Zhili and Shaanxi, and in the meantime the Hunanese members of the clique had become resistant to external interference. Officials of

Hunanese origin quickly memorialized the court to request that Liu Jintang be reinstated as governor, and soon after, Tao himself requested dismissal.[59] His given reason was his frustration with the British incursion into Kanjut, which Xinjiang's garrison soldiers were meant to combat. Tao's difficulties sprang from the army's unwillingness to follow his commands. The army was still staffed in the majority by Xiang Army veterans, who had now been settled in the region for fifteen years. Dong Fuxiang's Hui had likewise become an increasingly independent power in Yarkand and Khotan.[60] Nevertheless, Tao spoke the language of *jingshi*, and it was in this paradigm that he responded to the financial crises of the 1890s.

Without the support of other members of the provincial administration, Tao reached out to merchant groups, who in China proper had long since become indispensable to the everyday operations of local government.[61] These merchant groups became critical to maintaining the province's financial stability. It had been agreed in 1884 that the province would receive an annual subsidy of 3,360,000 taels from China proper.[62] While there was technically a land tax in place to supplement the subsidy, exceptions to the tax were very frequent: access to water was unstable in arid areas, much of the land chosen for "reclamation" was unworkable, people tended to move away from their places of resettlement, and the system for reporting and remitting taxes was fraught with the usual problems of the imperial hierarchy. Officials frequently lowered a given plot of land's tax quota following floods or droughts, under the mistaken assumption that later taxes would make up the difference. Moreover, inflation all over the Qing was devaluing local officials' already-meager salaries. As a result, many turned to selling government-controlled land for personal gain.[63] Meanwhile, merchants easily avoided internal trade tariffs (*lijin*), and so these provided almost no revenue whatsoever. Therefore, because the cost of levying the tariff was actually higher than revenue derived from it, Tao Mo abolished it in 1893.[64]

Tao's decision was added to the *jingshi* canon because it devolved authority further from the formal mechanisms of government to ad hoc partnerships between officials and nonstate actors. Merchants' native-place associations and temples held their own endowments of land, and it was theoretically possible to convince them to summon tens of thousands of taels in contributions, more than the internal tariff brought in in a year.[65] In short, merchant networks had significant cash on hand and a good logistical apparatus for the movement of goods when the provincial government simply did not.

Therefore, Tao encouraged merchants to purchase government-owned grain at reduced cost and transport it across the desert in the government's place.[66] That would bring in revenue and take the burden off of the province to distribute grain, but it essentially put private interests in charge of a government duty. While Tao decried merchants' exploitation of ordinary Musulmans, he still found them supremely useful, or at least admitted that they had become indispensable. Moreover, while these measures were dissonant with the Xiang Army's ideals of provincehood, they resembled established practices in real provinces.

Tao Mo may have meant his collaboration with merchants to be temporary, but by the end of his time in office, conditions had deteriorated further. Between 1895 and 1904, as the Qing struggled to pay the Sino-Japanese War indemnity, Xinjiang's subsidy was reduced to one-third of what it had been.[67] Beijing instructed the already-impoverished region to adopt austerity measures: reduce personnel and raise taxes. The new governor, Rao Yingqi, refused. He argued that Xinjiang was unable to dispense with the remnants of the Xiang Army, as there were effectively no local militias. Instead, he undertook a number of partnerships with mainly foreign commercial interests in an attempt to mine Xinjiang's natural resources and enrich the province's treasuries. These failed.

The Boxer indemnity and the subsequent further reduction in Xinjiang's subsidy forced the hand of Rao's successor, Pan Xiaosu. As Xinjiang could no longer pay its outsized force of garrison soldiers, in 1902 Pan disbanded half of them. He intended to reorganize the rest into farming colonies and so make the borderland garrison both hereditary and self-sufficient, as Zuo Zongtang had originally hoped. However, even this plan could not be funded. Pan was forced to reintroduce the internal tariff and increase land taxes, while he attempted to centralize control over provincial finances. As later documents reveal, during this period local officials often sold government-held land for their own profit and conspired with merchants and local Musulman elites alike to exploit farmers for short-term revenue and personal gain. Longstanding complaints about the province's inability to collect taxes were revealed as problems of corruption and fiscal discipline, as networks of Xiang Army veterans and their families and associates avoided provincial scrutiny of their finances.

In 1905, Pan established the General Office for Agriculture and Animal Husbandry (*tun mu zongju*) in an effort to counter local officials' corruption.[68]

The new office established a parallel tax administration, staffed by officials loyal to the governor, that circumvented the subregional authority of the circuit intendants. Two Xiang Army veterans, Pan Zhen (1850–1926, from Dangtu, Anhui) and Liu Chengqing (1843–1910, from Xiangyin), were given control over the North and the South, respectively. Both had a staff of clerks stationed in each county and prefecture to manage the surveying and purchasing of land and livestock, planning for new irrigation works, and even the recruitment of militias. Nevertheless, this measure too failed to extend the control of the provincial capital.

Effectively, *jingshi* policies had first devolved the authority and duties of government from the center to the locality, nominally in order to make administration more efficient. However, those policies were untenable: It turned out that the *jingshi* revolution from the middle, in which capable officials were trusted to stabilize and transform their localities, ultimately depended on the formal machinery of the empire to function. The decentralization policies led to the further entrenchment of local interests to the detriment of the basic functioning of government. Indeed, instead of re-creating Xinjiang as a formal province with what was notionally at least a meritocratic, rational system of appointments under central control, reconstruction had produced something like a covert landed aristocracy or a mafia, a set of families who used official positions with minimal oversight to derive profit from the land and resources under their control. Marriages, recruitment, and the "flexible" policy of internal promotion ossified the Xinjiang administration through the beginning of the twentieth century. The network of patronage that had begun with Zuo himself and was maintained by common origins and practices turned into an opaque governing elite. Meanwhile, the empire as a whole was moving on, and as the Hunanese community struggled to maintain Xinjiang province, Beijing maneuvered to dislodge them entirely.

The Fall of the Hunanese and Rise of the Imperial Cosmopolitans

Much of what we know about the Hunanese ruling community in Xinjiang circa 1904 comes from attempts by the Qing court to loosen its grip on the province by investigating corruption and appointing non-Xiang Army officials to its highest positions. Those efforts helped foster a new discourse of Xinjiang as a "colony" (*zhimindi*) and a concomitant shift in policy. However, the Xiang Army community's continued control of lower-level official positions tempered reform and shaped the factional struggle over how to define and rule the region.

The Hunanese had long since admitted that the civilizing project was essentially a failure. Over two decades of sending Musulman boys to Confucian schools had not produced the moral men that Zuo Zongtang had wished for. In 1896, with the withdrawal of imperial subsidies, the provincial government cut funding to the schools drastically.[69] "You can lead the people to follow [the relations]," Governor Rao remarked, "but you cannot make them recognize [their value]" (*min ke shi you zhi, bu ke shi zhi zhi*). Instead, the provincial government in 1900 decided to formalize the students' growing influence in local government, and they became village headmen, irrigation chiefs, or other submagisterial functionaries.[70] The begs were rehired as clerks and runners in the yamens, and magistrates learned to accommodate local cultures and practices, much as their counterparts had among the Miao.[71]

This on-the-ground reorganization was insufficient to save the provincial government. Soon the dysfunction within the Xiang Army clique was exposed through the efforts of a new governor-general in Shaanxi: Songfan (1837–1905, in office 1900–1905), a Manchu and Qing loyalist with no ties to the Northwest. Songfan effected the dismissal of Governor Pan Xiaosu on charges of embezzlement.[72] He immediately appointed a newcomer in Pan's place, Wu Yinsun (1851–1921, in office 1905–06). Wu had held high office before, but most of his career had been spent in the police training section of the Guangdong Military Academy. Wu suddenly found himself in 1904 transferred to Dihua, and then promoted the next year to acting governor. Xiang Army dominance of the governor's seat was over.

Wu immediately set about promoting the New Policies (*xinzheng*), a program of empire-wide reform that included the broad implementation of public education. These received support in Xinjiang only from the court's loyalists, such as the Old Torghut ruler Palta (1882–1920) and the Ili generals.[73] The Hunanese claimed, as they had in the face of every new policy, that Xinjiang was too poor and remote to take on any further administrative burdens. They were not wrong—Xinjiang operated at a deficit, provincehood had turned out to be impractical, and much of the New Policies demanded significant institutional reforms without providing funding to support them. Yet their reaction reflected a continuing resistance to central control. Ironically, while a fiscal crisis had prompted the Hunanese to pursue centralization and state-building on their own, they resented similar attempts by the imperial government to generate revenue.

It is hard to say whether the Hunanese regime in Xinjiang began to decline on account of political intrigue or simply natural causes. In 1905, the average "old Xiang Army" veteran was around sixty to eighty years of age. Many of the longest-serving and highest-ranking officials passed away within a few years of one another.[74] Lower-ranking officials were already in their fifties. The generation of Hunanese after them, who rarely achieved county-level ranks, also lacked the military experience that bound their superiors together. They, along with the Henanese, Gansunese, and Zhejiangese who made up most of the cohort of Qing officials after 1904, had almost universally purchased their ranks, buying their way directly to a low-level post in Xinjiang. When older Xiang Army veterans occupied top offices well into their seventies, there was little room for advancement, and so younger officials from this fourth generation lacked the opportunity to form a governing cohort of their own.

Meanwhile, Beijing wanted change. Xinjiang's next governor was Liankui (b. 1849, in office 1905–10), a Manchu official nearing the end of his career. Liankui had previously held high offices in Gansu, but he maintained little connection with the Hunanese. Liankui was thought to be busily appointing Manchus to provincial offices in place of the Chinese bureaucrats, much to the satisfaction of the Musulmans.[75] However, some saw him as a rather ridiculous character who held little conviction of his own. Liankui's own financial commissioner Wang Shu'nan (1852–38, in office 1906–12), the second-highest official in the province, characterized him as a "muddle-headed, mediocre, worn-out imbecile."[76] Perhaps because Liankui's own voice or convictions were weak, his memorials to the throne are dominated by a pair of contradictory voices who advanced competing plans for Xinjiang's future. Neither voice belonged to the Xiang Army. One of the combatants was Wang Shu'nan; the other, Education Commissioner Du Tong (1864–1929, in office 1906–11). Wang and Du were both representatives of the cosmopolitan reformism of the very late Qing, but they could not have been more different from each other. Wang Shu'nan, by his own account, came from a long line of scholar-officials, and he considered himself a distinguished literatus who pursued interests as diverse as climatology and Greek philosophy.[77] At the same time, Wang had a longstanding reputation for bribery and embezzlement. In Xinjiang, he again extracted large sums of money from the provincial treasury and built a network of influence among provincial officials, while his intellectual pretensions secured his reputation as a visionary.

Du Tong was the first to occupy the new post of educational commissioner, which the New Policies had created in an effort to establish universal schooling. Du was an academician of the imperial Hanlin Academy, but he was among the dedicated educationalists selected to study new pedagogical methods in Japan.[78] He was deeply impressed by Meiji Japan's accomplishments and the sociopolitical effects of Japanese education and militarization, which he then sought to implement in Xinjiang. While the Xiang Army–dominated government had all but abandoned the old Confucian schools, Du established hundreds of new schools focused on teaching liberal arts and practical skills, including instruction through the medium of the spoken and written Turkic language. To Du Tong, Musulmans possessed the basic moral inclinations shared by all human beings, and so integrating them into the revived Qing was a matter of gradual awakening to an identity shared with people across the empire, with the end goal of creating a strong national identity.

In contrast, Wang Shu'nan saw Xinjiang not as an inseparable part of the national body, but as an accessory to it, the Qing's colony—indeed, he was the first to use the term *colony* (*zhimindi*) in Chinese when referring to Xinjiang. Wang argued from a developmentalist perspective rooted in his reading of Herbert Spencer.[79] He too advocated abandoning Confucian education as a waste of funds, but also forgoing education for most Musulmans beyond the skills necessary to exploit resources for the empire. Musulmans were, in his formulation, akin to the autochthones of South Africa or Indochina, while the Chinese were the "Whites" (*bai ren*). According to Wang, Xinjiang's situation, in which a small number of "Whites" governed a "native" majority, required autocratic rule on the model of British India or French Annam. Only through autocracy could the Musulmans be brought to a level of "civilization" (*wenming*) necessary for participation in the planned constitutional monarchy. Wang also asserted that cultural difference was racial and inherent, and that progress for non-Chinese was unlikely. His idea of "civilization" was not that of a process of transformation-by-teaching (*jiaohua*), but that of an essential quality or state gained gradually through discipline and economic development. Wang therefore advocated a model for state-driven capitalist development on the backs of Musulman workers, which he proposed would be achieved through the state-merchant collaborations then popular in the Qing.[80] If anything, his plan was to make Xinjiang a classic site of colonial exploitation typified by the focused extraction of specific resources.[81]

While Liankui and Du Tong were both aligned with the court-sponsored reform project, Du enjoyed little support among officials.[82] Du's inspection in 1908 found that only a handful of idealists had implemented the New Policies, including the non-Chinese Ili general and the Torghut Mongol ruler Palta alongside only two magistrates. In contrast, the imperial censor Ruixian discovered that Wang Shu'nan enjoyed a wide network of influence through bribery and office-trading.[83] Nearly all of the officials in his network came from the post-1904 generation and circulated between a set of offices in Dihua, Yarkand, Ghulja, and Khotan. During the last years of the Qing, these magistrates flitted rapidly from one end of the province to the other, purchasing ever-higher offices and rarely reporting for duty. If one extreme case, there were four magistrates in Dihua County in 1911 alone. Moreover, these alleged conspirators either were precisely those censured by Du Tong for failure to implement the New Policies or were closely associated with those who were. Policy and personal interest aligned to create two distinct factions, neither of which mapped clearly onto the old Xiang Army elite.

Thanks to the Xinhai Revolution, which toppled the Qing, Wang and his associates were never prosecuted. Instead, Du Tong left in frustration, while Liankui was replaced by Yuan Dahua (1851–1935, in office 1911–12). Yuan arrived in Dihua just as the Brothers and Elders Society (*Gelao hui*) began uprisings that brought the tide of revolution to the empire's farthest-flung corners. The Society took root in the new Ili Model Army, which received a large number of soldiers from Hunan and Hubei.[84] Meanwhile, Xiang Army ties brought in revolutionary-minded intellectuals who served the Republican cause from within the civil administration. While Hunanese influence waned in the higher levels of government, Hunanese nevertheless filled newly created positions in the mid-level bureaucracy, especially the new judicial system.[85] Thus Hunanese police, officials, and soldiers conspired to overthrow the Qing. They were opposed by Wang Shu'nan's clique, including Yuan Dahua, who fully embraced Wang's program and abolished all that Du Tong had tried to build. In their place, Yuan outlined three guiding policies for governing Xinjiang, the foremost being "colonization" (*zhimin*).[86]

In Xinjiang, the revolutionaries lost, even as the Qing fell, creating a situation in which the monarchist Yang Zengxin (1867–1928, in office 1912–28) ruled this borderland in the name of the Republic. Yang, then the Aksu intendant, was among the post-1904 officials whom Ruixian accused of corruption, and he brought with him many other members of Wang's network: Zhu Ruichi (d. 1934) was later Yang's "model official" and even served briefly as the governor at the end of his life.[87] Liu Wenlong (b. 1879, Baling) remained a prominent figure in the Xinjiang government through 1933. Wang Buduan (b. 1859) rose to the rank of Tarbaghatai Intendant, where he gradually grew more independent of Yang. Pan Zhen, a Xiang Army affiliate whose opium addiction brought him into the embezzlement scheme, became the head of the provincial Ministry of Finance. Wang Shu'nan's "patron-disciple" relationship with Yang Zengxin ensured that Wang's ideas defined the province for years to come. A few revolutionary Hunanese briefly held power in the South before their expulsion in 1915. The Hunanese era came decisively to an end.

*   *   *

The political history of late-Qing Xinjiang was one of factionalism, entrenched interests, and the struggle to respond to periodic crises with the tools of *jingshi*. The arc of the Hunanese era began with an idealistic program for the sociomoral transformation of Muslim people such that they and their land would be integrated into the Chinese ecumene. That ambitious civilizing project was immediately frustrated by the realities of government. However, as long as Beijing continued to subsidize Xinjiang's reconstruction, the Xiang Army community was free to experiment with small-government policies meant to bring about a sociomoral transformation. Real fiscal crises prompted the same group to centralize its state and attempt a rapid penetration of society. This in turn effected the further entrenchment of aging Xiang Army members within the administration, which weakened their community's potential to maintain control in the long term and prompted Beijing's intervention into the regional government. Even this final attempt to return control of Xinjiang to the imperial court prompted networks of officials to align into two factions divided over the best means to exploit the region: allowing its people full participation in a future constitutional monarchy, or forcing them into colonial servitude.

In many ways, Yang Zengxin's Republican-era government was a realization of Wang Shu'nan's ideas: Yang was a strongman who used military might to consolidate his control at the upper levels of the administration, yet his state retreated from the Xiang Army's mission of interference in society. The fiscal crisis of the late Qing intensified under Yang, as Xinjiang became a de facto independent state only nominally owing allegiance to the Republic and receiving little support from it. Yang therefore minimized the government's nonmilitary functions, following Wang and Yuan Dahua, but pursued further collaborative ventures with foreign merchants to exploit the region's natural resources. Assimilating the Muslims was no longer an overt goal of government. State-building in the early Republic thus reflected the priorities of the earlier Qing, and the region's rulers acknowledged the similarity of their situation to those of imperial powers elsewhere.[88] Yang claimed to rule not as a Confucian revivalist, but as a Daoist sage, under whom minimal government permitted the common people to live in blissful simplicity. The civilizing project was over.

Yet its legacies persisted, if not through the policies of the provincial government, then in the society the civilizing project had altered. Over the course of three decades of *jingshi*-inspired Hunanese rule, its interventions changed how Musulmans, Hui, and Chinese alike interacted and represented themselves and others. The promotion of "the rites" (*li*) and attempts to enforce them within a zone of exception did not succeed in transforming Muslims into Confucians. Yet the institutions of the civilizing project gained lives of their own among people still struggling with the violence of the Muslim uprisings and their aftermath. Let us turn now to their effects on Musulmans, Hui, and Chinese, their modes of self-definition, and relations between communities as they were manifested in memory, in the creation of a new social elite, and in the reshaping of intimate relationships.

THREE

Frontier Mediation

The Rise of the Interpreters

IT WAS SEPTEMBER 3, 1920, and Xu Youcheng was being sued again.[1] In his statement to the Turpan magistrate, he laughed the charges off. Xu had worked for over thirty years as an interpreter, one of a small cadre of men trusted to move text and speech between Chinese and Turkic languages, and between the idioms familiar to the Muslim majority and those of the former imperial and now Republican governments. In that capacity, he wrote, he had been accused countless times of corruption and extortion. Such allegations were simply a hazard of the job—people were often disappointed in Xu's efforts because they expected his skillful manipulation of language to induce the Chinese authorities to work in their favor.

Nevertheless, the people of the village of Qarakhoja brought very serious charges against Xu. Not only had he extorted over a thousand taels of cash from the villagers, he had sold hundreds of acres of government-controlled land and pocketed the profits. The village leaders pursued justice for nearly a year. The Turpan magistrate refused to consider their case, and so they wrote to Governor Yang Zengxin in Dihua. Yang asserted that local affairs no longer concerned the provincial authorities and rebuffed them once again. Next the villagers traveled the rocky road to Dihua to present their grievances in person, but Yang refused them a final time. Now the Turpan magistrate agreed with Xu Youcheng: interpreters were constantly being accused of corruption, and the magistrate could not adjudicate every dispute. The case was remanded to mediation by one of the magistrate's underlings, Section Head Zhou Jiyu, who promptly dismissed the charges against Xu.

We may suspect that the villagers spat in anger at the obvious injustice, for Xu Youcheng and Zhou Jiyu belonged to the same class of men. Both were born to Musulman families but bore Chinese names adopted during their educations in Zuo Zongtang's Confucian schools. Their specialized knowledge of the Chinese language and intimate understanding of the local administration enabled them to work as interpreters, the indispensable individuals who could transform spoken and written Turkic into the Literary Chinese used in the organs of the state. These culturally and linguistically bifluent intermediaries were necessary to the functioning of local government. Xu and Zhou were both interpreters, not just in rank, but in identity: what the Chinese called a *tongshi*, meaning "intermediary," the Musulmans derisively label a *tongchi*.[2] As Musulmans described it, *tongchi* were dangerous and unreliable communicators who amassed significant power and ultimately served only their own interests.

Tongchi were not new in Xinjiang, or in China. Before the Muslim uprisings, begs and Qing officials employed tongchi who came mostly from the aristocratic families of Qumul and Turpan.[3] These tongchi mainly worked between Chaghatay, Manchu, Mongol, and sometimes Persian and developed a peculiar idiom that officials used to communicate with their Qing overlords. Several old tongchi remained active in post-reconquest Xinjiang. However, the tongchi of the late Qing had different origins, careers, and social statuses. They were not necessarily aristocratic, and some came from poor backgrounds. They did not work between Turkic and Manchu or Mongol, but directly with oral and written Chinese and Turkic. Their power was tied not to the hereditary wangs, but to the new site of government in Xinjiang: the local magistrate's office. In this sense, the tongchi of the late Qing were akin to the widely despised clerks and runners who operated local government all over China.[4] They were the face of government for the majority of people, but many also worked outside of the yamen, more like the "litigation masters" (*songshi*) or vernacular lawyers of China proper, who could be paid to write petitions to secure their clients' legal victories and coach them on effective courtroom conduct. A late-Qing tongchi was capable of turning a petition written in the Islamic idiom of justice (Arabic ʿadālah) into one that spoke to the Chinese concern with the rites. In this light, *tongchi* is not easily translated simply as "interpreter," "translator," or "intermediary." Rather, "mediator" would be an appropriate rendering: an actor "endowed with the capacity to translate what they transport, to redefine it, redeploy it, and also to betray it."[5]

The social persona of "the tongchi" was inherently bound up with the nature of translation and mediation. Tongchis were "subjects in transit" who operated at sites of fluidity and transfer.[6] That site in the late Qing was an information gap that local administrations in the provincial system strategically maintained between the yamen's understanding or representation of the people it governed and the reality it kept hidden from itself, the disorder of everyday life. This gap opened up a space for multiple intermediaries to engage in the politics of representation, some more effectively than others, while facilitating the operation of the common set of symbolic vocabularies and institutional morphologies that enabled a Qing subject to communicate across the distance with the emperor, and vice versa.[7] In order to operate effectively in that gap, a tongchi needed to adopt a position that cast him as a normative subject, in this case as an educated Confucian. That representation of sameness or simultaneity through translation and its embodiment in the translator paradoxically engendered a heightened awareness of difference among those who engaged in the process of translation and interpretation.

The system of mediation in Xinjiang was therefore more or less identical in form to that which was common in China proper. After all, a clerk or litigation master in a Chinese-speaking area needed to convert the speech of deponents or clients into a formal register that was legible to the magistrate and other officials. The rules for how a person's speech could be represented were very strict and formulaic and even included specific ways of voicing individuals and presenting the text, such that even "colloquial" speech was altered to suit the conventions of the bureaucracy.[8] It was also necessary to render speech in one of the many divergent varieties of Chinese into formal Mandarin. In China proper, however, the pervasive idea of fundamental cultural similarity between officials and commoners and the longstanding presence of a system of common vocabularies and morphologies of power had habituated people to interacting with local government. In Xinjiang, all of this was new to the Musulmans, who now faced the same apparatus as a strange and alien imposition. Mediation in Xinjiang thus draws into stark relief the role of mimesis in the judicial system.[9] The practice of a tongchi was to create a representation of reality, in accord with a moral universe that the magistrate understood, in order to grant that representation's power to the represented person.

The Search for Intermediaries

The Xiang Army, too, found themselves in unfamiliar circumstances that challenged their assumptions about the society they encountered. At first, the administration attempted to displace Islamic legal authority, as ideology dictated, by bringing marriage and property disputes firmly into the yamen's jurisdiction.[10] However, the practical realities of government, and in particular the need to demonstrate the fairness of provincial justice, forced them to work through various kinds of intermediaries.

Given the existence of longstanding institutions of Islamic law, the Xiang Army could have worked through the myriad grassroots legal authorities known as *ākhūnds*.[11] However, the Chinese were suspicious of the akhunds for several reasons. First, Hui akhunds (Chinese *ahong*) were familiar from China proper, as well as from older accounts of Xinjiang.[12] From the Xiang Army's perspective, Hui akhunds bore much of the responsibility for the Muslim uprisings. Moreover, these educated men, which was more or less the meaning of akhund in this context, appeared to make their livings by trading their knowledge of writing for money. Chinese observers imagined that they did so strictly for personal profit, and that, since akhunds recited the Quran rather than the Classics, they lacked the moral grounding that a Confucian official received during his education. Worse, the akhunds were accused of advancing a corrupt version of the law: "The Muslims have punishments, but no statutes or substatutes," wrote Zuo Zongtang's clerk Xiao Xiong. "Everyone listens to the akhund, who from time to time reads the scripture to make a judgment."[13] In short, where *jingshi* imagined a paternalistic local society guided by moral men, an akhund represented a debased moral man following the wrong scripture and enforcing a primitive, irrational kind of law.

A case from 1879 illustrates the persistence of Islamic authorities as primary mediators in family law, the administration's intolerance of their role, and how the yamen was already engaged in a politics of representation that cast Muslim society in terms of Confucian moralism. That year, the petty official Thābit Dorgha arranged a marriage between his son Wāsīṭ and a woman half his age named Tokhta Banu, the daughter of a poor trader and farmer.[14] Within a year, however, the young couple was already quarreling and considering divorce. Tokhta Banu's mother took them to Rāshid Akhund (Lashier Ahong), who in turn consulted the mufti. The mufti advised him that, "according to the scripture" (zhao jing), if the parties could be reunited, that was for the best—if not, they could divorce, but Wāsīṭ ought to apologize with the gift of a sheep. Unfortunately, the mediation process went afoul when Wāsīṭ quarreled with his mother-in-law and injured her. Rāshid reported the matter to the village headman, according to what he understood to be the proper procedure, and in the meantime approved the divorce. "I truly handled it according to the scripture," he later attested in a deposition, satisfied that he was morally in the right. However, Wāsīṭ soon murdered Tokhta Banu, which revealed the dispute to the magistrate and his staff. The yamen identified Rāshid Akhund as a disruptive force in this story, as he had usurped the magistrate's authority to approve their divorce. He was given a suspended sentence of eighty strokes of the heavy stick as a warning not to interfere again.

Meanwhile, clerks at the yamen set about crafting a narrative that would minimize Wāsīṭ's culpability in the murder and blunt the crime's potential to cause further disruption.[15] Their summary of the case emphasized that Tokhta Banu was a much-married woman whose first husband had died and second had abandoned her. The clerks impugned her mother's sanity, suggesting that madness had driven her to take the couple to Rāshid Akhund, a mere farmer who happened to read scripture and led the young couple astray through his incompetence. Wāsīṭ and Tokhta Banu were still legally married, the report asserted, as Islamic law had no authority to separate them. That assertion justified the murder: Tokhta Banu, they wrote, had falsely been divorced against her husband's wishes so that she could seek pleasure with yet another husband, violating the principle of wifely obedience. Qing justice had long been responsive to the idea that a flash of masculine passion and moral outrage could drive a reasonable man to murder his wife.[16] Here they narrated the murder to show that Wāsīṭ, enraged by her violation of Confucian propriety, was only holding the knife against her neck as a threat when Tokhta Banu had twisted her head at just the wrong moment, cutting her own throat. Wāsīṭ, presented as the good Confucian man he probably never was, received clemency.

Precisely such manipulations of the record persisted throughout the late Qing, and they should lead us to reconsider the value of reading social history through the reports delivered to Beijing.[17] Not only does Tokhta Banu's case demonstrate that the yamen's process of judicial reporting and reasoning produced a fictional image of the society it governed, it shows that knowledgeable grassroots actors such as akhunds were punished for reporting their actions honestly. Other cases in the Turpan archive show that Rāshid Akhund was not punished for granting a divorce so much as for claiming the authority to do so. Indeed, where the akhunds failed to deliver a desired result such as divorce, the yamen could step in as a legitimate legal alternative. According to Islamic law as it was practiced in East Turkestan, a woman was entitled to a divorce in the event that her husband disappeared for some length of time and left her without financial support (*nafaqa*).[18] The Turpan yamen received many such complaints in the years that followed, but translators now stepped in to clothe them in proper moralistic language.[19] In divorce pleas presented to Islamic authorities, formulaic phrasing emphasized the wife's financial difficulties: a husband "abandoned me without support and disappeared . . . and my support was not enough" (*bī-nafaqa tashlap, ghāyib bolup . . . nafaqa yätmädi*). In pleas to the Turpan prefect, however, writers emphasized the family's collective suffering caused by supporting a daughter who could not be married off. The latter strategy sometimes secured a divorce from the yamen where Islamic authorities would not grant it, as it enabled a supposedly wanton Musulman woman to settle down in a stable family unit, preventing her from engaging in sexual impropriety. Sometimes the goals of the civilizing project could align with those of Musulmans.

Of course, *jingshi* thought emphasized the primacy of morality over law, and when officials found divorce to be ubiquitous among the Musulmans, they attempted to use local Islamic moral authorities to prevent it. "Marriage by Musulman customs is beyond the proper human relationships," Liu Jintang wrote. "They marry privately at a moment's notice and just as quickly divorce and remarry. These sorts of obscene practices are deeply despicable."[20] In 1881, the province appointed "preacher (*khaṭīb*) village headmen" (*haidipu* or *haidibu xiangyue*) specifically for the purpose of propagating orthodox ideals of marriage. This office combined the title of the Muslim cleric who reads the sermon (*khuṭba*) at the Friday prayer with that of a village headman, who would read out imperial proclamations to villagers in China proper. Officials saw these roles as analogous. On the occasion of a marriage proposal, the preacher was to ensure that the bride and groom were a good astrological match and both willing to enter their partnership. Nor were they to permit a divorce without an investigation. Nevertheless, the Xiang Army's faith was misplaced: preacher village headmen were elected by Musulmans in their own communities, and their appointments were then confirmed by the prefect. They probably had little interest in Confucianizing marriage. The title of preacher village headman disappeared just as quickly as it appeared, probably because the administration had misidentified preachers as willing participants in the civilizing project.

Instead, the Turpan prefect and his staff chose to rely on a preexisting hierarchy of local functionaries whose authority did not derive primarily from Islamic learning or piety. The yamen typically interacted with three officials, each of which could be found in most of the villages: the superintendent, the *aqsaqal*, and the irrigation master.[21] The highest ranking among these was the superintendent (*dorgha*), who was mainly charged with tax collection and mobilizing temporary militias.[22] Councils of local notables elected a superintendent, whose appointment the magistrate generally approved. This superintendent in turn supervised an *aqsaqal*, literally "white beard," another elected leader whom Chinese officials considered equivalent to a "village headman" (*xiangyue*), albeit not a preacher. An aqsaqal in Turpan not only assisted the superintendent's collection of taxes but was usually the first point of contact for Musulmans when they reported a dispute or crime. Aqsaqals, as village headmen, also delivered the fortnightly lecture, realizing the function of the preacher village headmen but without explicit religious authority. Rather, aqsaqals functioned more like communal representatives, much like those found on the Sino-Russian frontier, where each community, including that of Musulmans from China, would be led by a "trading headman."[23] In those villages of Turpan where many Chinese and Hui lived alongside Musulmans, these communities elected separate aqsaqals, who were usually prominent merchants. While nearly every village in Turpan had a superintendent and an aqsaqal, only those that bordered major water sources elected an irrigation master (*mīrāb*).[24] The irrigation master's traditional role was to coordinate the distribution of water resources. Nevertheless, the division of labor between these three functionaries was unclear. From the magistrate's perspective, all three of these local powerholders were of roughly equivalent rank to the common clerks and runners who worked in his own offices, and so he commanded them accordingly.

The same was broadly true of the nominally independent Turpan Wang, an old Turco-Mongol vassal of the Qing whose court was in Lükchün. Previously, the Qing court communicated with the wang through the Lifanyuan. After 1877, however, this formal vassal reported mainly to the Turpan prefect, whose office now processed ritual communications between the wang and the Qing and fielded complaints regarding his administration. The Turpan Wang, much like the aqsaqals elsewhere, sent many cases from his demesne up to the Turpan yamen for investigation and adjudication.[25] The wang's land formally extended over a large part of the Turpan Depression, and it included many of the locations that appear regularly in the Turpan yamen archive, such as Subashi, Shengjin, and Qarakhoja. Until 1907, the wang also maintained an independent police force, collected taxes, and in many ways projected the image of a sovereign ruler. That was reflected in the wang's communication with the magistrate: the yamen's point of contact with the wang's court was usually through one of his close male relations, whom the magistrate knew as a "prince" (taiji) in Chinese.[26] In Chaghatay, however, this official referred to himself as a "governor" (ḥākim beg), reflecting a higher rank in the pre-uprisings hierarchy of begs and equal with that of a magistrate. Although the Qing abolished the wang's control of his own serfs, it appears that the liberated farmers simply became tenants on the wang's land. Ultimately, such problems of representation, as well as the provincial administration's ideological commitment to minimal formal government, mean that it is difficult to establish precisely how these hierarchies worked in practice.

The vagueness of political organization from the yamen's perspective was compounded by its poor sense of Turpan's social organization. In 1878, the prefecture was meant to establish the baojia mutual-security system, which had been in place to a limited degree among Chinese settlers before 1864.[27] The order included taking a population survey and distributing nameplates for local households. However, it appears that no population survey was carried out until very late, perhaps only in 1909, when Musulmans were required to register their marriages at the yamen.[28] Moreover, the *baojia* system never reappeared in the archive, suggesting that it was never even formally created. The Turpan archive does include a number of lists of households, such as those registers of children's names created in the course of a smallpox eradication campaign in the mid-1880s. However, there is no evidence that the yamen produced knowledge about population in anything but an ad hoc way throughout the Hunanese era.

That the yamen possessed minimal knowledge about the society it governed also reflects the era of its establishment, as by this time provincial officials in China proper were accustomed to relying on merchants for information and for many of the functions of local government. The Turpan prefect attempted the same but eventually found that the Chinese merchant networks that dominated the local economy were unreliable actors. In one explosive case from 1890, a merchant from Shangzhou, Shaanxi, died of an apparent accident in a fire.[29] His own relatives and co-locals were tasked with investigating the death, which they construed as a conspiracy on the part of the Musulman landlord from whom the merchant rented his room. Their reports fabricated and altered evidence extensively in order to frame the landlord, from rearranging the physical configuration of the courtyard house in which they both lived to creating a murder weapon discovered in the landlord's home, still bloody many months later. The yamen regained control of the case, ruled the death an accident, and realized that merchants made poor informants, especially given the strength of their internal cohesion and minimal connection to local society. It was shortly thereafter that debt cases led to an increase in violence, and Tao Mo proposed curtailing merchants' power.

Eventually, the same practical considerations that led the provincial government to formalize its relationships with Chinese merchants and former begs also brought mullahs and akhunds into the local yamen. In 1887, the Turpan prefect employed a "mullah for translating Muslim language" (*fanyi Huiwen maola*).[30] By 1905, "official mullahs" (*guan maola*) appeared and stayed on the payroll.[31] At the yamen, these Muslim clerics were valued primarily for their literacy, and their work supplemented that of the yamen's chief manipulator of language and narrative, the tongchi. However, scholarship and documents demonstrate that not only did Islamic legal authority survive in Turpan, it appears to have undergone somewhat of a revival there and across East Turkestan, where new "Shariah courts" (*maḥkama-ye sharʿī*) composed of panels of judges appeared in major towns and cities.[32] Its apparent covertness is simply an artifact of the politics of the archive, and indeed, Islamic judges were clearly also playing roles at the yamen.

As the following pages will show, unlike a mullah or akhund, a tongchi presented himself as a normative Chinese-speaking Confucian and possessed the education to support that identity. The tongchi could gather intelligence locally, and then produce information in a format the yamen could understand, making a locality such as Turpan knowable to its Chinese administrator. More importantly, however, a tongchi was meant to be a ritualist, a replacement for the preacher village headmen who could not only transmit orthodox texts but embody the Classics in his comportment and social performance, transforming the Muslims from below and from within.

A Typology of Translation

The problem of speaking across languages and cultures dogged the provincial administration through the end of the Qing, when Du Tong observed that when a Chinese person and a Musulman attempted to communicate, it was "like staring at each other across a vast distance."[33] Many methods of bridging that distance were tried, but most were ineffective because they relied on a method of translation that maintained faith to the form and content of Chinese source material. Better communicators, the tongchi chief among them, learned to transform not just the words, but the form of text. The most effective translation, as we will see, involved the movement of text from oral deposition or Islamic petition into the formal documentation of the Qing politico-juridical system. That process of transmediation created a porous boundary between symbolic worlds by fabricating a new reality in the gap that divided them.

Different varieties of translation in late-Qing Xinjiang displayed varying degrees of faith to the form and content of the source text. David Brophy has described the emergence of a distinct variety of Turkic infused with Mongolic terminology that he calls "Yamen Uyghur."[34] This written language emerged in the documents of the wangs of Qumul and Turpan through the translation of messages to and from the Lifanyuan. That mediation aimed at terminological clarity by shaping Turkic writing according to the expectations of a distant interlocutor. It is consistent with the Manchu-centric language ideology apparent from such imperially commissioned works as the Qianlong-era *Pentaglot Dictionary* (*Wuti Qingwen jian*), which matched vocabulary equivalencies between Manchu, Mongol, Tibetan, Chinese, and Chaghatay through pronunciation guides in Manchu.[35] The pre-uprisings government and travelers to the borderland also relied on Manchu-centric phrasebooks that presented dialogues of interest to merchants and diplomats by placing equivalent phrases side by side.[36] This juxtaposition enforced a sense of parallelism between Manchu, Mongol, and Chaghatay, which possess very similar morphology and syntax. A Manchu traveler or Musulman merchant could easily see how parallel words and sentences displayed cognate structures.

One of the last vestiges of such Qing-centric translation appeared in 1892.[37] In 1891, the Qing government decided to propagate the Shunzhi emperor's *Moral Exhortations to the People* (*Yuzhi quanshan yaoyan*), originally distributed in 1656.[38] Originally, the *Exhortations* attempted to legitimize the Qing's then-fledgling rule over China by presenting its emperor as a Confucian moralist. The goal of the new printing was a popular revival of imperial ideology through the widespread recitation of the text at the village lectures. In Xinjiang, however, the Chinese version would be incomprehensible to Turkic-speakers, and so Governor Tao Mo, ever the supporter of sociomoral propaganda, commissioned a Chaghatay translation.[39] Kashgar Intendant Li Zongbin (1834–98) took up the task and recruited Fušan, an interpreter at the Ili Solon Camp, to come to Kashgar and lead the effort. Fušan knew Chaghatay well and had worked as a tongchi in the Ili military government, where he consulted regularly with educated Musulmans to refine his products. In this case, two of Intendant Li's clerks joined the effort, a Muslim judge (*qāżī*) and irrigation master. Rounding out the crew was a secretary (*mīrzā*), then working with a Protestant missionary to translate the Bible into Kashgari Turkic.[40]

Fušan's team produced a monolingual text in Chaghatay with a trilingual cover page in Manchu, Chaghatay, and Chinese.[41] However, they worked from the Manchu version of the *Moral Exhortations* and followed the phrasebook writers in maintaining a one-to-one equivalence between words and suffixes whenever possible. Whereas the *Book of Li* had insisted on the expression of concepts through specific Chinese terms to the detriment of clarity and grammaticality, Fušan produced a fluent Chaghatay text. Moreover, the translation adapted the *Moral Exhortations* to the vocabulary of popular Islamic pamphlets (*risāla*) that presented apocryphal revelations, usually a legend of the sacred transmission of craft knowledge.[42] It thus took the Chinese moral cosmology of Heaven, the Way, and numinous response to human deeds and translated it into the language of popular Islamic piety. Moreover, the work mimicked the format and appearance of such a pamphlet, including a pair of chronograms (*tārīkh*) commemorating the text's translation and printing.[43]

Nevertheless, as Rian Thum has pointed out, it is unlikely that this last resurgence of old Qing translation had its intended effect, as printed text was regarded with much less respect than manuscript. Other printed texts, such as the *Book of Li*, juxtaposed passages in Literary Chinese and awkward Chaghatay and maintained the basic format of a Chinese book.[44] Lingering tensions between Musulmans and Chinese-speakers would have made such prints unappealing, particularly given their explicit association with the civilizing project. More importantly, their language was awkward to the point of incomprehensibility, as it enforced a one-to-one correspondence between the Chinese character-word (*zi*), which is isolating and uninflected, and the morphologically complex Turkic word. The idea of the word as the minimal and indivisible bearer of meaning derived from the mystification of Chinese characters in Neo-Confucianism, in which contemplating a character, or even embodying it through dance, was thought to transmit the underlying principle behind the character. It was ineffective at transmitting meaning outside of the sociocultural context of China proper.

One such text that embodied this approach to translation was a primer for use in the schools, the *Sino-Muslim Concordance* (*Han-Hui hebi*).[45] The *Concordance*'s history began in 1880, when a teacher in Wensu named Sun Shouchang grew frustrated with the slow progress of his Musulman students in grasping the Chinese language. That slowness is no surprise: the Confucian schools taught through rote memorization of the standard school curriculum beginning with primers such as the *Three-Character Classic* (*San zi jing*) and then progressing through the Classics. Sun was curious why his students took no interests in the Classics, since after all Musulmans were humans like anyone else and should therefore be receptive to universal truths: " 'Round heads and square feet'; they have human forms, so they must have human natures!" (*Yuan ding fang zhi, juyou ren xing, ji you ren xing!*) The problem, Sun explained, was that his predecessors had "used what is Chinese to transform the outlanders" (*yong Xia bian yi*). A new primer would hasten students' learning and clarify the meaning of the Classics: "Once they are illuminated, they will believe and follow, and once they believe and follow, they will grow attached to us." (*Ming ze xincong, xincong ze qinfu yi.*) Sun's logic resounds with the colonialist belief in pedagogy, that the universal truth held by the colonizer will become immediately apparent to the colonized and transform them, if only they are exposed to it.

Sun's *Concordance* consisted of a series of glosses in three columns: the first held a single Chinese character, the last its translation in Chaghatay, and in between them a rough pronunciation guide for the Chaghatay in Chinese characters. Where the *Pentaglot Dictionary* had presented Manchu as the mediating language, here Chinese played that role. An instructor or student was meant to point to a character and its translation when it was necessary to communicate. However, conversation would have been impossible, as the *Concordance* focuses not on practical terminology, but on those characters that were central to Confucian moralism and cosmology. The list begins with Heaven (Chinese *tian*, Chaghatay *āsmān*) and proceeds directly through a series of untranslated words. Some of these untranslated terms have a clear connection with Confucian ideals, such as *wen*, which indicates everything from literary culture to the warp and weft of the cosmos. We might easily suspect that Sun found some words in Chinese so essential as to be untranslatable. Yet most of the untranslated words in the *Concordance* are actually concrete terms that had already been translated in the *Book of Li*, as well as in long-established Chinese-Persian glossaries. It is therefore likely that the *Concordance* reflects the knowledge of Sun's Musulman informants, perhaps his own students. Blank spaces in the printed text could have been filled in in class, as the teacher gradually collected vocabulary. If that were the case, however, it suggests that Sun and his colleagues possessed extremely thin knowledge of the language used around them, as did the person who carved the woodblocks used in the printing.

The *Concordance* demonstrates how lower-level Chinese actors participated in the project of sociomoral transformation by innovating tools to support it, to the exclusion of preexisting texts from the earlier Qing. It also shows how the Xiang Army, per Zuo Zongtang's stated intent, tried to colonize Chaghatay-language discourse with a translingual sociomoral vocabulary, again failing for the most part to take advantage of more effective practices based on Manchu-Turkic translation.[46] While Chinese scholars had studied language on the level of morphology and phonology for centuries, nevertheless the isolating structure of Literary Chinese seemed to preclude the analysis of a more synthetic morphology such as that found in Chaghatay. Late-Qing observers of Xinjiang thus analyzed the Turkic word as an equivalent to the character-word, making lists of vocabulary without considering grammar. It was not until about 1908, as the Hunanese period drew to a close, that one exceptional gazetteer-writer attempted to study the phonology of spoken and written Turkic and present it in terms of traditional Chinese linguistics.[47]

Character-centered teaching oriented toward the internalization of the Classics was the foundation of the Confucian schools that Zuo Zongtang and his followers established across Xinjiang. It represented a break from the Manchu-centric translation practices of the pre-1864 regime and reorientation away from Beijing and imperial authority toward imparting the Sino-normative practices that, according to *jingshi*, were best preserved in Hunan and the Chinese-majority South. The following pages will show how this system produced not the moral men who were intended, but instead linguistically and culturally bifluent functionaries who used their grasp of the Chinese language and official culture to their own advantage.

The Confucian Schools

Zuo Zongtang combined Lu Yao's plan for the cultural assimilation of the Muslims and the example of Chen Hongmou's "charitable schools" (*yishu*) in Yunnan into a plan to Confucianize Muslim families through education.[48] His plan had clear parallels with colonial schooling and cultural violence in the civilizing projects of contemporary European empires. In residential and mission schools across the British, French, and Spanish empires, children were separated from their families and forced to assimilate linguistically and culturally.[49] In the longer term, residential schools became a central tool of politics and social change in many colonies. On this basis, Stevan Harrell has characterized similar efforts elsewhere in the Ming and Qing as Confucian civilizing projects in which the dominators "were concerned not with race or language as determining characteristics of peoples, but with modes of livelihood."[50]

Indeed, Zuo's rhetoric is curiously close to that of his contemporary Thomas Babington Macaulay (1800–1859), who in 1835 argued for the colonization of the Indian mind with the concepts of "science." Macauley sought to form "a class [of] interpreters . . . Indian in blood and colour, but English in taste, in opinions, in morals, and in intellect . . . render[ing] them . . . fit vehicles for conveying knowledge to the great mass of the population."[51] Macauley, like Zuo, argued that indirect rule was costlier than assimilation in the long term, and he rejected the notion that Islamic and Hindu traditions made for as solid a foundation for government as did Western "science." What Macauley meant by "science" was not of course the practice of expanding knowledge through experimentation, but rather a mass of shifting assumptions about proper behavior that we might call "Euro-normative." Such Euro-normativity was predicated not only on racial or ethnic distinctions, but on class.

Similarly, Zuo Zongtang's idea of civilization proposes that, in order to bring the Musulmans to accept a putatively fixed and transcendent standard of behavior called ritual, it will be necessary to teach them a set of customs (*feng*) associated with the dominant people: language, clothing, and engagement with a certain textual canon. Confucius himself might have balked at the idea of teaching the rites through the modern Chinese language, as it is reported that the sage sought to recite the Classics only in the speech of the ancients. Chinese clothing in the Qing had changed significantly from that worn in the golden age of the Western Zhou, but photographic evidence shows that Musulman boys were dressed in contemporary Chinese clothing.[52] Zuo's project in this sense was Sinonormative: it superficially claimed to inculcate transcendent and universal truths, but instead enforced a set of shifting norms that reflected the cultural assumptions of the dominant party. As we will see, many Chinese assumed that their own behaviors and the ancient rites were equivalent.

Cultural violence has been the focus of nearly all previous scholarship on the schools, and one frequently cited anecdote has created the impression that they were therefore equivalent to Euro-American residential schools. The Uyghur nationalist leader Isa Alptekin (1901–95) in particular recalls how his father, Yusuf, was sent to one those schools and made to dress in Chinese clothing.[53] When little Yusuf returned home, his mother refused to see him as long as he wore that costume. Here the anecdote ends, leaving an illustration of how Chinese colonizers separated Uyghur boys from their parents, and metaphorically from their heritage. However, the imposition of Chinese dress does not appear as a point of contention in the Turpan archive or in the manuscript record, while a Yarkand magistrate who purchased Chinese robes for the students was nevertheless very popular among Muslims.[54] In this light, it is worthwhile to reassess the nature of the cultural violence in the schools and how Musulmans perceived and reacted to it. Moreover, previous scholarship on the schools has characterized the program as "doomed almost from the beginning"[55]—however, as we will see, it failed not because of its idealism, but despite its usefulness.

Reconstruction agencies established schools as a central part of their sweeping mandate to remake Xinjiang.[56] The first three were founded in Turpan in 1878 as the army was still concluding its campaign in the South: in Toqsun, the Old (Chinese) City, and the New (Muslim) City.[57] Another followed in Pichan in 1879, Lükchün in 1882, Qarakhoja in 1883, and Handun in 1884. Further schools appeared in Lämchin and Tuyuq soon after. Each enrolled about nine to twelve students, or more when the number of schools was reduced. While detailed documentation is only available for Turpan, it is striking that at any given moment during reconstruction, Turpan had at least sixty boys enrolled in the reconstruction agencies' schools. Previous scholarship based on provincial-level figures from the end of the dynasty indicated that there were only about sixty schools in all of Xinjiang, and two in Turpan.[58] Instead, if Turpan is typical of Xinjiang overall, then there were perhaps 250 schools throughout the province at their height, suggesting total enrollment in the thousands.

While the school's explicit purpose was indeed to assimilate Musulmans, archival documents from Turpan indicate that enrollment was more diverse. In any given school, roughly one-third of students were listed as Musulman (*Chan*), one-third as Hui, and one-third as Chinese. Given that Chinese and Hui made up roughly 17 percent of the local population, this indicates a much higher rate of enrollment of native Chinese speakers. However, Musulman families with children enrolled in the schools had a special relationship with the state. Although Zuo's original plan and Liu Jintang's orders called for mandatory schooling,[59] it was not the case that boys were separated from their families. Rather, a given family was selected to provide a son to study at a local school until he had completed the curriculum. If a child passed away, disappeared, or needed to withdraw for other reasons, the Turpan prefect would pressure the family to enroll another son.[60] In this sense, the relationship of a Musulman family to the state was one of obligation, rather like the duty of a hereditary military household in the Ming to provide an able-bodied man for garrison duty. However, it does not appear that the Turpan administration had the means or the will to actually coerce families to send their sons. From the beginning, the Xinjiang provincial project was founded on the idea that Musulmans could be brought to Confucian norms by attraction, rather than by force, and officials were loath to do anything that might cause resentment.

The diversity of enrollment in the schools resulted both from their appeal to Chinese-speaking people and from their unstable funding system. While higher officials demanded supervision of the schools at the provincial level, they nevertheless expected magistrates to fund them locally. This early ad hoc organization of the school project opened it up to local manipulation. When the first schools were established in Turpan, the magistrate located a nearby patch of land and a karez in Yarghol to act as their endowment, providing income from rent and food for the staff and students.[61] However, the local Musulman officials who managed the endowment had little personal investment in the project. In 1879, the instructor at the Toqsun school, Bai Zhenyu, furiously reported to the magistrate that a superintendent had embezzled grain from the school's endowment. The superintendent countered that the endowment had never been formalized, nor had anyone specified the amount of produce meant for the school. From this point onward, the yamen took responsibility for the endowment, and Musulman officials continually attempted to gain control. While the primary mission of the schools was linguistic, cultural, and ritual transformation, these funding constraints encouraged them to accept fee-paying students as well.

Moreover, the traditional Classical curriculum that the schools offered appealed to Chinese-speaking families who wished for their sons to study for the imperial examinations. The government in Dihua recruited clerks and functionaries from the schools by means of an examination in the Classics, so even those who only passed lower-level exams could secure an official position.[62] While Musulman students did take the exams, the most successful examinees usually came from Chinese or Hui families.[63] In 1889, top students from schools across Xinjiang were first sent to Dihua's Boghda Academy (*Boda shuyuan*), about which little is otherwise known. The best of Toqsun were between the ages of nineteen and twenty-one *sui*, had studied for at least seven years, and were all from elsewhere: one Chinese student was apparently the son of a merchant or official, while his colleagues came from Shanxi, Sichuan, and Shaanxi. In order to excel in the schools, it would appear, one already had to be engaged in the Chinese tradition more broadly. On the other hand, Musulman students maintained their student status as long as possible. Instructors consistently reported that their Musulman students progressed all the way to reading such elevated books as the *Book of Odes*, but somehow rarely completed the curriculum or graduated.[64]

This was apparently due neither to a love of Confucian culture nor to a desire to remain immersed in it indefinitely. To the contrary, instructors at the schools expressed derision for their Musulman students, finding their task confusing and all but impossible to accomplish. As a frustrated Bai Zhenyu exclaimed, "The wrapped-headed Muslims despise this culture of ours!" (*Chanhui mianshi si wen!*) Bai disagreed with the Xiang Army administration's assertion that force was unnecessary to convince the Musulmans to assimilate. He was not alone, as reports of Chinese teachers' violence against Musulman students came in from across Xinjiang in the early years. In one case, provincial authorities ordered a secret investigation into the suicide in 1884 of a Musulman boy called Hua Guo at a school in Ush.[65] The boy's teacher had beaten him for failing to memorize the readings. Two days later, Hua Guo went into an empty room in the school's rear courtyard and hanged himself. The school's Musulman custodian vouched for the connection between Hua's treatment and his suicide. Hua Guo's case was sent back to the circuit to be reinvestigated, quietly, so as not to endanger the introduction of "Confucian customs" (*Ru feng*). Not long after, another report came from Guma, a town in southern Xinjiang. There, the same scenario had played out with an eighteen-*sui* Musulman student called Guo Hulin. Governor Liu Jintang ordered Guo Hulin's teacher expelled back to China proper, as the boy was over the age where his teacher was permitted to beat him. As a result of these cases, the province strictly banned harsh punishments for students.

Such incidents demonstrate that provincial officials took seriously the notion that they were engaged in a paternalistic project of transformation by education (*jiaohua*), and that this entailed concern for students' well-being, even if lower-level actors did not share their idealism. An incident in Turpan illustrates the role of the magistrate in maintaining the stable and unitary family unit as the building block and central metaphor of a good society. In 1885, a young Musulman boy named Yu Xueshi was enrolled in the school at Qarakhoja.[66] According to archival documents, his father, ad-Dawlah, was a former superintendent who sent his son to the school to "grow up." Instead, the boy, then only about eight *sui* old, was unable to focus on his studies as he was prone to fits of crying. Yu Xueshi's emotional state was reported to the magistrate's office, and an investigation ensued. They found that ad-Dawlah had decided to divorce Yu's mother, which prompted the boy's anxiety but also presented a threat to the project of creating and maintaining stable nuclear families. The magistrate summoned ad-Dawlah to his office and convinced him to call off the divorce. That the magistrate's power was brought to bear on a family conflict so that a Musulman boy would focus on his studies suggests that the administration was genuinely invested in the students' futures as servants to the state.

Such cases also suggest that coercion, although not physically violent, took the form of Sino-normative discipline that could be far more insidious. Scholarship on the schools has noted the tendency for Musulman students, like Hua Guo and Guo Hulin, to have Chinese names.[67] Indeed, roughly one-third of Musulman students are known in the archive only by a Chinese name that implies a fervent love for Chinese culture: Hua Guo's 華國 name literally meant "China Country." The schoolmaster of Qarakhoja wanted one of his Musulman students to "Treasure China," and so gave him the name Hua Gui 華貴. The Turpan Old City school had students named Gao Hua 高華 "High China" and Hua Li 華理 "Principle of China." *Han wen* 漢文 "Chinese Writing (or Culture)" was a common character combination as well, either as a given name or incorporating the surname Han. Most names, however, were not so obvious in their origins or implications. Another third of Turpan's Musulman students bore a surname derived from their Muslim name and a given name reflecting educational aspirations. Yu Xueshi's 魚學詩 name meant "Yūsuf (or Yūnus?) Studies-the-Odes," suggesting that Yu would complete the classical curriculum by learning the difficult *Book of Odes*. His classmate Ai Xueshu 艾學書 (d. 1926) was probably "Aḥmad Studies-the-History," indicating the *Book of History* (*Shujing* or *Shangshu*) of the Neo-Confucian canon. The name A Yingxuan 阿應選 "'Abdullah(?) Passes-the-Exams" expressed an aspiration that this student should not only absorb Confucian culture but master it. However, yet another third of students were called in a way that simply reflected the phonetics of their Muslim names: Sajiti (Sājid) was the top student at the Lämchin school in 1892. He was joined by students like He Luoban (Qurbān), whose Chinese name integrated a common Chinese surname but was homophonous with his own given name, and Yahubu (Yaʿqūb), whose name incorporated characters commonly used for transliterating non-Chinese names and thus marked him as an outsider.

While schoolmasters granted some of these names to students, others reflect their families' performance of loyalty to the Qing empire. Each student was required to submit a genealogical table showing his ancestry going back three generations, in order to demonstrate his understanding of and reverence for genealogy.[68] The available tables show a common pattern: the students' fathers, who all came of age under Yaʿqūb Beg, are listed under Turco-Muslim names, while grandfathers and great-grandfathers mostly have Chinese names. It is possible that the students in question were descended from people who were educated in Chinese, as there were a few academies (*shuyuan*) that trained students for the examinations in pre-uprisings Xinjiang, and although their known graduates all had Chinese names, some could certainly have been Turkic-speaking Muslims.[69] During the uprisings, when the students' fathers grew up, an outward affiliation with Chinese culture would have been dangerous, while a Turco-Muslim name would express loyalty to an Islamic state. Some may have been descended from culturally Chinese people, or from the many individuals who successfully navigated multiple flexible identities. However, it is just as likely that some of these ancestors were fabricated in order to give the impression of a multigenerational devotion to Chinese learning. Moreover, because the Xiang Army constantly criticized the Musulmans for supposedly lacking genealogical knowledge, being able to list honored ancestors demonstrated a degree of "civilization."

In short, the schools operated according to a logic of discipline and social control that was Confucian in origin and Sino-normative in content. Where residential schools in the Americas sought to separate children from their parents, those in Xinjiang were meant to inculcate filial piety. To do so entailed disciplining not just the student, but his whole family, which was singled out for service to the provincial government. As we will see, this self-discipline was less a mask for a subtle art of resistance and more of an "art of being governed"—of using the state and its institutions to one's own advantage.[70] That is, Musulman students on the whole did not become good Confucians, but rather tongchi—people like Xu Youcheng who used their indispensable positions to benefit their families and themselves.

The Rise of the Interpreters

At first, officials were pleased with the rate of assimilation. Zuo Zongtang's secretary, Xiao Xiong, as he traveled through Xinjiang, composed poems to celebrate the gentle victory of Confucian culture:[71]

> There are some of ability and distinction
> Who rise above the mob's foul reek;
> Their intelligence is no less than that of Li Bai—
> They finish their outlandish books and study Chinese writing.

Xiao Xiong noted with pleasure that students across the province, having completed their Classical educations, could recite "hundreds" of poems from the *Book of Odes*. Such hyperbole was either optimistic to the point of self-delusion or a means for a member of Zuo's circle to propagandize the civilizing project. Rather, as we will see, studentship brought a range of advantages to oneself and one's family.

The basic advantage of studentship was the ability to learn the Chinese language, specifically those forms that made it possible to argue one's case before a magistrate. That is, tongchi spoke the language of Chinese power. The Xiang Army's occupation of Turpan had proven the value of Chinese-language skills, as those Musulmans who could communicate with the army had an immediate economic advantage as intermediaries and suppliers.[72] Abū 'l-Mahdī, the young man whom we met in the introduction, came down from the hills of Turpan to find that the army had razed his home to the grounds and ransacked all of the family's belongings, save for some rudimentary supplies that he and his brothers had been wise enough to bury. Soon the brothers were forced to part ways, and Abū 'l-Mahdī and his new wife found themselves scratching out a living by foraging and trading. Abū 'l-Mahdī's Islamic education was less useful under this new regime, and so he joined the masses of people gathering fodder for the army's horses or sewing roughspun cloth into bags to sell to the soldiers. While a mullah starved, Abū 'l-Mahdī wrote, an interpreter could eat well.

Archival documents show that the Musulman students leveraged their linguistic and cultural knowledge in order to defend their families. While the archive only identifies them by their Chinese names, they nevertheless served Muslim relatives by aiding their appeals to Chinese power. Yu Xueshi and another Musulman student from the Qarakhoja school, Shi Min, found themselves on opposite sides of a conflict over an arranged marriage between their families.[73] Shi Min's uncle ʿAsad had been negotiating an engagement with Ruohesha, who was the older sister of Yu Xueshi's father, ad-Dawlah. The match would have joined two prominent families together. Because Ruohesha may have been infertile, ʿAsad discussed adoption with her as a means to secure an heir. During the negotiations, however, ʿAsad took another, younger wife. This precipitated a fight between the young woman and a jealous Ruohesha. ʿAsad took ad-Dawlah and Ruohesha to the akhund for mediation, but there another fight broke out, ending in ʿAsad's injury. Shi Min, as the member of the family with the best Chinese, then brought a suit to the yamen on his uncle ʿAsad's behalf. Yu Xueshi handled Ruohesha's defense. Thanks to Shi's and Yu's educations, these families could square off in different legal contexts and seek advantages through forum shopping.

Benefits could also be more direct. A turning point in the theory and practice of the schools came in 1882, when the provisional government, led by Liu Jintang, became deeply worried about the region's preparedness for provincehood. Following Zuo, Liu proposed to the Board of Rites in Beijing that the Musulman students could be the region's salvation: if a student could speak Chinese well and demonstrate that he had read one book of the Classics, he proposed, then the student should be granted the rank of sti-pendiary student (*jiansheng*) and appointed as a beg to administer a town.[74] Previously, he wrote, the schools had prioritized simply "Chinese dress and understanding Chinese language" (*Han fu, tong Hua yu*) in an effort to "bring the other kind of this strange land to assimilate to our Chinese customs" (*shi shufang yizu tong wo Hua feng*). Yet, they had failed to teach them the Classics. Now it was time to follow the example of academies in China proper and recruit minor officials from the schools, even if they were only marginally competent. The Board of Rites rejected Liu's proposal, as it did not accord with the substatutes governing ranks and appointments. Eventually, Liu and the provincial director of schools (*xuezheng*) bargained Beijing down to a compromise: rather than force every student to go through the county and prefectural exams, some could instead be rewarded with the title "ritual dancer" (*yisheng*). The title meant not only that the student had the highest result on the school examination, but that they would have ritual obligations at the temple of Confucius. Material rewards therefore required an investment in the ceremonies that defined one's membership in the community of educated men. Indeed, when the magistrate led local officials in the rite of welcoming spring by parading a paper ox around the city, Musulman students participated.[75] The same demand to engage in ritual appears to resonate in Chaghatay-language writings that depict Musulmans who were promoted into the Chinese administration as participating in idolatrous ceremonies, going to the temple, bowing to a statue, and eating pork.[76] Ritual served as a symbolic boundary between Musulmans and Chinese, as a mark of elite status became, through resentment and the violation of religious strictures, a mark of having betrayed one's community.

Following their selection, these top students went on to careers in local administration. The top student of the Lämchin school, Sājid, was made an apprentice to the Chinese doctors working to eradicate smallpox in Turpan.[77] This was done partly as a cost-saving measure, as it had been determined as early as 1886, five years after the smallpox inoculation program began in Turpan, that a locally trained Musulman could be paid half as much as a specialist from China proper to do the same job.[78] Perhaps low pay for dangerous work was why Sājid eventually fled his "apprenticeship," which was more like indentured servitude, an obligation to the province for providing his education.[79] Consequently, the yamen attempted to track Sājid down and compel him to return to his studies, but here the archival trail disappears, and so perhaps did the authorities' grip on Sājid himself.

Other students received better incentives. In 1894, two top students, Ai Xueshu and Gui Xin, were granted adjacent parcels of excellent land along the highway.[80] This was a turn in both men's fortunes, as neither one received any family support. Ai was soon moved from the New City school to the Old City school, where he could be available for his new job clerking in the rites section of the prefectural yamen.[81] From that time forward, Ai's star rose as he climbed through the provincial ranks.

The material benefits of student status were therefore clear, and families fought to keep the schools open when they were threatened with closure. In the first known instance, in 1882, the Turpan prefect declared that the Pichan school was to be closed on account of its instructor's ineffective teaching.[82] Musulman students' families protested in a petition to the yamen and expressed their hope that the instructor could continue, if not indefinitely, then until such time as a suitable replacement could be found. That Musulman parents actually asked the administration for more Chinese schooling merely five years after the reconquest indicates that a certain sector of society at least benefited from this resource, probably a relatively elite stratum such as ad-Dawlah's that the provincial government would have wanted to mollify. An ineffective teacher from the province's perspective was one who failed to transform his charges into good Confucians, but the same individual could be ideal for Musulman families who desired language skills and a mastery of official writing.

Meanwhile, crises of local government also inspired officials to make more extensive use of the schools' students and graduates. Because the magistrates brought the sensibilities and practices of government in China proper to their yamens in Xinjiang, investigations and prosecutions proceeded in a familiar way. However, hyperbolic problems of translation and cultural interpretation meant that routine procedures could play out in unexpected ways. In one key case, a murder committed between Musulmans in Bay (Baicheng) in February 1886 was not reported to Beijing until September 1890, long after the statutory limit.[83] It was not an especially complicated case to resolve. However, the Bay magistrate attempted to interrogate all of the concerned parties without the benefit of speaking Turkic. This fact was not discovered until his superior, the Aksu circuit intendant, found the depositions to be inconsistent and ordered a second interrogation, which a new magistrate failed to carry out. As it turned out, the yamen in Bay had no employees who could properly conduct the interrogation because this incident occurred during the period of transition following the formal establishment of the province, when begs had been dismissed from office and the yamens had not yet reemployed them as functionaries. Rather than locate an interpreter, the new Bay magistrate simply ignored the case. The intendant then performed the interrogations personally, this time with an interpreter. That intendant was Chen

Mingyu, the Xiang Army veteran who had purchased his office and who the next year became the provincial judicial commissioner. The palpable frustration he expressed in his report as a circuit intendant then translated into a new effort to ensure that interpreters would be on hand at every yamen. Elderly tongchis who were trained before 1864 or attained their positions without attending the schools were replaced with young graduates.[84] Thanks to Chen, no further linguistic troubles or resulting delays were reported in the judicial system thereafter, while Musulman families could now be assured of a path into officialdom for their sons educated in Chinese. Nevertheless, it had taken fourteen years for the province to require that every yamen employ a tongchi.

A new threat appeared in 1896, following the withdrawal of subsidies from Beijing. By this time, inspections of the schools demonstrated that they had failed in their central mission to inculcate Musulman children with "the value of the Classics" (shi shu zhi gui) and Sino-normative familial relations (lun).[85] Therefore, the province ordered each Musulman-majority county to close all but two schools, leaving one main school (zheng shu) and one auxiliary school (fu shu). The plan also reduced teacher and custodian salaries, as well as stipends for students. Main school teachers, who usually taught Chinese-speakers, were paid twelve taels each month, while those at auxiliary schools, who taught Musulmans, were paid eight, which was the rate originally established in 1877. In Turpan, eight schools were reduced to two, and top students were transferred to the Old City and Handun schools, which began training Musulman students almost exclusively.[86] In 1899, the provincial government, realizing that Chinese and Hui had begun to establish their own private schools that did not lead students directly into government, quickly formalized the schools' segregation according to language, giving the main school to Chinese-speakers and the secondary one to Musulmans.

New policies reflected Chinese officials' acceptance that the civilizing mission had not succeeded. In 1901, the Ush subprefect Yi Shousong was fed up.[87] Each governor in turn had continued the schooling policy, he wrote, but the only effect had been to produce cohorts of Musulman men with no skill but the Chinese language, and now too many of them to guarantee their employment. As a last-ditch effort to derive some benefit from the students, Yi advanced a plan, which Beijing eventually approved, to appoint them to preexisting positions within local society: the best students would be sent out to proclaim imperial edicts orally in the villages, as they were considered trustworthy. Others, however, would be aqsaqals, irrigation chiefs, or other petty officials. Since 1877, the magistrates had been approving these officials following elections by their communities, but now they were to be appointed directly. Gone was the pretense that the students would realign society—now the government sought only to co-opt Musulman elites to keep the province running.

That year, the propagation of the New Policies demanded the integration of preexisting schools into an empire-wide public system. Xinjiang was wildly ill equipped to comply. Ultimately, its only three academies were converted into an upper school and two middle schools, while Confucian schools were turned into elementary schools (*mengguan*).[88] The curriculum changed not at all.[89] Instead, the reforms presented local officials with an opportunity to do away with what they now considered the hopeless task of civilizing the Muslims. The Turpan prefect petitioned the governor with the complaint that, while Chinese and Hui students in the Old City were "striving to be the best" and memorizing the Classics, the Musulmans in Handun were simply learning to speak Chinese. They closed the Handun school and instead employed Chinese-speaking Musulmans as language instructors at three elementary schools in Handun, Lükchün, and Toqsun. There, students would learn nothing but language for fixed three-year terms—after all, it was reasoned, they showed no interest in anything else. Yuan Dahua's brief tenure as governor and Wang Shu'nan's policies meant the formal end of Confucian schooling. Nevertheless, the schools survived in some form at least through 1919.[90] Indeed, the material benefits of Chinese-language study were still clear after the fall of the Qing, and it is in this period that the success of many of Turpan's school graduates, now adults at the height of their influence, becomes clear.

After the Xinhai Revolution, the successful graduate Ai Xueshu was appointed to Shāhyār County (Shaya) as the first magistrate born a Musulman.[91] It was difficult for people to accept his authority, and the provincial government received dozens of letters claiming to expose his shortcomings. For the first few years, the province assumed that the complaints related solely to Ai's peculiar origins, but in 1915, inspectors nevertheless discovered that Ai was corrupt and had him demoted. He spent several more years in the government as a tax collector and inspector of waterworks before working his way back to magistrateships in Yuli (Lop Nur) and

Shawan, moving around the province like any other official.[92] The other top student in Ai's school had been Gui Xin, whose career trajectory was similar, if not as stellar. Gui eventually became a village headman and by 1929 had joined the yamen himself. As of 1926, Gui and Ai were still neighbors, along with several other school alumni. Most of those neighbors worked outside the yamen, where they were indispensable intermediaries. Xu Youcheng, whom we met at the beginning of this chapter, appears with exceptional frequency in the Turpan archive as a mediator in a broad range of disputes all the way through 1928.[93] Some of his success derived from a longstanding association with his classmate Tömür, who became an inspector for the local government. There is otherwise little mention of Ai's or Gui's ethnicity in these documents or any others after Xinhai, or for that matter of the origins of Zhou Jiyu, Xu Youcheng, Mi Jiashan, or a host of other tongchis. In the archival record, having completed their schooling, they lost the label *Chan*, "Musulman," and became known by their titles. Accordingly, biographical detail for any of these individuals is frustratingly sparse. Few documents discuss any marriages or children, and those that do are in Chaghatay, suggesting that tongchis attempted to keep their Chinese and Musulman identities separate.[94]

Indeed, the documentary record bears out the widespread impression of tongchis as corrupt, grasping officials who amassed fortunes by exploiting the boundary between the interior of the *yamen* and the society outside while maintaining their own communities. In 1922, when Yang Zengxin issued a decree encouraging private investment, Ai Xueshu and his brother 'Abdul responded by using Ai's property and official connections to open their own textile mill.[95] The mill itself was successful, and was apparently built on the land that the Qing authorities had awarded Ai Xueshu for his diligent study so many years before. However, Ai engaged in an elaborate scheme to cheat his employees out of their salary. He managed to avoid the resulting lawsuit until his death in 1926, when his family inherited a small fortune.

Let us return to Alptekin's anecdote about his father's wearing of Chinese clothes and rejection by his mother. Alptekin presents it as an allegory for the alienation of a nation from its heritage: by speaking the language of the colonizer and wearing their clothing, a person loses touch with their origins. In the late Qing, such an essentialized definition of groupness, which reflects the belief in common traditions connected to a myth of common descent, was still being worked out. At the same time, recorded Musulman complaints against the tongchis are based on their abuse of power and power that derived from the ability to mediate across languages and cultures. Given this context, I would argue that a disruption of the socioeconomic system was just as significant for the identification of a group as was the violation of linguistic and cultural boundaries.[96] Tongchis' backgrounds, as far as they can be discerned, included both aristocratic and commoner families. Whatever their origins, they displaced the literate Muslim men who had previously commanded respect and control over communication with authority. Not only did their rise therefore displace some of the power of preexisting elites, but it created conditions in which the boundaries between peoples were constantly reified by the tongchis' act of translation across them. Let us turn now to the substance of that act.

Mediation and Mimesis

An Uyghur saying holds that "a bad tongchi can kill" (*chala tongchi adäm öltürür*).[97] Oral history traces the origin of this saying back to an incident during the Xiang Army's reconquest wherein an interpreter's mistranslation led to the senseless deaths of dozens of innocent imams at the army's hands. Dozens more were saved only by the timely intervention of a good tongchi, who understood the grammatical error that had been made. Yet a single event does not make for a saying. Tongchis wielded power over life and death, and many smaller boons and injuries, through their skillful manipulation of language. They did so not in the realm of mere translation, but in that of mimesis. That is, the task of the tongchi was to use narrative to fabricate a reality that imitated the assumptions of the moral world of official Chinese writing as well as its underlying beliefs about human action and psychology. That fabrication granted different degrees of power to people through their representations in text.

Chaghatay had other words for "translator" and "interpreter," such as *tarjumān* (from Arabic) or *tilmach* (from Turkic), but *tongchi* specified the boundary-crossing Musulmans who operated in the realm of official Chinese writing. The etymology of the term points to the distinctiveness of their activity as an interplay of meanings across languages: in Chinese, *tong* 通 means "to cross through, to connect," as well as "to understand."

One then adds the Turkic suffix -*chi*, "one who does," and so *tongchi* is "one who *tongs*," that is, a person who gets meanings across, through, from, and to Chinese. The word *tong* also became verbalized, as in the phrase "He should have it communicated (*tonglatip*) to the other *tongchi*" (*bashqa tongchigha tonglatip bärsun*).[98] This verb was used to describe information only in an official Chinese context, where text passed through the medium of the Chinese language.

Tongchis controlled the representational play that took place in the linguistic and cultural gaps between Turkic Muslim society and the administration. A tongchi's task was therefore to make Musulman subjects "speak" in ways that were intelligible to the yamen. They did so in four ways: First, during interrogations, a tongchi "interpreted" a person's oral speech for the benefit of other clerks, so that it could be written down directly in Literary Chinese. We are fortunate that the Turpan archive contains many copies of testimonies apparently written down during interrogation. In another case of a husband murdering his wife, this one from 1890, several witnesses presented detailed accounts: the accused, a young Musulman man; the dead woman's mother, also a Musulman; her younger and older brothers; their Hui landlord; two Musulman neighbors; and the aqsaqal Tömür.[99] Their testimonies are heavily redacted. Editing marks indicate the elimination of inconvenient passages of text that challenged the narrative that the yamen wanted to advance, followed immediately in some cases by contradictory statements. For example, the victim's younger brother, who was all of ten *sui*, left a testimony that shows signs of prompting and editing:

> I was fast asleep, and I don't know what happened. He took my elder sister and cut her to death. He also jabbed me and ~~jabbed~~ stabbed me, ~~and he made a lot of noise~~, and my mother went to save her. I was startled awake, and I got up. My sister's husband ~~Wāṣil was holding the knife and doing the deed~~ had already run off.

The boy's words reflect the position of a child confused about what his interrogators want to hear and unsure of whether he ought to have helped his dead sister or perhaps been a more useful witness. Ultimately, the boy's words were expunged from the record, along with the child himself. Instead, the victim's mother became the key witness. Her first deposition shows the same marks of redaction and insertion: "My daughter, because she was gravely wounded, passed away immediately. ~~I got dizzy and fell to the ground, so I don't know how Wāṣil escaped~~," her testimony reads. By the end of the months of investigation and interrogation, the official record was changed to state that this woman had seen everything.

In the meantime, we are in the awkward position of interpreting an act of which there is no direct historical record, but only traces of Turkic speech in a written text in Chinese. It is remarkable that no known transcripts of oral depositions are written in Chaghatay, as doing so would have saved the trouble of translating on the fly. Many of the editing marks are not related to an attempt to alter the factual content of a testimony, but rather compensate for the radical differences between Chinese and Turkic syntax. A simultaneous oral interpretation might have resulted in text that seemed "out of order" in Chinese, and so needed to be placed into a logical sequence. Yet there is no systematic way to illuminate the practice of interpretation without access to source texts. What is certain is that the interpreter was present as a means of communication, but also as a barrier separating an interrogee's voice from the workings of the judicial system.

Yamen staff needed to advance a coherent narrative that carried the quality of truth. Therefore, second, a tongchi needed to engage in ventriloquism, the projection of a voice into a speaking subject.[100] Musulmans in the archive often "said" things they had never uttered, or at least probably not in idiomatic Literary Chinese. In this case, the victim's mother not only was turned into the sole eyewitness, but was made to say something that in the eyes of a Chinese magistrate justified a woman's murder: her dead daughter had been acting like a "shrew."[101] That is, the mother's final, formal testimony described a history of impropriety and disobedience on the part of her daughter. In her narration of the events of her daughter's death, the daughter does not simply "scold" her husband, but "scolds shrewishly" (hanpo hunma), using a fixed expression in Chinese that was well known in the judicial system. The purpose of this depiction, as in the case described earlier, was to justify the murder and grant the husband clemency. The mother's testimony is written mainly in a very colloquial (baihua) Chinese as well, in order to suggest its authenticity to a Chinese reader, who would expect such rough speech—but only in Chinese—from a commoner.[102] Yet the use of this phrase was aimed at achieving a specific legal consequence, the downgrading of the crime from premeditated murder (*mousha*) to the lesser offense of murder with intent (*gusha*).[103] The murderer's own testimonies received a similar treatment.[104]

However, it was not enough for a Qing subject to be spoken for in writing. The judicial process required that all parties to a case must provide a final testimony, so that all accounts matched.[105] Therefore, and third, the tongchi helped to elicit speech from the subject. The Turpan yamen staff took this requirement seriously. The murderer in this case was held in a jail in Turpan's New City, a stinking and windowless enclosure reserved for violent criminals.[106] On at least three occasions, the jail's staff transported him back to the yamen, where the tongchi and clerks walked him through new oral testimony. Ultimately, the murderer would need to say out loud that he accepted his punishment as a consequence of the events described.

Each deposition was an opportunity for the murderer's interpellation as a Qing subject—the yamen called upon him through their labels and categories, and as a prisoner he had little choice but to comply.[107] They obliged him to describe himself through those categories and to narrate his own experiences through their reality and the logic of cause, effect, and culpability that was legible to the judicial system. The term that Chinese yamen staff called Musulman subjects was *Chantou*, "wrapped-head," sometimes simply *Chan*, "wrapped," for short, or *Chan min*, "wrapped-head commoner." This term diffused gradually from higher-level official discourses of difference, as well as common speech, into the practice of the yamen, and early documents in Turpan label Turkic-speaking Muslims more ambiguously, often simply as *min*, "commoner," or *humin*, "tax-paying commoner." In the early 1890s, however, *Chantou* entered Musulmans' own Turkic-language oral and written discourse in Turpan.[108] Meanwhile, every petition from a person identified as a Musulman, and every oral testimony, began with a statement of the speaker's name, age, place of origin, and now ethnic category: *Chan*. It is unclear what a Musulman might have said to the initial question of their identity when speaking in Turkic—perhaps "Musulman." Nevertheless, they would have heard "*Chantou*" in the immediate translation of their speech or would have been made to recite the term themselves at the conclusion of a case.

This is one way that colonial law forces the subject to accept the categories of the state, through their repetition and affirmation of those categories in their own speech. *Chantou* denoted no legal category. Rather, it was a category of practice in the discourse of difference that Chinese officials and commoners alike considered natural. The Sino-normative assumptions that pervaded the politico-juridical system, and the fact that political power rested firmly in the hands of Chinese people, nevertheless granted *Chantou* a law-like status. *Chantou* indicated the docile kind of Muslim subject, as opposed to the Hui, that Xiang Army leaders had described as being close to civilization, and being identified as such implied not only tractability, but simplicity and naïveté. Nevertheless, to be regarded as a fool could be advantageous, as Chinese officials easily pitied a *Chantou*.

We may end this section on a lighter note, with a fourth example of the tongchi's role in making a Musulman subject speak, by imitating the forms of text that officials found acceptable. A tongchi could replace Musulman categories with their perceived Chinese equivalents and thereby represent their clients as normative imperial subjects. One particularly clear example comes from a petition that a group of akhunds sent to the Turpan prefect in 1887, complaining about the moral corruption brought by Chinese prostitutes.[109] The Chaghatay original read:

> To the great *dalaoye*, a petition from all of your underlings from Pichan, Liushi Hu, Er Gong, and San Gong:
>
> Every spring, our runoff from the mountains comes in the fourth month. Now, however, it is the tenth day of the fourth month. The water is still not coming from the mountains. We gathered the akhunds and went about everywhere, praying. The water still does not come. We asked very, very old people who have lived for a very long time, "Why should it be so?" They said, "If there is much prostitution in the land, the water won't come."
>
> We find: there are some bad women in this area. These women engage in prostitution. They neither take their leave, nor go about peacefully doing their business, but always do bad things. Because of the badness of their acts, our water does not come. Bugs eat our crops, and the wind blows them away. We submit this petition on these matters.

As we will see in chapter 4, "bad women" (*yaman khatunlar*) became a common term for women who had sex outside of their communities, whether it be Musulman women with Chinese men or Chinese women with Musulman men. The petition itself is a fairly transparent attempt to mobilize the perceived biases and interests of the Chinese magistrate. First, there are clues indicating how these akhunds themselves sought to imitate the structure and language of a Chinese-language petition from the provincial system: The opening line uses a Chinese word that was already common in Turkic discourse, *dalaoye* (Chaghatay *dālawyä*), which is a respectful term for the magistrate. "We find" (*bakhsaq*) is parallel to Chinese *cha* or Manchu *baicaci*, terms used in official writing. It was not commonly used in this way in Chaghatay. More to the point, the akhunds suggest a magical relationship between sexual activity and the availability of mountain runoff. Certainly, we can imagine a metaphorical relationship between sexual fluids and water, and between the fertility of the fields and of human beings. However, the suggestion that this knowledge was gained from "very, very old people who have lived for a very long time" (*tola uzun yashighan chong chong ādamlär*) invokes stereotypes about Chinese respect for the elderly, as reflected in the stories of extreme filial piety that the Xiang Army was distributing through the *Book of Li*. This part of the petition also uses oddly stilted and repetitive language that may seek to imitate Literary Chinese. Finally, the akhunds emphasize their use of prayer and ritual, in this case probably referring to using the *yada* stone to summon rain in times of drought. While Muslim commentators were skeptical of Chinese rituals—"They have this stupid idea that it's beneficial, that it keeps people from getting sick or the city from catching on fire"—they nevertheless recognized that this kind of magic was central to the workings of Chinese power.[110]

This petition's Chinese translation presents these events and their supernatural dimensions rather differently:

> The superintendents, mīrābs, and chiefs of Pichan, Liushi Hu, Er Gong, and San Gong petition the *dalaoye*.
>
> We petition: the lands farmed by those households that we Muslim chiefs administer are all lacking water. Every year, they depend on mountain runoff to irrigate them. Before, mountain runoff always flowed down to irrigate the sprouts in the first ten days of the fourth month. This year, up until now, there has been no water at all.
>
> We Muslim chiefs find: We asked old folks around here, who said that the reason that the mountain runoff still has not arrived is all because there are extremely many prostitutes here. Because they have offended local spirits, they have blocked up the mountain runoff, so it does not flow. Right now, the sprouts are all dry. We Muslim chiefs jointly petition to ask the magistrate to forbid

prostitution and clear the land, in order to receive the spirits' manifest response and save the myriad people.

Again, the key strategic framing of the petition involves the deployment of "spirits." Turpan Musulmans lived under a regime that appeared obsessed with ritual and magic, and with respecting the demands of the spirits. In 1877, Chinese settlers in Turpan had "borrowed" a mosque to perform a ritual drama, after which settlers and officials alike considered the mosque to have become a Chinese temple.[111] A conflict ensued that persisted into the Republican period, demonstrating that spirits were more powerful than earthly demands. Not long before the akhunds wrote their petition, the Turpan government had collected funds to renovate a temple for Turpan's city god. While the collection was nominally voluntary, documents indicate that Musulmans considered it mandatory, although the magistrate permitted them to donate anonymously.[112] Yet the most mysterious of Chinese spirits were those that dwelled in the mountains. The Board of Rites designated the rituals used to worship those mountains at fixed times of year, and Musulman students participated in them. Therefore, the akhunds' petition attempted to appeal to what they imagined as Chinese spirituality in order to ask for the expulsion of Chinese prostitutes.

It did not work. The magistrate and his staff perceived the motives behind the petition. He replied,

Local prostitutes and itinerant whores all ought to be banished, to support the transformation of customs. As for the poor flow of mountain runoff, it is only that the weather has been cool lately, and the snows are not melting. What does this have to do with prostitution? What has been petitioned is truly fabricated nonsense.

The magistrate rejected the notion that outsiders caused spiritual instability, which in this context was a device for talking about a kind of social instability thought to be caused by sex between members of different groups, and calling on state power to act upon it. Other interpreters were much more successful, and we will see in the next chapter how Musulmans could use the Xiang Army's resettlement project to expel or confine Musulman women they believed to have violated the boundaries of their community. In this case, the magistrate might have faced strong opposition from

Chinese settlers, merchants, and soldiers if he had followed the Musulmans' wishes, both for denying Chinese men sexual partners and for obeying the suggestions of akhunds.

A tongchi was powerful, but not omnipotent. Malfunctions in the system of communication, such as the translation of the akhunds' petition, point to the imperfect nature of mimesis as a means of appropriating the power of the state. When a deposition or petition favored the magistrate's priorities, or something obscure could be represented in appealing language, a tongchi's work could favor a client or interrogee, Musulman or otherwise. It was more difficult to mobilize the state's symbols and forms against it. A bad tongchi could indeed kill by incompetence or malice, but an effective tongchi provided the magistrate with an image of the people he governed, an image that he could present in turn to his superiors. Representing a Musulman murderer, for example, as a moral Confucian person could save their life, while eliciting a Chantou identity from a dominated Musulman subject granted them the limited power to evince sympathy or pity from the magistrate.

*   *   *

"A bad tongchi can kill," as the saying goes, and as we will see in chapter 6, a tongchi could also be perceived as causing historic disruption to the cosmic and social order. These actors who lived in between languages, religions, and cultures were nevertheless obligated to present themselves as normative Confucians, as the kinds of moral men whom the Xiang Army sought to foster among the Muslims. While the tongchis did not necessarily embrace the army's ideology, their educations nevertheless allowed them to embody a Confucian and Chinese subjectivity, particularly in the realm of the written word, in which they could present not just their own identities but Muslim society in terms that were acceptable and legible to Chinese officials. The tongchi's constant motion across a gap between two modes of representation drew attention to the difference between them, and it did so in a context that was increasingly routine and intimate. Musulmans especially were exposed to new reminders of their linguistic difference and the alienness of Chinese, now embodied in a figure who also appeared to be losing the marks of Muslim identity.

The civilizing project's centerpiece, the Confucian schools, therefore had an ironic result: First, the Xiang Army hoped to transform society from below and within, and then to use its agents of transformation as bilingual and bicultural intermediaries. Instead of information, however, they received images of society crafted for their consumption according to the forms and limitations of judicial documents such as petitions and depositions. As we will see in the next chapter, the power of translation was not used to transmit elite values to Muslim subjects and effect their assimilation into the Chinese ecumene, but instead to police the boundaries around the Muslim community. Nevertheless, the tongchi played the key role in causing Musulman subjects to speak, and so their oral interpretation enabled the routine interpellation of Musulman subjects according to the categories that were active in the state, granting informal categories the power of formal, legally recognized boundaries. The institutions of assimilation therefore caused estrangement, while the apparatus meant to facilitate communication instead demonstrated people's separateness while assigning them a distinctive label: Chantou.

FOUR

Bad Women and Lost Children

The Sexual Economy of Confucian Colonialism

YANG RONG'S GRANDSON went by "Pockmark" (*Mazi*), in reference to his acne-scarred face. He was a habitual gambler, which Yang tolerated until the evening of May 5, 1890, when a young Musulman woman named Mehrish (Mairesha) pounded on his courtyard gate.[1] According to Yang, she was drunk and declaring in a loud voice that she was betrothed to Pockmark and would marry him that very day. They had apparently met at the tavern. Mehrish was insistent, and as people awoke and emerged from their doorways to marvel at the display, Yang found himself paralyzed with shame. He deputized a neighbor to lie and tell Mehrish that the wedding date had been postponed.

Yang Rong's troubles were not over, however, and shame drove him eventually to the magistrate's office. Yang was a village headman, charged with delivering fortnightly lectures on morality, and therefore played a critical role in civilizing the borderland. Yet his own grandson, he complained, caroused with Musulman women! He begged the magistrate to punish Pockmark and Mehrish in ways that he could not, threatening them with prison and beatings for gambling and prostitution. The magistrate replied, however, that there was no evidence that Mehrish had committed any crime. Marriage, after all, was considered a stabilizing force and precisely what was needed to settle a rowdy young Chinese man and a lascivious Musulman woman. At this point, the archival trail fades away. Perhaps they married.

Pockmark and Mehrish's case illustrates the problems that emerged in late-Qing Xinjiang as culturally distinct modes of sexual exchange clashed in ways that led to a reification of ethnic boundaries. Relationships between Chinese and Musulmans were usually products of coercion, necessity, or prostitution and came to be considered appropriate to lower-class men, but below the dignity of officials. On either side of that relationship, very different practices surrounding marriage and prostitution, and very different definitions thereof, created confusion about the nature of intimate relationships, compounded by a politics of representation that sought to obscure sexual violence in the language of Confucian orthodoxy. Frequent boundary-crossing led to a hardening of those boundaries predicated on perceived threats to masculinity, namely, male mastery over women's bodies. Descent as a sign of membership in a bounded community gradually took precedence over the more flexible embodied identities of religion and language.[2]

There arose in this context the haunting figure of the "bad woman" (*yaman khatun*), a pariah excluded from the Musulman community for her sexual relationships with non-Muslim Others. The lives of such "bad women" illuminate the conflicts that emerged around the attempt to transform the Muslim family. That intervention, like the other aspects of the civilizing project, took place on two levels: The provincial project not only attempted to seed Muslim society with the patriarchal norms and practices espoused by the *jingshi* group by inculcating Musulman boys with Confucian values, as described in the previous chapter; they engaged in a comprehensive resettlement program that forced men and women—mainly lower-class Chinese men and Muslim women—into marriages meant to civilize both parties. Meanwhile, under the difficult economic circumstances of the Reconstruction era, many Musulman women sold themselves as wives to Chinese men, or else were kidnapped and trafficked by brokers, who were mainly Hui.

In this new sexual economy, Musulmans, Hui, and Chinese came to occupy new structural positions that corresponded to commodity, broker, and consumer, respectively. These positions gained a new degree of social reality as they were compounded by economic inequalities. However, economic status alone did not produce a more coherent sense of a bounded Musulman identity. Rather, the sale of Musulman women presented a threat to Musulman masculinity, which in turn encouraged Musulman men to tighten their control of women's bodies. First, Musulman leaders ostracized women who had sex outside of the boundaries of the community. Second, they leveraged the institutions of the civilizing project to discipline these women through spatial segregation. As boundary violation and mixed descent became increasingly salient sources of social tension, the idea of Musulman-ness shifted away from a community of practice defined by common language and participation in certain forms of Islamic piety, and toward an imagined community rooted in an idea of common descent.

This chapter builds on previous work in historical ethnography to explore how norms and practices were challenged in times of change.[3] It takes a "sexual economy" approach in order to illuminate how power and belonging were articulated in the exchange of sexual, domestic, and reproductive labor. Thinking in these terms helps us to explore racial supremacy and male supremacy simultaneously by illuminating how certain people valued others' lives and labor.[4] At the same time, it highlights women's agency or lack thereof in transactional exchanges of sexual labor that were meant to build social or economic capital in times of crisis.[5] That transactionality takes on new meanings in borderlands and colonies, wherein the macro-level relationship of domination between one group and another plays out in complicated ways in everyday intimacy and boundary maintenance.[6]

It also concerns intimate relationships that were almost universally violent and exploitative.[7] I attempt as far as possible to honor and emphasize the voices of victims. However, the systematic suppression of women's voices was central to the creation of legible narratives at the yamen and to the maintenance of imperial and Xiang Army ideology. In that sense, this chapter is a history of patriarchies in competition—of interactions between two different ways of deploying women's bodies and voices so that men could remain in control of them. The documents must be read through that politics of representation.

Marriage and Sex: Practices and Perceptions

The Xiang Army found Musulman marriage practices morally repugnant. While their derision may have been unwarranted, they were correct in identifying great differences between Confucian and Musulman norms. However, Chinese writers at least since Sima Qian (ca. 145–86 BCE) have accused their enemies of violating the principles of good sociomoral order through outlandish marriage, to the point that it became a trope of Chinese ethnographic writing.[8] It is necessary to outline how Musulman marriage tended to work in Turpan from a Musulman perspective, so as to disentangle the history of social change from the history of representations of difference.

The Xiang Army's main objections were to a pair of practices that were very common in East Turkestan, namely, serial marriage and temporary marriage. While polygamy was allowed under Islamic law, it nevertheless appears to have been uncommon for one man to have many wives in the same household.[9] Where men did have multiple wives, they were usually unaware of each other. The urge to hide such an arrangement and the fact that it sometimes caused conflict suggest that Musulmans did not accept it fully. Instead, serial marriage was the norm, as both men and women divorced with some frequency, and then remarried other partners. Indeed, a widow or divorcée could be considered more valuable than a first-time bride, especially if she had demonstrated her ability to produce children.[10] The result was that any individual might have a number of wives or husbands over the course of a lifetime, and blended families were common.

While statistical data is lacking, anecdotes abound, and one of the richest is provided by Mullah Abū 'l-Mahdī, our acquaintance from the introduction.[11] Abū 'l-Mahdī was married no fewer than four times between the 1870s and 1909. His parents arranged the first marriage when he was seventeen years old, to a woman that he and his young friends found unattractive. Looking back, Abū 'l-Mahdī criticized his younger self for being spoiled and petulant, as he had married her but refused to play the role of husband. His parents gave in and returned the woman to her family. Not long after, Abū 'l-Mahdī's parents died, and his older brothers, who were trying to rid themselves of their obnoxious sibling, arranged a new match. Abū 'l-Mahdī did not care for his second wife either, as she was unattractive and from a poor family. However, the reoccupation of Turpan in 1877 and the concomitant changes in the economy deprived him of means of support other than her labor and his own. While Abū 'l-Mahdī was considering divorce, she became pregnant, and they raised their son together. Between his dependence on doing backbreaking unskilled labor to survive and her apparently bottomless appetite—keeping in mind this is his narration, not hers—he grew weary of the marriage. He divorced his wife and left her with their son, whom he never saw again but believed would survive.

Abū 'l-Mahdī was satisfied with his next wife, who was an excellent businesswoman. The couple had eight children together and were married for twenty-seven years, during which time they married off two sons. Eventually, this woman passed away, and Abū 'l-Mahdī lived with his unmarried children as a single father. Later, during harder times, his fourth marriage was to a widow who brought two daughters of her own into his crowded house. At this point, Abū 'l-Mahdī had twelve people under one roof, and the fighting was endless. He and his wife tried marrying one of her daughters to one of his sons, but that only worsened the conflict. Marrying her second daughter to Abū 'l-Mahdī's older brother then seemed like a reasonable solution—until that turned both sides of the family against them. Only intervention by the local Islamic authorities succeeded in establishing peace in their household.

What is striking about Abū 'l-Mahdī's account is the degree to which his marriages were companionate. It is well established that Musulman women were relatively independent.[12] A man could value his wife not only for her company, but also for her ability to contribute to the household economy, as Abū 'l-Mahdī did. Even investigators sent to assess the state of Uyghur society in the 1950s, who were inclined to emphasize the injustice of "feudal" arranged marriages, conceded that women could have a great deal of independence in choosing a partner and running a household. Women also returned to their natal homes frequently to see family.

Families regularly divided their wealth between children, who were expected to start households of their own, and short marriages produced smaller, more atomized families with fewer obligations to an extended network of relatives.[13] New families tended to outgrow their quarters in the family courtyard and locate houses of their own, while the divorced and widowed might or might not return home. The Turpan archive rarely presents multigenerational courtyard homes but mainly describes families in which parents and adult children lived at enough of a distance from each other that visiting a family member required making a special trip. Available statistical evidence corroborates the idea that the Musulman family was relatively atomized: an undated late-Qing register of tax-paying households (*hu*) from the town of Handun, where Abū 'l-Mahdī lived for a time, lists 188 Musulman households ranging in size from two to nineteen members, with an mean household size of 6.2, including children.[14] This is only slightly higher than the average Musulman household size across Xinjiang, which was five people.[15] On the other hand, the register shows that Abū 'l-Mahdī's large family in one house was not a total anomaly, as a handful of households included more than ten members.

"Temporary marriage" (*waqitliq toy*) was common among Musulmans before and after the Yaʿqūb Beg period.[16] Generally speaking, a Muslim merchant far from home was encouraged or even pressured to integrate into his host community by taking a wife on a fixed-period contract. Temporary marriage, much like the *mutʿa* marriage known in Iran, was meant to supply the man with sexual pleasure, companionship, and domestic service while he was in residence.[17] In exchange, the woman's family received contractually specified goods. Temporary marriages were licensed by the religious authorities, including an akhund's performance of a marriage ceremony. At the same time, temporary marriage is not described in manuals of jurisprudence from the Kashgar Islamic court, suggesting that local Muslim authorities did not distinguish it in ritual or legal terms from ordinary marriage (*nikāḥ*).[18] Overall, temporary marriage was not taboo. Nevertheless, as Ildikó Bellér-Hann points out, a woman's relative security in a temporary marriage was related to class, and those who entered into such an arrangement out of their or their parent's need to survive tended to suffer greater abuse.[19]

Temporary marriage thus occupied an uncertain space between marriage and prostitution. Yaʿqūb Beg's regime forbade it, as it did not conform to normative Islamic practice in the nearby Ferghana Valley, whence they had come.[20] While late-Qing Chinese observers did not identify temporary marriage by name, they interpreted the practice in different ways, identifying temporary wives as "wives" (*qi*) or sometimes "concubines" (*qie*). "Wife" (*qi*) implied a normative, legal, and morally orthodox arrangement, but in the historical record, the term euphemized a range of relationships, including those that a modern observer would construe as sexual slavery or prostitution. Concubinage in traditional China was a legal, orthodox practice, although one that many found morally questionable. In the Turpan archive, people deployed the word *concubine* (*qie*) in order to cast certain relationships in an unsavory light, relationships that again ran the gamut from companionate marriages between consenting adults to a man's ownership of a trafficked woman. In rare cases of polygyny, this Chinese word for "concubine" could indicate a Muslim man's secondary wife. Of course, when an interested party addressed the yamen, it would have been unwise to point out that a Muslim man could legally marry several wives of nominally equal status. Instead, people were obliged to represent their lives as those of normative Chinese subjects, so as to avoid moral censure. The politics of translation ensured that the Chinese authorities did not have a firm grasp of how Musulmans' marriages worked.

Chinese observers nevertheless interpreted temporary and serial marriage as a sign of Musulmans' fallen moral condition. Zuo Zongtang's clerk Xiao Xiong described Musulman marriage thus:[21]

> If a man marries several women, no one thinks it strange, and if one does not suit him, he simply gives her up. . . . The ladies lack proper teaching, and most are wanton. On summer days, they invite girl pals to bathe in the river without shame. In the fertile lands of the Southern Eight Cities [the Tarim Basin], their extravagant and wanton customs are even more extreme, meaning that there are actually fewer women who act overtly as prostitutes. . . . If a husband marries a woman and then learns she is "flawed," and if he is moved to break off the marriage, then the bride's family has nothing to say against it. It is like the customs of Yue.

Xiao's ethnographic eye saw Musulmans in terms of ancient China's deep South, the country of Yue, once the periphery of the Han and Tang empires and, from this perspective, the edge of the civilized world. Xiao Xiong's comments had at least as much to do with a longstanding tradition of essentializing the Other in terms of deviation from Confucian sexual norms, including the trope of exotic women bathing together in a stream.[22] Those tropes were usually associated, however, with the peoples of the southern borderlands, such as the Dai or Miao, while excluding the steppe peoples of the North. Not coincidentally, the Southern peoples lived under the provincial system or in ad hoc arrangements in which magistrates collaborated with local chiefs (*tusi*). Depicting Musulman women as "Southern" peoples reflects Musulmans' new relationship with Chinese power under the provincial system, the administrative shift of Xinjiang from the bureaucratic "North" to the "South." Yet Xiao Xiong was also one of the first in a long series of Chinese officials who identified Musulman marriage and family structure as the root reason for Musulmans' need for civilization. The blame and responsibility for Musulman sexuality, in the eyes of Chinese officials, fell squarely on Musulman women, who, according to Xiao Xiong, were so accustomed to lasciviousness that there was no clear distinction between prostitutes and ordinary women in the Musulman heartland.[23]

The depiction of Musulman women as "wanton" was not entirely new. Earlier Chinese observers of the "Western Regions," including those visiting Turpan, had commented on the ease with which Musulman women divorced their husbands.[24] They were not incorrect, as Hanafi jurisprudence allowed for a relatively easy divorce for women, especially for those whose husbands had abandoned them.[25] Gazetteers commented on what officials considered Musulmans' debased family morals. Officials complained about how Musulmans lacked surnames but used patronymics instead—this was not only an administrative inconvenience, but a sign that they were incapable of maintaining lineages.[26] In more extreme formulations, Musulmans were said to lack any concept of filial piety because they could not trace their ancestry.[27] Musulmans were therefore flawed subjects and people without history, in that they lacked moral guidance from the past. Such an analysis of Musulman society appears absurd, given the importance of the veneration of the dead in local religious life and the range of children's obligations to their parents. Nevertheless, it would take until the very end of the Qing for a high official to note the significance that Musulmans placed on tombs.[28]

That notion of Musulman immorality continued to inform how provincial leaders articulated policy. In 1882, Liu Jintang endorsed a report from Chen Mingyu, then general inspector of reconstruction (zongcha shanhou shiyi), affirming the army's basic view that the key to stability was the moral transformation of the Musulmans.[29] The core of propriety (liyi), he argued, was disciplining familial relationships and gradually altering customs under the strict guidance of the distant sovereign. Chen's assessment was the basis of a proclamation that explicitly forbade divorce. The Qing Code already prescribed very narrow conditions under which a husband could repudiate his wife, while women were simply not allowed to dissolve a marriage.[30] However, Chen and Liu argued that this law needed stricter implementation among Musulmans: magistrates facing a divorce case would be required to avoid customary leniency out of sympathy for the accused, and instead seek harsher punishments. That meant, for example, that a wife who fled her husband, or who divorced him under Islamic law but without the permission of the Qing state, would receive at minimum the statutory punishment of one hundred strokes with the "heavy stick," a bamboo pole about three inches thick, the blows of which could kill or permanently injure a human being. Liu granted magistrates the latitude to impose even harsher punishments.

The army leadership's prejudices were based not only on cultural difference, but on class anxieties about the violent potential of the sort of unmarried, uprooted men who composed the rank and file, the so-called "bare sticks."[31] When it came time to demobilize, army leaders immediately depicted their former soldiers as obvious threats, just as other members of the *jingshi* community did in Hunan and Hubei.[32] They ordered the men who won them the Northwest to be carefully monitored on the roads back to Hunan, lest they turn to banditry. At the same time, thousands of demobilized soldiers simply settled in Xinjiang, where they farmed, traded, and labored. Ironically, these "dangerous" men had been part of the plan all along. *Jingshi* thinkers from Gong Zizhen and Wei Yuan onward had dreamed of simultaneously civilizing Xinjiang and taming the unattached men of China proper by sending them to colonize the borderland.[33] In their vision, a bare stick and a Muslim woman could marry and, through their cultivation of the husband-and-wife relationship, each bring the other to conform to Confucian norms. Gong and Wei's vision was almost Jeffersonian in its faith in the frontier's ability to create moral people through labor.[34] Yet Gong, Wei, and later Zuo Zongtang's plans also reflected anxieties about the bare stick—who was implicitly homosexual—as a threat to the reproduction of the normative family.

Marriage was therefore at the heart of the Xiang Army's project in Xinjiang. The idea that marriage produced certain kinds of subjects points to the consonance between class prejudices and beliefs about ethnoreligious difference articulated in the central texts of Hunanese *jingshi* thought. Yet it was also part of a broader and in many ways much older discourse about difference that informed representations of Musulmans in subtler ways. Before Chinese officials arrived in Xinjiang, they expected to find an alien society as it was depicted in their books, one in which heterodox marriage produced widespread immorality. The ambiguities of serial marriage and temporary marriage confirmed their preconceptions and the necessity of their mission to civilize.

Displacement Through Violence and Resettlement

The main mechanisms that the provisional and provincial administrations used to impose Sino-normative family relations were forced marriage and resettlement. Resettlement seemed necessary, as the Muslim uprisings and reconquest had displaced large numbers of people. Early estimates from the Xiang Army indicate massive depopulation, especially across the North, where many Chinese-majority settlements had been razed and their residents killed, enslaved, or scattered.[35] Pro–Ya'qūb Beg chronicles describe events in which his armies forcibly removed Hui and Chinese from their homes and drove them into servitude in the South.

One of the Xiang Army's early imperatives was therefore to separate groups of people—Chinese, Musulman, and Hui—where members of each group cohabited. An order from Zuo Zongtang in 1877 commanded the Reconstruction Agencies to inspect Musulman households for Chinese children they had taken in.[36] Warfare, he reasoned, was an opportunity for Muslims to kidnap or enslave Chinese, particularly orphaned children, but restoring these children to their families might save their lineages. The agencies indeed liberated many people from captivity. One man, a Musulman named Qādir, was found to have held a Chinese woman and man in bondage.[37] Qādir claimed that, during his service to Ya'qūb Beg, he had been "ordered" to marry the woman. His assertion was in keeping with an apparent pattern of sexual violence: Ya'qūb Beg's troops sometimes murdered Musulman women engaged in temporary marriages to Chinese soldiers.[38] Meanwhile, Chaghatay-language accounts and the observations of outsiders attest to the widespread forced conversion of Chinese men to become "new Muslims." However, very little is said in the historical record about the fates of those Chinese women who did not "martyr" themselves, and their conversion perhaps involved forced marriage. Qādir's second Chinese cohabitant was a young man, whom Qādir claimed was a "renter." During the inspections, Qādir coerced both Chinese people into representing themselves as a married couple renting a room, but both escaped and begged the agency to free them.

During the inspections, a Chinese woman from Gansu, Li *shi*, told the magistrate her story, which attests to a deeper history of sexual violence: Early in the Muslim uprisings in Gansu, a Hui rebel killed Li *shi*'s family and took her as a "concubine" (*qie*).[39] He took her with the Hui leader Bai Yan-hu's army beyond the Pass and settled in Dihua, where the Xiang Army eventually executed him as a rebel. The dead man's brother, Ma Fuyuan, compelled her to stay as his own concubine. Li *shi* escaped and fled to Turpan, where she begged for food. Eventually, a Chinese officer named Yang San took her in, apparently into an informal domestic relationship. Ma Fuyuan accused Yang San of having kidnapped his "wife"—not "concubine"—of twenty years or more. Ma Fuyuan testified that she was not named Li *shi*, but Ma *shi*, suggesting that she was a native-born Hui with a typical Hui surname, but only masquerading as Chinese. Ma Fuyuan was found out, however, and Li *shi* won her freedom. The establishment of Qing military and political power in Turpan afforded all of these people a chance to seek better conditions by claiming ethnic or religious difference. Forced marriage or slavery was not, however, in itself grounds for liberation—one needed to be a Chinese victim of a Muslim to be freed.

While some people now gained their freedom, the resettlement created new forms of displacement. The sheer scale of resettlement is apparent only from scattered documents, but some settlements were sizable. In the town of Dabancheng, for example, the Refugees Agencies (*nanmin ju*) settled twelve hundred refugees, each of whom was supplied with grain and blankets.[40] Yet resettlement demanded the enforcement of the normative family, and so the agencies took displaced people, married them to each other, and gave them plots of fallow land to undertake reclamation. This act was described as a man "adopting a refugee . . . as a wife" (*shouyang nanmin . . . yi zuo qishi*).[41] Documents recording their assignations were brief and routine: "Zhao Guixing is now ordered to the yamen; he is ordered to be paired with a Chinese woman," reads one.[42] The effort was meant to create families for those who had none, cultivate the desert, and civilize the borderland. It more than incidentally enforced a patriarchal family structure in which women, who tended to be Muslims and often had children, were brought into the households of single Chinese men.

Frequently, the agencies actually divided families. In the introduction, we met Wei *shi*, a Hui woman who was running just ahead of the Xiang Army in 1877. Wei *shi* had been traveling with her husband, Ma Zhenghai, and their children all the way from Shaanxi, where Ma feared he would be executed for rebellion.[43] They were headed to the Ili Valley and the stability afforded by the Russian occupation when, somewhere near Qumul, the family was separated. Wei *shi* found her brother-in-law, and they went together to Kashgar. There the Refugees Agency took her in and assigned her to a Chinese named Zeng Changming as his "wife" (*qi*). The agency granted them a plot of land in Aksu, where they farmed and raised two children alongside Wei *shi*'s own. Ten years later, Ma Zhenghai finally tracked his wife down, half of China away from home. Ma and Wei *shi* intended to move away together, but Zeng refused to release her, and so Ma sued him for "kidnapping his wife." In the ensuing investigation, Wei *shi* testified that "A Muslim woman and a Chinese each follow different teachings" (*Huizi furen yu Hanren, ben bu tong jiao*). She probably thought the magistrate would understand that it was natural for a Hui woman to be with a Hui man, or that the separation of peoples applied not only to those imprisoned in other's households, but to free people as well. Ultimately, however, the Xinjiang government enforced the principle of paternity: Zeng was to retain his children, and Ma his. Meanwhile, no one "kidnapped" Wei *shi*, it was concluded, because the Refugees Agency had decided their pairing, and that arrangement was final. Regardless of her previous marriage, the magistrate added, time and the bonds of family life had confirmed the match—Zeng and Wei *shi* stayed married.

Wei *shi*'s argument that she and a Chinese man could not belong together, as they followed different religions, ought to have resonated with the effort to separate Chinese, Hui, and Musulmans. Indeed, we will see a Muslim official make that same argument—and successfully—later. However, Wei *shi* did not succeed. How, then, are we to understand the logic of forced marriage under the Xiang Army? First of all, its goal was not simply to control women's sexual and domestic labor, but to instrumentalize that labor in the service of a further objective: to establish a Confucian genealogical consciousness and the practices of filiality that the Xiang Army leadership believed were necessary to maintain an orderly, family-based society. The conclusion of this case points to the supremacy of patrilineal descent over all other concerns. Second, resettlement was a means for the army to enact its exceptional power over human life. A challenge to the decisions of the Refugees Agency was a challenge to the raison d'être of the civilizing project.

Yet resettlement also formalized and legitimized the sexual violence of the Xiang Army's reconquest of the Northwest. Many officers took Hui wives by force, and in light of cases recorded in the Turpan archive, rumors that Liu Jintang had taken a Hui concubine in Gansu after killing the woman's family seem plausible.[44] Other stories circulated about soldiers who traded women plundered from Muslim families. Musulmans who remembered the reconquest of Xinjiang could be more explicit. A chronicler writing in 1899 described the conquest of Kashgar: "All the Andijanis, they killed. The Chinese took their wives as their own wives. Many women refused to submit and were martyred."[45] Resettlement, from the perspective of provincial leaders, would have solved the problems of soldiers' aggression by satisfying what appeared to be soldiers' central desire to succeed as family men on the frontier. Muslim women, whom the army perceived to be wanton and readily available, as well as only peripherally civilized given their lack of family consciousness, could be forced into obedience as the lesser partners in husband-wife relationships.

Chinese Men Purchasing Musulman Brides

Where resettlement failed to supply Chinese settler men with wives, wife purchasing, self-sale, and trafficking stepped in. Many of the survival strategies that displaced Musulman women employed were familiar from China proper, as were the practices of brokerage that trafficked Musulman women into Chinese hands. Yet in Xinjiang these practices gained an ethnic character, as a minority of Chinese men employed Hui merchants to secure wives from the Musulman majority.

After the Xiang Army's arrival, the scarcity and expense of food forced people, women especially, to seek alternative means of survival. One solution was to marry someone with money, usually a soldier. Han *shi*, a Hui woman from Turpan, made this choice when her family was on the edge of starvation.[46] First Ya'qūb Beg's army had sent her husband on the long march into slavery during their siege of Turpan. Han *shi* gave her husband up for dead and worked to sustain her family until the arrival of the army and rising grain prices made it impossible to survive on her own. Han *shi* responded to these worsening conditions first by marrying off a daughter, and then by finding a new husband who could maintain her. That her second husband, Li Chaorong, was Chinese mattered little—after all, the agencies were marrying Muslims to Chinese, and Han *shi* at least located a husband before being assigned one. Like many demobilized soldiers, Li Chaorong sought out some land to farm in one of the Chinese-majority towns in the North that the uprisings had reduced to ruins. The couple traveled northwest to their new home, but along the way, Han *shi*'s last child died, and the couple's relations soured. Han *shi* returned to Turpan to stay with her son-in-law, at which time her first husband reappeared, leading to a dispute much like that surrounding Wei *shi*.

Demobilized soldiers easily found wives under such conditions. Soldiers who married generally did so through simple purchase by contract, which blurred the perceived lines between marriage, temporary marriage, and prostitution. In many disputes, one party accused another of kidnapping (*guai* or *lu*) a woman, while the accused would defend himself by arguing that he had in fact bought her (*mai*).[47] In one early case, a pair of Hui soldiers from Shaanxi, Ma Jinfu and Yang Wushizi, took leave from the army in 1875.[48] They went ahead along the Hui-dominated trade routes into Xinjiang, and settled in Jimsar to trade. There they married two Chinese women, Huang *shi* and Niu *shi*. In 1877, the couples moved to Turpan, where Ma moved in with a Sichuan Army commander and sold beef, while Yang rented a plot of land in Tuyuq. Both went for a few days to harvest Yang's crop, and when they returned, they found that their wives and goods were gone. Some investigation found that a man living nearby named Yu Dabi had kidnapped both, selling one of the wives to another man while keeping the other for himself. When confronted, Yu laughed at the men and told them, "those are women the soldiers have cast off" (*ju xi bingyong yiqi funü*).

Yu was expressing a common sentiment that soldiers' marriages were merely temporary relationships contracted for servitude and sex, and therefore no cause for emotional attachment or moral indignation. Realistically, a soldier was not married in the sense of having had a match arranged by his family, and not necessarily even in the minimal legal sense of having conducted the necessary marriage ceremony. Even after arriving in Xinjiang, he was likely to move around rather than settle into a stable household. According to the population registers of Turpan, which were made many years after the reconquest, Chinese tax households (*hu*) usually consisted of groups of unrelated men living together under one roof. Of the twenty-one Chinese households registered in Handun, for example, only eight had any woman members at all, in contrast to 99.5 percent of the 188 Musulman households and nearly all of the twenty-seven Hui households.[49] Unmarried single men living alone were clearly only common among Chinese. It is telling that conflicts involving prostitution that escalated into violence were more common in the Chinese-majority North, where large numbers of men competed over a very small number of women, as compared to the Musulman-majority South. In some cases, the circumstances of a conflict make it clear that a man would prostitute his wife to others in a situation resembling informal polyandry.[50]

The paucity of marriageable Chinese women persisted for many years after the reconquest, prompting aging soldiers to seek marriages to Musulman women throughout the late Qing. Until 1882, marriages between Chinese settler men and Musulman women were described in the archive strictly in terms of "purchase." After this point, however, settlers began to use the term *bride price* (*li yin*) to refer to the money given to a Musulman woman's family for her. This shift in discourse reflects the gradual normalization of relations between Chinese, Hui, and Musulmans, and it is simultaneous with a decrease in the reports of kidnappings and forced marriages that were very prominent immediately after the reconquest. While it was not necessarily the case that sexual violence decreased in Turpan, people at least learned to represent domestic relationships in ways that conformed to the yamen's expectations.

Indeed, Musulmans would not normally have understood marriage in terms of "bride price." According to Bellér-Hann, exchanges of gifts and cash in marriage in the Musulman context cannot be read straightforwardly, or from an emic perspective, as purchase or the presentation of a bride price.[51] Rather, *toyluq*, which has often been translated as "bride price," pointed to a range of transactions between families, brides, and grooms, which could be normatively rendered in the language of purchase, but were more often one stage in a long series of symbolic exchanges in the building of community. Documents from Kashgar and accounts of elite marriage in Qumul alike indicate that the exchange of goods, particularly livestock, clothing, and food, was central to contracting a marriage between Musulmans.[52] In the multiethnic society of Turpan in the late nineteenth century, however, the nature of *toyluq* changed. It consisted more often of silver when a Musulman daughter married outside of her community, while clothing and other goods remained the norm in marriages between

Musulmans.[53] While Musulman families sought to maintain community with one another through ritual exchanges of goods over time, they may have seen marriages out to Hui and Chinese more as strategies for short-term financial stability or gain. Chinese could easily have interpreted a cash *toyluq* in terms of bride price, which would therefore be reminiscent of survival strategies common in China proper.[54] Moreover, the exchange of a women for money became closely tied to problems of debt, in which lenders were usually Chinese or South Asian merchants who readily accepted daughters in lieu of payment.[55]

Wife-selling and self-sale in particular were familiar from China proper, where such practices were common in this time of upheaval, but also censured by the Confucian moralists who now held political power. Indeed, in the core provinces, the exceptional punishment of "execution on the spot" was explicitly deployed against people who trafficked in women or forced marriages.[56] That fact effectively made execution on the spot a punishment for the desperately poor, or for those who took advantage of them. In Xinjiang, however, marriage of any kind served the central purpose of the civilizing project, to create family units, and so there are no records of execution on the spot for traffickers in Xinjiang. Instead, the provincial authorities followed a substatute of the Qing Code, according to which kidnapping and selling a woman with her apparent agreement was punishable with the sentence of three years' imprisonment and one hundred strokes.[57] Someone could therefore be executed swiftly for being a rootless "bare stick" who stole clothing from a corpse, but not for selling another human being into slavery, as the latter was seen as creating families.

This punishment, while debilitating, was not necessarily a death sentence, and the potential for profit from trafficking in Musulman women was high. Moreover, yamen employees were often involved. In 1880, for example, two Musulman runners working for the Pichan subdistrict magistrate were accused of kidnapping a young Musulman woman and selling her to a Mr. Li.[58] According to the kidnapped woman's brother, the runners had assumed that the family was without a father, as theirs was away cutting wood, and saw an opportunity to kidnap an apparently "displaced woman" (*nüliu*) and "settle" her with a new husband. This was far from the only time that a Chinese man acquired a Musulman woman by money or force in Turpan while her male relatives were away. Late one night in 1886, a woman named Piyaza (Biyazi) was awakened by a banging on the door.[59] A

Chinese man named Zeng Yucheng burst in and demanded to marry her daughter. The presumptuousness of his request aside, Piyaza's daughter already had a husband, who was away on business in Aksu. Piyaza's daughter fought Zeng, biting his hand and drawing blood, but he managed to knock her unconscious and carry her off. Zeng imprisoned the young woman in his house for several days. In the ensuing investigation, he claimed to have paid for the daughter several months beforehand through a Hui intermediary. He was under the impression that Piyaza's daughter was a prostitute, and the Hui merchant had apparently taken advantage of Zeng's confusion to defraud him of a substantial "bride price." Zeng lost the case, while the Hui broker disappeared with the money.

Zeng Yucheng was credulous of his ability to purchase a Musulman woman with no male guardian present both because of the widespread perception that "unattached" Musulman women sought Chinese husbands and because of the ongoing trade that facilitated such arrangements. Liu Yun, a young Chinese man from Shanxi who sojourned in Qitai, similarly claimed to have been drawn unwittingly into human trafficking.[60] In 1889, he paid thirty taels to marry a twelve-*sui* Musulman girl from Turpan named Rawżallah (Ruozangle), who came to live with him. This was a typical arrangement for a sojourner in a temporary marriage: he effectively acquired a girl and placed her in bondage, first as a domestic servant, later as a sexual partner. In late 1892, Rawżallah's father Ablimit sued Liu Yun before the Qitai county magistrate. Ablimit claimed that Rawżallah had a previous husband, and that Liu Yun had kidnapped her. Liu objected and pointed out that Rawżallah was by then four months pregnant. Further investigation led to a settlement from the magistrate: Liu would pay twenty taels as a fine, and he would keep the baby once it was born, while Rawżallah would return to her mysterious "previous husband." Liu Yun, baffled by the situation but powerless to change it, later ran across Rawżallah in the house of a Hui man, Zhang Shi. He later learned that Ablimit and Zhang Shi were known to be in cahoots, kidnapping girls, whom they presented as Ablimit's "daughters," and selling them as wives.

The apparent obsession of one Chinese man in Turpan illustrates at length the complex interactions between different parties' perceptions of marriage.[61] The man was Zhang Xi, a forty-five-*sui*-old Xiang Army veteran, and he clumsily attempted to leverage the yamen's authority to secure his marriage to a Musulman girl only six *sui* old. Zhang's strategy was to present himself as a moral individual who sought a normative marriage and the fulfillment of a contract with the girl's father, Aḥmad, whom he depicted in his complaints as a swindler who extracted a bride price but failed to deliver the daughter. Between Aḥmad and Zhang stood a Hui broker, Jin Shaoyuan, who lived with Aḥmad and acted as a translator for this seemingly well-to-do merchant. In 1891, Zhang Xi approached Jin Shaoyuan with a request to marry Aḥmad's daughter Nurlan (Niuliang) in exchange for a hefty bride price, including cattle, grain, and a sum of money. Aḥmad was interested in marrying the girl off, as her mother had died, and a young woman's utility lay in her ability to bring wealth into the family. Jin wrote up a contract with two copies, one in Chinese and another in Chaghatay, which were witnessed by a superintendent and an akhund. Zhang supposedly produced the bride price and expected to marry the girl immediately, bringing her into his home for domestic labor and, once she had reached sexual maturity, in order to produce an heir. However, Aḥmad delayed the marriage, possibly because he detected something disturbing in Zhang Xi's intentions. Zhang Xi lived with a number of other Chinese men, and while he may have possessed the necessary wealth to pay the *toyluq*, Aḥmad may rightly have feared that Nurlan would be abused in her marital home. At the same time, Aḥmad may have doubted Zhang's ability to pay, and indeed, it is unclear whether Zhang actually produced the *toyluq*. Zhang approached Aḥmad and Nurlan as though he could secure the girl easily with his outsider's wealth and status, but in fact Zhang, despite being Chinese, had less economic capital than Aḥmad. As noted earlier, temporary marriage could vary according to socioeconomic status, and while Chinese soldiers and merchants could pressure the poor into giving up their daughters, better-off Musulmans deployed their daughters' domestic and reproductive labor in ways that drew others into their families and communities. Aḥmad was certainly insulted by Zhang's demands.

What happened next showed Zhang Xi's frustration at having his Chinese supremacy denied, as he subsequently brought a series of complaints to the yamen in rapid succession, each of which summoned a different trope of Chinese-Musulman relations. He claimed that the contract had been violated and demanded restitution, which he apparently received following mediation. Next, however, Zhang pressed the matter further. He invoked the stereotype of Musulman trickery and claimed that Aḥmad was conspiring with Jin to defraud Chinese men by promising wives and absconding with the bride price, as other Hui brokers had done. Zhang made two demands, which the magistrate pointed out were incompatible: he wanted Aḥmad and Jin to be punished for an illegal act, and yet he wanted the original agreement to be enforced because he had believed it to be legal. Zhang demanded a refund of an even more exorbitant bride pride than he had originally claimed, in order to assuage his wounded pride, but also Nurlan's hand in marriage. Ultimately, the magistrate refused to hear the case and sent it to mediation, and so all parties met on the neutral ground of a Hui-run tavern. Over a sizable feast, apologies were made in the presence of a mullah and the local superintendent. Aḥmad, through his interpreter, explained Nurlan's reluctance to marry at such a young age but promised to fulfill the contract. At this point, Zhang would appear to have won the conflict by threatening to involve the Chinese administration and painting Aḥmad as an immoral criminal.

However, Zhang Xi pressed the matter again. He then claimed to have seen Nurlan at a Musulman man's house, which indicated to him that Aḥmad had "sold his daughter for a price" (*mai jia wei qi*) to that man while she was engaged to Zhang, or else was conspiring to traffic in women. After all, the same practice had come to light in other cases. This time, Zhang demanded four times as much money as he had originally claimed to have paid, a large plot of land, several cows, and even an entire karez, one of the underground irrigation tunnels that allowed Turpan's lifeblood to flow. The magistrate was now keen to see this conflict conclude, as it threatened to put Chinese, Hui, and Musulmans at odds, and so he convinced Zhang to demand compensation only in silver—the usual means for a Chinese man to purchase a Musulman woman as a wife. At this suggestion, Zhang complained that Aḥmad was discriminating against him as a Chinese person! If marriage between peoples of different teaching was permitted, Zhang argued, then Aḥmad should be happy to marry his daughter to him at a reasonable price.

Zhang Xi never received the money, or the girl, and the entire process resulted in nothing but animosity. The magistrate also refused to hear any more from the obnoxious Zhang, and so the archival trail grows cold at this point in the story. However, it reveals how Chinese settlers conceived of their place in the post-reconquest sexual economy: as consumers. Musulman women became commodities, whom Hui brokers acquired and resold. Typically, the Turpan *yamen*, like any other in the Qing, upheld contracts, and Zhang expected them to do so in the matter of marriage as well. Indeed, Zhang took marriage to be a contractual matter of purchase, and he submitted his complaint to the yamen's "punishments section" (*xingke*). However, the *yamen* then placed it into a separate category of law and a different office: the rites section (*like*), governing matters of family, ritual, and education. That distinction points to a broader disconnect between how the yamen treated marriage—as a matter of sociomoral propriety—and how marriage functioned in the society it governed, as a matter of economic exchange.

Indeed, the positions of "Musulman," "Hui," and "Chinese" were not simply ethnic, religious, or linguistic categories, but positions in a system of exchange. The exchange of silver—or in this case, a refund—for a Musulman woman denoted her movement outside of her own community. To "return" other goods to Zhang Xi would have suggested that the exchange was meant initially to bring him into that community, while offering to return only cash marked instead a distancing of Zhang from those who might have been his in-laws. This logic is reminiscent of rituals in which Musulmans symbolically exchanged a child for cash in order to ward off the evil eye by suggesting that a newborn was not a natural child of their family, but an adoptee who had been "bought"—hence the common name Setiwaldi, meaning "gotten by purchase."[62] In contrast, temporary marriage of Muslim sojourners to local women typically involved the same exchange of goods seen in long-term marriage. The exchange of cash as a way of distancing the husband from the wife's family superficially resembled the exchange of cash in prostitution, reinforcing the idea in Chinese eyes that Musulman women were simply sexually available for money.

As for Hui brokers, it is striking that the Turpan *yamen* does not seem to have dealt with cases like Nurlan's among the Hui. One Khwaja Nāy Khan in 1892 observed that Hui in Turpan avoided sexual contact with outsiders, and the archival record seems to confirm his assertion.[63] Instead, Hui people appear almost universally in these matters as intermediaries arranging the sale of women, and not as customers or victims themselves. The ethnic triad of Xinjiang was therefore an economic one: Chinese consumers, Hui brokers, and Musulmans as the producers of a desirable and marketable good, women's domestic and sexual labor.

Musulman Martyrs for Confucian Patriarchy

The bifurcation between the yamen's treatment of marriage as a ritual concern, and thus one that was ideally decided within the family and village, and the social acknowledgment of marriage as a matter of exchange of property facilitated and justified the ongoing trafficking of Musulman women. This took place under the cover of what Janet Theiss has called "the chastening state," the tendency of the Qing to propagate imperial norms of gender and sexuality through the politico-juridical apparatus.[64] For the most part, the Turpan yamen remanded issues of marriage and wife-sale to local authorities, who were expected to maintain the sociomoral order independently. However, some extreme cases emerge in the archive, and one will illustrate how Qing law and Xiang Army ideology justified the ethnicized sexual economy.

In 1881, Ruwayda Khan (Yueweiti Han, Reweidi Han), a widow with no remaining family, married Zhu Chunting, a Xiang Army soldier.[65] Within a year, she was pregnant, and Zhu returned to his hometown in Ningzhou, Gansu. According to a deposition later taken from Zhu, he had been compelled to leave to care for his aging parents, and so entrusted his wife and unborn child to his friends Yao Zhengrong and Chen Desheng. In Zhu Chunting's absence, Ruwayda Khan bore a daughter named simply "Peach Blossom" (Taohua'er). Peach Blossom had no surname, suggesting that she was not to be considered a formal member of Zhu's family. Shortly after Peach Blossom was born, Yao and Chen wrote to Zhu claiming that Ruwayda Khan had committed adultery. Zhu subsequently responded with instructions to sell her and Peach Blossom. According to travelers' accounts, Chinese soldiers in Yarkand and Kashgar had the same practice: a departing soldier would sell his wife to a former companion and take any resulting sons with him, but sell the daughters.[66] The two friends thus located a pair of Hui brokers, Zhao Da and Wang Si, who in turn found a buyer named Yang Bencheng. Yang, whom we met briefly in the introduction, was an older Chinese man and Xiang Army veteran in search of a wife to carry on his family line. In 1885, he negotiated a steep bride price and agreed to pay a stipend for Peach Blossom as well.

Ruwayda Khan was clearly unwilling to go through with the sale. She had originally sold herself to Zhu Chunting to secure her survival, and never expected to be left behind, even less to be traded by others. According to later testimonies, when Yao and Chen told Ruwayda Khan that she was to be sold to Yang, she refused to eat for several days and swore that she would rather die than marry him. Meanwhile, a man named Şābir, who claimed to be Ruwayda Khan's older brother, sought her freedom by threatening a lawsuit, while her captors spirited her away. Eventually, Ruwayda Khan arrived at Yang's house, which despite its depiction in depositions was far from a family home. According to archival records, Yang instead lived with other Xiang Army veterans, and it is possible that this colony of single men intended to share Ruwayda Khan as a servant, or in a form of polyandry not unknown in China.[67] Ruwayda Khan feigned illness and successfully avoided Yang's bed. Instead, according to the official account, she located a lump of opium, swallowed it, and died in what we may hope was a deep and peaceful sleep.

Yang Bencheng and his housemates kept Ruwayda Khan's death a secret for ten days, at which time Yang reported her suicide and sent Peach Blossom to the village headman for safekeeping. Meanwhile, Şābir had attempted unsuccessfully to intervene at the yamen, where the magistrate reasoned that matters of marriage and family were private concerns. Suicide, however, triggered an inquiry if it was suspected that the victim was driven to kill themselves, and now Şābir attested that Yao, Chen, and the Hui brokers had done so to Ruwayda Khan. The investigation that followed resulted in a thorough account of Ruwayda Khan's identity and fate. Şābir could hope for Ruwayda Khan's kidnappers to face justice under Qing law.

However, Governor Liu Jintang replied to a report on Ruwayda Khan's suicide by praising her: "Ruwayda Khan was a chaste woman who sacrificed herself in the end for chastity—such an intention is eminently praiseworthy! We must urgently praise her, in order to promote the transformation of customs!"[68] Liu's decree erased the difficult circumstances under which Ruwayda Khan originally sold herself to Zhu, and instead upheld her suicide as a sacrifice for the civilizing project. This meant that no one bore responsibility for Ruwayda Khan's death except Ruwayda Khan herself. Ruwayda Khan thus died a hero—but in doing so was denied her agency.

Vivien Ng and Janet Theiss have shown how suicide was one of the few means for a woman who experienced sexual violence to secure justice in the Qing, at least posthumously, by bringing the law to bear on those who harmed her.[69] Yet the Xiang Army's civilizing project denied even that by subsuming nearly any marriage—whether it resulted from forced settlement or self-sale—under the rubric of family ritual. It was possible for a practice such as wife-sale that thrived in China proper, even if it was nominally forbidden, to thrive where officials promoted marriage as the core of their mission.

Patriarchy and Boundary Policing

On the whole, it was not harm to women's lives that troubled Musulman men, but rather their own loss of control over women's bodies. Non-Muslim purchase of Musulman women became a major source of tension, as temporary marriage was replaced by the permanent transfer of Musulman women into outsiders' hands through sale, usually under coercion, and by prostitution conducted without an akhund's blessing. Discourses around prostitution and intercommunal intimacy and Musulman authorities' attempts to police these activities shed light on the renegotiation of communal boundaries. Musulman elites used the civilizing project to enforce the spatial and social segregation of women who violated the bounds of their religious and linguistic community.

Khwaja Nāy Khan, who had observed that Hui avoided sex with Chinese and Musulmans, attested that prostitution between Musulmans was routine, at least when it included men's heterosexual encounters with women, while sex with other men and with young boys (bachcha) was tolerated but outwardly stigmatized.[70] Chinese prostitutes, Nāy Khan stated, were more expensive, but available to Musulmans who could afford them. Stigma emerged when a Musulman woman had sex with a Chinese man: "If one of the Chinese takes a local girl, she will be known as a whore," Nāy Khan explained. "If someone who is a whore goes into a Chinese's house, no one can stop her" because stark inequalities between Chinese and Musulmans in terms of economic power and the ability to threaten violence meant that, in practice, there was no effective legal recourse to do so. The trouble, from Nāy Khan's perspective, was that sex with a Chinese man meant leaving the Musulman community: "There are even local whores who have come into the possession of Chinese and become Chinese." After all, the state preferred that Muslim women adopt Chinese customs.

It was not quite true that such a woman "became Chinese," however—instead, these so-called "bad women" remained excluded from both communities. Prostitution cases involving Musulman women indicate a pattern of naming that reflects this betweenness and a logic similar to the adoption of the term *Chantou* to refer to Musulmans who took on Chinese characteristics: An older generation of women, born before 1877, tended to be known by Turco-Islamic names, while their daughters were almost always labeled with Chinese names bearing eroticizing or objectifying connotations. Just as Ruwayda Khan and Zhu Chunting's daughter was called Peach Blossom, a woman and prostitute named Niyāz Khan lived with her two daughters, named in Chinese "Silver Flower" (*Yinhua* or *Yinhuazi*) and "Osmanthus Fragrance" (*Guixiang*). As of 1898, all three were involved in sex work, and Silver Flower and Osmanthus Fragrance were likely the biological children of Chinese men. Another woman is named in the archive as "White-and-Black Sugar" (*Baiheitang*), implying mixed origins.[71] Other women had names that indicated their "sold" status, as did "Eight Cash and Fifty" (*Baqianwu*).[72] In this sense, Musulman sex workers resemble the Confucian school students, who demonstrated their descent from men with Chinese names and often took on Chinese names themselves in order to demonstrate their membership in the elite—whereas these women received Chinese names that indicated their exclusion and subordination.

That exclusion was spatial as well as social. Nāy Khan's description of Musulman and Chinese prostitution distinguished between "locals" (*yärlik*) and Chinese (*Khiṭāy*), figuring the difference between the groups as one between natives and newcomers. The same logic was reflected in the akhunds' argument in the previous chapter that prostitutes from "outside" were disrupting the social, moral, and cosmic orders, angering the spirits and drying up the spring runoff. Accordingly, Musulman women who had sex with Chinese men were thought of as occupying a third space. Consequently, they were not buried in the Muslim cemetery, but instead interred outside the city walls, in or near the Chinese cemetery, remaining pariahs even in death.[73] Nor would the Quran be recited over their graves, unless someone paid a madrasa student to do it in secret.

That was the case with Silver Flower, who was buried twice in the Chinese cemetery.[74] In December 1897, Niyāz Khan had married her to a newly arrived instructor at the Turpan garrison, Yang Qiting. Silver Flower was considered a good match, as her mixed heritage allowed her to pass easily as Chinese. In April 1898, Silver Flower quarreled with her mother and took poison. Yang hired a Daoist priest to read scripture over Silver Flower's body for three days, and then buried it in the Chinese cemetery outside the East Gate. For some time, Yang Qiting continued to support Niyāz Khan, whom he considered a woman who "did not keep the womanly way" (bu shou fu dao): as he and the official reports described it, "all day every day, strangers walk in and out of her courtyard." This was a transparent euphemism for sex work. Soon the revelation that Yang Qiting had married the daughter of a Musulman prostitute scandalized Yang's superiors. Silver Flower had been a "Chantou woman dressed in Chinese array" (Chan nü yi Han zhuang), for whom Yang had purchasing fine clothing. Apparently Silver Flower gave the impression of a well-heeled woman newly arrived from China proper. The knowledge of her origins, however, made Yang's fellow officers uncomfortable. Chinese soldiers might have such relationships, but it was considered at best an embarrassment for officers, officials, and their relatives, such as Yang Rong's grandson Pockmark. Eventually, Yang was pressured into ceasing his support for Niyāz Khan.

In response, Niyāz Khan hired a man named Parhat who on the night of December 30 helped her exhume Silver Flower's corpse from the Chinese cemetery. They slipped past the guards and managed to deposit her body at the shop of Yang's friend Mao Linfu, in the marketplace, where he and hundreds of others would see it immediately in the morning. Niyāz Khan would later claim that she was bewitched when she hatched the plan to exhume Silver Flower's body. Perhaps in an attempt to appeal to Chinese officials' sense of magic and mistrust of Islamic clerics, she testified that a traveling mullah from Ili had recited "dark scriptures" (hei jing) that baffled her mind. Regardless, when Yang Qiting awoke to learn that the body of his departed wife was at Mao Linfu's gate, he swiftly ascertained the reasoning behind it and ran to rouse the magistrate. A Chinese man such as himself could recognize a strategically placed corpse, as it was not uncommon in China proper to leave the remains of the dead at the home of the person blamed for their suicide.[75] Such an act would ideally trigger an investigation into the suicide, as in Ruwayda Khan's case, that could result in compensation for the family of the deceased.

Yang Qiting assumed that the body was meant to threaten him, and Niyāz Khan later confessed that she planned to extort Yang in precisely such a manner. Nevertheless, its placement at the shop of Mao Linfu ought to have implicated Mao. Perhaps Niyāz Khan originally blamed Mao for Silver Flower's suicide or intended to weave a more complicated story. A similar case from Dihua suggests that, while Yang purchased clothing for Silver Flower and sheltered her, she as a Musulman courtesan may have received gifts from multiple Chinese patrons who competed for her affection, Mao Linfu among them.[76] Indeed, given the exoticizing imagery that Hunanese officials and settlers had absorbed, perhaps they found Musulman women especially desirable. Regardless, rather than consider the complex causes of the case, the magistrate ordered Niyāz Khan, her hired man, and her surviving daughter to return to Kashgar, whence they had come, and receive their punishment for exhuming a corpse. Yang Qiting was ordered to pay their travel expenses.

Niyāz Khan and her family illustrate not only the naming patterns common to sex workers and women of mixed parentage, but also the spatial and social separateness that characterized them. While in death a woman who had "become Chinese" would be buried in the Chinese cemetery, in life such women were known for living not in town, but in houses along the desert highways and in real or fictive families. In 1883, Musulman authorities in Turpan attempted to leverage for their own purposes an order from the magistrate to clear some of these houses out and relocate the women living there.[77] While the original order's Chinese text is lost, the Chaghatay translation is quite vivid: "Until the bad women within this land are eliminated, trouble will come to it, plagues will enter it, rot will appear, insects will descend on the crops, hard winds will blow, and all this will come from the trouble of the bad women. By the imperial grace, you will eliminate these bad women." In response, the akhunds prepared a list of specific individual women to be punished for immoral behavior. They chose as their targets "degenerate Musulman women" (Chinese bu xiao zhi chan fu, Chaghatay andūḥliq qiladurghan maẓlūm) who had established themselves in brothels on the road to and from China proper. Khwaja Nāy Khan stated that these women charged more for their services than streetwalkers, but this also meant that their trade was much more open, and so more easily assailed.[78]

Clearly, the akhunds were familiar with the women in question. According to the petition, some of the "bad women" living in Turpan were part of a family: One Maṣtura was the wife of a man named Jahān Bāqī and the daughter of the widow Anäl. Officials considered both women to be willingly engaged in sex work, along with a third woman, Gülüsh. These clerics and the *yamen* collaborated to resettle all of them. Maṣtura and Jahān Bāqī, already a married couple, were settled on a plot of land at the Number Six Karez in Lükchün, alongside Anäl and Gülüsh, who were assigned Musulman husbands.[79] The akhunds took responsibility for locating appropriate land for these families to farm, along with the "men to look after these women" (*shubu maẓlūmlarni saqlaghan ādamlär*). The state provided each with a stipend. These and other resettled "bad women" found themselves confined to desert farms mostly in Lükchün and in Lop Nur, apparently on land controlled by the Turpan Wang.[80]

Eventually, in 1896, as conflicts over sex and indebtedness between Musulmans and Chinese came to a head, Lop Nur became the exclusive site of exile for "bad women."[81] Lop Nur, the name of the desolate salt lake in the desert south of Turpan, indicated an area of marshy land where Musulmans lived in great poverty. Muslim elites and foreign travelers alike depicted them as backward or wild people. There a "bad woman's" exclusion could isolate Turpan from her alleged sexual immorality, blamed for increasing tensions between groups, while civilizing these women through marriage and cultivating the wild land. In the words of Financial Commissioner Rao Yingqi, the purpose of this ongoing relocation was that "The Muslim masses shall immediately be put into order, which is to say made subjects" (*Hui zhong ji jing shoufu, ji shu zimin*). That is, Musulmans were to be reordered in a way that put women's reproductive labor to work for reconstruction and the creation of a moral, agrarian society based on the family.

Meanwhile, soldiers were expressly (though ineffectively) forbidden from taking Musulman women by force, on pain of punishment through military law. Any women whom those soldiers had raped were likewise sent with their resulting children to Lop Nur. This last decision calls into question the nature of the perceived threat to social stability: Perhaps the authorities construed a raped woman as sexually wanton. Otherwise, perhaps it was not sexual violence that was the problem from their perspective, but rather the appearance of children with mixed heritage, who had become increasingly common in Turpan and served not as a sign of Musulmans' assimilation, but as a reminder of their subordination to Chinese.

The system of exile created yet another horrible irony in that some of the women sent to Lop Nur never arrived at their assigned destinations but remained in captivity in the court of the Turpan Wang. A year after Jahān

Bāqī and Maṣtura's exile, while the clerics reported that both were happily and peacefully living a life of simple farming, Jahān Bāqī wrote to the contrary that his wife had still not been released to him.[82] The same was true of one Khushnān Khan, a young woman whose mother had sold her in desperation to a Chinese moneylender in payment for her debts.[83] The Turpan Wang seized Khushnān Khan from her Chinese husband by paying the debt from his own coffers, claiming that "Chinese and Muslim teachings are incompatible" (*Han Hui liang jiao bu he*) and so the couple would "each return to their teaching" (*ge gui ge jiao*). While the Turpan Wang thus acted contrarily to the province's goals of assimilation, Xiang Army leaders nevertheless regarded him as a reliable ally in the civilizing project, a man who was able to rectify corrupt women's morals by putting them into the service of their betters.[84] Yet if such reports were true, then the Xiang Army's attempt at moral rectification through marriage had resulted instead in the potentially greater immorality, from a Confucian perspective, of what Nāy Khan described as the Turpan Wang's very own collection of women.

The boundaries between communities were therefore reified in the partition of space. Sex workers living in a liminal space were capable of mobilizing their bodies in ways that did not serve the Xiang Army project. At the same time, Musulman women's intimacy with Chinese men came to symbolize a loss both to the Muslim community generally and to the Musulman community whose members were the specific object of exchange. On one side, Confucian patriarchy demanded that women settle into monogamous marriages in order to build a more ideal society in which cultural and linguistic boundaries would blur as people Sinicized. On the other, Musulman patriarchy demanded control over women's sexual and domestic labor as well, so that the exploited community would remain whole, regardless of other consequences.

Ethnicity in the Family

We have so far seen how the sexual economy of Xinjiang's reconstruction encouraged certain forms of transgressive social mobility, of movement between relatively fluid categories that in turn reified and deepened the differences between those categories.[85] Those differences could be marked spatially through exclusion in life or death, or socially by different positions in a system of exchange, or ritually through inclusion in certain lifecycle rituals such as wedding and funerary rites. Yet these larger-scale dynamics of exclusion and inclusion also came to play a role within families. This is not in itself surprising. Some states have focused overwhelmingly on the family as a site of moral and social discipline.[86] This makes the family, as Ann Stoler argues for colonial cases globally, a proxy for other policies and anxieties, and so people encounter the state's categories within the family.[87] Two case studies of adoption and disinheritance will illuminate how ethnoreligious categories served people's interests in family conflicts. In this context, although the categories of Chinese, Hui, or Musulman had little or no formal legal status, nevertheless they could be mobilized under the right circumstances to demonstrate either common descent or estrangement. That is, as of the mid-1890s, a Chinese belonged to a Chinese family, a Hui to a Hui, and a Musulman to a Musulman—these labels no longer pointed simply to language or religion, but to descent.

In 1864, a Chinese boy only six *sui* old was living with his parents in Qarakhoja when the uprisings broke out.[88] A Musulman man named ʿĀṣim attempted to shelter the family, but all were slaughtered in the violence, save for the child, whom ʿĀṣim named "Islām" and raised as his own adoptive son. When in 1877 the Xiang Army separated Chinese children from Musulman families, Islām was nineteen *sui* and aware of his origins, but he refused to leave the man who had raised him. Islām was, by all accounts, an ordinary member of ʿĀṣim's family, albeit with his own ambiguous social identity. Islām appears here and there in mundane archival documents, as when in 1880 the yamen ordered him to offer a cow to his opponent in a minor dispute.[89] At this point, ʿĀṣim had recently passed away. Shortly thereafter, his wife—Islām's adoptive mother—bore ʿĀṣim a posthumous, natural son, perhaps the very son they had dreamed of having for years. While Islām was known as ʿĀṣim's son, documents alternatively call him a "Musulman commoner" (*Chan min*), "tax-paying commoner" (*humin*), or "commoner" (*min*). The latter two unmarked categories usually implied a Chinese identity.

"Islām the Musulman" lived an otherwise ordinary life until 1897. That year his adoptive mother and brother conspired to deny Islām his share of the remaining inheritance from his father. Musulman men such as ʿĀṣim frequently left much of their fortunes to surviving wives, after whose death it fell in equal shares to the remaining sons (and in smaller proportion to any daughters), and this case was no different. However, Islām's adoptive brother Tokhta Akhund was now twenty *sui*, and we may suspect that the mother favored him over the adopted son. Indeed, the name Tokhta may be a clue to Islām's family life. The name literally means "stop," and it was typically given to children when the parents wished to have no more. Perhaps ʿĀṣim and his wife had borne several unmentioned daughters, and the mother now saw Tokhta at last as his father's heir, or else no other children had survived. Regardless, they drove Islām from the home, expelling the single "Chinese" member of the family, and denied him the promised right to inherit. The *yamen* sided with Islām: his ethnicity made no difference in the argument, while what mattered was his identity as a son, a member of a patriline who had served his parents filially. Islām's mother, the magistrate ruled, must not show prejudice in matters of ancestry. This official logic is reminiscent of the *jingshi* analysis of the lineage as a ritual construct in which practicing family relations alters one's substance, making them a part of the family regardless of parentage. The magistrate's ruling was valid under Qing law and enforced the maintenance of the patriline, but it was dissonant with the treatment of difference on the ground.

Cases involving adoption favored the adoptive father's wishes, while cases involving marriage introduced the conflicting interests of both a father and a husband. In one example, Liang Benkuan came to Xinjiang as a member of the Xiang Army, and in the spring of 1877, he settled in Turpan's New City.[90] How he acquired his home is unclear, but it had enough rooms that he could rent them out to other Chinese soldiers and settlers. A Musulman peddler woman named Khāliṣa visited regularly. One day, Khāliṣa approached Liang Benkuan to inform him that she and her husband had fallen on hard times. The reconquest and its chaotic aftermath forced them to consider marrying off one of their daughters, a girl who had just come of age. Indeed, the girl had been a baby during the uprisings, when her Chinese biological parents passed away, and so Khāliṣa offered the girl as a concubine to produce an heir for the aging and unmarried soldier. The girl's Chinese origins, Khāliṣa suggested, would make her an appropriate match. Liang was enthusiastic, and they agreed on a modest bride price of twenty taels. The girl moved in. (She is nameless in the documentary record and called only "concubine," *qie shi*.) In 1880, however, Liang was released from his duties, and he planned to move to China proper with his concubine in tow.

Khāliṣa and her husband were outraged. They had taken the arrangement to be a temporary marriage for the sojourning Chinese soldier, they asserted, not a permanent exchange. The girl, they stated, was to be married to other men. Liang himself did not care to press the matter with the *yamen*, apparently having realized that he had unwittingly contracted a "soldier's marriage," while Khālisa and her husband attempted to raise it at the Islamic court. While Liang would not file a suit, one of his lodgers did so on his behalf: This Chinese man named Zhang Zhongyuan had become friendly with the girl, and he went to the *yamen*, arguing that she "was originally a Chinese" (*yuan xi Hanren*) and therefore ought to be removed from her Musulman adoptive home, as so many had been in the resettlement in 1877. However, the clerks in the rites section informed Zhang that only evidence of kidnapping would serve to free her.[91]

Therefore, Zhang made a second attempt, and this time accused Khālisa and her husband of abducting the girl. If that were proven to be the case, they would have been in violation of a statute of Qing law sufficient to bring this issue to the prefectural authorities. He could now leverage the yamen's power in this matter, and indeed, the case was transferred from the rites section to the punishments section. If Khālisa and her husband had captured the girl in order to profit from her sale as a daughter, then they might be subject to physical punishment and imprisonment. If on the other hand she were properly their adopted child, and if the wedding ceremony had been performed, then she was Liang Benkuan's responsibility. Meanwhile, Liang had known Khālisa and her husband for some years, and a certain affection had grown between them, as they visited their daughter frequently. Liang was unwilling to force the girl to make a choice between her family and himself.

As a result, the girl's own testimony became the central evidence in the case, as it could indicate whether she were truly an adopted daughter and a loyal spouse, or merely a captive forced to play a role. Her statement was hardly ambiguous, and rather than simply explain the issue of adoption and marriage, it invoked ethnic categories:

I am originally a Chinese! (*Wo ben Hanren!*) Because of the military chaos, I was captured (*bei lu*) and raised by you. But now I've been married to Mr. Liang for a few years. All of you depended on me to survive. I have already repaid the kindness you showed in raising me. I've married a Chinese husband—I'll never go back and marry a Musulman! If you force me to return, then I'll surely die!

This statement was edited for the consumption of Chinese authorities, of course. We may suspect that the girl's declaration of identity was suggested by Zhang, or that the girl made it instrumentally to secure her release, or that the prefect hoped to enforce the integrity of marriage. What the testimony demonstrated, however, was something more ambiguous: Family could be many things. The girl was "captured"—by whom is not specified—and then raised by her adoptive parents, who used her to secure income. Nevertheless, she expressed gratitude for their care. Now she was a "concubine," intended as a temporary wife, but emotionally attached to her husband. Ultimately, the girl's ethnic self-identification mattered not at all to the yamen—her marital status and relationship to her parents did. The prefect determined that her parents' actions were improper, but not criminal, and that years of living as a family had indeed made her their daughter. Liang and his wife then journeyed to China proper and faded into history.

These two cases show how Chinese and Musulmans could represent difference and membership in families when facing the authorities. In Islām's case, his adoptive mother and brother unsuccessfully used the language of ethnic and religious difference to undo a family tie; in the girl's case, people successfully used the state-recognized language of family to separate people by group. Whether or not people genuinely believed ethnicity to be related to common descent is of course difficult to determine, although it would appear that Zhang Zhongyuan thought so. Rather, Chinese expressed that this was the case, and Musulmans learned how to mobilize the same language. To put it another way, it became reasonable to state that a person who lost Chinese parents—non-Muslim, Chinese-speaking parents—naturally ought to be reunited with the same kinds of people. In the next chapter, we will encounter more people who drew analogies between lost family members and lost patrimony, and who believed that an orphan was not just their parents' lost child, but the lost child of an imagined community.

*　　*　　*

It is not necessary for a civilizing project to intend to engender ethnicity in its objects—rather, the civilizer's concerns leave a trace in the reactions of the civilized. This bifurcation is apparent in the way the Xiang Army approached their transformation of Muslims: ideology and law stated that the family unit was the fundamental building block of a harmonious society. However, during the reconquest, they also separated people from households according to ethnoreligious groups, presupposing that ethnic and religious difference was sufficient evidence for kidnapping, while leaving it to inspectors to determine group membership. Many of those displaced people were forcibly settled into households and into marriages they did not desire, which tended to cross ethnoreligious boundaries, as it was believed that marrying Muslim women to lower-class Chinese men would civilize both of these "dangerous" parties. Vertical class hierarchies elided with horizontal religious and linguistic differences. At the same time, the facts of economic and demographic inequality, in which many impoverished Musulman women were faced with the opportunity to survive by marrying Chinese men, encouraged transactional domestic and sexual arrangements facilitated by Hui brokers. The very fact of these exchanges, however, disturbed Musulmans who complained of losing "their" women to wealthier non-Muslim Chinese, often through coercion or kidnapping. Their complaints fell deaf on the ears of the prefect when they attempted to nullify Musulman-Chinese unions, as it remained in the government's interest to create families. Therefore, some learned to use resettlement, euphemized as the creation of stable households, as a means to control women and maintain the boundaries around their communities. The language of family was a means to articulate claims about difference in a way that could invoke the power of the state.

The constant reinscription of the homology of Chinese-Hui-Musulman to consumer-broker-commodity reified boundaries between groups previously defined more by linguistic and religious practice. An ideological discourse of family at times justified, obscured, or facilitated those inequalities in the sexual economy. Yet, somewhere between exchange itself and the discourse of exchange, there emerged a sense that these categories were natural, and rooted in the very questions of belonging raised by the selling of wives and daughters. The norms and language of family that the state deployed in order to enforce the patriline and bring about assimilation were also a means to articulate difference and police boundaries. By the mid-1890s, Musulman elites' attempts to sequester boundary-crossing women and their children not only had become matters of popular practice, as in the burial of such women in or near the Chinese cemetery, but also were formalized in Turpan prefecture's enforcement of sexual mores. The drive to assimilate through marriage had produced instead division, resentment, and a stronger sense of the inherent difference between groups.

FIVE

Recollecting Bones

The Muslim Uprisings as Historical Trauma

ON DECEMBER 3, 1878, an eight-year-old boy named Mämät was gathering kindling from the cold ground of a vineyard in the town of Tuyuq, just east of Turpan proper, when he happened upon a human head.[1]

Tuyuq was and remains famous for two things: grapes, which grow in abundance and remarkable variety in Turpan's short but intense summers, and the Shrine of the Seven Sleepers.[2] Pilgrims came from as far as India to visit the grave of these "Companions of the Cave" (aṣḥāb al-kahf), who according to the Quran, and as elaborated upon in legend, fled persecution for their faith. God protected them by giving them three centuries of sleep in a cave, long enough to awaken in a world where their beliefs were practiced openly. This story is attached to a number of different sites across Eurasia, but Musulmans regarded the shrine in Tuyuq as the Sleepers' authentic resting place. Tuyuq is thus one of the holiest sites in all of East Turkestan.

Yet what Mämät discovered was hardly holy. A body was attached to the head, buried under the ground, which the coroner estimated had decayed for about thirteen years, dating it to the outbreak of the Muslim uprisings. Clearly, no one died in a vineyard on purpose, and the human remains scattered across Turpan's landscape served as constant reminders of the recent violence. Sayrāmī describes how entire settlements had been cleared of "nonbelievers," and so many battles had been joined that, in one place, "as the years passed, until the Chinese returned, their bones lay desiccating in the road."[3] Now rumors spread quickly, as people sought to assign blame for the corpse's disposition. The magistrate—ill-fated Yang Peiyuan—determined to manage the potential for violence by discovering "whether the body was Chinese, Hui, or Musulman." However, Yang's investigation was met with the usual local resistance that later led to his suicide. That resistance strengthened when it was revealed that the head sported a long queue and a shaved pate, a sign of submission to Qing authority that Chinese and Hui wore, but from which common Musulmans were normally exempt. The remaining clothing marked him as Chinese. Moreover, the dead man in the orchard had been tortured before his execution. The body's hands showed marks where they had been bound. Dozens of stab wounds perforated his body, but it was the long, deep cut along his throat that ended his life. While the body told a story, the Musulman farmers in whose vineyard Mämät had discovered it offered only silence, as did their Hui neighbor. Yang dropped his investigation.

Identifying the body would have resulted in a number of potential complications. If the victim's identity were known, then the Reconstruction Agencies might have needed to prosecute someone—or, in the coroner's estimation, a group of people—for murder. Furthermore, a body necessarily belonged to a person, who in turn had belonged to a family, the remaining members of which could claim the property their deceased relative had held in life. Practicality dictated silence.

However, human remains also gained a new aura of power and danger in the course of the uprisings and reconstruction. Even before 1877, as Yaʿqūb Beg's forces retreated before the Xiang Army's rapid advance, the pointlessness of the uprisings had become apparent. Mullah Mūsa Sayrāmī, whose vision of the past we will address in detail in chapter 6, describes how the great optimism of the "time of Islam" (*Islām waqti*) had quickly given way to a sense of confusion and frustration, as Yaʿqūb Beg's taxation and constant battles laid ever heavier burdens upon common people.[4] He figures the pre-1864 Qing regime as an age of peace now irrevocably lost. Nevertheless, loss demands recovery, and Sayrāmī relates how Musulmans came to suffer under the increasing exactions of Yaʿqūb Beg's regime and cried out for the emperor of China's return. Sayrāmī describes the restoration of Qing rule as a horror story, comparing it to an old tale about three dervishes lost in the desert who came across the bleached bones of two long-dead animals. These curious dervishes prayed three times, restoring the creatures to life, only to find that they had recovered the bodies of a tiger and a bear. The tiger and bear had died of hunger, and upon their revival, these ravenous beasts devoured the dervishes who had saved them.

Others told stories that were more intimate and personal and yet resonated with the broader experience of loss.[5] Indeed, Chinese and Musulmans alike came to regard human remains as emblematic not only of personal or familial loss, but of the imagined community's loss of collective heritage. A corpse could stand for many things: a personal threat or a sign of impending disaster; a lost parent, or a lost national hero. In this chapter, I will argue that the lingering presence of the Muslim uprisings formed an important discursive space in which people articulated claims and communal identities through the topos of human remains. As Dominick LaCapra puts it in his study of historical trauma, "In converting absence into loss, one assumes that there was (or at least could be) some original unity, wholeness, security, or identity that others have ... made 'us' lose. Therefore, to regain it one must somehow get rid of or eliminate those others—or perhaps that sinful other in oneself."[6] The history of the Muslim uprisings became attached not only to present corpses, but to absences: bones and monuments that people expected to find, but that had disappeared from the landscape in the violence. This "evacuated past" of the pre-uprisings period implied the existence of a prior golden age, the imagination of which displaced recent memory. The discourse of traumatic loss to which the Chinese state responded therefore provided a means to articulate grievances between and within communities. In this sense, while the complex violence of the thirteen-year interregnum had involved the mobilization of groups against one another, it was reconstruction that encouraged people to reify their boundaries and ground them firmly in discourses of common descent.

Familial Trauma and Collective Trauma

In order to illustrate the transubstantiation of the mundane into the sacred and the personal into the collective in the course of traumatic loss and recovery, let us consider a journey across the Qing empire that two men made together and yet experienced and wrote about in wholly different ways. This is the story of Feng Junguang, who traveled from Guangdong to the edge of Xinjiang to retrieve his father's bones, and of Wang Zhensheng,

Feng's clerk and companion who envisioned that same experience as a quest to reclaim lost heroes. Their narratives illustrate the slippage between duty to family and duty to country, and between the recovery of bones and the recovery of territory.

Feng Junguang (1830–78) was a scholar-official from a well-regarded family in Nanhai, Guangdong, on China's southeastern coast.[7] His father Yuheng (1807–61) was an official until he was convicted as an accessory to embezzlement and exiled to the Ili Valley in northern Xinjiang on the other end of the empire. In 1858, Junguang and his younger brother accompanied their father and his concubine to his place of exile, where they left him in good company, as a Cantonese community had grown up in Ili. Yuheng joined his sister-in-law and her husband, as well as his own second cousin, who was the garrison commander. A native-place association provided a space for Cantonese to gather and worship, and even a cemetery where deceased exiles could be interred until their families managed to retrieve their bones for burial at home. Junguang and his brother made the long journey back to Guangdong, where they now found their native land torn apart by the Taiping war. Junguang joined the Xiang Army as a clerk. In 1861, news arrived from Ili of his father Yuheng's untimely death. Junguang wished to retrieve Yuheng's bones, but he was now leading a reconstruction agency in Anhui. It was not until the end of the war in 1864 that Junguang managed to make the journey west once more, just in time to hear of the outbreak of the Muslim uprisings. Midway through his journey, he fled back to China proper and to a series of administrative jobs, landing eventually in Shanghai. For thirteen years, he heard no news of his relatives in Ili.

In 1877, as the Xiang Army was reconquering Northern Xinjiang, Junguang's uncle Peiqing was in Lanzhou. Merchants accompanying the army could once again deliver letters from Russian-occupied Ili, and Cantonese members of Zuo's armies sent news of their countrymen. Some told Peiqing about Yuheng's bones and the fate of his family, which he conveyed back to Junguang: When the uprisings broke out, the Cantonese of Ili moved Yuheng's remains into the native-place association's cemetery, but rebels destroyed the hall and desecrated the coffins of the dead. The caretaker of the cemetery fled to Jimsar, where death met him in the Ürümchi faction's conquests. Meanwhile, the garrison commander had died during the siege of Ili in 1865, and no one could say where he was buried. Yuheng's concubine took poison that day rather than face capture, while her daughter,

Junguang's half-sister, ran away, her fate unknown. A pair of nieces fell into the hands of the Muslim armies. As for Junguang's aunt and uncle, some related that they had fled and disappeared. Others claimed that they had joined Yuheng's concubine in suicide when the walls fell. Still another related a more heroic story: his uncle had died alongside the garrison commander, and incidentally Junguang's half-brother, in a bold defense of Ili against overwhelming odds. They had held the native-place association to the last man. Of course, the dead could not speak for themselves, and these stories had the advantage of providing their heroes with morally satisfactory endings.

The Feng family paid for one last journey to the ends of empire to retrieve Yuheng's remains. Junguang asked to resign early from his office in order to undertake the trip, and the court in Beijing approved, as "the emperor rules all-under-Heaven by means of filial piety," and a loyal son could not be denied an act that supported the will of Heaven and the empire.[8] Nephew and uncle maintained a frequent correspondence as Junguang traveled from Shanghai to Lanzhou, and Peiqing from Lanzhou to Ili. (Peiqing actually traveled the greater distance—Xinjiang, it must be remembered, is vast.) Junguang spent his idle hours on the road reading. He found it relaxing, and the *Romance of the Three Kingdoms* in particular could give him an afternoon of quiet contemplation. Junguang took little notice of his intended destination, perhaps because he no longer found the "Western Regions" (*Xiyu*) strange or wondrous. Unlike many of his contemporaries, who obsessively practiced their erudition by connecting their journeys to the places described in ancient texts, Junguang only took notice of history when he was desperately bored: weeks of waiting in Lanzhou for news of his father's casket finally inspired him to verify the name of a local river.

Meanwhile, his uncle Peiqing kept writing letters. When Peiqing arrived in Ili, he was stunned to find the Cantonese cemetery in total disarray— but, through prayer and divination, he recovered twenty-eight of Yuheng's bones and placed them in an attractive ossuary made of Tianshan red pine.[9] At this news, Junguang chastised himself for dereliction of his filial duty. In his diary, he mourned for his father's laughing face. Eventually, Peiqing and his nephew met at the boundary of Xinjiang and Gansu, where they exchanged Yuheng's bones. Junguang wrote to his family, made the necessary arrangements, and prepared to bring his father home. Hardly a day after Junguang returned to Shanghai, he himself passed away.

Junguang's clerk Wang Zhensheng tells the story differently. While Junguang mentions his companion only as one of his servants, Wang expresses a deep connection to his mentor and depicts their journey as a shared quest.[10] His account begins with a blunt autobiographical statement that indicates the significance of parentage to his experiences: "I was orphaned at a young age."[11] Wang lost his parents early in the Taiping war, after which the educated young man wandered between semiskilled jobs until finally Junguang took him under his wing. Wang's account confirms that Junguang was distraught at the news of his father's death. In 1877, he struggled for months to secure the necessary permission from his family and the bureaucracy to travel into the war zone, meeting resistance from friends who begged him not to risk his life. In this telling, Junguang is a heroic figure who journeyed bravely into the jaws of death. Junguang's own account suggests something quite different, that the route across China was now largely peaceful, well trafficked by merchants and protected by the Xiang Army.

If Feng Junguang was the hero of this journey, then Wang Zhensheng depicted himself as the faithful sidekick who tearfully agreed to share it. A subtle contrast between the titles given to either diary upon publication emphasizes their difference of perspective: Feng Junguang called his account the *Diary of a Journey to the West* (*Xi xing riji*), while Wang preferred *Diary of a Campaign to the West* (*Xi zheng riji*). Feng's term *xing* 行 straightforwardly indicates a "journey" in the sense of movement through space. In this sense, *xing* understates the personal significance of Feng's efforts to retrieve his father's remains, which involved traveling for the third time across China. Wang chose *zheng* 征, which carries the base meaning of a journey to somewhere distant but also emphasizes an act of recovering territory through a military campaign. *Zheng* overstates Wang's role by characterizing the journey as a historical undertaking.

It is no wonder that Wang chose a military theme, as he spent his time on the road reading chronicles and collections of poetry about Xinjiang.[12] These poems, written in the Evidentiary Learning (*kaozhengxue*) tradition, tied the Qing conquests of Xinjiang in the eighteenth century to the ancient geographies of the Han and Tang dynasties, both of which had garrisoned the Western Regions. Along the way, Wang composed eight "Elegies of Xinjiang" (*Xinjiang yongshi*) of his own. He wrote in the Evidentiary style, replete with notes, in order to memorialize the Xiang Army's historical accomplishments:

They feared not death on the sandy field, nor transformation into corpses;
They followed the army for 10,000 miles (*li*), waiting long to return.
The spring winds in the willows on the road to the western Pass,
The autumn moon round as a lute playing songs above the redoubts . . .
An artful strike, a surprise at night, and the barbarians rode away—
Army drums boomed forth sad songs of Chu. *Note: Many of those soldiers who
    marched west were men of Chu (Hunan and Hubei).*
I pity them: in that far-off land, the songs of home were distant.
To gamble it all for country and glory, they endured separation.

Wang, however, never entered Xinjiang. Like earlier poets who wrote
"shepherd's songs" for a distant herdsman, he was engaging in a broader
imagination of the borderland.[13] For Wang and many others like him, the
history of the Northwest was now intimately tied to the heroic struggle of
the Xiang Army, which now appeared to be the savior of China's ancient
territory. In this poem, Wang invokes images that both tie Xinjiang to China
proper and emphasize its alienness and distance: the men of Chu traveled
far to the west and, as Zuo actually did, planted red willows along the way.
The Xiang Army's movements are inscribed on the landscape in a trail of
trees that symbolize not just the marking of territory, but also the transformation of the land and its people at the very root. To Zuo, they probably
meant more as readily available firewood for the army.

Wang also showed himself to be invested emotionally in the reconstruction of Xinjiang as a province and its sociomoral transformation through
the agency of the Xiang Army "heroes":

One is never promoted by renouncing the pen;
Most of these heroes were ordinary men.
Divided North and South, this army of fame
Went among Fan and Hui,[14] of strange teachings and ken. *Note: To the south of the
    mountains is the land of the Chantou tribes; to the north, the dark barbarians of
    the west predominate.*
Nowhere to live, their houses of skin. *Note: Beyond the Pass, they have no houses, but
    set up tents here and there, most of which are made of cow leather and horsehide.*
Women dress differently, pearls in their hair. *Note: Outsider women's braids hang
    to the ground. Wealthy merchants decorate them with jewels. The poor use seashells
    in their place.*

Xinjiang, now a province, created again—
The farthest reaches transformed by moral power!

Wang experienced the reconquest vicariously, and he was not alone: across China proper, people celebrated "the righteousness and heroism of the martyred dead," the empire's heroes who fell in battle bringing the war to a close, at the expense of the memory of those killed early on in the violence.[15] For Wang Zhensheng, focusing on the Xiang Army's territorial recovery and Feng Junguang's familial recovery means that he never returns to reflect on his own orphaning. Following Xiaofei Tian's analysis of post-Taiping traumatic literature, we can read Wang's work as a narration away from the self, an attempt to cope with personal loss by covering the individual subject's absence through the successful agency of the collective subject—a vicarious heroism.[16] Where trauma demands its repetition and acting out, Wang acts out other, analogous journeys that lend an alternative structure and meaning to his own. In this case, descriptions of those journeys rely on Chinese tropes of East Turkestani peoples to lend an exotic gloss and a historical significance to the Xiang Army's agency.

The circumstances of the two diaries' publication indicate the role either one played in the construction of memory. Feng Junguang's *Journey* was released in 1881, not long after his death, by a cousin who hoped that it would stand as a monument to filial piety. Wang Zhensheng sought publication of his own *Campaign* in 1900. At the time, there was a burst of popular publishing on Zuo Zongtang's campaigns. An illustrated, novelized, "exciting" account of the Xiang Army's battle against the Taiping called *The Xiang Army Pacifies the Rebels* (*Xiangjun ping ni zhuan*) was printed in Shanghai in 1899.[17] Its woodcuts presented the Xiang Army heroes and Taiping villains in dramatic poses. *Prince Zuo Pacifies the West* (*Zuo gong ping xi zhuan*) was produced as a sequel that same year. The novel features Zuo and his heroic compatriots fighting romanticized visions of Nian and Muslim leaders and ends just before a planned third novel about Xinjiang that, sadly, appears never to have materialized. In the final scene, Zuo receives a letter from the fictional king of Khotan begging for help combatting the Muslim rebels.[18]

Wang Zhensheng's diary thus reached the market just as there was rising interest in the Xiang Army campaigns, approximately twenty to thirty years after their conclusion, and a concomitant rise in fantasy in how people remembered that part of the past. This was the emergence of "heritage," that which allows history, as a formal recollection of the past, to dominate memory, as an ongoing repetition of the past in life.[19] Per Pierre Nora's estimate, it typically takes about three generations from an event for it to slip from living memory into the social discourse about the past, while after about fifteen or twenty years novels about events begin to appear. By that benchmark, the publication of Wang's diary and the Xiang Army stories about thirty-five to forty years after the death of Feng Yuheng and the end of the Taiping war seems to fit the model. Indeed, Sayrāmī also frames his history as a project of recovery, and he began it around 1900 when "forty years had passed."[20] It was the earlier moment in time, the general civil war across China proper and the outbreak of the Muslim uprisings, that subsumed the recent history of Xinjiang into what Chinese called the "Military Disaster" (*bingxian*), the chaos of the mid-nineteenth century associated primarily with the Taiping conflict. The name worked on multiple scales and levels, and chroniclers of the Xiang Army's campaigns in both China proper and Xinjiang used it to indicate all of the wars of that period.[21]

This slippage between familial loss and the loss of the greater imagined community was expressed in stories of Chinese who perished in the uprisings. Accounts abound in the gazetteers of Gansu and Shaanxi of righteous widows whose husbands sojourned "beyond the Pass" in search of livelihoods. The women of Fuping County, Shaanxi, seem to have suffered inordinately.[22] These women married in their teenage years, and some never bore children by their young husbands, who disappeared into Xinjiang before the outbreak of the uprisings, never to return. Propriety demanded that widows maintain their chastity, but given that those who actually did so were probably in the minority, the large number of celebrated "righteous widows" in Fuping implies that even more women lost their husbands in Xinjiang.[23] Official accounts such as these confirmed that women's sphere of agency was limited: to be celebrated in death, a widow could raise her husband's children or serve her in-laws, preferably until she starved or froze to death.

In contrast, sons who lost their fathers and sought them out were depicted as possessing a heroic power to reunite both family and territory. According to one narrative, Hui Sicong from Fuping County was small when his father Hui Dayou went to sojourn in Xinjiang.[24] Sicong grew up during the uprisings. He would ask his mother where his father was, and she would tell him "10,000 miles (*li*) away, and no one knows where he might be found."

Because the boy so longed for his father, he fell into incurable melancholia. One day in 1884, Sicong ran across a Fuping man who had returned from a sojourn beyond the Pass, and this man told him that his father still lived in a place called Daheyan. When Sicong heard the news, he was torn. He could heed his mother's warning: "Daheyan may as well be in Heaven, and my boy hasn't wings to fly!" Or he could do what he knew to be his filial duty: "If he is on Earth, what reason is there that he can't be reached?!" With a fortune-teller's aid, mother and son found an auspicious day for the westward journey to begin, and so Sicong traveled alone through the winter, dressed in rags to save money, over freezing mountain passes. Sicong's story recalls the fables of the *Twenty-Four Filial Exemplars*, the same collection of stories that Musulmans encountered in the *Book of Li*, in which young boys often endured the cold to spare their parents, lying on the ice to catch a fish or going without clothing to keep a cruel stepmother warm.[25]

Finally, when father and son were reunited, they immediately recognized each other, thus demonstrating natural recognition of the parent-child relationship. An elm tree now grows there, says the gazetteer, named for Sicong the filial son, and people from every community, Chinese, Hui, and Musulman alike, all honor it and refuse to cut its branches. In the *Filial Exemplars*, cruel stepmothers witness the filiality of their abused sons, which transforms them into loving parents. Similarly, in this biography of a supposedly real filial exemplar, the tree stands as a beacon of true morality of the kind that everyone could understand: a Chinese or Confucian value was self-evident, even in the wild borderlands. Sicong and Dayou's story is one of the recovery of territorial and familial integrity through a meritorious act of moral transformation. It reflects stories about the bodies of the virtuous, which did not decompose, but were preserved to be reunited with their families.[26] Their story is one of reconstruction (*shanhou*) playing out on the interpersonal level as well as that of the imagined community.

Such narrative transformations of personal tragedy into heroism are common in the wake of war trauma.[27] Moreover, transforming painful scattered memories into heroic collective history would have been both politically useful for a state recovering from mass violence and potentially empowering to ordinary people. The Military Disaster thus became the limit event of the history of Xinjiang's people, a reference point for both policies aimed at speeding the region's recovery and the complaints of commoners who felt the speed of that revival was lagging.[28] When local gazetteers were composed in Xinjiang, the Military Disaster featured prominently in their accounts of history.[29] Officials were overwhelmingly concerned with the maintenance of family lineages, and they attributed the erasure of this most central institution to "suffering repeatedly from the Military Disaster" (*lü zao bingxian*). Indeed, in the eyes of Xiang Army officials, the problem was not that the uprisings had killed people, but that the violence destroyed family lines—for without a family line, an individual was wild, uncivilized, a person without history in the eyes of orthodoxy. Rebuilding the ancient ties of family was metaphorically and actually central to the rebuilding of the empire.

The Haunted Landscape

When the Xiang Army entered Xinjiang, seemingly bringing the Military Disaster to a conclusion, it was both a moment of triumph and a realization of the totality of destruction that they faced. Confucians' relationship with the past was mediated not just through text, but through objects, particularly stone or metal artifacts that also carried inscriptions. These stood as physical embodiments of the Chinese literate tradition and proofs of history. However, the army encountered instead an absence of the heritage they had expected to find in Xinjiang. Those inscriptions and ruins had fallen instead to a destruction that remained in living memory. The army's response was to rebuild the ancient past of the Han and Tang that they depicted themselves as reenacting through reconquest.

Accounts from the early reconquest point not only to the widespread loss of human life, but to the built environment that had once sustained Chinese, Manchu, and other non-Muslim communities. Initial estimates indicated that up to three-quarters of arable land in the North had been abandoned, and nearly every Chinese person displaced or killed.[30] Officers returning to their former posts found them in ruins. In August 1876, Ürümchi general Yinghan returned to his old garrison town.[31] All that was left of the Chinese city, he reported, was a set of walls, while the Manchu garrison had been "flattened." It took two months for him to reconstruct the events of the uprising: In the summer of 1864, his fellows in the Manchu city held out under siege for eighty days before they were massacred. Now, nearly all of the arable land was fallow and untended, save by two or three Hui farmers who had once come from China proper looking for a better life. Such stories of loss during the Muslim uprisings became common in the Chinese official culture of the reconstruction period. One author wrote in 1907 about the ruins of the old settlement of Jimsar.[32] In 1865, Jimsar resisted a wave of Hui assault. While the garrison escaped to fight again, the city itself was ruined, and the walls lay "shattered" on a lonely plain. Now the observer wrote that "Peace has reigned for over thirty years, but the spirit of this place has been gravely injured. The wounds have not healed. It makes one sigh." Other writers were less dramatic, even as they emphasized the total destruction of the former Chinese presence: Qitai "vanished from the face of the Earth" when the Muslims burnt it.[33]

However, most of the officers that reconquered Xinjiang possessed no prior connection to the region, having only imagined it, as Zuo Zongtang had. Instead, they knew Xinjiang according to its Han- and Tang-dynasty geography, which Zuo's circle hoped in many ways to revive in their new era of Chinese and Confucian dominance. The Tang artifacts that these men expected to find in Xinjiang resonated because they saw their community as continuing the successes of the dynastic past. Much as the classically educated British elite in India depicted themselves as Romans engaging in a revived imperial project,[34] so did Chinese writings constantly invoke the conquests, generals, and garrisons of the Han and Tang. One magistrate described his own arrival in Turpan in terms of the Han-era march into Loulan.[35] It was no coincidence that Zuo, working from Gong Zizhen's plan for Xinjiang, proposed names for counties that reflected those of Tang garrisons.[36] His follower Xiao Xiong frequently made reference to the Tang in his notes on poems and borrowed obscure facts from Tang-era ethnography to explain what he saw in the present: under his brush, the Kyrgyz became the descendants of the Tang tributary state of Jiankun, while Qumulese saw long braids as a sign of beauty because the Tang-era elite of Qiuci grew their hair out.[37] It mattered not that Qiuci was quite far from Qumul, having been centered in latter-day Kucha, or that many of the ancient kingdoms reinscribed on Xinjiang's landscape had been similarly dislocated. Shanshan County, when it was established in 1907, was far north of classical Shanshan. Other places ended up displaced in time, as Kashgar was once again named for the pre-Islamic Shule kingdom.

The Xiang Army found every landmark of old Chinese geography absent from the landscape. In the days before the uprising, a broken iron bell had lain half-buried in the soil near Jimsar.[38] Its visible part displayed a Tang reign name, "clear as day," declaring a Chinese presence dating from a golden age. "Afterward," lamented an official writing in 1907, "it was probably broken up by the locals and tossed into the forge to make farm implements, melted down into nothing. There is no other trace of the past." Writers blamed the Musulmans for looting Chinese relics, and while people did take building materials and artifacts from ancient sites, accounts of lost ruins played into ideas of the Muslims' avariciousness and lack of respect for history.[39] The Han and Tang sites that remained were spooky, but never threatening: northwest of Suilai, one could visit the ruins of a Tang-era temple.[40] The walls had fallen, but five wooden idols remained, desiccated and preserved by the dry steppe winds. Or perhaps visitors merely took a more recent Mongol Buddhist temple to be an ancient Chinese structure. Regardless, "the old folks said," on a quiet night you could still hear the sound of drums and bells within.

The erasure of structures attested to a final break with a history that could not be recovered, a negation of two processes of territorialization on paper that literati found especially significant—what Laura Newby has called "the literary conquest of Xinjiang" and James Millward the process of bringing Xinjiang "onto the map."[41] Those conquests sustained a geographical imagination that made this strange region familiar, denied its present inhabitants the authority to speak about their own history by characterizing them as historical relics, and instead placed them and their homeland squarely within the imperial territorial inheritance.[42] Indeed, officials even had difficulty understanding the connection between Islam as practiced by Turkic Muslims and that of Chinese-speaking Muslims in China proper, so that local Islam appeared to many as a strange cult. Some speculated that it was a relic of ancient Manichaeism or Zoroastrianism with no apparent connection to Mecca, or for that matter to Xining or Lanzhou. Others treated Islam as a curiosity and repeated the same stories about Muḥammad and the early years of Islam over and over, as though hearing them for the first time.

Meanwhile, the Xiang Army's recovery of Xinjiang's history also obscured the Qing conquest of the 1750s. For example, the army made no effort to restore the system of temples constructed around the garrison at

Ürümchi during the Qianlong (1735–96/99) and Jiaqing (1796/99–1820) reigns.[43] Instead, they favored instead relics that represented the Han and Tang legacy. For example, in 1876, General Jinshun ran across a Tang-era stela dating to the year 640 atop a peak at Dawan in the hills between Qumul and Barköl.[44] The inscription recorded the arrival of Tang general Jiang Xingben (d. 645) during a conflict with the king of Gaochang. Its content may have resonated with Jinshun, who read it aloud as a demonstration that, contrary to rumor, he was in fact literate. Actually, it was not a wholly new discovery: the stela had attracted the attention of travelers for some time, and an earlier Qing official had incorporated it into a temple to Guandi. That Qing-era temple was destroyed in the uprisings during the long siege of Barköl. In 1882, Barköl imperial agent Mingchun (d. 1887) rebuilt the temple and moved the stela inside. In 1901, a new inscription was made that explained the history of the place from the perspective of Chinese officialdom. This inscription provided a series of temporal signposts of significance to that elite: in the reign of Emperor Gaozu of Tang (r. 618–26); at the moment of the temple's destruction in 1866; at Mingchun's arrival in "Yiwu," which was the name of a kingdom in Barköl dating to the Han and Tang; and at the restoration in 1901. The pre-uprisings attention to the stela was ignored in favor of a connection to the ancient past. Indeed, while Guandi was actually not widely worshiped until the Ming and did not even possess his title of *di*, "emperor," until 1615,[45] late-Qing writers came to believe that the Qing-era temple had itself stood there in the Tang.

Similarly, reconstruction did not revive the geography of what was destroyed in 1864. The people of Barköl themselves had resisted the uprisings and somehow survived them, an achievement that they attributed to the intervention of their local deity.[46] Nevertheless, the Xiang Army erased their gods from the landscape, while Tianjinese merchants redirected trade away from the town, emptying its once thriving market. In transforming the garrison towns of Dihua, Ürümchi, and Gongning into a provincial capital, the Xiang Army erased its banner identity, chose the name of the Chinese garrison (Dihua, meaning "civilizing the barbarians"), and turned the dual city form more common in the borderlands into a single-city complex like those of China proper.[47] What did survive the uprisings, and yet did not fit into the Xiang Army's narrative of history and its agency as the heroes of Xinjiang, could not survive reconstruction.

Yet for many people, the spirits of the pre-uprisings period would not remain silent. Qurbān ʿAlī Khālidī in 1889 published an account of his pilgrimage from his adopted home in Tarbaghatai to Turpan.[48] It begins with a ghost story: There is a place, he tells us, called Qarasun. There was once a beautiful Hui mosque there, but it was destroyed "in the time of tribulation" (balwa waqtinda), the Muslim uprisings and the factional violence that followed. Just southeast of that mosque was a shrine (mazār), the holy resting place of a saint, which would have been one of Khālidī's first stops along his pilgrimage, had it not been leveled, erased but for the memory. By Khālidī's time, the site was marked only by the flags planted by pilgrims, signs of devotion to a saint whose presence was felt but whose name was lost to history.

Nevertheless, the saint had been seen. After the reconquest, Khālidī relates, a Chinese man and his family settled near the tomb. The Reconstruction Agency granted him a parcel of land, on which he planted an orchard and some crops. As we will see, the people of Turpan frequently accused one another of destroying family graves by farming atop them, and resettled families such as these would have possessed either no knowledge of or no regard for the Muslim human remains on their land. That indeed was the Chinese family's downfall: One day, this man's two small sons went to play by the river, where they saw a ghostly man who wore a white turban on his head and a green garment on his body. A Muslim hearing this story would know that the green garment symbolized descent from the Prophet and immediately marked the man as holy, but a Chinese person probably lacked such knowledge. All the children knew was that this spectral figure "drew water from a different stream" not used by the Chinese, a stream by the ruined Hui mosque. Here the symbolism of the water is obvious, as the Muslim ghost belonged to a different religion from the Chinese. We may interpret it also as a reference to the Sufi idea that Law (shariah) and ultimate truth (ḥaqīqah) are akin to two waters, where the latter is only attainable by those who make exceptional effort, as a saint interred in a tomb would have done in life.[49] In that case, the comment about "drawing water from a different stream" confirms the specter's saintly status, rather than or alongside its ethnic difference. The turbaned man carried the water back to the tomb and disappeared.

The boys ran home to tell their father about the vanishing man. He did not believe them, saying, "It was just a passing Chantou." However, the children were not convinced. They returned to the river regularly and continued to witness the spirit rise from a patch of flat ground marked only by pilgrims' flags. Eventually, the father witnessed this specter's disappearance for himself, upon which he declared, "It's the tomb of a Chantou!" Khālidī's depiction of this poor farmer thus suggests ignorance not only of Islam and of hagiolatry, the worship of saints that was central to Islamic practice in East Turkestan, but of the proper naming of peoples. To the Chinese farmer, a Muslim is simply a "wrapped-head" (Chantou).

At their father's urging, the boys returned to play among the flags atop the tomb. Suddenly, they fell ill and died. Their mother, stricken with grief, blamed the tomb and took her revenge by defecating on it. Soon after, she too passed away. The children and the mother, in ignorance and rage, violated the shrine's sacred space and its ritual purity, effecting a double desecration. In his sorrow, the Chinese farmer approached the magistrate to beg for resettlement elsewhere. The magistrate responded, "Other people need a place to live, too! If you hadn't gone to the shrine, this wouldn't have happened." He was refused resettlement.[50]

Khālidī reports that this story began to circulate among the Musulmans, and that, when he heard it, he approached some Chinese, who confirmed the account. Khālidī volunteered to find a superintendent (mutawallī) for a new pious endowment dedicated to the shrine, to build a dome atop it and offer prayers to honor the saint within. A Hui official in Qarasun enthusiastically welcomed this proposal, but met some resistance from Musulmans, who claimed the whole story to be an invention of the infidels. They proposed to open the tomb and see who was actually inside—Muslim or not? Khālidī was wiser than Yang Peiyuan and knew to let the body rest, or risk disturbing the tenuous peace between Musulmans, Hui, and Chinese. Instead, he reasoned with the petitioners: as the tomb was known to have possessed a dome and walls, and was oriented to Mecca, it was surely that of a Musulman. The skeptical were invited to hold a vigil of forty nights at the shrine and await a vision, but no one was brave enough to volunteer. Khālidī, by mobilizing his powers of reason and rhetoric, presented the people of Qarasun with a moral message for the post-uprisings age: one ought to recognize difference and respect the boundaries of communities ordained by history and sacred authority. Moreover, a scholar could discern those differences by observing concrete signs in the world.

With Khālidī's story, we arrive at the place of slippage between a site of memory and the remains of a human being, and so we will soon return to the question of corpses. Meanwhile, what do a saint's shrine and the temple to Guandi have in common? Both of them mark places where memories were ordinarily fluid and underwent negotiation and affirmation through ritual, but where trauma compelled people to fix these memories in place according to new historical narratives. Rian Thum persuasively argues that a shrine in the East Turkestani context is a site for creating and relating to history as a sacred act, that "Local historical practice was . . . a ritual act linking the community to God through historical personages."[51] A shrine is not necessarily the tomb of a physical body—rather, it is the place where a saint who brought Islam is imagined to have died or been interred. Pilgrims from across East Turkestan traveled along a network of shrines and through these journeys encountered other pilgrims and engaged in the recitation of hagiographies kept at each shrine. Hagiography thus provided a framework for understanding the self simultaneously as part of a broader community and in relation to a fixed point in history and geography. Nevertheless, that understanding was "modular," as pilgrims mixed and matched stories to imagine the religious community in different ways. The Qarasun shrine, however, gained a new meaning by being destroyed: it was no longer a fixed point, but self-evidently something that could be erased from the landscape, and so demanded recovery. Many people around Khālidī sought to connect the body within to a bounded group and so determine the natural ownership of the land above, ending the fluidity of memory and openness of interpretation that gave the site its meaning. Khālidī demonstrates his wisdom—which seems to be one of the main goals of his writing—by affirming the site's Islamic meaning and leaving it open to interpretation within Islam.

Similarly, worship at a Chinese temple was an opportunity to reaffirm or negotiate the boundaries of community through ritual, and often through performances of historical narratives.[52] However, the Xiang Army, when they entered Xinjiang, experienced the "loss" of something they had never owned but only expected to exist. Their own sense of belonging to the region was meant to be confirmed by Han and Tang ruins. When that connection was already severed, its palpable absence demanded its recovery at the expense of the legacy of the recently dead. The Guandi temple's potential to make a historical statement that connected the present-day Xiang

Army to a Tang-era conquest led the temple's curators to present its history selectively. Where Wang Zhensheng experienced the reconquest of Xinjiang vicariously, so could members of the Xiang Army project themselves into the role of ancient heroes, recovering what had been lost not for thirteen years, but for a millennium.

Making Claims with Corpses

The ubiquity of human remains nevertheless mitigated against attempts to expunge the recent past and live in heritage. To the contrary, people became adept at deploying discourses of flesh and bone in order to induce action on the part of officials. Indeed, a corpse's power in the Chinese context derived in many ways from how seriously the state regarded the disposition of human remains. Chinese settlers meanwhile benefited from participation in a common discourse about human remains that had its roots in traditional Chinese thought but also in the specific circumstances of the nineteenth century. Tobie Meyer-Fong argues that, for the people of China proper, the Taiping war itself was an apocalyptic event that induced a widespread sense of the need to save a faltering sociomoral order through personal moral rectification.[53] One of the chief signs of collapse was the sale and consumption of human flesh, which was an ancient trope in Chinese culture but gained a terrifying reality during the war. At the same time, anonymous bones, "stripped of their identities, . . . were in effect a blank surface onto which an account of dynastic balance and restored community could be inscribed." Under these circumstances, the bodies of the dead gained profound political and emotional meaning, opening up the potential for a "mortuary politics" in which people mobilized practices, ideas, and materials surrounding death for other purposes.

On one level, cases from reconstruction suggest that arguments about corpses were instrumental, as they offered potential economic benefits. One of the earliest cases filed at the Turpan yamen was by Luo Yang *shi*, a Chinese woman who claimed to have roots in Turpan.[54] Luo Yang *shi* testified that her father's former landlord, a Musulman named Raḥīm, was among those who massacred her family. In the face of this disturbing allegation, Luo Yang *shi* had a simple demand: her father had been killed before his lease was up, and so she wished to continue renting the land until the contract expired. The dissonance between Luo Yang *shi*'s loss of her closest family and her desire to rent from her father's alleged murderer is striking; equally so, that between the seriousness of the allegation and the compensation she demanded.

Nevertheless, it was not abnormal for Chinese settlers to seek the means of subsistence by making claims against Musulmans. The very day that Luo Yang *shi* went to the yamen, a Shaanxi man named Zhang Guishu was behind her in the line of petitioners.[55] Zhang had a slightly stronger claim, as the vineyard of which he sought ownership, he contended, was stolen when Musulmans murdered all nine members of his uncle's family. If Zhang's uncle had been the deed-holding owner of that vineyard, surely, he ought to have a valid claim to it as his inheritance. However, Zhang was awarded only a five-year rent on less than half of the vineyard's grape trellises. Luo Yang *shi* lost her case outright. Indeed, in the broader Turpan archive, there are almost no cases in which a Chinese settler successfully claimed property rights over a Musulman. Magistrates probably denied them because they were skeptical about claims to land advanced by poor farmers without deeds or other physical evidence of ownership. Chinese settlers or returnees were generally desperately poor, so much so that they fled family farms in Shaanxi and Gansu for a chance to scratch out a living in the desert. Whatever archive existed in Turpan before the uprisings had been destroyed, along with any deeds that might have verified someone's claim to land or the name of a family member. Moreover, to expropriate the land of a Musulman for the benefit of a Chinese farmer so soon after the end of the uprisings would have seemed foolish to an official on the ground. (Indeed, a strategy of favoring autochthonous people in property disputes generally correlates with a low instance of violence in frontier zones.)[56] These disputes over family death and land also show that there was a very narrow path for a Chinese person to file suit successfully against a Musulman for violence related to the uprisings. Zuo Zongtang had declared a general amnesty for combatants, which shielded a substantial number of Musulmans from prosecution, but also foreclosed the possibility for people to seek justice on the basis of the uprisings themselves.[57] Instead, the provincial judicial system allowed them to file suits on the basis of unfulfilled contracts or claims of theft.

Either Zhang Guishu's or Luo Yang *shi*'s claim would have been bolstered by the presence of a Chinese corpse on the land concerned. Qing law specified harsh corporal punishments and exile for those who disturbed or destroyed others' graves without reason.[58] Moreover, if one sold land with the knowledge that there was a corpse buried on it, and that sale resulted in the disruption of a grave, then the law required that land to be returned to a relative. The ubiquity of remains in Turpan therefore opened up the possibility of litigating the losses incurred in the uprisings, not through accusations of murder, but through proximal discourses surrounding the remains of the dead.

As a result, the politics of human remains became such a common means of making claims in Turpan that it was sometimes unclear whether a corpse actually existed. In one exceptionally convoluted case from 1909, four different parties all claimed ownership of a single cemetery.[59] An elderly Musulman man named Haierlang sued a Hui man named Wang Wanfu, claiming that Wang had buried a Hui corpse in his family's graveyard in the dead of night in order to claim falsely that it was his ancestral land. Wang Wanfu asserted, in turn, that the corpse was authentic, and that the cemetery indeed belonged to him. Wang countersued Haierlang for damaging it. Wang's paternal grandparents had been buried on that land since before the uprisings, he claimed, and the elderly Musulman was attempting to destroy the bodies by tilling the remains into the soil. Haierlang had dug an irrigation ditch, flooding the land—and lamentably, but conveniently, destroying any trace of any ancestors' remains.

When Haierlang was called to the yamen, he suddenly shifted his position: Wang, he said, did not actually bury a body on his land, and it was never a cemetery to begin with! Wang, he testified, had spread a rumor that Haierlang sold Wang land to bury his ancestors, whose corpses remained disinterred. Haierlang presented himself instead as the victim of a plot to bamboozle him, an elderly man, out of his remaining scrap of farmland. Haierlang apologized for making a fuss, but at least Wang's scheme was exposed. Meanwhile, seventy local Musulmans petitioned in support of Haierlang, who they now claimed was the custodian of their communal cemetery, open to Musulmans, but not to Hui. Another petitioner, a Musulman named Sulṭān Niyāz, then appeared with another claim entirely: Haierlang was the custodian of *his* family's cemetery, who had abused his authority by farming on *his* ancestors' graves.

The prefect was now confused. Haierlang called the land in question farmland but had earlier claimed that it was a cemetery; Wang claimed it was his ancestral cemetery; these Musulmans said it was a communal graveyard; and Sulṭān Niyāz asserted that it belonged to him. Each party accused the other of some malfeasance with regard to corpses, but no one was able to produce any evidence to prove their case one way or another. After several months, the magistrate remanded the case to a pair of village headmen, one Hui and one Musulman, at which point it drops out of the archival record. Tellingly, all of the land surrounding the plot in question had recently been opened to "reclamation" and farming, which suggests that each of the parties in the dispute was actually the owner of an adjacent plot attempting to secure a claim over this remaining scrap of land. The only certain way to do so, however, was to have ancestors buried under the surface. Such instrumentalization of corpses meant that human remains were a recognized and powerful topos for the articulation of communal grievances. Haierlang's original complaint hinged on the ethnoreligious identity of Wang Wanfu's alleged corpse, and the assumption that this identity was simultaneous with familial descent. Wang Wanfu, in turn, advanced a historical claim, that his ancestors had been buried in that cemetery since before the uprisings. Haierlang's supporters made a claim to the land based on communal ownership, arguing that their own ancestors' bodies proved their ownership. Sulṭān Niyāz's claim, in turn, was based on family. In the end, all of them were probably false, but the fictions themselves are interesting.

Similarly, there was a large cemetery outside the north gate of Lükchün where Chinese merchants claimed to have buried their dead many years before the uprisings.[60] In 1878, it was alleged, some Musulman officials leveled much of it in order to build a new irrigation channel—again, conveniently destroying any trace of human remains. The merchants were furious but failed to convince the provincial authorities to intervene on their behalf. Four years later, Chinese merchants from several provinces took the same complaint to the Pichan subdistrict magistrate. The subdistrict magistrate was just then leaving office, and so ordered the Musulman officials to rebuild the cemetery, along with its walls and ossuary. However, a year later, no progress had been made. The newly elevated Turpan Wang Maḥmūd saw no reason to enforce the ruling but instead approved the sale of the land to an interpreter.

Early in 1884, a group of merchants from Shanxi, Shaanxi, Sichuan, Hunan, and Hubei sent a joint petition on behalf of "the Chinese" (*Hanren*) following up on the case. While the precise number of Chinese in Turpan at this time remains unclear, there was a rapid influx of Chinese-speaking, non-Muslim people through this important center of trade.[61] This suggests that in-migration into an area of scarce resources would have put significant pressure on religious and social institutions that served Chinese-speaking, non-Muslim people, such as cemeteries and native-place associations, to expand their services beyond narrow groups defined by collocal identities. After all, native-place associations frequently opened their doors to sojourners from adjacent homelands whose communities were too small to construct their own lodges. People from Shaanxi and Hunan could be buried in the same ground, and others would tend their graves and advocate for their corpses despite differences of geographical origin. The merchants could therefore advocate on behalf of this internally diverse body that was gradually learning what they had in common, and how they differed from the Muslims among whom they lived.

The merchants channeled their fury into a clear statement of their beliefs regarding the Musulmans in general:

> Ohh, the Chinese (*Han*) bones, how angry they are at the Chantou! The Chinese spirits (*shen*), how frustrated with the Chantou! Those who dig the Chinese graves, they anger the Chinese people! . . . If our Emperor wishes to guide these people to transform into "Chinese" (*hua Zhong*), he must make these people walk within the law (*fa*).
>
> The royal code states that the digging of graves and destruction of temples is to be punished at one grade above that for "disrespecting one's bodily inheritance and the country's grace." If you excuse these Chantou because they "are ignorant of the law," then try asking them, what about Chantou graves? Can Chinese people dig them up? What about Chantou temples? Can Chinese people destroy them? If they really have no emotional reaction (*nuwei*) at all when they are dug up or destroyed, then that *really* means the Chantou are ignorant of the "law"! This means the Chantou can't be considered under the law!

This statement reveals much about the concerns and attitudes of Chinese people in Turpan seven years into reconstruction. It demonstrates the confluence of concerns over parentage and the disposition of the dead, which were intimately related in Confucian thought and culture. Genealogy was the essence of civilization, and just as schoolteachers were frustratedly suggesting that their Musulman charges lacked the basic ability to comprehend orthodoxy, so did these Chinese-speakers feel that their neighbors were too ignorant to be fully human. Moreover, it shows how these merchants perceived moralism and the rites as the essence of imperial law, and therefore agreed with the civilizing project's premise that Musulmans needed to understand the rites before "walking within the law." While these petitioners presented themselves as natural allies of the government, they also criticized the civilizing project for its seemingly favorable treatment of Musulmans and encouraged it instead to engage in the kind of cultural violence necessary to force them to recognize the superiority of Chineseness. Finally, it shows how Chinese in Turpan were gradually coming to see themselves as part of the same community, common defenders of Chinese bones and patrimony, rather than members of different native-place groups.

Concerns about lineage intersected with definitions of Chineseness—and, for that matter, Hui-ness and Musulman-ness—that transcended not only family but native place. In Turpan, different merchant households competed with one another. However, the demands of maintaining a cemetery had imposed a certain institutional reality on the Chinese population as a whole, while disruptions of Chinese graves on the backdrop of other forms of violence and conflict mobilized a larger-scale identity. In life, the Chinese buried in that cemetery were individuals with families who maintained their tombs. In death, with their children gone, they became "the Chinese bones," sites for the inscription of new meanings stripped of their fleshy identities. That rhetoric was shown to be powerful in Turpan time and again, as people of varying backgrounds mobilized real or fictional remains of ancestors, whose identities could allegedly be proven by their ethnic characteristics, in order to claim land. In Turpan, a collective Chineseness erased the geographical differences between Chinese-speaking, non-Muslim people and tied that identity to the defense of ancestors against a Muslim Other.

The Exiled Soldier Sends Chinese Souls Home

The same common Chineseness was articulated and institutionalized through worship of a deity who simultaneously naturalized the presence of Hunanese people in the borderland and allowed the souls of dead Chinese people to return home to their native places, even when their remains could not.[62] Dingxiang Wang was the city god of Shanhua County, which constituted one half of the city of Changsha. He first became the Xiang Army's patron deity, and then gained a new life in Xinjiang as the reimagined god of Hunanese settlers. Over time, his popularity grew until he came to be seen as a sort of "postmaster general" for the prayers and souls of Chinese-speaking non-Muslims.

Dingxiang Wang's origins are murky, but his identity was persistently tied to deep and treacherous waters and the military defense of Changsha and of China. He may have begun his existence as a river god, the "King who Pacifies the Xiang River." Changsha was built on this river's banks, and its rising floodwaters periodically imperiled the city, but they could be calmed by a sacrifice. Later, a heroic defender of Hunan against the Qing invasion became attached to the legend, and some construed Dingxiang Wang as this hero's drowned spirit. Others claimed that he was an upright magistrate from the early Qing and descendant of a Tang official, and that he defended Changsha's people against demons. According to the historical record, Dingxiang Wang emerged by 1847, when he flowed out of the river into the body of a water-seller. The possessed man proceeded directly to the Shanhua County yamen, where Dingxiang Wang reported for duty as the county's new city god. According to the theory current at that time, which *jingshi* scholars also adopted, city gods are the "doubles" of the towns, counties, prefectures, or even provinces that they represent. Indeed, "city god" is a somewhat awkward translation, albeit the usual one in English— "god-of-the-wall" captures its broader meaning, as well as the metaphor that *jingshi* writers used to explain how they worked: the city god's relationship to an administrative unit was like that between a city and its walls and moat. Proper ritual worship of the god ensured the unit's safety, harmony, and integrity. That worship frequently involved performing plays in front of the deity's statue, as well as transporting it around its territory on yearly inspections.

It was therefore appropriate when, during the Taiping siege of Changsha in 1852, the Shanhua County magistrate and a group of local gentry carried Dingxiang Wang's statue to the top of the city wall and faced it toward the attacking forces, inviting the god to inspect the situation. According to the local gazetteer, Dingxiang Wang immediately intervened in the battle, as the Taiping soldiers scaling the walls tumbled as if repelled by an unseen force. The siege was broken, the Taiping army turned, and Changsha saved. The next year, the Board of Rites bestowed honors upon Dingxiang Wang for his service, just in time for the formation of the Xiang Army. This new army's soldiers, many of whom hailed from Shanhua, now took Dingxiang Wang on an extended inspection as they marched with their city god across Hunan, and then across China. Dingxiang Wang observed combat from Changsha to Kashgar and Khotan—and later still in the Sino-French War—and at each resting place stayed in a "temporary residence" (xinggong). Dingxiang Wang became an object of fascination and pride as a city god who had far outgrown his boundaries. "The god-of-the-wall of our Changsha does not only orient inward, but can also orient outward," wrote the Hunanese intellectual Yi Baisha (1886–1921). "Not only does he stay in Hunan—he goes on campaign to other provinces as well!"[63] The Hunanese officials of Xinjiang continued to celebrate their hometown deity as well, publishing his image in their sponsored work of morality literature in 1885.[64] His inspection tour of the far corners of the empire indicated the expansion of Shanhua's territory to encompass all of that space which the Xiang Army had reconquered, as images of Dingxiang Wang could now be found from Fujian to the Pamirs.

In Xinjiang by the mid-1890s, Xiang Army veterans rewrote Dingxiang Wang's legend and gave him a new name, "Fangshen."[65] This shift coincides with the community's settling down and entrenchment in the provincial bureaucracy, but also with the strange erasure of Dingxiang Wang from chronicles of the army's exploits written in China proper. "Temporary residences" to him were built across Xinjiang and maintained by Hunanese native-place associations and donations from veterans and their families. The deity's legend now figured him not simply as a heroic defender of Changsha and China, or simply as a drowned god. Rather, he was described, as "Fangshen," as an ordinary farm boy from Hunan who had once accepted exile in Xinjiang as a consequence of defending his brother in a conflict. His exile to Kashgar coincided with Jahāngīr's incursion from Khoqand in the 1820s, the same event that had prompted scholars at the Yuelu Academy to rethink frontier policy. During the battles with Jahāngīr, the farm boy sacrificed himself by diving into a flooded town and rescuing his brothers-in-arms, as well as saving the Qing from invasion. To be clear, there is no evidence that Fangshen was worshiped in Xinjiang prior to 1864—rather, evidence from these texts, travelers' accounts, and writings by members of Dingxiang Wang's transregional community of worshippers makes it clear that Fangshen was a reimagining of Dingxiang Wang. His new story naturalized the presence of Hunanese settlers on the frontier by showing that a Hunanese presence predated the uprisings, and also valorized their efforts by showing how they reenacted a heroic narrative from the past. (Indeed, one legend of Dingxiang Wang gives his name in life as that of a popular Xiang Army commander who had died in Xinjiang.) It reflected Wang Zhensheng's perception of Xiang Army soldiers as heroes reclaiming a lost patrimony dating to the earlier Qing.

Dingxiang Wang's interconnection with his other main temple in Shanhua made him appealing to non-Hunanese as well, and gradually his "temporary residences" came to be tended by Chinese people of various origins.[66] He long outlasted the period of Hunanese dominance, and by the 1930s, the chief priests of his temple in Dihua were Gansunese. There worshipers far from China proper could send letters to their hometown distant deities, if they paid a fee for a special stamp labeled "Dingxiang Wang's Palace" (*Dingxiang Wang fu*). Thereupon the letters would be burnt so that Dingxiang Wang could spirit them to their recipients. The temple did especially brisk business around the Lunar New Year, when migrants were too far from home for a return visit to be feasible. This charming scene reflects a darker practice: Xiang Army soldiers were typically too poor for their remains to be transported home for burial. Dingxiang Wang, it was said, could instead transmit their spirits across the distance. Documents from the Turpan archive demonstrate the tremendous difficulty that most Chinese settlers had in this regard, as families and merchant groups approached the yamen seeking funds for coffins and the price of carrying bones down the long highway to Hunan, Shaanxi, or Guangdong. Dingxiang Wang's inherent and immediate connection with China proper was therefore appealing, as it could ensure that a person buried in Xinjiang would nevertheless rest with their ancestors in the homeland.

As Wang Penghui has also argued, Dingxiang Wang helped blur the distinctions between kinds of Chinese people in the borderland.[67] By the 1930s, the deity was known as the "city god of the Chinese (*Han*) ethnic group" (*Hanzu zhi chenghuang*), refiguring the city god's spatial function as one of preserving the integrity of a group defined by common descent. His temple was the only temple to a city god in the provincial capital of Dihua as well, despite the fact that Dihua ought to have hosted separate temples for county, prefectural, and provincial city gods. This suggests that Dingxiang Wang came to be perceived as the city god of Xinjiang, as well as that of the Chinese, and that of the Hunanese, specifically of Shanhua County. His story of borderland defense and self-sacrifice valorized and legitimized the Chinese presence in Xinjiang.

*   *   *

Memory as the repetition of lived experience is a matter of ongoing and situational recollection, and so it is easily colonized by history, the formal account of the past. This is especially true when traumatic loss—experienced directly or vicariously in narrative—causes these different modes of remembering and forgetting to interact. In the attempt to make sense of absence, narrative subsumes the individual subject's story of loss into the collective experience. The imposition of a grand historical narrative is not necessarily a negation of personal experience. To the contrary, individuals like Wang Zhensheng or the Hunanese stranded in the borderland could find it deeply empowering to present their own experiences through those of heroes. Members of the Xiang Army could be motivated to recover lost territory by their own romantic notions of a golden age, imagined partly through antiquarian culture and partly through their own experiences of struggle. The sons of Fuping may well have taken inspiration from the stories of boys who sought out their sojourning fathers, comforted by the notion that Confucian ideology saw power and goodness in their pain—so might the widows of Fuping, even as they struggled to fulfill the obligations of orthodoxy. The people who lived and settled in Turpan could learn to advance effective narratives of loss that had legal bearing, and thus legitimized a mortuary politics that could have been instrumental, sincere, or both.

The imagined community as it was articulated in late-Qing Xinjiang was at least in part the product of mass conflict and its concomitant imagination of collective struggle, the transformation of mundane aspects and actions into characteristics and deeds with ethnic and historical meaning. Others have suggested that the institutions of warfare, such as military service and the instrumental need to articulate an ideology that justifies conflict, produce the experiences and symbolic vocabularies necessary to engender a strong sense of group feeling.[68] However, the relationship between armed conflict and the reimagination of one's group is not so straightforward. Killing someone may demand that one articulate the reasons for it, to prevent "combat" from becoming "murder"—however, because hardly anyone in Turpan would admit publicly to their participation in the Muslim uprisings in the historical record, that justificatory narrative was not part of the discourse. Loss and recovery were more powerful in the field of representation. People could resist identifying the bodies of the dead, or they could identify them, even fabricate them, to advance their purposes and those of their communities, and in so doing state their belonging to a group with common grievances based on a common history.

That common history, as the people of Turpan articulated it, attached individuals to genealogies. In Rogers Brubaker's terms, Chinese, Hui, and Muslims all participated in a set of "deeply taken-for-granted and embodied identifications" that were primarily religious in their nature and context, and yet implied the existence of a larger imagined community based on language and piety.[69] For Musulmans, that was the identity system formed through shrine pilgrimage, while for Chinese, it meant participation in native-place associations and temples that tied the individual to a community that crossed and even transcended Chinese territory. Genealogy was already an implicit part of Muslim and Chinese identities. The saints believed to be buried at shrines could be interpreted as the fictive ancestors of Muslim groups, although they were the people who had converted their ancestors to Islam, not their biological parents.[70] A missing saint could be construed nonetheless as a powerful being defending its sacred territory against the incursions of infidels. Dingxiang Wang, too, was a hero from the past who emerged from the absence or obliteration of history to defend his territory. In Turpan, it was the dead—the absent or invisible ancestors—who gave those communities common purpose and power and defined their mutual grievances. In their combat at the yamen, they filled the fictive cemeteries and the flattened tombs with imagined ancestors.

SIX

Historical Estrangement and
the End of Empire

MULLAH MŪSA B. MULLAH ʿĪSA SAYRĀMĪ was twenty-eight years old
when the Muslim uprisings broke out in Kucha.[1] By this time, he had completed his education and taught students of his own. As his old schoolfriend
Maḥmūdīn Khwaja was among the leaders of the new Islamic state, and so
was his former teacher Mullah ʿUthmān, Sayrāmī naturally supported
their efforts. He soon received an intimate view of the progress of the uprisings and the factional violence that followed, the optimism of the restoration of Islamic rule and its shocking failures.

Sayrāmī joined the Kucha khwajas' disastrous first campaign westward
to Aksu. In the confusion of the Battle of Qara Yulghun, he fled eastward
and soon found himself wandering in the desert, limping by stages back
toward Kucha. He took refuge at the ʿArshuddīn Shrine and waited prayer-
fully for good news. When the roads were safe, Sayrāmī traveled north and
west into the mountains, hoping to return home to the town of Sayrām.
Over a century earlier, the Zunghar Mongols had forcibly removed his
ancestors from their ancestral home in Old Sayrām, in today's Kazakh-
stan, and after many tribulations, his people had settled in a place where
no one would bother them. Now, however, as Mullah Mūsa stood upon the
mountain pass overlooking his childhood home, he realized that its circumstances had changed forever. No shelter awaited him there, he later
wrote. It was impossible to come home. He turned back for Kucha.

Decades later, as Mullah Mūsa's beard was turning white, some acquaintances importuned him to write his experiences down in a history of the uprisings, as he possessed a mind and disposition peculiarly suited to scholarship. Sayrāmī writes of his trepidation at the task of reclaiming events now crossing out of memory. "Since the beginning of the Time of Islam to the present," he wrote, "over forty years have gone by. Most of those who witnessed those happenings have passed on to the eternal realm, and past events fallen out of the people's memory. Perhaps their stories were forgotten."[2] Sayrāmī, however, had seen nearly everything: After turning back to Kucha, he had become an adviser to the khwaja leadership and later served Ya'qūb Beg as a tax collector. His life after the Xiang Army's reconquest is less clear, and some contend that he spent his years wandering the pilgrimage routes and collecting stories.[3] Somewhere along the way, Mullah Mūsa learned some Chinese and became familiar with the workings of the new state. He therefore grasped a broad-ranging understanding of the past century, as well as a deep knowledge of the Quran, the hadith, and the chronicles of past rulers. Moreover, Sayrāmī's friends believed that reading and writing history were his only source of joy. Mullah Mūsa sat down to write.

The work that he produced and then revised over the course of a decade, the *Tārīkh-i Ḥamīdī*,[4] is not only a discerning chronicle of the events of the nineteenth century, but a work of often grand scale that delves into the depths of history to excavate the reasons for the present. Sayrāmī describes his work as a monument to the forgotten martyrs of the uprisings. Yet it was not sufficient simply to recount the recent past, for the uprisings and their failure presented a puzzle: How had an Islamic state beaten the infidel back, but then fallen again to a non-Muslim power, which had now returned in a new and more aggressive form? The *Tārīkh-i Ḥamīdī* was an attempt to answer that question by rallying oral and written sources together into an argument. Sayrāmī's perspicacity has therefore attracted the praise of modern historians.[5] However, the *Tārīkh-i Ḥamīdī*'s most striking aspect is its use of traditional Perso-Islamic historiography to undermine established discourses of political legitimacy, juxtaposed with its selective mobilization of other narratives and explanatory devices from that tradition in order to legitimize specific manifestations of Chinese power and delegitimize others. Sayrāmī not only used the Perso-Islamic past to explain the Qing, but also drew on Chinese sources and on the institutions and forms of imperial rule. By relating Chinese rule to the ancient past, and the periphery to the imperial core, Sayrāmī explains not only the uprisings, but the relationship between diverse peoples and how they came to be estranged.

In this chapter, we will see how Islamic history writing in Chaghatay written by Musulmans for a Musulman audience reflected concerns with Chinese power and the social change that it wrought. The experience of historical loss, I argue, demanded an explanation through the rewriting of history, just as it did for Chinese people. To explain the Muslim uprisings and their aftermath was to reimagine a golden age prior to them in terms of a special relationship between Muslim subjects and the Qing sovereign that was licensed by God and expressed in terms of descent, followed by a shattering of that covenant through the violation of the same principle. That story placed China near the center of humanity's primordial history, and Xinjiang in turn at the center of Chinese history. It was told through adaptations of preexisting Islamic narratives inflected with the specific experience of imperial rule. That imperial context in turn engendered discourses and categories of difference that Musulman writers engaged with beyond the yamen.

How the Emperor of China Became a Muslim

There is a peculiar tension or contradiction in Sayrāmī's work, from the perspective of a modern historian, between his often-acerbic criticism of established legends and his assertions of the veracity of others that many people might find just as unconvincing. By attending to Sayrāmī's selective deployment of narratives, however, one can see how he adapted arguments from Islamic history and scripture in their specifically East Turkestani manifestations to advance arguments about past and present. Much of his argumentation about Chinese power and empire relates to genealogy of one sort or another: biological descent, chains of transmission, or inherited offices.

Mullah Mūsa opens the introduction of the *Tārīkh-i Ḥamīdī* with a critique of the fabrication of genealogies for political purposes that openly assails a longstanding tradition about the origins of the Chinggisid royal house. The majority of Islamic historical writings about Turco-Mongol rulers since the Mongol conquests had included the legend of Alanqoa, who conceived a child with a beam of light and thus begat the line of Chinggis Khan. This story was meant to demonstrate the partly divine descent of the world-conqueror, and official chronicles commissioned by his real or fictive descendants accent it so as to emphasize the ruler's special nature.[6] Sayrāmī, however, debunks this myth in the first chapter of the introduction.[7] He attacks it on scriptural grounds: the only virgin birth was that of ʿĪsa to Maryam (the biblical Jesus to Mary). Here Sayrāmī contradicts the *Akbarnāma*, the monumental Mughal history that proclaims, "If you listen to tales of Mary, then incline likewise to Alanqoa."[8] He then disassembles the foundation of a popular belief that the light-being was in fact ʿAlī b. Abī Ṭālib (601–61), the cousin of the Prophet and the fourth caliph, whom Shiites consider the first imam. Sayrāmī notes that ʿAlī lived long before Alanqoa, and so their union was impossible. Moreover, he casts doubt on the very concept: even if they were contemporaries, why would ʿAlī turn himself into a beam of light and travel to the other side of the world to lie with an infidel in a tent? To the contrary, Sayrāmī argues, the myth of the virgin birth was invented to disguise the Mongols' incestuous origins and justify the misdeeds of Chinggis's descendants. Mullah Mūsa is obviously a skeptical historian, and his willingness here and elsewhere to overturn common wisdom is striking. It makes it all the more intriguing that he accepts a range of other narratives of origins that other scholars may find difficult to believe.

The historical construction of groupness in Central Asian Islamic history-writing took legends of Islamization, the conversion of a people to Islam, as origin myths for Muslim peoples. Many such legends concern the encounter between an Islamizing saint—usually a Sufi—and a ruler who accepts the faith and in turn brings about a mass conversion to Islam.[9] Ethnogenesis is therefore inherently related to the historical realization of Islam. Appropriately, the *Tārīkh-i Ḥamīdī*'s introduction (*muqaddima*) consists of a series of familiar stories of Turco-Mongol rulers' "dual conversions," their realization of Islam in two stages. Either the ruler must hide his Islam until the time is right to reveal it, or else a father begins the process, while his son must complete it.[10] Sayrāmī begins with Oghuz Khan, the legendary Turkic leader who upon birth spoke and named himself.[11] The infant Oghuz refused to suckle at his mother's breast until she accepted Islam, but hid his Islam from his father until achieving his majority and undertaking a holy war against him. Later, the conversion of Sutuq Bughra Khan (d. 955), the historical Qarakhanid ruler of Kashgar, was said to be predicted by a hadith. Sutuq likewise remained a secret Muslim until his nonbelieving father got wind of his encounter with Abū Naṣr Ṣāmānī, a noble sent to convert the Turks. A war ensued, which Sutuq won, followed by further battles to establish Islam in place of the Buddhism then common throughout East Turkestan. The shrines of Sutuq Bughra Khan and Abū Naṣr Ṣāmānī in the mountains of Artush near Kashgar are famous pilgrimage sites and were objects of Yaʿqūb Beg's patronage.[12] Finally, Sayrāmī relates the dual conversion of the Chaghatayid ruler Tughluq Temür Khan (r. 1347–62), first through an encounter with Jalāl al-Dīn Katakī, and then with his son Arshād al-Dīn. Arshād al-Dīn's descendants were the very Kucha khwajas whose state emerged during the Muslim uprisings. This past of Islamization was therefore very much present in turn-of-the-century Xinjiang as the shrines of historical Islamizers played a role in precisely the politics that Sayrāmī sought to explain.

The last chapter of the introduction jumps forward in time to the recent past, and then back into the depths of history. It begins with the events of June 6, 1864, when the Muslims of Kucha set fire to the Chinese settlements.[13] Sayrāmī lays out his typically rational, source-based approach to these events: "Everyone tells the story differently. One's account differs from another's." He decides to discern which stories are correct, rather than simply repeat them on the page. Given Sayrāmī's approach, and his stated skepticism toward legend, his next rhetorical choice seems odd. Sayrāmī, in order to locate the origins of the uprisings, immediately casts the point of his reed into the depths of the inkwell of history, down to the days of the Tang dynasty and the Prophet Muḥammad himself, and relates the story of "How the Emperor of China Long Ago Became a Muslim" ("Ḥikāya-ye zamāna-ye awwalda Khaqan-i Chīn musulmān bolghani").[14] Here as elsewhere, Sayrāmī uses the term *Khaqan-i Chīn* to indicate the emperor of China, invoking a mysterious, magic-wielding sovereign from the Persian *Book of Kings* (*Shāhnāma*). Now that the *Khaqan-i Chīn* had stepped off the page and into the lives of Musulmans, his presence demanded attention.

Once upon a time, Sayrāmī begins, there was a just and benevolent ruler in the country of China. His name was Tang Wang Khan. That name indicated the "King of Tang," in this case Tang Gaozong (r. 649–83), to whom the caliph ʿUthmān (r. 644–56) sent a diplomatic mission. One night, Tang Wang had a dream in which a dragon entered his window and wrapped itself around a pillar. As the dragon turned to attack the king, an imposing man in a green robe with "a white thing wrapped around his head" appeared and split the dragon in two with his staff, killing it. The next morning, Tang Wang called his dream interpreters into his chambers to explain his dream. They informed him that the man in the dream matched the description of someone named "Muḥammad," far to the west, who had taken up the mantle of prophethood. Tang Wang's court packed a trove of Chinese treasures—silk, tea, and porcelain—to send to Muḥammad with an invitation to the imperial court. After many travails, Tang Wang's messenger located the Prophet.

However, Muḥammad refused to travel overland to China, but instead sent a magical letter in his stead: when the khan opened the envelope, Muḥammad said, he too would arrive in person. On the long road from Arabia to China, Tang Wang's messenger was tempted to open the envelope containing the Prophet's missive. When he did so, "it seemed as though someone emerged from it, and then left." That is, the magic meant to transport Muḥammad through the envelope was used without the presence of the emperor, and so he could not materialize. So, when the emperor himself opened the letter, the surprise was ruined, and Muḥammad did not appear. There was nothing inside the envelope but a letter in Chinese. This interrupted transmission represents the failure of the final revelation, literally the "message," borne by God's Messenger (rasūl) Muḥammad in its pure Arabic form, to reach China.

The messenger confessed to disobeying both prophet and emperor and, as just punishment, was sent back to try again. This time, a disappointed Muḥammad selected three men from among his companions, Waqqāṣ, ʿĀs, and ʿUkkāsha. He sent them with seven other people to travel with the messenger to China. One member of the party died at the Pass at Jiayuguan, leaving behind a famed shrine at the traditional boundary between China proper and the Islamic world. ʿUkkāsha's resting place, the legend says, is at Bügür in the northern Tarim Basin, while another's body is buried in China proper. Eventually, however, most of the embassy entered the khan's capital to great fanfare.

Nevertheless, Tang Wang was disappointed again, as the man in his dream had not come in person. Still, the emperor consulted with his ministers about accepting Islam. According to Sayrāmī, "Some of them agreed, while others did not. . . . They say that the khan secretly exalted the faith, without letting his ministers know" (khan wazīrlaridin maḥfī sharīfgha musharraf boldi, dedürlär).

Tang Wang furthermore established laws protecting Islam and Muslims, including limiting Muslims' tax obligations to those specified by the Shariah. The ancient rule of the emperor of China, Sayrāmī relates, is that his subjects should follow their own religion without interference.[15] In order to shelter these travelers far from home, Tang Wang Khan established a colony of Muslims in China by exchanging forty Chinese for some four hundred Samarqandis.[16] Sayrāmī, ever skeptical, argues that Samarqand was not a Muslim country in the seventh century, and so its king must have been a just nonbeliever, in the manner of the pre-Islamic Anushirvan. In any case, the resulting population of Hui claims a lineage stretching back to the time of the Prophet. That population resulted not only from the colony of Samarqandis, Sayrāmī relates, but from a festival that the emperor held at which the men among the new arrivals were permitted to choose whatever wives they wished. Since then, the Hui have never deviated from their religion, but have brought others into it as "(secret) Muslims" (*maḥfī musulmān*).[17] This fact accounts both for the numerousness of the Hui and, according to Sayrāmī, for their tendency to abuse their privileges under the law. With this story, Sayrāmī establishes the Hui as a relatively new group of people, and one that occupies an unstable position between Chinese and Islamic communities, just as the Hui appeared to do in late-Qing Xinjiang.

Over time, Tang Wang's descendants forgot their Islam. Nevertheless, they kept their ancestor's promise to ensure that Muslims would always be ruled by Shariah. Sayrāmī thus explains that the emperors of China entered into a covenant with their Muslim subjects, a special relationship between the ruler, the people, and God. They preserved this all the way through an unbroken line of descent from Tang Wang to the emperors of the Qing.[18] Anthony Smith defines such a "covenant" as an agreement between a usually monotheistic God and a kin community, according to which that community must carry out God's will in exchange for his protection.[19] In Sayrāmī's narrative, the fusion of such a covenant with a hierarchy within the community is not unlike what Smith sees in the Ethiopian case: a line of kingship is appointed by God to maintain the commandments revealed for the chosen community.

For Sayrāmī, however, the covenant is presented in order to explain its breaking. According to him, the imperial order fell in the Muslim Northwest, including Xinjiang, because of corruption among lower-level officials. Sayrāmī relates that Qing authorities sold offices that had previously been held hereditarily.[20] As Hamada Masami has argued elsewhere, this hereditary relationship with the Qing was a legitimate source of power, but its violation signaled a disruption of the natural order of justice.[21] Corrupt officials began to favor Chinese and permitted them to allow their pigs into Muslim sacred spaces. Others levied taxes that were beyond the scope of Islamic law. According to Sayrāmī, Muslims in East Turkestan wrote petitions to the emperor begging for him to restore justice and preserve the boundaries around their places of worship and the laws of their community. However, the same corrupt officials prevented those pleas from reaching Beijing, and so it was simply the duty of the Muslim subjects of the empire to establish justice themselves. The legend of the Muslim emperor explains that need as a historical consequence.

The source of Sayrāmī's legend is clearly the "Origins of the Hui" ("Huihui yuanlai"), a legend that emerged among the Sino-Muslims of China proper and appeared in print in the Ming.[22] It is generally thought of as a Chinese-language text, and the published narrative was closely tied to the identity struggles of Hui who were involved in both Confucian and Islamic scholarship. In the Ming version, the arrival of the ambassadors at the Tang court sparks a conversation demonstrating the ultimate compatibility of the two traditions, as well as the emperor's protection of Islam. An oral version of the same story circulated among Hui in Central Asia who had migrated from Xinjiang in 1877, and it includes several elements that are apparent in the Chaghatay manuscript accounts described here.[23] Like Sayrāmī's narrative, the Hui story explains how men from Central Asia settled in China along with the Prophet's emissaries and married Chinese women, thus giving rise to a people with roots in both worlds.

Both versions likewise identify certain sites as the resting places of the emissaries, which mark the historical arrival of Islam itself.[24] Per the logic of East Turkestani shrine pilgrimage as described by Rian Thum and Elif Dağyeli, the steps of the saint and their resting places have a chronotopic quality, in that they draw together the memory of origins, in this case the community's roots in the moment of Islamization, and the spatial dimensions of it, through the journey of the Islamizer and their transportation of Islam to the new land, as symbolized by the saint's body. For Hui readers, the chain of tombs marked the difficult journey from Central Asia into China, the Islamizers' sacrifice, and the persistent distance that separated Hui in China from Muslims to the west. To a Musulman, the journey *through* East Turkestan signaled something else entirely: the oases were themselves part of the emperor's journey, and the journey of the people of China, toward Islam.

The "Origins of the Hui" story circulated in Xinjiang in multiple forms, one of which is recorded by Qurbān ʿAlī Khālidī.[25] His correspondent Sayrāmī was also aware of this version but chose to present a different narrative. Khālidī's version is on some points identical to Sayrāmī's, but Tang Wang is visited in a dream by two figures: the first is a white-haired man clothed in a white turban and green trousers and carrying a staff. In the dream, this figure explains Islam in all its details to the khan. Tang Wang's ancestors, the figure explains, were mired in ignorance, but this ruler is just, and so has been found worthy of receiving Islam. He vanishes, leaves behind his staff and turban, as well as a copy of the Quran. After this first figure disappears, a second comes in through a back door and warns Tang Wang not to abandon the religion of his ancestors, for if he does, the common people will rise up and kill him, ending the royal line. When Tang Wang awakes, the staff, turban, and Quran remain, which his courtiers take as a sign that the former visitor was telling the truth.

Tang Wang promptly sends messengers to search for someone who can read the Quran, and they find such individuals in Samarqand. (According to Khālidī's analysis, Samarqand had been a Muslim state for some decades.) The king of Samarqand dispatches three scholars with three thousand men to go to China, where the scholars teach Tang Wang to read the Quran. Tang Wang promptly recites the Muslim declaration of faith, the shahada, the sound of which rings out across the lands. Next, he smashes the statues in the idol-temples and sparks a brief civil war in which Islam is victorious, resulting in a mass conversion of the Chinese people. In the aftermath, the Samarqandis settle in China, where they are protected by a special status. The scholars die, and their tombs become shrines. Finally, Khālidī relates how the country fell into war again as the Muslim emperors declined, and the government moved to North China (*Khiṭāy*), reflecting how the center of imperial power shifted to Beijing more or less permanently after the Mongol conquest. Nevertheless, the later rulers, too, were just and maintained the covenant between Tang Wang and the Muslims. Over time, however, tyranny grew until the day that the Muslim uprisings began in Gansu and Xinjiang.

It therefore appears that there was a story circulating in several versions among both Chinese- and Turkic-speaking Muslims to the effect that the emperor of China was secretly a Muslim and overtly a protector of the Sha-riah. Given the deprivations that the Xiang Army visited upon the Musul-mans in the late nineteenth century, as was described in the preceding chapters, it is worthwhile to ask why such a narrative would be popular. For Khālidī, this story is a curiosity, and as is his custom with regard to popular belief, he essentially dismisses it. He presents an impossible history—he knew, as we do, that no Tang emperor led a Muslim holy war. Moreover, Khālidī would have dismissed other, similar narratives: According to one such story, the transgressive dervish-poet Shāh Bābā Mashrab (1657–1711) brought the Zunghar khan to the faith, while another held that the Dalai Lama himself had accepted Islam.[26] The value of such stories lies in part in their demonstration of the power of Islam, the faith of the conquered, to transform the non-Muslim ruler. An East Turkestani variant on the Alexan-der romance (*Iskandarnāma*) presented a similar inversion, as Alexander the Great's legendary conquest of China is revealed to be his defeat at the hands of the charms of Chinese women.[27] Other satirical stories inverted tropes about the wealth and power of the distant emperor.

However, in Sayrāmī's *Tārīkh-i Ḥamīdī*, written by a scholar who took oral sources seriously, the story of the Muslim emperor is a crucial point of explanation about the history of East Turkestan and China. In his account, the emperor of China does not fully convert to Islam, but instead begins a dual conversion that remains unfinished. The shrines to the Prophet's ambassadors that dot the route from Central Asia to China proper mark the transportation of Islam directly into the heart of Chinese power, so that East Turkestan becomes central to the hidden history of China. This gesture is reminiscent of others from colonial contexts in which culturally hybrid authors wrote the narratives of core and periphery together.[28] Sayrāmī shows that the Muslim uprisings were not the end of Chinese power, or even the overthrowing of an unnatural relationship, but a hiatus in the enforce-ment of an ancient covenant of justice between a sovereign and his people.

The Politics of Japhetic Descent

Yet the genealogy of the emperor of China could run even deeper than the conversion of the Tang ruler to Islam. Following its thread backward in time brings us to the aftermath of the Flood and the peopling of the world by the children and grandchildren of Nūḥ (Noah). With Sayrāmī's presentation of this story, he participates in a tradition of accounting for the contemporary politics of empires and peoples by narrating them back into human origins. Specifically, Sayrāmī blames the profusion of languages in the world—and the inability of peoples to communicate with one another—on the interventions of tongchi between the grandsons of Nūḥ, leading to their primordial conflict. The distribution of and relationships between the children of Nūḥ's son Yāfith (Japheth) reflected ideas about the closeness or estrangement of the peoples of Eurasia.

The primary means of talking about the origins of peoples in East Turkestan was through the paradigm of Islamic sacred history, the broader collection of explanatory material and historical narratives that expand upon the Quran.[29] Stories from Syriac, Jewish, Byzantine, and other traditions traveled alongside the Quran and hadith. They came to be compiled separately and gained a life of their own, read both for entertainment and for enlightenment. Islam thus provided a new narrative system for the reframing and sacralization of stories of diverse origins within collections of tales about the pre-Islamic prophets and the early period of Islam. These "stories of the prophets" (Ar. qiṣaṣ al-anbiyāʾ) present the origins of the world's people through the chapter on Nūḥ and how his sons peopled the world in the aftermath of the Flood.

In most narratives, Nūḥ's first son, Sām (Shem), settled the Arab and Persian lands, and other places that a given author holds in high esteem; his cursed son, Ḥām (Ham), Africa, Hindustan, and countries that the author dislikes; and his third son, Yāfith, the "other" lands, usually those to the East of the known world. The main traditions of the stories of the prophets therefore posed a problem for a Musulman living under Qing rule, as they failed to provide a satisfying historical explanation for the present condition of East Turkestan. The main traditions did not describe the origins of the Chinese people—indeed, they hardly even acknowledged the humanity of the Turks, attributing their ancestry instead to the monstrous Jūj and Maʿjūj (Gog and Magog).[30] However, the Turkic-language stories by Nāṣir al-Dīn b. Burhān al-Dīn al-Rabghūzī (d. before 1310) attributed human ancestry to the Turks as descendants of Yāfith.[31] This attribution of Japhetic descent neatly captured the position of the Turkic peoples in the Islamic world as a rising power that demanded respect in the period after the Mongol conquest and yet separate from the Arabs and Persians who dominated the established cultural and political center. Nevertheless, the question of China, an unquestionably significant power in the eyes of a Musulman, remained.

The intervening centuries of post-Mongol historiography did not resolve the question satisfactorily either. While the works of history that are familiar to scholars, such as Rashīd al-Dīn Ḥamadānī's (1247–1318) *Compendium of Chronicles* (*Jamiʿ al-tawārīkh*), were also known in East Turkestan, their accounts of China were dry and sketchy.[32] Sayrāmī references Ḥamadānī's work but does not quote its discussion of China, which after all does not present the emperors in terms of primordial and continuous lineage. Some Muslim travelers' narratives describing China were copied in East Turkestan and yet do not appear to have been integrated into other works or the popular discourse.[33] Nor did those officials who had extensive contact with Chinese power appear to transmit their knowledge very far.[34] For that matter, before 1864, even Musulman officials who had been to Beijing for audiences seemed unclear on who exactly was the emperor or under which ruler Kashgar had been conquered.

The specific legend that eventually informed Sayrāmī's account of the origins of the world's peoples can be traced to the *Compendium of Histories and Stories* (*Mujmal al-tawārīkh wa ʾl-qiṣaṣ*), an anonymous Persian-language work dating to 1120.[35] This *Compendium* tells us that Nūḥ gave all of the lands east of the Amu Darya (Oxus River) in Central Asia to Yāfith. Yāfith's sons included not only Turk, the ancestor of the Turks, who was wise and cultured, but Chīn, the ancestor of the Chinese, whom the *Compendium* describes as intelligent and a skilled craftsman, and also Rūs, ancestor of the Russians, who is said to have been shameless and scheming. Soon after, Mongol rulers began a new royal tradition of legitimation through sacred history that drew significantly on such stories of descent.[36] Rashīd al-Dīn's *Compendium of Chronicles* was influential in its presentation of the origins of the peoples of the East in a way that was favorable to his Mongol Ilkhanid patrons and also suggests a natural alliance between them and Muslim Turks.[37] He makes the Mongols out to be two lateral branches of the Turkic family, descended from two uncles of Oghuz Khan. Yāfith is here the "father of the Turks," and not of monsters.

It is with the Timurid politics of genealogy that we begin to see the outlines of the Qing-era East Turkestani account of the origins of peoples in the legends that members of the dynasty propagated to legitimize their rule. Khwāndamīr (1475–ca. 1535) in his *Companion of Biographies* (*Ḥabīb al-siyar*, 1525) claims Rashīd al-Dīn as his source, but in most respects his account follows instead the *Mujmal*.[38] Yet the narrative elaborates on the *Mujmal* in significant ways: Turk is "extremely intelligent, manly, polite, and wise," the best of the sons of Yāfith, who abandons wood and mud-brick houses for tents made of animal skins and dispenses justice among his people. Rūs is mentioned as a mild-mannered brother, and Chīn again as a clever and artistically oriented father of a race of inventors and craftsmen.[39] However, war breaks out between these brothers: Ghuzz, father of "the worst of the Mongol tribes," the Oghuz, contests with Turk for control of the *yada* rainmaking stone. This stone, part of Central Asian rainmaking rituals, is given a special origin in sacred history, as Nūḥ requests the original stone from God, who has the archangel Jibrā'īl (Gabriel) carve the name of God upon it. Khwāndamīr comments, "And still to this day strife and enmity rage between their offspring." That is to say, the conflict that raged in Khwāndamīr's time between the Eastern Turkic Timurids and the Western Turkic Oghuz of the Ottoman Empire actually dated to the earliest days of the peopling of the Earth. In the legends of the origins of peoples that later circulated in East Turkestan, we will also see the use of sacred history to explain present conflict.

The Mughal emperor Akbar (r. 1556–1605) drew not only on his Timurid heritage for legitimacy, but on a further claim that he was descended from Yāfith, "the most just of Nūḥ's sons," by way of Turk.[40] The implication is that genealogy itself can confer rulership, or that justice is heritable, not unlike the assertion Sayrāmī later made with regard to the Muslim emperor. This account of sacred history is again drawn from the *Compendium of Histories and Stories* via Khwāndamīr's *Companion of Biographies*. Khivan ruler Abū 'l-Ghāzī Bahadur Khan's (1603–63) *Genealogy of the Turks* (*Shajarah-i Turk*), also a source for Sayrāmī, repeats the legend, but Abū 'l-Ghāzī writes his present geography into sacred history by emphasizing only regions proximate and important to him.[41] These narratives, as legends about the ancient past that explained people's origins, circulated in complex and often obscure ways, sometimes in manuscript and sometimes orally, and they interacted with popular retellings of the Persian *Book of Kings*. Rian Thum has argued in particular for the interpenetration of these peri-Quranic stories with the Persian *Book of Kings* (*Shāhnāma*) tradition, and in turn with local historical traditions in East Turkestan.[42] This process created the peculiar fusion of legend and sacred history—narratives derived from Persianate hero tales and Islamic scripture alike—with which Mullah Mūsa Sayrāmī was familiar.

The endpoint of this process—or perhaps its reemergence in the historical record—is what I have come to call "pseudo-Rabghūzī," an East Turkestani product of the fusion of "stories of the prophets" and the Timurid rewriting of sacred history.[43] Manuscripts of pseudo-Rabghūzī claim to be the work of Nāṣir al-Dīn Rabghūzī, the author of the Turkic-language stories of the prophets. While the general outlines of Rabghūzī are present, however, they are filled with material from a variety of sources, apparently including local folklore. Across the known manuscripts, dating from 1752 to the 1930s, the text of the chapter on Nūḥ varies mainly in terms of the enumeration of the sons of Yāfith, and in ways that reflect the shifting geopolitical circumstances in which the stories were copied. The earliest pseudo-Rabghūzī, copied near Kashgar in 1752 during the period of Zunghar domination, uses the framework of the *Compendium of Histories* to sketch divisions between Turkic-, Persian-, and Tibetan-speaking peoples of the region and yet draw the Zunghar Mongols into common ancestry with the peoples of Yarkand, Turpan, and China.[44] The narrative describes both a family tree and a geography that link together the Turco-Mongol peoples of Inner Asia then involved in the Qing-Zunghar War, rendered here a conflict between cousins much like that between the Eastern and Western Turks presented in the *Mujmal*. Later manuscripts' lists of people reflect the integration of the Khalkha Mongols into the Qing and the arrival of treacherous Europeans (*Farang*), but the close relationship between Turks and Chinese through Yāfith remains.[45]

The very first chapter of Sayrāmī's history is likewise taken up with a narrative of Nūḥ and his sons that draws on this tradition but makes key interventions in it.[46] In Sayrāmī's account, Chīn, the eldest son of Yāfith, settled the land of China first. Chīn is presented not only as the ancestor of all of the Chinese people, but as the direct ancestor of the current emperor of China. From there, each of Chīn's younger brothers dispersed across the East. Sayrāmī narrates the war of the *yada* stone and other conflicts between the brothers, who deny one another land or hunt one another's families, explaining, as Sayrāmī puts it, why certain peoples have been in conflict since time immemorial. That peaceful order, Sayrāmī writes, was disrupted by the divergence of languages, of which he numbers eighty-two.[47] In order for fathers, sons, and brothers to speak to one another, they now required the intervention of a tongchi. These interpreters, these Chinese-speaking Muslims who were known in their own time for using their boundary-crossing for their own advantage, and who were the agents of miscommunication and separation as much as of translation, therefore appear in Sayrāmī's account at the beginning of history. Tongchi were agents of the division of a familial relationship between peoples analogous to the division between families in Sayrāmī's present. In this account, a people is defined both by language and by descent, the former of which is presented as an artificial, divisive intervention into the natural, unifying force of kinship.

The sons of Turk in turn became the peoples of Inner Asia. While the lists differ slightly between manuscripts, the *Tārīkh-i Ḥamīdī* copied in 1911 maintains the usual list of the sons of Yāfith, including Chīn, Turk, and Rūs. The sons of Turk in turn are presented thus: Mongol, Tatar, Kyrgyz, Qipchaq, Uyghur, Manchu, Nayman, Cherkez, Daghestani, Torghut, Noghay, Barlas, Churas, Jalayir, and Qing.[48] This final member is Dāching, from Chinese *Da Qing* 大清, "Great Qing," and Sayrāmī clarifies that he means the Great Qing. Its inclusion reflects a narrative that Sayrāmī learned from Khālidī and that established the Manchus and the tribe of Dāching as the product of an alliance between Mongols and Tatars, who then conquered the land of Beijing.[49] Historically, the Qing was founded by the Aisin Gioro house, members of the Jürchen people, who proclaimed the new name "Manchu" in 1636, along with their new dynasty. The Qing rose to power through strategic coalitions between the Aisin Gioro and Mongol groups, so Sayrāmī and Khālidī are right to say that it was a multiethnic state founded on an alliance.[50] However, this story shows that the Qing had reunited two houses whom most histories characterized as being divided by ancient enmity, the Mongols and Tatars, and thereby mended a primordial schism between cousins.

The Great Qing, from this perspective, is an agent of the maintenance of peace between peoples through separateness. The tongchi, in contrast, create enmity by standing between those who are naturally meant to be united. Sayrāmī's account of the sons of Nūḥ therefore reflects the configuration of the Qing empire as a state made up of distinct groups all ruled through different idioms by a royal house,[51] while his explanation of the division that plagues the world reflects the conditions of the late-Qing civilizing project. Difference in this narrative is defined by language and a myth of common descent. At the heart of this imagination, the emperor of China, as a direct descendant of Chīn and heir to millennia of unbroken kingship, remains a mediating force of stability and source of justice. The stories of the prophets literature provided a means to imagine communities centered on both God and empire, and thus to critique the new Chinese regime as a corruption of relationships licensed by God.

The Indomitable Empire

The primordial ancestry of the emperor of China, his descent from Chīn b. Yāfith b. Nūḥ, provides Sayrāmī with an explanation for the resilience of Chinese power. From his perspective, the fall of Qing rule in East Turkestan represented a disruption in the order of the world that could only be explained by cosmic forces. Across the text, Sayrāmī shows that, while the emperor's ancestry made him a potential just ruler, the stability of Chinese rule depended on the sovereign's astrological fortunes, as well as his and other rulers' different abilities to defend the Shariah. In this sense, Sayrāmī's account places Chinese power into the framework of traditional Perso-Islamic history-writing.

On one hand, Sayrāmī's stories reflect the realities of interacting with the Qing, while on another, they depict the Qing sovereign as a just ruler in the mode of Perso-Islamic kingship in the post-Mongol era.[52] This "sacral model" emerged after the death of the last caliph in Baghdad in 1258, which profoundly disrupted the order of authority in the Islamic world. According to the sacral model, a ruler is himself appointed by God, who endows him with divine support and charisma. The king demonstrates and maintains this mandate of sovereignty (*dawlah*) through conquest and benevolent rule, combatting tyranny (*ẓulm*) while promoting justice (*'adālah*). In this vision of rule, the just king is a distant and disinterested arbiter, not unlike the idealized emperor in Beijing. He is not idle, nor does he intervene in society, save to promote the Shariah, God's will on Earth. These new ideas of kingship grew out of the experience of the Mongol conquests, which, like the events of mid-nineteenth-century Xinjiang, demanded historical explanation. Generally, this explanation entailed recasting Chinggisids as just rulers despite their slaughter of Muslims. Discourses of legitimation claimed, for example, that Chinggis was a "tool of God" and a means for the broad establishment of Islam.[53] Similarly, the Ilkhanid ruler Hülegü (r. 1256–65), known mainly as a destroyer of Islam and the very man who ordered the caliph's execution, came to be depicted not long after his death as a convert himself.[54] (Sayrāmī of course later disagreed with these assessments.) Soon, astrology, as the calculation of destiny from the stars under which one was born, was also used to support the idea of the Mongol conquests as events ordained by Heaven. This is to say that the adaptation of Mongol power to an Islamic paradigm took place very rapidly and was initiated mainly by the subjects of the new khans, rather than by the rulers themselves.

These elements of the political theory of post-Mongol Islamic Central Asia were expanded and refined under Amir Timur ("Tamerlane," 1336–1405) and his descendants in Central and South Asia.[55] Throughout that time, descent from the "world-conqueror" Chinggis Khan remained a necessary condition of political legitimacy, but mysticism and astrology came to play an increasingly important role in the histories of Turco-Mongol Muslim rulers. Timur, for example, was depicted as a mystical repetition of the previous world-conquerors Alexander the Great and Chinggis Khan. The rise and fall of states could thus be depicted as a matter of predestination, whether by the legitimacy or illegitimacy of descent, the justice or tyranny of the ruler, or the rise and fall of their star. Sayrāmī applies this Perso-Islamic framework of kingship to Chinese power in order to make the unfamiliar intelligible. The Qing could indeed produce justice, but only through the instruments of Chinese bureaucracy.

Sayrāmī, as discussed in chapter 1, attempted to unify the history of Islamic revelation with the ancient history of China in order to demonstrate the imperfection of Chinese rites (li). He contrasts this Sino-normative, Shariah-like system of rules derived from scripture with the formal written law of the Lifanyuan, where the latter typified pre-1864 Qing rule and was a reliable source of justice. An extended anecdote demonstrates that the old Qing emperors, when petitions from their Muslim subjects could reach them, assiduously investigated the misdeeds of corrupt officials and determined their punishments according to statutes (lü, from Chinese lü 律).[56] While the statutes of the Qing Code could be made commensurate with Shariah, the corrupted Chinese revelation reigning in the late Qing could not.

Similarly, Sayrāmī explains the rise and fall of each ruler in the nineteenth century in terms of justice (ʿadālah) and tyranny (ẓulm), two concepts that suffused Islamic political discourse in Central Asia and beyond. "Justice" meant protecting the Shariah, which was of course what the emperor had agreed to do when, according to Sayrāmī, he converted secretly to Islam. "Tyranny," or the violation of the Shariah, resulted from the disruption of ancestral covenants. Sayrāmī thus explains that the chaos of the Muslim uprisings was not isolated to the Northwest: rather, as of 1864, the Qing was plagued by enemies both internal and external, mired in civil war and defending against British invasion. Sayrāmī's reason for this shattering of the state is simply that the Tongzhi emperor (r. 1861–75) was ill starred—that is, born under an infelicitous alignment of celestial bodies.[57] According to Sayrāmī, Tongzhi's astrologers advised him that "the alignment of the spheres" dictated that China's ill fortune could not be lifted until Tongzhi himself died.

Meanwhile, on the other end of the empire, Yaʿqūb Beg's star rose. At the request of some of the combatants in Kashgar, the khan of Khoqand had sent Yaʿqūb Beg along with a khwaja from a famed lineage. The Kashgar faction hoped that a khwaja would possess the religious authority necessary to establish a legitimate government, while Khoqand sought to expand its power into the vacuum left by the Qing withdrawal. Instead, Yaʿqūb Beg seized power for himself.[58] To Sayrāmī, who was himself a partisan of the khwajas of Kucha, Yaʿqūb Beg's dishonorable usurpation was the first act of a tragedy. The energetic ruler established Islamic rule across East Turkestan, but he did so tyrannically, at the expense of other Muslims. Moreover, Mullah Mūsa tells us, he was prone to fits of wrath (ghażab) that undermined his ability to produce justice.

For Sayrāmī, the idea that the line of Chinese kings is extremely ancient, and that China is under God's special protection, helps to explain the downfall of Yaʿqūb Beg: Each of the great world-conquerors, Sayrāmī asserts in various places, tried and failed to conquer China.[59] The first was Alexander, who established a kind of temporary mastery over China, but was ultimately seduced by its women's charms.[60] The same was true of Chinggis Khan, who fought the ruler of China to a draw and instead expanded his realm eastward by marrying a Chinese princess. Such an assertion flies in the face of all of the world histories, local histories, and collections of strange stories known to have circulated in East Turkestan at the time, including Sayrāmī's source texts.[61] Lastly, Amir Timur, upon directing his armies toward China, was struck dead by God's will. This appears to be

Sayrāmī's own interpretation of Timur's death on the eve of his China campaign, but while it contradicts his sources, it speaks to the dangers of hubris. It reflects in turn on the reasons for Yaʿqūb Beg's own failure—and indeed, Sayrāmī calls Yaʿqūb Beg a "second Timur."[62] Khālidī and Sayrāmī both relate that Yaʿqūb Beg, by the time he received the caliph's recognition, seemed capable even of conquering China. This is not necessarily a flattering comparison, as Sayrāmī takes pains to relate Timur's cruelty and demonstrate that he was an enemy of Islam.[63]

As the optimism of the early Yaʿqūb Beg era gave way to the realization of his cruelty, the Tongzhi emperor made the fateful decision to fake his own death. Tongzhi publicly was interred in the Qing imperial tombs but secretly lived out his life elsewhere on the surface. Tongzhi's son (in reality cousin) Guangxu ascended the throne in his stead but was too young to rule. So, through what Sayrāmī calls a "bizarre ritual," Heaven, Earth, and the boy's mother all gifted him extra years of age. The astrologers found that young Guangxu's star was at its zenith, and so he ordered the reconquest of Xinjiang and the rest of China, bringing the time of chaos to an end. From this perspective, such justice was only possible because of the emperors' original protection of Islam. The brief period of tyranny could not be attributed to any action that Tongzhi had taken, but rather to a cosmic weakening of his ability to maintain the institutions that ensured justice. Nor was Guangxu's ability to restore the imperial order a matter of his ethnicity, but rather a combined function of his ancient descent, the covenant between the Tang emperor and his Muslim subjects, and the alignment of the stars.

In May 1877, Yaʿqūb Beg was in his palace in Kucha as the tide of war closed in upon him. Sayrāmī, for his part, attributed the cause of the holy warrior's death to the same wrath that had led him to massacre innocent Muslims. According to Sayrāmī, that rage increased until it could no longer be suppressed, and Yaʿqūb Beg turned his cruel hand to the fatal beating of a loyal retainer.[64] In his exhaustion afterward, he called for cold tea to refresh himself. Yaʿqūb Beg raised the cup to his lips and "did not drink the cold tea but drank the wine of death. He tumbled, fell to the floor, and stayed there." Sayrāmī thus lends Yaʿqūb Beg's life a tragic narrative by casting him as a force for justice and holy warrior whose wrath drove him to unjust actions, and therefore cost him the throne.

Qurbān ʿAlī Khālidī (1846–1913) provides a less mystical, but no less damning, explanation for the fall of Yaʿqūb Beg and restoration of Qing rule.[65] According to his account, Ya'qūb Beg lost the loyalty of the people through his own cruelty at the height of his victories against the khwajas of Kucha. Like Amir Timur before him, Ya'qūb Beg was thought to be capable of conquering China—but as with Amir Timur, who died on that eastward campaign, such hubris signaled his downfall. Instead, the advancing Xiang Army quickly gained the loyalty of the exhausted natives of Moghulistan by giving them supplies to farm and feed themselves. Ya'qūb Beg, in this account, realized that he could not oppose the Chinese without fighting his own people, and ultimately, "he set himself to ruin."[66]

Sayrāmī's assumption of the ancientness of China and its emperor's line of descent permitted him to explain the temporary hiatus in Qing rule. The logic of justice and tyranny in turn showed how a just non-Muslim emperor could defeat a tyrannical Muslim ruler. His recognition of two forms of law operating within the empire solved the mystery of the empire's transformation as the usurpation of the power of a just sultan-like emperor by lower-level agents spreading a corrupt revelation. Astrology fated one ruler or another, however, to success and failure beyond their earthly control. After all, Sayrāmī, quoting scripture, frequently reminds his readers that God grants the crown to whom He will and removes it from the heads of those He will. China must also obey these rules.

The Eternal Emperor and the End of the World

When taken together, this complex of ideas from Perso-Islamic tradition, refigured through the experience of Chinese rule, forms a powerful means to explain the vicissitudes of history. So much is clear from a continuation of the *Tārīkh-i Ḥamīdī* by Ghulām Muḥammad Khan of Yarkand (n.d.).[67] Ghulām Muḥammad began this chronicle around the time of Sayrāmī's death in 1917 and continued writing it through April 1927. He not only picks up where Sayrāmī leaves off but adopts and expands upon Sayrāmī's analysis of politics in order to account for the fall of Qing power in the Xinhai Revolution of 1911–12. He does so by arguing that the Qing fell because of the disruption of Muslim families in Xinjiang, and the end of the genuine imperial line.

The chronicle begins its story not in Ghulām Muḥammad's hometown of Yarkand, but in Beijing in 1911 with a succession crisis. The Xuantong emperor, he relates, had no children, and so the future of the royal line was in question. One corrupt minister sees in Xuantong's predicament an opportunity: he poisons the emperor, whose loving mother dies of grief, wailing upon the ground with her son in her arms. Both are interred in the Qing imperial tombs in a scene evoking Sayrāmī's depiction of the burial of Tongzhi. Meanwhile, the minister has conspired to place his own child upon the throne, and so end the ancient line of Chīn. Again, a "bizarre ritual" ensued, ensuring that the small child gained several years of age and reached the point of maturity necessary for him to become emperor. Actually, the events of this crisis as Ghulām Muḥammad presents them reflect not those of 1911, but instead the ascent of the Guangxu emperor's cousin Puyi to the throne in 1908, including the near-simultaneous deaths of Guangxu and of his famed aunt, the empress dowager Cixi (1835–1908). Guangxu at the time of his death was indeed childless, and it was his two-year-old cousin who was crowned the Xuantong emperor. Rumors abounded that Cixi poisoned her nephew rather than see him gain substantial power after her own death—and indeed, Cixi had aborted the Hundred Days' Reform that would have made Guangxu an emperor in fact as well as in name. Such intrigue made the goings-on at the court in Beijing an object of interest across the empire. Puyi was a toddler when he began his reign, but this is immaterial to the substance of Ghulām Muḥammad's story: that the end of the genuine royal line of China brought about a new era of chaos.

For reasons that Ghulām Muḥammad never makes clear, the corrupt adviser is obsessed with the destruction of the Muslim people and violation of the ancient covenant between the Muslim emperor and his subjects.[68] He, through his son the false emperor, commands that schools be built across Xinjiang. These schools force young boys to learn the Chinese language so that fathers and sons can only speak to each other through an interpreter—a tongchi. Ghulām refers of course to precisely the program of education that Zuo Zongtang and the Xiang Army undertook in the late Qing, but also to the role of tongchi in creating and maintaining enmities between the sons of Nūḥ. The reemergence of tongchi indicates the shattering of the imperial order embodied in the Qing and foreshadows the return to chaos, the reenactment of the divisions that threw the world into conflict.

In Ghulām Muḥammad's telling, God is unwilling to countenance such injustice, and so he shatters the Qing, which then falls into civil war. What follows is the collapse of hereditary empires across Asia:[69] the Russian Tsar is deposed by Bolsheviks, while Salafis gain power in the Hejaz and destroy pilgrimage sites in Mecca and Medina that other Muslims considered sacred. Ghulām Muḥammad attributes both actions to the rise of Christianity and European influence. Soon Jadidism, Islamic modernist reformism, undermines the caliph in the Ottoman realm, and then spreads in Afghanistan and Kashmir. Ghulām Muḥammad compares the breakdown, and in particular the assault on the holiest sites in Islam, to the Day of the Elephant, the event in the year of the Prophet's birth in which the ruler of Ethiopia besieged Mecca with his armies of elephants. Time appears to fold back on itself in this account, as the events of the period of revelation reappear just as the imperial and Islamic orders both break down. Ghulām Muḥammad is a traditionalist in this regard, as the repetition of events from the early days of Islam heralds the coming apocalypse.

Throughout this narrative, however, Ghulām Muḥammad maintains the emperor of China as a character in his account of history. Amid the chaos he sees in the Republic (*mīnggūy* < Chinese *minguo*) and the Warlord Era, he depicts the emperor as a just ruler trapped in his palace, unable to communicate with his subjects. Finally, he writes in 1926,

> There is no khan, but they have put a man named Yan [Huiqing] in his palace. . . . The highest official of each province and its general, they are not loyal to the khan but have become kings themselves. They take taxes from their lands and collect them in their treasury, and they appoint officials according to their own will. If the khan orders them to send soldiers, they do not send them. If he orders them to send money, they do not send it. They take matters into their own hands, and if there is a capital case, they do not inform the khan as they did before, but command as they will. Nor is Yan [Huiqing] a descendant of the khan. He cannot do anything.

According to this depiction, the crisis of the collapse of the Qing and its aftermath was fundamentally one of legitimacy. The Chinese president Yan Huiqing (in power July 1926–June 1927), Ghulām Muḥammad points out, is no royal. The khan has no power to command or mobilize—and indeed, Puyi was living out his days in the royal palace as a powerless figurehead. Ghulām Muḥammad realizes in 1926 those things that changed about Chinese rule in Xinjiang with the arrival of the Xiang Army in 1877: capital cases are not reported to Beijing, but judged locally, per the rule of "execution on the spot." No taxes reach the treasury, but they fall into officials' own hands. Indeed, it is as though it took fifty years for Sayrāmī and his continuator to come to terms with the end of the old regime—or, per our discussion of trauma in chapter 5, the usual amount of time for an event to slip from living memory into collective memory.

The end of the empire results from the end of justice and the violation of the covenant between the sovereign and the people, which is in turn the result of the end of the royal line of the Muslim emperor converted during the Prophet's embassy. The Chinese do not lose power because they are infidels, or gain it because of the infighting that followed Ya'qūb Beg's death—rather, the empire fails because cosmic forces determine that it will, because the royal line of just kings is corrupted, or because those factors lead it to violate a sacred covenant with its Muslim subjects. Its success, conversely, derives from the uninterrupted flow of imperial justice. Ghulām Muḥammad's history of the post-Qing world bears out Sayrāmī's combination of these explanatory mechanisms into a theory of kingship.

Being Chantou in Khaqanistan

Where Sayrāmī and those like him could be explicit and systematic about the reasons for the shattering of the sons of Yāfith into communities defined by language and descent, popular discourse could be more or less explicit or sophisticated. Yet the same basic questions about the nature of difference were being worked out in society, as shown over the past several chapters. These questions coalesced around the identification of Chantous, as opposed to Musulmans, and their relationship with Chinese power.

'Abdullah Poskāmī, an acerbic observer of East Turkestani life, wrote an uncharitable verse about those who sought associations with Chinese power and Chinese settler culture:[70]

> Some Chantous married and never professed their faith,
> Going about looking like Muslims, but not in their hearts.
> Mothers and fathers, elder brothers and teachers, masters and disciples
> separated

And went about madly in the grip of avarice, forgetting their "Oh, Master!"
   (Yā pīrim!)[71]
Conquered, they became successors to a Shariah-less order (ṭarīqat).[72]
I was shocked—they cannot grasp that it is commanded to do ablutions once
   one is married;[73]
"Muslim" (Musulmān) does not suit them—they are animals! . . .
In this world, there's no more waiting period between a bitch's divorce and
   remarriage . . .
With such women, and with their husbands, there is nothing licit;
Their belief in man-and-wife is just a show.
They get their way of being Muslim (Musulmānchiliq) from their way of being
   Chantou (Chantoluq).[74]

Plainly, Ṗoskamī objected to those Musulmans who violated what he
understood to be traditional marriage, the "bad women" whom his contemporaries made into pariahs. He was likewise critical of those who clam-
ored for office and submitted to the plan to "make the people into Beijing-
style mullahs" (khalāyiqni Beyjinchä mullā qildim).[75] The studying of Chinese
could be a great advantage to some, but a traditionalist Muslim scholar
such as Ṗoskamī derided it as a means to seek a fortune at the expense of
faith. Ordinary people became Chinese "mullahs," the clerics of a corrupted
revelation.

In Ṗoskamī's account, marriage and the family subsequently fell apart,
as though changes in schooling and sexual relations were part of the same
disruption of Islamic society—indeed, as we have seen over the course of
this book, they were the two chief elements of the civilizing project. A
"Chantou," in Sayrāmī's estimation, does not respect Islamic law, but
instead turns to the Chinese, whose law serves their purposes differently.[76]
Implicitly, association with the administration, wherein a Musulman would
regularly encounter the label chantou, affects their treatment of family
matters, pointing to the Xiang Army's interventions in the fundamental
unit of social organization and the locus of moral education. After all, as we
have seen in Turpan, a Muslim could challenge the Islamic order at the
yamen. For Ṗoskamī, illicit sexual relations are an affront to the boundedness and integrity of the Muslim, and specifically Musulman, community.
Finally, whereas normative Islamic practice in this period and place
included shrine visitation and participation in Sufi rituals, the Chantou

have ceased to engage with it. In short, Ṗoskamī says that Chantou are Musulmans who have forgotten how to be Muslims. Instead, when they pretend to practice Muslim-ness (*musulmānchiliq*), they in fact act according to behaviors learned in the pursuit of personal benefit through association with the Chinese, their Chantou-ness (*Chantoluq*).

Ṗoskamī's objections are reflected in an essay written from a very different perspective, as nationalist revolutionaries also drew on sacred history to reject the term *Chantou*. On October 30, 1933, as fighting in Kashgar continued between Turks, Kyrgyz, and Hui, an editorial appeared in the official paper of the Turkist revolutionaries, *Life of East Turkestan* (*Sharqī Turkistān Ḥayāti*). One writer, soon to be a founder of the East Turkestan Republic, wrote under the title "Are We Turks? Or *Chantous*?":[77]

> The whole world knows that the people of East Turkestan come from the revered and famous Greater Turk nation. There is no need to discuss this. Although this fact has become clearer and clearer, we have been given a named by the ignorant, bigoted Chinese people: Chantou. . . .
>
> Our country, our land, is Turk! Not Chantou! . . . How did it come to be that the nation of East Turkestan is not called by its own name, but Chantou? It is said that Chantou comes from the Chinese for "wrapping a turban around one's head," because the Chinese say *chan* to mean "wrapping," and *tou* means "head," so this means "people who wrap their heads."
>
> Regardless, we are the children of Turk, son of Yāfith! Unlike those who have taken on this name Chantou that an alien nation has called us, we cannot discard the true name that our fathers have passed down to us for a thousand thousand years!

The author, probably the editor Qutlugh Shawqī (1876–1937), also invokes the Turks' possible descent from Alexander the Great. His anger at the use of "Chantou" points not only to its pervasiveness in East Turkestan, but to its incompatibility with the Turkist vision of history. "Chantou" makes no claim to familial or historical origin—from the perspective of ideological Turkism, it is antinational, a misidentification of a group of people that denies them their heritage. In its place, Shawqī appropriates sacred history and the story of Japhetic descent to formulate a myth of common descent.

Ṗoskamī and Shawqī both reacted against the popular adoption of the term *Chantou* as a term of self-identification.[78] As much is clear from the interviews that Katanov conducted in Turpan and Qumul in the early 1890s, wherein his informants frequently use the term. However, their attitudes toward it confirm what Poskāmī suggested—that a Chantou is somehow a lesser form of Musulman, and that to call oneself a Chantou is to accept one's fallen state, as the word is used in the contexts of prostitution and venereal disease. Nevertheless, some used the term in a way that lent it power and historical specificity. As David Brophy has pointed out, the Qumul rebels whose efforts led to the East Turkestan Republic early on referred to themselves and the nation they represented as the "Chantou peoples," apparently pointing to all of the different groups whom the Chinese had so labeled.[79]

Indeed, as we have seen, widespread use of the term *Chantou* emerged from conflicts over history, property, and belonging that took place in the context of Chinese power. While Chantou was not a formal label, in that it had no legal meaning, nevertheless its semiformal use in documents and as a pervasive term in Chinese discourse lent it power. As is often the case in colonial contexts, such categories gain social reality, and sometimes larger-scale identities coalesce around them.[80] In this case, Musulman and Turkic nationalist elites both sought to combat the use of *Chantou* as a term of self-identification, as it indexed the oppression and assimilation that they sought to end. Sayrāmī and Khālidī would seem to agree, as they place the word *Chantou* into the mouths of ignorant or corrupt Chinese: "It is just a passing Chantou," said the father, before his sons died at the hands of an angry ghost.[81]

The definition of groupness with reference to the empire also implied a spatial relationship with the imperial center. Musulman writers frequently contrasted their own position as "locals" (*yärlik*) with the immigrant Chinese. In the late Qing, writers began to characterize the origin of Chinese people as "within Khaqan" (*khaqan ichidä*), suggesting that the term was synonymous not with the emperor (the *Khaqan-i Chīn*), but with the empire.[82] The first known appearance of this translation is actually in a Chaghatay translation published in the 1880s of a Chinese text (itself originally in English) on smallpox vaccination that the provincial government distributed.[83] It describes someone fleeing into China as going "into the interior of Khaqan." Similarly, some sources refer to the Chinese as "from Khaqan" (*khaqanī*), analogous to being "from Turkestan" (*Turkistānī*).[84] This conception of China transformed again into *Khaqanistān*—"Khaqan-land" or "Emperor of China-land," like Afghanistan, Hindustan, or even *Orusistān*, "Russia."[85]

We see Khaqanistan again, and without comment, in the schoolwork of children at the Swedish mission in Kashgar in the years 1924–28.[86] (See map 6.1.) These maps were produced bilingually in Chaghatay and Chinese by both Musulman and Chinese-speaking children, who also learned English at the school. In Chinese, the Republic is labeled "complete map of China" (Chinese *Zhongguo quantu*), and yet there is written above it in clear Arabo-Persian script "Khaqanistan." The map is a scrap, nestled between a hospital report and a recipe for almond buns—such is the state of the archive of Xinjiang's history in the early Republic. Nevertheless, we can look around the rest of the map to see how a child writing in Kashgar in the 1910s might have labeled his or her place in the Republic: Tibet is both (English) *Tībät* and (Mandarin) *Xizang*; Hong Kong is *Hūng Qūng* and *Xianggang*; Korea is *Kūryā* and *Chaoxian*; Mongolia *Mongholiyā* and *Menggu*; and Manchuria both *Mānchūryā* and *dong san sheng*, "the three (north)eastern provinces"; and so

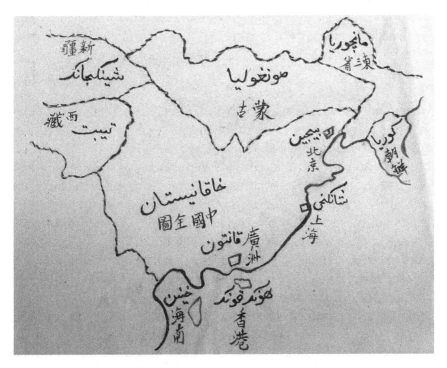

MAP 6.1 Map of China drawn by a schoolchild, 1924–28. Riksarkivet, Stockholm, SE/RA/730284/6/130, file of Rachel O. Wingate. Photographed by the author.

on. As such, it juxtaposes in nearly every case an Anglophone term, written in Chaghatay script, with a Chinese one. The exceptions are Khaqanistan and, of course, Xinjiang, the name of which is written solely in Chinese (*Xinjiang*) and in Chaghatay transliteration (*Shīngjāng*).

Yang Zengxin's nominally Republican regime had self-consciously maintained imperial institutions and values, meaning that the Xinhai revolution in Xinjiang as seen from the ground was not so much the end of the Qing as a reversal of late-Qing policies of assimilation.[87] However, the infrastructure of late-Qing rule remained in the form of yamens, Chinese officials, and the boundaries between administrative units. There was no more empire—instead, the Chinese people had declared a new era that, as far as most Musulmans knew, was called the *Mīnggūy*, the "Republic," and consisted mainly of chaos in China proper. The old imperial territory of Xinjiang was functionally independent yet claimed to be part of China. This coexistence of the imperial and the postimperial fostered a strange cultural effect, particularly as the region increasingly fell under Russian, and later Soviet, influence and the domination of Britain and its Indian subjects continued. The image of the emperor in Beijing persisted, as did the categories of difference that the empire had blindly helped to produce.

*   *   *

We conclude with a reversal: a Musulman might refer to themselves by Chinese terms, as a Chantou living in Shingjang, which was within an empire defined in Perso-Islamic and Turkic terms, as the khan in Beijing ruled Khaqanistan. Such a formulation was understandably anathema both to the gatekeepers of Islamic orthodoxy and to Turkic nationalists. And yet, it speaks to a set of symbols that for a time became powerful in the East Turkestani context. Those images of the emperor became relevant both because of the civilizing project and despite it: the just, secretly Muslim emperor stood not for something present, but for something that was believed to have been lost, an idealized imperial past of justice and protection for the Muslim community, a nostalgia for a state of affairs that to some degree had existed before 1864 but that in retrospect had accrued a host of other meanings. Sayrāmī's history of ancient peoples is not just an explanation of the alliances and enmities that he saw, or for the central place of Chinese power in the definition of Xinjiang's communities, but an expression of nostalgia.

His and Ghulām Muḥammad's work is strikingly similar in approach and content to the post-Qing reimagination of the past by the Mongolian Buddhist monk Zava Damdin Lubsangdamdin (1867–1937), who likewise used theology to construct a discourse of presence and absence in the wake of the empire's collapse.[88] Like the writers from East Turkestan, Zava Damdin tried to reclaim the diverse peoples of Inner Asia through a sacred textual tradition, framed the decline of the Qing in terms of cosmic time, and tied the history of Mongolia intimately to that of the lost empire. His "hybrid, counter-modern Buddhism" also incorporated popular stories and transmitted knowledge about the outside world, just as Sayrāmī and Ghulām Muḥammad brought specific elements of the local experience of imperial rule and vernacular texts to bear on their histories. Their specific depiction of the tongchi as the agents of disruption, for example, would have made little sense in other Islamic contexts. While Zava Damdin surely never knew Sayrāmī or Ghulām Muḥammad, their writings speak to the same concern with loss and recovery, the persistence and absence of the Qing. In this sense, all of them are more in harmony with someone like Liu Dapeng (1857–1942), the Shanxi Confucian who long outlived the Qing and spun his own antimodernist beliefs from the traditions he held dear.[89] Much as Ghulām Muḥammad, or for that matter ʿAbdullah Ṗoskāmī, criticized the Republic, so did Liu interpret omens and consult the *Book of Changes* to understand the chaos that emerged around him.

None of these writers, as Henrietta Harrison points out, is "typical"—no one is. To the contrary, their efforts to synthesize and explain the world around them are exceptional for how they reflect the encounter of Qing-era common sense with the post-Qing order. On the one hand, we have witnessed the ways in which Muslims explained their world in the absence of a clear effort on the part of the Qing to create an identity for them. At the same time, we see in the label "Chantou" the state's ability to interpellate subjects into particular positions and identities. Where there is a politics of representation, groupness emerges unbidden in complex and unpredictable ways as the dramas of everyday conflict play out in the theater of justice. Therefore, while we expect colonial categories to contain traces of the systems that made them, we should not suppose that Chantou-ness was the perfect impression of the Qing empire. To the contrary, it emerged through the institutions of local law and politics, combined with the Musulman imagination of China. While the "just emperor" that Ghulām Muḥammad imagined having been locked away in Beijing was a fiction, it was neverthe-less a powerful one, and one that simultaneously legitimized the system under which Muslims had once lived and explained the chaos of the present. Across the bureaucratic distance, the emperor became an abstract figure. This figure took up residence in the strategic information gap between government and society that left such room for representational play.

Conclusion

ON MARCH 10, 1909, in a house in Mayfair that no longer stands, George Macartney mounted the dais at the Central Asian Society.[1] Macartney (1867–1945) was arguably Britain's greatest living expert on East Turkestan, having been the British representative and later consul at Kashgar for some twenty years. The historical record, at least as the India Office recorded it, would appear to support that judgment, as Macartney indeed carried out his duties with a singular regard for the nuances of the society in which he lived, albeit for the benefit of the British Empire. The title of Macartney's lecture was "The Chinese as Rulers Over an Alien Race," and in it, he outlined the activities of Chinese officials, whom he regarded as follow imperials, and their colonial project in Xinjiang. It seemed to him that the old Qing regime had represented a more rapacious and exploitative government, while under the new one, Chinese sought to rule their "docile" subjects gently and by persuasion.

One could easily regard Macartney's argument as the historical smoking gun: an imperialist knew empire when he saw it. Macartney himself had been chosen for the assignment to Kashgar in part because of his own peculiar heritage: he was a relative of the Lord Macartney, who led the famous British embassy to the court of Qianlong in 1792. George Macartney's mother was also Chinese, and although he rarely spoke of her, other Westerners found in his face the implication of a special connection to and knowledge of China. George Macartney's history was bound up with empire.

Perhaps his self-awareness provided a certain insight into the complex society in which he was stationed, or perhaps it was his study of the Persian language—either way, the audience at the Central Asian Society expected Macartney to hold forth with authority on a land they considered singularly exotic and fascinating.

To the modern scholar of empire, however, Macartney's remarks appear simplistic, so much so that they betray his significant knowledge and experience. It must be remembered that Macartney spoke to an audience of relative neophytes, and ones whose minds were preoccupied with the so-called "Great Game," the competition between British and Russian interests in Central Asia. Macartney invoked the game, as his purpose was evidently to communicate the need to consider the Qing itself an empire with interests in Central Asia, and one engaged in comparable techniques, so that the captains of empire might regard it with the respect and perspicacity due to a worthy foe. Macartney was intimately familiar with the Xiang Army community's officials who were stationed in and around Kashgar, and often worked closely with them. Macartney highlighted how, before the uprisings, the Qing had been content to govern the Muslims from a distance, while after, the Xiang Army had taken advantage of "the natural docility of the governed race" to engage in a new kind of government. It was not for the "self-aggrandizement" that European imperialism displayed, he said, but rather for the defense of China and the benefit of its subjects under "the moral equipment of a superior order." In the terminology of today's historical analysis, Macartney was describing precisely the shift from a decentralized imperialism to a civilizing project predicated on the simultaneous inclusion and exclusion of a culturally distinct people.

Provincial Treasurer Wang Shu'nan, writing in the same year, would have agreed. In chapter 1, we saw how Wang compared Xinjiang to French Indochina and British India and found it wanting in comparison. Xinjiang, Wang argued, ought to abandon its civilizing project and pursue instead a brutal colonial autocracy driven by resource extraction. Had the Xinhai Revolution not broken out in 1911, this component of Wang's plan might have succeeded. The revolutionaries failed, but the damage to the provincial system was done: the Xiang Army, for all their venality and ideological inflexibility, had at least maintained a commitment to govern. Yuan's successor, Yang Zengxin, took Wang Shu'nan's vision to heart but largely lacked the means to implement it.

The Wang-Yuan-Yang revolution in Xinjiang's government throws into relief those things that were distinct about the reconstruction period. Hunanese rule was colonial in the sense of the drive to assimilate and to enact violence against an internal Other; it was not as obviously colonial in the provincial government's approach to resources. Was Xinjiang colonial? I argue that the situation that obtained under Xiang Army rule in Xinjiang was similar enough to colonialism to merit productive comparison. However, it is the vicissitudes of the colonial process that are revealing—its manifestations in the everyday, in the social and cultural—more than the often abortive and bungling plans that its rulers made.

In sum, reconstruction was intended to ameliorate differences between people and assimilate them to an elite norm. Instead, its institutions provided a new and powerful language with which to represent difference. The practical effects of reconstruction meanwhile fostered new tensions that mainly surrounded issues related to family: sex, marriage, parentage, death. Effectively policing vertical boundaries between groups, whether over membership in a family or ownership of a plot of land, often meant invoking the power of the yamen through the language of patrilineal descent and the patriarchal institutions, such as resettlement of "bad women," through which the civilizing project operated. The yamen in turn interpellated its Musulman subjects into the position of "Chantou" via interpreters whose identity and activity seemed so uncanny as to warrant the special pseudo-Chinese label "tongchi." In such a social and cultural context, as people sought to explain history and reclaim a heritage lost to war, they imagined a special connection between the Chinese center and the Muslim periphery located not in the recent turmoil but somewhere deep in history. These are phenomena we may expect from colonialism.

Colonialism

This study began with a seemingly simple question about Xinjiang's reconstruction era: How did Turkic Muslims write about Qing or Chinese rule? Reading Chaghatay sources closely and placing methodological priority on the lives of the dislocated and dispossessed revealed a set of central concerns that arose when Musulmans encountered and wrote about China and the Chinese: family, translation, justice, and the dead. Reading across the historical record, and placing manuscripts into dialogue with the bilingual archive, illuminated in turn institutions and ideologies that directly and intentionally shaped those concerns, as well as conflicts that surrounded the same tensions. New subjectivities formed in the encounter with a new legal system along with the transgression of intimate boundaries. The research was drawn ineluctably into a comparison with other colonial cases, as the literature on colonialism addresses the same problems of life under conditions of heteronomy.

Nevertheless, it is wise to be cautious of the comparative project, especially as there is a scholarly tendency to contrast the Qing empire with a sort of European hyperreal—an imagination, stripped of the details, of the history of Euro-American colonialism that forms a benchmark for comparison, as though Europe were the subject of all colonial histories.[2] An imagined British India, in particular, is frequently invoked in discussions around Qing coloniality, although colonial India itself was a vast region in which multiple projects of domination operated in different and overlapping spaces and different ways. As Jerome Cohen once put it, Western legal historians used to compare a Chinese reality with a Euro-American ideal, posed as a universal theory, and consequently found that China never stacked up to their imaginations of themselves.[3] The denigration of Chinese imperial law was insulting and unproductive, and we are right to pursue more finely grained comparative projects. At the same time, the fact that some aspect of the Qing does not look precisely like what we imagine France to have been, or that its expansion is not a perfect reflection of British Indian history, does not absolve that state and its myriad actors of the potential to engage in some kind of colonialism. To the contrary, imperialism and colonialism are transhistorical phenomena that manifest more intensely or diffusely in different contexts, and we should not be surprised when investigating any expansive state to find projects adjacent to colonialism in form, content, and results.[4] This "imminent logic of colonialism" is a useful object of analysis, while typology is simply a means to formulate questions about it. I have therefore endeavored to take up Emma Teng's call to use colonialism as a grounds for argument and exploration.[5]

As Macartney remarked in his speech in Mayfair, the mode of domination in late-Qing Xinjiang appeared surprisingly gentle, too gentle for Wang Shu'nan's taste. Indeed, an examination of capital cases from late-Qing Xinjiang reveals a surprisingly low incidence of violent conflict between people whom authorities identified as belonging to different categories: Chinese, Musulman, Hui, and so on. The Musulman-majority regions of southern Xinjiang in particular were calm and stable, pacified by strong local traditions of dispute resolution and the presence of established Islamic legal institutions. In contrast, the Chinese-majority North demonstrated the characteristics typical of a frontier society, with high levels of violence surrounding debt and sex, the latter owing to low numbers of marriageable Chinese women. Where Musulmans and Chinese came into conflict, it was usually over debt, a problem that the provincial government identified as Chinese merchants' taking advantage of impoverished Musulmans. Nevertheless, that same government advanced a narrative of the region's instability and the need for exceptional measures to control its Muslim population. That discourse justified the continual renewal of the exceptional violence of "execution on the spot," an instrument of politics and the performance of sovereignty that posed a Hunanese conservative moralism over and against imperial law. We can therefore identify two aspects of late-Qing Xinjiang that are commonly associated with colonial empire: external merchant networks that expanded into a new region alongside their military allies and exploited the region's people, and a narrative of chaos and civilization justifying a program of extrajudicial punishments. Indeed, there is something of British India in this story, certainly of the zone of exception in the frontier regions.

The complement of that program was the establishment of schools, which has long been noted in the scholarly literature. Tracing the intellectual lineage of the school program reveals that it was not simply a result of the compulsion of the dominant to acculturate the Other, but that its intellectual roots lie in a specific lineage of Confucian thought. The ramifications of the Xiang Army group's preoccupation with transforming the family truly become apparent only upon opening the archives of the "rites section" of the Turpan yamen, which document a torrent of cases revolving around resettlement, marriage, and sexual assault, represented through the euphemistic language of "chastity." Following the archive forward points to a shifting politics of belonging centered on the family that emerges not only from legal documents, but also in broader discourses of loss and recovery. As the Hunanese period continued, a politics of mixing came to the fore. These dimensions of domination and estrangement invite comparison with civilizing projects in places as diverse as Canada, with its residential schools that forcibly converted and acculturated indigenous people, and the Dutch East Indies, with its complicated politics of race and intimacy.

All of this points to clear parallels with colonialisms elsewhere, particularly of the settler and missionary varieties, but more importantly speaks to the kinds of tensions that emerge in heterogeneous societies in which one group is more closely affiliated with the dominant governing class but is also dominated by them. That is, Turpan was a place in which Chinese sojourners, settlers, and soldiers of varying identities and affiliations came to articulate a common cause and identity over and against the Muslim Other, despite their subordination to elite Chinese officials, who possessed their own common identity. Albert Memmi reminds us to attend not only to the colonialist, as we have done in the discussion of the Xiang Army elite, but to the colonial and the colonizer, outsiders of lower standing with complicated relationships to the colonial project.[6] A fuller account of Chinese settler life in this period remains to be written, as does a history of the merchant groups that extended into Xinjiang. Nevertheless, it is clear that life in Turpan was not defined solely by ethnic conflict, but that socioeconomic differences were at least as important a factor in shaping the tensions of everyday life, and that ethnoreligious identities and economic positions were interrelated. The sexual economy especially drew those intersections into stark relief.

Nevertheless, it is important to nuance the comparison between the East Turkestan case and colonialisms elsewhere. The specific manner in which the provincial system integrated non-Chinese peoples focused the action of government and resulting discourses of difference on matters of ritual and propriety, which is to say, family. The peculiar textual apparatus encouraged certain modes of self-presentation and self-narration that implied a subject with the emotional responses and speech that a magistrate expected from normative Chinese subjects. Musulmans therefore made themselves legible to Chinese power in strategic ways, and while the tongchis who enabled that process allowed them to gain power through representation, Musulmans also learned through that encounter the consequences of being a Chantou. Such self-fashioning as a Chinese-speaking subject is arguably the essence of the oft-touted power of Chinese culture to attract and transform the Other: where the institutions and ideology of the empire were useful, people learned to engage with them, and gradually became accustomed to them.

The provincial system's built-in preference for moral guidance over legal intervention and maintenance of a strategic information gap conditioned the channels through which intercultural contact took place. The more formalized integration of Muslim authorities into the government in some parts of the Russian empire included the creation of a muftiate through which to regulate the affairs of Muslim subjects.[7] The late-Qing Xinjiang government's formal rejection of those authorities, but covert engagement with them, shifted the site of contestation between legal systems and forms of authority to the local level, below the veil that separated a magistrate or prefect from the society he nominally governed. A closer parallel to the Xinjiang case may be Russian Central Asia following its abortive de-Islamicization.[8] There too the Russians ruled with a relatively light hand, in that their attempts to establish schools reached only the elite, while participation in the Hajj and Islamic institutions such as pious endowments, although perceived as potential sources of danger, "barely registered in the official consciousness." Instead, Islamic law and legal practitioners were integrated into the Russian administration in a manner not dissimilar to British India, in that officials attempted to codify Islamic law and local custom and to regulate the operation of the Islamic courts. It would be curious to see how Chinese administrators in Xinjiang would have attempted to codify Islamic law, or to reconcile the magistrate and the Muslim judge. Instead, the work of dispute settlement, and consequently of gradual acculturation, mainly took place below the veil and only emerged occasionally into the official consciousness.

Xinjiang in the late Qing was in these ways similar to any province in the late Qing, although its problems of communication and mediation across cultures made the distance between the magistrate and his subjects even more apparent. The Xiang Army's invocation of Hunan and the patterns of cultural difference they encountered in the South was therefore apt. This also suggests that a better point of comparison would be a provincial project in

Taiwan, which was similar to Xinjiang's in its origins but diverged in its path of development. Taiwan's provincehood was no foregone conclusion, as its population was mainly non-Chinese. The Qing had been content to maintain part of the island as a prefecture of Fujian and leave the rest to ad hoc arrangements that frequently integrated aboriginal custom into structures of authority and dispute resolution.[9] In that sense, Taiwan was like much of the southern frontier, including the Miao borderlands, where special "Miao statutes" emerged for dealing with interethnic disputes.[10] However, in 1871, a shipwreck of Japanese sailors on Taiwan's eastern coast led to a crisis of Qing sovereignty not unlike that which Zuo Zongtang invoked in his arguments for reconquering Xinjiang. That crisis resulted in 1874 in the appointment of Shen Baozhen (1820–79) as Taiwan's first governor. Shen, like Zuo Zongtang, developed a close relationship with Lin Zexu and attracted the attention of Zeng Guofan during the Taiping war. When Zuo received his assignment to the Northwest, he passed his Fuzhou Shipyard project on to Shen. Their efforts on either end of the empire ought to have run parallel to each other.

Nevertheless, Zuo and Shen belonged to different factions within *jingshi* and the Self-Strengthening Movement. Where Zuo was a traditionalist, Shen encouraged Western-style education and adopting Western technology on a much larger scale.[11] In Taiwan, Shen's schools did not teach the aborigines the Classics, but instead the Minnan variety of Chinese spoken in Fujian.[12] Their purpose was not to inculcate the Confucian tradition so much as to assimilate peripheral subjects to normative Chinese life. Where Zuo desired a direct relationship between the Musulmans and their magistrate, Shen established new formal intermediaries who would speak for aborigines. While both men and their followers encouraged agriculture, Shen was more concerned with the exploitation of Taiwan's land and resources. Shen's successor, Liu Mingchuan (1836–96), likewise bore a striking resemblance to Zuo's protégé, Liu Jintang, in that he began life in rural Anhui, fought against the Nian in the Xiang Army, and came to govern a new province in its first years.[13] Taiwan became a province in 1885, one year after Xinjiang, but neither Liu Jintang nor Liu Mingchuan believed that their charges were prepared and instead asked to delay provincehood. Despite those concerns, Taiwan's development proceeded in a manner that reflected the priorities of a modernizing state-building infrastructure to maximize the productivity of natural resources. This developmental trajectory continued after the Japanese annexation of the island in 1895.

Some of the reasons for Taiwan's and Xinjiang's divergence are obvious: Taiwan was not undergoing reconstruction after years of violence, nor was it a vast, arid region of questionable economic value to the empire. Rather, it was an island easily accessible to trade that had been exporting resources to the mainland for decades and had been under some form of colonization since the seventeenth century.[14] Shen's reforms, which included the construction of railroads and telegraph lines well before these were introduced in the Northwest, contributed to the island's earlier development of manufacturing. In many ways, he followed a longstanding tendency in Qing government whereby policy in Taiwan was driven mainly by fiscal needs, while cultural concerns remained secondary.[15] In Xinjiang, the balance was reversed, as subsidies supported the project of education and resettlement, and the economy remained underdeveloped. Zuo Zongtang's followers early on attempted to derail the civilizing project and creation of the province when it became clear that the schools were not producing the expected moral men. Nevertheless, the early focus on reconstruction, as they had practiced it in post-Taiping China proper and in the Muslim Northwest, shaped their governance from that point onward, while Shen and Chen's Taiwan more immediately pursued a gradualist policy of assimilation. Both regions saw the importation of the provincial system, but its effects differed.

Attending to the core-periphery dynamic also illuminates broader systemic change. Imperialism is a cycle of development, and as a diagnostic we may apply a simple typology of imperial legal regimes: the Qing in Xinjiang was once a confident, pluralistic state, but by its last decades, it displayed features of a weakened empire, in which sovereignty was usurped by the elite class of one of its subject peoples.[16] Lauren Benton characterized this as a shift from the decentralized early modern empire to "high colonialism." The Hunanese elite's homogenizing enterprise was a desperate attempt to save the imperial system in order to safeguard Confucian sociomoral principles, a law without law. However, they believed that doing so required the abrogation of the plural imperial system itself and homogenization of the people within its territory. This shift in strategies has long been acknowledged in the scholarly literature, including the special role that Hunanese leaders played in it and the implicit redefinition of the Qing as a Chinese, rather than Manchu-led, state.[17]

From the theoretical perspective offered by critical colonial legal studies, however, Xinjiang's designation as a persistent zone of exception points to a change not simply in thought and strategy, but in the very conception of sovereignty.[18] The imposition of an extralegal, law-like regime of moralism, accompanied by the unchecked power to punish, shifted the power over life and death from the hands of the emperor into those of Xiang Army leaders who had proclaimed themselves the guardians of the rites. This indicates the emergence of a separate zone of sovereignty within Qing territory but one governed by Chinese elites—specifically Hunanese adherents of *jingshi*—according to Sino-normative ideas of imperial subjecthood. Its legal regime prefigured that of the early Republic, when extrajudicial capital punishment was also instituted broadly early on, nominally as a means to control a chaotic society.[19] From this perspective, Xinjiang's exceptional position within the late Qing points to an inchoate Chinese imperial project, within which this borderland territory was a site for the performance of sovereignty through violence.

That project, however, was abortive. The intervening century has witnessed instead a layering of multiple forms of imperial and colonial projects. Wang Shu'nan's plan for Xinjiang was predicated on the subordination of Musulman subjects to Chinese in service of resource extraction and the dominated people's assimilation through punishment, and it was explicitly crafted in a European mode following the brutally violent colonialisms of the French and others, along with their theories of racial inequality. Yet it was short lived, as the state rarely possessed the capacity to intervene forcefully in society or the economy, at least not until the arrival of Soviet hegemony in 1934. Instead, the aftereffects of the civilizing project endured throughout the Yang Zengxin era as the state retreated further. The Soviet Union's imperialism of free nations followed, as well as the Republic of China's flailing attempts to co-opt Uyghur nationalists, and then the false promise of ethnic autonomy under the People's Republic of China. It was not until the late 1950s, however, that the practices and traces of the late Qing faded away at the local level. This local history in East Turkestan bears further investigation.

Identity and History

The other persistent concern of Xinjiang historiography, apart from empire, is identity. Scholars sometimes speak of "ethnogenesis," the creation of ethnicity, as though a collective identity were glass to be melted in a crucible or metal forged at a certain heat. Certainly, Qing empire and reconstruction shaped Musulman-ness or Chantou-ness as we have encountered them in this book. However, postcolonial historians have long sought to rescue history from the nation, to disentangle our analytical frames from the endless search for ethnonational categories, and search instead for the hidden genealogies of groupness that nationalism obscures.[20] After all, as Rogers Brubaker argues, religion, language, and ethnicity are all ways of acting and performing group belonging that seem natural and fixed.[21] Such identifications resemble one another and naturally tend to flow together and apart. Yet this book has shown how certain kinds of friction engender a hardening of boundaries, a fixing in place of history, territory, and belonging.

One key factor is historical trauma. Theorists have pointed to the importance of collective struggle in the formation of national consciousness, which seems almost self-evident. The evidence presented in this book reminds us that we ought to think more about the ways in which the losses incurred in that struggle gain meaning through memory and the repetition of the past. Many metaphors are available to explain suffering, but the one that dominated in Xinjiang was estrangement, alienation from family and the familiar. The violence of the uprisings, expressed in Chaghatay as "tribulation" or "shattering," marked a break in autobiographical time as well as collective experience, not unlike the "Military Disaster" and how it punctuated the mid-nineteenth century for Chinese people. Perhaps for the articulation of new collective subjectivities, it is necessary for some event to produce this sense of loss, to demand reason and agency for personal suffering, and for this sense in turn to transcend the individual through the language of trauma. In Xinjiang, we see the ways in which trauma played out not just in commemoration or ritual, but in the everyday representation of self and Other, as loss creates a powerful grounds for making legitimate claims and pursuing them on the basis of history and the group. Yet in conflict and loss there was hope of resolution and recovery. Where a modern nationalist sees optimism in the wide horizons of the future,[22] so did someone like Sayrāmī see the potential for justice in his imperial present, the sacred past, and the person of the emperor; the petitioner, in the magistrate and the provincial system; and Wang Zhensheng, in the person of the Xiang Army. Discourses of nationalism have obscured those kinds of historical imagination that emerged in this period, much as they have in other colonial and postcolonial contexts.[23]

Economic inequality also played a central role in creating difference. The arrival of the Xiang Army evidently threw the regional economy into even more turmoil than it had seen for the previous thirteen years, particularly because it led to another realignment of access to economic and political resources. The new elite included those who could use the Chinese language effectively to extract desired results from the yamen. Ordinary Musulmans, meanwhile, were often excluded from the new economy as well as displaced, or simply lacked the wealth necessary to afford basic necessities. From economic inequality arose a new sexual economy in which Musulman women became objects of exchange, Chinese men exchanged them, and bilingual Hui acted as brokers. The reinscription of these positions granted them a social reality enforced by new patterns of exchange as well as a strong sense of resentment. Musulman elites learned to collaborate with provincial authorities to effect boundary-crossing women's spatial exclusion and that of their mixed-heritage children. They created a discourse that characterized "mixing" as a problem of boundary violation. While human trafficking, wife sale, and similar phenomena were common in China proper, it was linguistic, religious, and cultural differences in East Turkestan that fostered the emergence of a sense of inherent difference.

Much the same was true of the tongchi. The idea of translation itself, or of *tong*, indicates getting something across from one space to another. Tongchis not only refigured text to fit Chinese and Islamic forms and languages but embodied the paradox of the mediator, as they presented themselves as normative subjects even while making their livings in fluidity. It is appropriate that Sayrāmī and Ghulām Muḥammad located them in moments of historical disruption, but also that tongchis were a conduit for the movement of ideas from the yamen into the popular discourse. One was "Chantou." Achille Mbembe argues in *Critique of Black Reason* that, if one were to trace the genealogy of the term *Black*, one would delineate the history of a global mode of domination through its quintessential subject.[24] Similarly, albeit on a rather smaller scale, the term *Chantou* points to a certain kind of subject in the system of Chinese dominance of Turkic Muslim people. Chantou-ness emerged by the 1890s as a discourse of the internal Other through which Musulmans could identify and expunge people who seemed to subvert an increasingly essentialized Turkic-speaking Muslim identity. A Chantou was notionally a Turkic-speaking Muslim who nevertheless engaged with Chinese settler culture and Chinese government, and thus deviated from Islamic religious practice. More concretely, a Chantou could be an object of the new sexual economy, or someone who debased themselves in search of a job at the yamen. Later, as Chantou-ness became naturalized, and the label drifted into the realm of ethnic identity, it was caught up in the backlash against the Chinese dominance that the term itself symbolized. It is no wonder that "Chantou" today is a vile slur.

Therefore, this book is not an argument that the Uyghur nation sprang from the Qing. Other scholars have offered finer accounts of the emergence of Uyghur nationalism in the 1930s, and still others identify structures of association that prefigured it.[25] Rather, this book is concerned with such structures of association and their manifestations. Uyghur nationalism's rise was bound up in the politics of nationality in Soviet Central Asia and the policies that a Soviet satellite implemented to institutionalize ethnicity in Xinjiang from 1934 onward. Chantou-ness, instead, was an artifact of the late-Qing state's encounter with Musulman society and culture in all its richness and complexity. Both encounters led to an essentialization of groupness and a hardening of boundaries between peoples, but on very different terms. Moreover, while the Stalinist state could impose a system of nationality through its exceptional capacity to build the infrastructure of education, the Qing state with its strategic information gap left space for the imagination of the community. To oversimplify, Chantou-ness was articulated primarily on the local level, whereas Uyghurness was transnational. Chantou-ness merits exploration as research on Xinjiang's history turns from the Great Game to the little games of the everyday.

Epilogue

In the spring of 2017, messages began to trickle out of Xinjiang that hinted at a renewed effort not only at control, but at reeducation. Individuals who had lived abroad, scholars who studied Islam, people who prayed at home, and countless others were intimidated, watched, and "invited to tea" with the police. Rumors circulated that others were not so lucky, that Uyghur men who had lived in Muslim countries were being disappeared upon their return to China. Soon the rumors proved horrifyingly true.[26] An estimated one million Uyghurs, Kazakhs, and others disappeared into indefinite detention, some into prisons on vague charges. This was and remains true even of high-profile scholars, artists, and Party members, now accused of being "two-faced" (*liangmian*), as if a lifetime of service were insufficient to prove one's loyalty.[27] That is to say nothing of countless others of less-privileged status whose stories do not enjoy international attention. A further one and a half million families in Xinjiang host "guests," government workers who monitor their behaviors and speech. The guests especially target children as vectors for introducing Sino-normative behaviors and Party loyalty.

The state demands loyalty not only of behavior, but of the heart, and in this sense the present program of detention and transformation may resemble that of the late Qing. Where China once denied the existence of a network of reeducation camps, under international pressure it not only acknowledged their existence, but insisted that indefinite detention and mandatory schooling were positive for Uyghurs. Like Wang Shu'nan, Xinjiang claims to be training Uyghurs, Kazakhs, and others in "job skills." Yet the outward goal of the education program is to cause non-Han Chinese to speak and sing in Chinese, and to engage in ritual and bodily performances that are imagined to be quintessentially Chinese. Before the rise of the reeducation camps, contests across Uyghur areas in Southern Xinjiang obliged members of work units to choreograph and perform dances to the "Little Apple" song, a sort of Chinese Macarena, with the claim that this insipid pop number was a "patriotic song" (*aiguo ge*).[28] Being patriotic, being a proper citizen of the modern state, therefore meant engaging with the popular culture of central China—Sino-normativity. Today, alcohol in Xinjiang is likewise a patriotic beverage, and pork the meat of a "political animal" (*siyasiy haywan*), while refusing to partake in both is considered a sign of extremism.[29] There are echoes of Musulmans going to the temple and crossing over into Chinese life. A long list of "Islamic" names is banned. Meanwhile, skirts must be short, cheeks clean-shaven, Chinese opera appreciated and sung.

It is striking that this effort is meant to turn Uyghurs into what one official characterized as "normal people."[30] Once again, a China-based power seeks to expunge the Muslimness from its Muslim subjects, demanding instead not simply a general appreciation of Chinese culture, but the adoption of manners, tastes, and behaviors that cause a person to resemble an imaginary ideal citizen. That is, there are plenty of Han Chinese who do not drink, who grow facial hair, or who despise the "Little Apple" song, but Uyghurs no longer have those freedoms.

In other respects, the reeducation camps present a stark contrast to the Confucian schools of over a century ago. Where the Xiang Army hoped to preserve the integrity of families, and to seed home life with Confucian values, today's camps separate families. Where transformation-by-teaching in the Qing appears to have been a drain on the resources of an already cash-strapped province, prison construction and prison labor in today's Xinjiang are sources of profit. The disciplinary tools of the digital age serve to realize these modern dreams in ways that were probably unimaginable to the Xiang Army. Modern Xinjiang is entirely the opposite, as the state collects biometric and geospatial data on millions of minority citizens. From a certain perspective, this information-gathering apparatus is more what one would expect from the documentary compulsions of Euro-American colonialism, and perhaps it shows how the complex genealogy of modern government in Xinjiang owes a great deal to the regimes of surveillance and discipline that have emerged in the "liberal" West.[31]

I emphasize these differences in order to counter a tendency to essentialize about the nature of Chinese control in East Turkestan and its historical antecedents. The reader may easily walk away from this book mistakenly believing that the reeducation of Musulmans in the late Qing was a direct ancestor of today's reeducation program. For all of the claims that China is somehow exempt from the laws of history, it is clear that the modes of domination that China-based states have pursued in Xinjiang have changed with time and will continue to do so. Attending to these changes is important to addressing the realities of violence, not as stereotype, but as lived experience.

I never set out to write a "relevant" book. The history of Xinjiang as region, as the story of "great men," and as the schematic transformation of relations between groups was and remains a chief site of contestation between the Party-state and Uyghur nationalists, and I felt that radically reorienting my methodological priorities would help me avoid politicizing the work, or at least open up new avenues of inquiry. So, ever contrarian, I set out to write a history that began with the sources no one thought were relevant: an oral account about venereal diseases; a scathing poem about tongchis; telegraphic reports of capital punishment; mundane fights over cows. All of these sources, I felt, spoke to the points of connection and negotiation more than the discourse of intractable historical conflict. They addressed the worldviews and experiences of ordinary people who were not, at least in the accounts they left behind, overtly engaged with questions of national liberation. There was, it seemed, a third party to the narrative struggles between the Party-state and Uyghur nationalists: "the people," on whose behalf everyone claimed to speak. I set out to let those sources speak for themselves, without a predetermined theoretical framework, and to let their concerns guide the research. The result was nevertheless a story about colonial discipline, of the terrible things that people do to one another, the consequences of those actions, and how they tend to follow certain patterns. I hope the book honors the people of the past and their stories. I hope that it honors my colleagues, now silenced, who encouraged me to pursue this history from below in the hopes of depoliticizing the scholarly discourse around their homeland. Yet it seems we cannot escape these terrible machines.

Notes

A Note on Conventions

1. H. S. Brunnert and V. V. Hagelstrom, *Present Day Political Organization of China*, trans. A. Beltchenko and E. E. Moran (Shanghai: Kelly and Walsh, 1912).

Introduction

1. A myth of common descent is a textbook characteristic of ethnicity. John Hutchinson and Anthony D. Smith, eds., *Ethnicity* (Oxford: Oxford University Press, 1996), 7. "Imagined community" has likewise become a theoretical commonplace in studies of ethnicity and nationalism. Critically, let us recall that, in Benedict Anderson's formulation, it does not refer solely or strictly to the modern nation. Anderson points the reader toward various ways of imagining a community greater than one's face-to-face community, each of which is dependent on the conditions of cultural production in a given time and place. Anderson, *Imagined Communities: Reflections on the Origin and Spread of Nationalism* (London: Verso, 2006). This book is also concerned to a degree with imagined communities, but not necessarily with the origins of the modern nation.
2. This brief historical overview is based mainly on David Brophy, *Uyghur Nation: Reform and Revolution on the Russia-China Frontier* (Cambridge, MA: Harvard University Press, 2016), 26–39, 44–52; Nicola Di Cosmo, "The Qing and Inner Asia: 1636–1800," in *The Cambridge History of Inner Asia*, ed. Nicola Di Cosmo, Allen J. Frank, and Peter B. Golden (Cambridge: Cambridge University Press, 2009), 333–62; Hodong Kim, *Holy War in China: The Muslim Rebellion and State in Chinese Central Asia, 1864-1878* (Stanford: Stanford University Press, 2004), 1–36; James Millward, *Eurasian Crossroads: A History of Xinjiang* (New York: Columbia University Press, 2007), 1–77; and James Millward, "Eastern Central Asia (Xinjiang), 1300-1800," in *The Cambridge History of Inner Asia*, ed. Nicola Di Cosmo, Allen J. Frank, and Peter B. Golden (Cambridge: Cambridge University Press, 2009), 260–76. I encourage the reader to

consult these works for more detailed introductions, as limitations of space demand that I exclude certain events and phenomena.

3. The Qing was founded in 1636 but did not capture Beijing until 1644. The latter event provides its traditional founding date in Chinese history.

4. The Xiang Army (*Xiang jun*, sometimes "Hunan Army") is generally thought of as the army led by Zeng Guofan. The army that remained under Zuo Zongtang after Zeng's departure in 1864 was called the "Chu Army" (*Chu jun*). However, throughout the Northwestern campaigns and beyond, Zuo's Chu Army was the nucleus of a larger fighting force, the members of which habitually and continuously referred to it as the "Xiang Army." Later writings also consider the Zuo-era campaigns to be part of the Xiang Army's history.

5. Sukanya Banerjee, *Becoming Imperial Citizens: Indians in the Late-Victorian Empire* (Durham, NC: Duke University Press, 2010), 1–3; Partha Chatterjee, *The Nation and Its Fragments: Colonial and Postcolonial Histories* (Princeton: Princeton University Press, 1993), 5–6, 173; Prasenjit Duara, *Rescuing History from the Nation: Questioning Narratives of Modern China* (Chicago: University of Chicago Press, 2005), 10.

6. Gardner Bovingdon, *The Uyghurs: Strangers in Their Own Land* (New York: Columbia University Press, 2010), 42–79.

7. Brophy, *Uyghur Nation*; Laura Newby, "'Us and Them' in Eighteenth and Nineteenth Century Xinjiang," in *Situating the Uyghurs Between China and Central Asia*, ed. Ildikó Bellér-Hann, Cristina Cesaro, Rachel Harris, and Joanne Smith Finley (Aldershot, UK: Ashgate, 2007), 15–30; Rian Thum, *The Sacred Routes of Uyghur History* (Cambridge, MA: Harvard University Press, 2014).

8. See for example the essay "Insān wa ʿirfān" in *Sharqī Turkistān ḥayāti* 9 (October 16, 1933). Romantic nationalism inflected with Chinese Communist developmentalism was a dominant mode of history-writing among Uyghur elites in East Turkestan until recently and persists in the diaspora today.

9. For critiques of official histories with references to further literature, see Gardner Bovingdon, "The History of the History of Xinjiang," *Twentieth-Century China* 26, no. 2 (April 2001): 95–139; Alessandro Rippa, "Re-Writing Mythology in Xinjiang: The Case of the Queen Mother of the West, King Mu and the Kunlun," *China Journal* 71 (January 2014): 43–64.

10. Brophy, *Uyghur Nation*, 72–74; Justin Jacobs, *Xinjiang and the Modern Chinese State* (Seattle: University of Washington Press, 2016), 13; Millward, *Eurasian Crossroads*, 124–25. Cf. Thum, *Sacred Routes*, 158–60.

11. The exception is Nailene Josephine Chou's dissertation ("Frontier Studies and Changing Frontier Administration in Late Ch'ing China: The Case of Sinkiang, 1759–1911" [PhD diss., University of Washington, 1976]), which, while a classic, is arguably due for an update. Kataoka Kazutada's work on Qing Xinjiang was of course a constant point of reference for this book, and much of what Kataoka states is repeated here for the benefit of an English-speaking audience (Kataoka Kazutada, *Shinchō Shinkyō tōji kenkyū* [Tōkyō: Yūzankaku, 1990]). However, Kataoka's work was limited by the availability of sources, which were entirely in Chinese, and, with due respect, a sometimes-superficial treatment of them.

12. Jacobs, *Xinjiang and the Modern Chinese State*; Judd Kinzley, *Natural Resources and the New Frontier: Constructing Modern China's Borderlands* (Chicago: University of Chicago Press, 2018).

13. Rogers Brubaker, *Ethnicity Without Groups* (Cambridge, MA: Harvard University Press, 2004), 41–44.

14. I follow Ann Stoler in reading the archive as a site of the inscription of power relations, but also of complex representational play. Ann Stoler, *Along the Archival Grain:*

Epistemic Anxieties and Colonial Common Sense (Princeton: Princeton University Press, 2009).

15. Several scholars have advanced the argument that the Qing was "colonial" on the basis of its use of indirect rule for managing a multiethnic empire. I would argue that heteronomy and legal pluralism are not sufficient conditions of imperialism or colonialism in themselves. Michael Adas, "Imperialism and Colonialism in Comparative Perspective," *International History Review* 20, no. 2 (June 1998): 371–88; Nicola Di Cosmo, "Qing Colonial Administration in Inner Asia," *International History Review* 20, no. 2 (June 1998): 287–309; Ruth W. Dunnell and James A. Millward. "Introduction," in *New Qing Imperial History: The Making of Inner Asian Empire at Qing Chengde*, ed. James A. Millward et al. (London: RoutledgeCurzon, 2004), 1–12, 3; Peter C. Perdue, "Comparing Empires: Manchu Colonialism," *International History Review* 20, no. 2 (June 1998): 255–62.

16. My heuristic typology of imperialism and colonialism is influenced by Lauren Benton's discussion of legal pluralism in imperial contexts (*Law and Colonial Cultures: Legal Regimes in World History, 1400-1900* [Cambridge: Cambridge University Press, 2002], 11–12, 29), Jürgen Osterhammel's differentiation of colonialisms, which included modes of domination that are primarily cultural rather than economic (*Colonialism: A Theoretical Overview* [Princeton: Markus Wiener, 2005], 4); and Charles Maier's emphasis on securing the collaboration of preexisting local elites as a central technique of imperialism (*Among Empires: American Ascendancy and Its Predecessors* [Cambridge, MA: Harvard University Press, 2006], 7).

17. Alice Conklin, *A Mission to Civilize: The Republican Idea of Empire in France and West Africa, 1895-1930* (Stanford: Stanford University Press, 1997), 1; Jürgen Osterhammel, *The Transformation of the World: A Global History of the Nineteenth Century* (Princeton: Princeton University Press, 2014), 327, 827.

18. Emma Jinhua Teng, *Taiwan's Imagined Geography: Chinese Colonial Travel Writing and Pictures, 1683-1895* (Cambridge, MA: Harvard University Asia Center, 2004), 8–12, 256–58.

19. Brubaker, *Ethnicity Without Groups*, 28–63; Brubaker, *Grounds for Difference* (Cambridge, MA: Harvard University Press, 2015), 87–89; Frederick Cooper, *Colonialism in Question: Theory, Knowledge, History* (Berkeley: University of California Press, 2005), 59–65; Ann Stoler, *Race and the Education of Desire: Foucault's History of Sexuality and the Colonial Order of Things* (Durham, NC: Duke University Press, 1995), 7–13; Stoler, "Rethinking Colonial Categories: European Communities and the Boundaries of Rule," *Comparative Studies in History and Society* 31, no. 1 (January 1989): 143–50.

20. Similar case studies of sociocultural change in borderland areas under the provincial system within Qing China tend to be located in the South, such as Mark Allee, *Law and Local Society in Late Imperial China: Northern Taiwan in the Nineteenth Century* (Stanford: Stanford University Press, 1994); David G. Atwill, *The Chinese Sultanate: Islam, Ethnicity, and the Panthay Rebellion in Southwest China, 1856-1873* (Stanford: Stanford University Press, 2005); Jodi Weinstein, *Empire and Identity in Guizhou: Local Resistance to Qing Expansion* (Seattle: University of Washington Press, 2013).

21. For an early overview of the field, see Joanna Waley-Cohen, "The New Qing History," *Radical History Review* 88 (Winter 2004): 193–206. For a landmark work on Qing empire and ethnic identity, see Mark C. Elliott, *The Manchu Way: The Eight Banners and Ethnic Identity in Late Imperial China* (Stanford: Stanford University Press, 2001). Johan Elverskog (*Our Great Qing: The Mongols, Buddhism and the State in Late Imperial China* [Honolulu: University of Hawai'i Press, 2006]) provides a nuanced approach to the Manchu-Mongol relationship, while a similar move is

made in the Tibetan case in Max Oidtmann, *Forging the Golden Urn: The Qing Empire and the Politics of Reincarnation in Tibet* (New York: Columbia University Press, 2018). For the multiplicity of Qing sovereignty, see Pamela K. Crossley, *A Translucent Mirror: History and Identity in Qing Imperial Ideology* (Berkeley: University of California Press, 1999), 11–12.

On Islam and Qing sovereignty: Joseph Fletcher, "The Heyday of the Ch'ing Order in Mongolia, Sinkiang, and Tibet," in *The Cambridge History of China*, vol. 10, *Late Ch'ing, 1800–1911*, pt. 1, edited by John K. Fairbank (Cambridge: Cambridge University Press, 1978), 351–408, 407; Evelyn S. Rawski, *The Last Emperors: A Social History of Qing Imperial Institutions* (Berkeley: University of California Press, 1998), 199; Rian Thum, "China in Islam: Turki Views from the Nineteenth and Twentieth Centuries," *Cross-Currents: East Asian History and Culture Review* 3, no. 2 (November 2014): 134.

22. *Qingdai Xinjiang dang'an xuanji*, 91 vols. (Guilin: Guangxi Shifan Daxue Chubanshe, 2012). (Henceforth *QXDX*. In order to conserve space, I will specify documents by volume and page.) These documents are held in the Xinjiang Regional Archives in Ürümchi and are still organized according to the "section" (*ke*) to which they belonged in the local Turpan yamen, each section reflecting one of the six ministries of the Ming and Qing: "appointments" (*li*), which deals with officials and any disputes involving them; "revenue" (*hu*), recording taxes and land disputes; "rites" (*li*), including issues related to family, marriage, ritual, and education; "war" (*bing*), for the mobilization and accounting of the instruments of state violence; "punishments" (*xing*), the largest section, which we may think of as encompassing most violent and nonviolent disputes and the work of criminal investigations; and "works" (*gong*), for construction projects. Within each section, the documents are organized roughly by date, so that there are no clear "cases." Sometimes a single case will be documented across multiple sections, since a dispute over inheritance, for example, might involve personnel from both the revenue and the rites sections. This collection includes an estimated fifty thousand or more documents. While they have certainly been censored to some degree, there is no unambiguous evidence of tampering, and the documents include content that would be considered "sensitive" or unflattering to the Party-state. Many documents have been mislabeled by the compilers, and some unnoticed, particular the roughly 10 percent of the documents that are written in Chaghatay. These are generally labeled simply "Uyghur language document." Moreover, the sequence of the materials, which is not strictly chronological, and the uneven quality of the images suggest a hurried reproduction process in which documents were simply fed into a scanner in the order in which they were found. I am inclined to believe, on the basis of what was included in the collection and in what condition, that any censorship was minimal and careless. For the Republican archive, see "Zhongguo dang'an" online at archives.gov.cn, accessed April 14, 2014. This online collection is less extensive, presenting only eight thousand or so digitized documents, although many are organized into cases. Similar patterns of censorship seem to have governed their digitization.

23. Some will reasonably question the use of some manuscript sources from Kashgar and Yarkand when those places are some 1,150 kilometers distant from Turpan, and even of Kucha, which is much closer but is anyway a separate oasis. One may also question the representativeness of Turpan with regard to Xinjiang more broadly—after all, it is only one oasis among many. I would firstly remind China historians of the long tradition of writing the social history of "China" according to documents found in a single county, such as the Dan-Xin archives of Taiwan or

the Ba archives in Sichuan, both of which also document life on the boundaries of imperial China.

However, there are also positive reasons to speak of Turpan and Xinjiang together. First of all, Turpan in the late Qing was a "directly-administered prefecture" (*zhili ting*). This meant that, although Turpan was technically part of the administration of the Zhendi Circuit in Northern Xinjiang, where the population was largely Chinese, Kazakh, and Mongol, it was actually ruled according to policies enacted across the Musulman-majority South, the Kashgar and Aksu Circuits. That distinction accorded with Turpan's demographics: as of 1911, even after thirty-four years of Chinese in-migration, about 70 percent of the valley was Muslim, and in the majority Musulmans. Wang Shu'nan et al., comps., *Xinjiang tuzhi* (Taipei: Wenhai chubanshe, 1965), *minzheng* 4–5, 5b–6b.

Moreover, in the late Qing, Turpan became a site of Chinese settlement as migrants from China proper came to Xinjiang to seek their livelihoods. Traders did not just pass through Turpan—merchant houses made it a key entrepôt in their trading networks. Turpan became a microcosm of the processes of domination and change taking place across Xinjiang. As Rian Thum has argued, Turpan and the oases that ring the Tarim Basin, the geographical core of the Musulman homeland, are joined by common religious practices that maintained a cohesive religious community with a shared historical imagination. Rian Thum, "Modular History: Identity Maintenance Before Uyghur Nationalism," *Journal of Asian Studies* 71, no. 3 (August 2012): 627–53. Where scholars once wrote of "oasis identities" as centrifugal forces mitigating the construction of a common identity, we now understand that belonging to an oasis helped locate one within Xinjiang. We will see over the course of the book how discourses of history and identity in Kashgaria reflected contemporaneous discussions in Turpan.

24. Benedict J. Kerkvliet, *Everyday Politics in the Philippines: Class and Status Relations in a Central Luzon Village* (Berkeley: University of California Press, 1990), 9–11; Michael Szonyi, *The Art of Being Governed: Everyday Politics in Late Imperial China* (Princeton: Princeton University Press, 2017), 7–8.

25. The term *Muslim uprisings* is a translation of Chinese *Hui min qiyi*. It refers not only to the period of 1864–77 of Muslim control in Xinjiang, but to related events in Shaanxi and Gansu in 1862–72. As we will see, there were many ways of referring to this period of events within a certain geographical scope, but for the sake of convenience, the Chinese term will stand for them. For a definitive history of the uprisings, see Kim, *Holy War in China*. For those interested in settler life in Xinjiang before 1864, I recommend Jia Jianfei, *Qing Qian-Jia-Dao shiqi Xinjiang de neidi yimin shehui* (Beijing: Shehui kexue wenxian chubanshe, 2012).

26. Kim, *Holy War in China*, 37–72.

27. QXDX 7:155–56. "'Ālam buzulup kätkändin keyin. . . ." The root meaning of the verb *buzulmaq* is "to be broken," which lends it the secondary meaning of "to rebel" or "to fall into disorder." Because in this document the speaker, a man named Sawut, speaks of the whole "world" (*ʿālam*) rebelling, and doing so quickly (*kätkän*), I am inclined to translate the phrase literally.

28. Kim, *Holy War in China*, 66–71.

29. TA/Pantusov 103–11; TH/Beijing, 128–35; Kim, *Holy War in China*, 42–44. Sayrāmī records that some 130,000 nonbelievers were killed in Turpan, while only some four hundred Muslims—Hui and Musulmans—perished in the fighting. The numbers are plainly overinflated, as Sayrāmī himself points out—the population of Turpan was less than half that.

30. TH/Beijing, 236–37; TA/Pelliot, 145r; TH/Jarring, 96v.

31. For a similar observation, see Thum, "China in Islam."
32. Brubaker, *Grounds for Difference*, 87–89.
33. TA/Pantusov, 193–205; TH/Beijing, 213–21, especially 214–15; TH/Jarring, 86v–90r. Sayrāmī indicates that eighteen hundred of two thousand Hui soldiers stationed at Toqsun were killed, and another six thousand at the gates of Turpan, but as Sayrāmī points out, these numbers are surely inflated.
34. H. F. Hofman, *Turkish Literature: A Bio-Bibliographical Survey*, section 3, *Moslim Central Asian Turkish Literature* (Utrecht: Library of the University of Utrecht, 1969), pt. 1, vol. 3, 110–13; IVR RAN C 759, ʿAshūr Ākhūnd b. Ismāʾīl b. Muḥammad Ghāribī, *Amīr-i ʿālī*, 44r, 51v–54r, 74v–75v. Hofman and the Institute's catalog both date the work to 1280 AH (1863/64). However, that is quite impossible, as many of the events described did not take place until 1870. Nor was ʿAshūr Ākhūnd's patron, Niyāz Ḥakim Beg, installed as governor of Khotan, where this work was composed, until after the conquest thereof in January–February 1867. The manuscript at the Institute is marked with the seal of an owner named ʿAshūr Beg (the author?) inscribed with the date 1288 AH, or 1871/72. We may conclude that the work was composed around the same time, just after the conquest of Turpan. IVR RAN D 124, Ḥājjī Yūsuf, *Jamiʿ al-tawārīkh*, 347r, and the *Tārīkh-i Khotan* (Hamada, "L'Histoire," pt. 1, 35 [=37v–38v]) also mention an ʿAshūr Beg as a close associate of Yaʿqūb Beg who supposedly later betrayed him—perhaps this is the same individual. British India Office reports may also refer to the same man, a former functionary under Niyāz Beg, as a struggling and untrusted petty official in Yarkand, some thirty-five years old in 1879. IOR L/PS/7/23, report for September 12, 1879. Niyāz by then was dead by suicide.
35. Kim, *Holy War in China*, xiv.
36. Muhammad Gherib Shahyari, "Ishtiyaqnamä," ed. Yasin Imin, *Bulaq* 17 (1985): 230–36.
37. Hodong Kim (*Holy War in China*, 166–69) details the Xiang Army's initial assault and the different accounts of Yaʿqūb Beg's death. For primary sources on the swift fall of Turpan, see IVR RAN B 779, Mullah Abū ʾl-Maḥdī, *Ushbu ötkän dhamānida*, 5r–5v; Wang Dingan, *Xiangjun ji* (Jiangnan shuju, Guangxu 15 [1889]), *juan* 19, 17a–18a.
38. TH/Beijing, 243; TH/Jarring, 99v.
39. IVR RAN D 124, Ḥājjī Yūsuf, *Jamiʿ al-tawārīkh*, 318r.
40. Hamada Masami, "L'Histoire de Hotan de Muḥammad Aʿlam (III), texte turque oriental édité, avec une introduction," *Zinbun* 18 (1982): 83–84; Kim, *Holy War in China*, 168; Lund University Library, Jarring Prov. 117, Ṭālib Ākhūnd, *History of Yaʿqūb Beg*, 91v–94r.
41. TH/Beijing, 322.
42. Karl Menges and N. Th. Katanov, eds., *Volkskundliche Texte aus Ost-Türkistan*, 2 vols. (1933, 1946; Leipzig: Zentralantiquariat der Deutschen Demokratischen Republik, 1976), 50.
43. Thum, *Sacred Routes*, 6.
44. TA/Pantusov, 318; TA/Pelliot, 204v; TH/Beijing, 340.
45. Ellsworth Huntington, "The Depression of Turfan," *Geographical Journal* 30 (July–December 1907): 254–73.
46. TH/Beijing 127; TH/Jarring 72r.
47. Cao Jiguan, *Xinjiang jianzhi zhi* (Taipei: Xuesheng Shuju, 1963), *juan* 1, 7b–11b; Wang Shu'nan et al., comps., *Xinjiang tuzhi, minzheng* 4–5, 5b; Millward, *Eurasian Crossroads*, 127; Lanny Fields, *Tso Tsung-t'ang and the Muslims: Statecraft in Northwest China, 1868–1880* (Kingston: Limestone, 1978), 83; Wei Guangtao, *Kanding Xinjiang ji* (Harbin: Heilongjiang jiaoyu chubanshe, 2014), *juan* 7, 2a–2b; Yixin et al., comps., *Qinding pingding Shan Gan Xinjiang Hui fei fanglüe* in *Qi sheng fanglüe* (Guangxu reign), *juan* 305, 4.

48. The *Tārīkh-i Ḥamīdī* notes the positive effects of grain price regulation, and so does the chronicler Ṭālib Akhund. Jarring Prov. 117, Ṭālib Ākhūnd, *History of Yaʿqūb Beg*, 128r–128v; TH/Jarring, 120v–122v.
49. Guoli gugong bowuyuan Gugong wenxian bianji weiyuan hui, comp., *Gongzhong dang Guangxu chao zouzhe* (Taipei: Guoli gugong bowuyuan, 1973–75), 7:18–19.
50. Cooper, *Colonialism in Question*, 29, 146–47.
51. One great regret in the composition of this book was that I was unable to undertake a thoroughgoing analysis of economic change in late-Qing Xinjiang sufficient to address the economic dimensions of alienation. The lack of prior scholarship on this issue, the difficulties of basic problems such as understanding local units of measurement, and the sheer number of apparently relevant but disorganized manuscript sources demonstrated that such an enterprise would take sufficient effort to comprise a separate project, and one that might last many years. Some initial results of that study appear in Eric T. Schluessel, "Water, Justice, and Local Government in Turn-of-the-Century Xinjiang," *Journal of the Social and Economic History of the Orient* 62, no. 4 (December 2019): 595–621; and Schluessel, "Hiding and Revealing Pious Endowments in Late-Qing Xinjiang," *Muslim World* 108, no. 4 (December 2018): 613–29.
52. On the Xiang Army, see, for example, Philip A. Kuhn, "The Taiping Rebellion," in *The Cambridge History of China*, vol. 10, *Late Ch'ing 1800–1911*, pt. 1, ed. John K. Fairbank (Cambridge: Cambridge University Press, 1978), 285–90; Stephen Platt, *Provincial Patriots: The Hunanese and Modern China* (Cambridge, MA: Harvard University Press, 2007), 23–25. This period and its cultural changes are illuminated in Tobie Meyer-Fong, *What Remains: Coming to Terms with Civil War in Nineteenth-Century China* (Stanford: Stanford University Press, 2013); and Katherine Laura Bos Alexander, "Virtues of the Vernacular: Moral Reconstruction in Late Qing Jiangnan and the Revitalization of Baojuan" (PhD diss., University of Chicago, 2016). For parallels in American Reconstruction, see, for example, Drew Gilpin Faust, *This Republic of Suffering: Death and the American Civil War* (New York: Knopf, 2008). Late in the process of revising this manuscript, I encountered Hannah Theaker's excellent dissertation "Moving Muslims: The Great Northwestern Rebellion and the Transformation of Chinese Islam, 1860–1896" (PhD diss., University of Oxford, 2018), which discusses the similar and related program of reconstruction in Northwest China undertaken by this same group before and during the period covered here.
53. My heuristic use of "horizontal" and "vertical" difference comes from reading Gellner (*Nations and Nationalism* [Ithaca, NY: Cornell University Press, 1983], 12), in which he invokes horizontal lines of difference between class strata and vertical lines of conflict between communities.
54. Platt, *Provincial Patriots*.
55. Duara, *Rescuing History from the Nation*.
56. This has led to suspicions on the part of modern historians that Naʿīm may have incited a revolt on behalf of the British, but his involvement therein appears to be entirely separate from his work for the Raj. Bai Zhensheng et al., eds., *Xinjiang xiandai zhengzhi shehui shilüe* (Beijing: Zhongguo shehui kexue chubanshe, 1992), 71–72; IOR L/P&S/10/825 File 2273/1919, No. 144, 30 June 1918, June diary; Tailaiti Wubuli and Ailijiang Aisa, "Yijian guanyu Minguo qinian Kuche panluan de xin wenshu—'Mahemude su Ali Hezhuo panluan zhuang' yishi," *Xiyu yanjiu* 2014, no. 3, 37–49; Yang Shengxin, *Qingmo Shaan-Gan gaikuang* (Xi'an: San Qin chubanshe, 1997), 97; Yang Zengxin, comp., *Buguozhai wendu* (Taipei: Chengwen chubanshe, 1982), 406–22.
57. On the similarly troubling "geo-body" of Manchuria and its constitution through different technologies of spatialization, see Mark C. Elliott, "The Limits of Tartary:

Manchuria in Imperial and National Geographies," *Journal of Asian Studies* 59, no. 3 (August 2000): 603–46.

1. The Chinese Law

1. IOR, L/PS/7/23 "Affairs in Yarkand," 1,220–32.
2. Benjamin A. Elman, *From Philosophy to Philology: Intellectual and Social Aspects of Change in Late Imperial China* (Los Angeles: UCLA Asian Pacific Monograph Series, 2001), 53–54; Joshua A. Fogel, *Politics and Sinology: The Case of Naitō Konan, 1866–1934* (Cambridge, MA: Harvard University Press, 1984), 60; Chang Hao, "On the Ching-shih Ideal in Neo-Confucianism," *Ch'ing-shih wen-t'i* 3, no. 1 (November 1974): 42–43; William T. Rowe, *Saving the World: Chen Hongmou and Elite Consciousness in Eighteenth-Century China* (Stanford: Stanford University Press, 2001), 2–4, 448–55.
3. Gideon Chen, *Tso Tsung T'ang, Pioneer Promoter of the Modern Dockyard and the Woollen Mill in China* (Peiping: Yenching University, 1938), 50–57.
4. James Millward, *Eurasian Crossroads: A History of Xinjiang* (New York: Columbia University Press, 2007), 133; Rian Thum, *The Sacred Routes of Uyghur History* (Cambridge, MA: Harvard University Press, 2014), 178. On the broader meaning of agriculture for Zuo, see Peter Lavelle, "Cultivating Empire: Zuo Zongtang's Agriculture, Environment, and Reconstruction in the Late Qing," in *China on the Margins*, ed. Sherman Cochran and Paul G. Pickowicz, 43–64 (Ithaca, NY: Cornell University East Asia Series, 2010).
5. Nikolai Katanov, "Man'chzhursko-Kitaiskii 'li' na narechii Tiurkov Kitaiskogo Turkestana," *Zapiski vostochnogo otdeleniia imperatorskogo Russkogo arkheologicheskogo obshchestva* 14 (1901): 33; Albert von le Coq, *Sprichwörter und Lieder aus der Gegend von Turfan mit einer dort aufgenommen Wörterliste* (Leipzig: Druck und Verlag von B. G. Teubner, 1911), 1; Albert von le Coq, ed., "Das Lî-Kitâbî," *Kőrösi Csoma Archivum* 1, no. 6 (1925): 439; Gustaf Raquette, *Eastern Turki Grammar: Practical and Theoretical with Vocabulary*, vol. 1 (Berlin: Reichsdruckerei, 1912), 27–28; School of Oriental and African Studies Archives, PP MS 8, Papers of Professor Sir Edward Denison Ross and Lady Dora Ross, #57. Katanov notes that the term in Chinese could also be rendered as the disyllabic word *liyi* but is apparently unaware that this was normally translated as "etiquette and ceremony." See also David Brophy, "He Causes a Ruckus Wherever He Goes: Sa'id Muḥammad al-ʿAsali as a Missionary of Modernism in North-West China," *Modern Asian Studies* 2009:13–18.
6. Confucius, *Analects*, trans. Edward Slingerland (Indianapolis: Hackett, 2003), 8. The relevant passage is *weizheng* 3.
7. Wejen Chang, *In Search of the Way: Legal Philosophy of the Classic Chinese Thinkers* (Edinburgh: Edinburgh University Press, 2016), 52–53, 58–60.
8. Angela Zito, *Of Body and Brush: Grand Sacrifice as Text/Performance in 18th-Century China* (Chicago: University of Chicago Press, 1997), 59.
9. Fernanda Pirie, *The Anthropology of Law* (Oxford: Oxford University Press, 2013), 103–5, 156.
10. Ma Dazheng and Wu Fengpei, comps., *Qingdai Xinjiang xijian zoudu huibian, Tongzhi, Guangxu, Xuantong chao juan (shang)* (Wulumuqi: Xinjiang renmin chubanshe, 1997), #66, 58–59, also in Liu Jintang, *Liu xiangqin gong zougao* (Taipei: Chengwen Chubanshe, 1968), *juan* 2:31a–34b. On the proclamation in Gansu, see Zhao Weixi, *Xiangjun jituan yu Xibei Huimin da qiyi zhi shanhou yanjiu: yi Gan-Ning-Qing diqu wei zhongxin* (Shanghai: Shanghai guji chubanshe, 2013), 88.
11. Chang, *In Search of the Way*, 53–54.

12. I derive the term *Sino-normativity* from the word *heteronormativity*, which indicates both the assumption that people are by default or ideally heterosexual and that which such an assumption masks, the constant uncertainty and negotiation surrounding the meaning of heterosexuality.

13. Xin Xia, *Shengyu shiliutiao fu lü yijie*, reproduced in *Zhongguo lüxue wenxian, di si ji*, ed. Zhang Yifan (Beijing: Shehui kexue wenxian chubanshe, 2007). Phonological evidence from the Chaghatay text, as well as its quick production, suggests that it was translated and carved onto wooden printing blocks in Qumul (Hami). Before 1884, one Niyāz was known as a skilled carver of Song-style Chinese characters and seal script (Xiao Xiong, *Xijiang za shu shi* [Suzhou: Zhenxin shushe, 1895–97], *juan* 3, 1b–2a). He or someone like him certainly participated in translating the text and preparing the blocks.

14. Yu Zhi, *Deyi lu* (Baoshan tang, 1885), 5r. On salvation in post-Taiping morality literature, see Katherine Laura Bos Alexander, "Virtues of the Vernacular: Moral Reconstruction in Late Qing Jiangnan and the Revitalization of Baojuan" (PhD diss., University of Chicago, 2016).

15. Katanov, "Man'chzhursko-Kitaiskii 'Li,'" 33.

16. The best translation of the Chinese term *Lifanyuan* is disputed, and many renderings into English, such as "Court of Colonial Affairs," have theoretically or politically loaded meanings that are not explicit in the Chinese name. It was in any case an originally Manchu institution called in Manchu the *tulergi golo be dasara jurgan*, and one whose function changed over the course of the dynasty. We might render it as "Ministry for the Management of the Non-Chinese Population" or "Ministry for Outer Regions," depending on whether we consider the Qing to have managed diverse peoples or diverse places. Dittmar Schorkowitz and Ning Chia, eds., *Managing Frontiers in China: The Lifanyuan and Libu Revisited* (Leiden: Brill, 2017), 6; Timothy Brook, Michael van Walt van Praag, and Miek Boltjes, eds., *Sacred Mandates: Asian International Relations Since Chinggis Khan* (Chicago: University of Chicago Press, 2018), 136.

17. TH/Beijing, 311.

18. TH/Beijing, 317–18.

19. TH/Beijing, 74, 86; TH/Jarring, 31v, 36v, 65r. Notably, nowhere in the Chaghatay-language record have I found *li* interpreted or translated as it was in an official textbook that the Xiang Army prepared for its schools: "courtesy," *adablik*. Chen Zongzhen, "Han-Hui hebi yanjiu," *Minzu yuwen* 1989, no. 5:49–72.

20. TH/Beijing, 26–29; TH/Jarring, 9v–10v. See also Nathan Light, "Muslim Histories of China: Historiography Across Boundaries in Central Eurasia," in *Frontiers and Boundaries: Encounters on China's Margins*, ed. Zsombor Rajkai and Ildikó Bellér-Hann (Wiesbaden: Harrassowitz, 2012), 151–76, 163. Sayrāmī, via Khālidī, works from a book he calls the *History of Khans* (*Khanlar tārīkhi*) or *Gāngjāng*. This is the *Gangjian yizhi lu*, an abridged version of the *Zizhi tongjian* used in the Confucian schools and elsewhere. Wu Chucai, comp., *Gangjian yi zhi lu* (Taipei: Chengwen, 1964).

21. It is possible that Sayrāmī made this connection through the theology of certain strands of Sufism practiced mainly by Hui, in which Shariah is sometimes rendered as *li*.

22. Jarring Prov. 207, I.48; G. N. Potanin, *Ocherki severo-zapadnoi Mongolii* (St. Petersburg: Tipografiia V. Kirshbauma, 1881), 14–15.

23. On the problem of Shariah and knowledge thereof, see Wael B. Hallaq, *Sharīʿa: Theory, Practice, Transformations* (Cambridge: Cambridge University Press, 2009), 1–13.

24. Guy Burak, "The Second Formation of Islamic Law: The Post-Mongol Context of the Ottoman Adoption of a School of Law," *Comparative Studies in Society and History* 55, no. 3 (July 2013): 580.

25. Jürgen Osterhammel, *The Transformation of the World: A Global History of the Nineteenth Century* (Princeton: Princeton University Press, 2014), 827.
26. Peter Bol, *Neo-Confucianism in History* (Cambridge, MA: Harvard University Asia Center, 2008), 238.
27. Philip A. Kuhn, *Rebellion and Its Enemies in Late Imperial China: Militarization and Social Structure, 1796–1864* (Cambridge, MA: Harvard University Press, 1970), 124–26, 148–49.
28. Lynn A. Struve, "Huang Zongxi in Context: A Reappraisal of His Major Writings," *Journal of Asian Studies* 47, no. 3 (1988): 475–85; Lynn A. Struve, "The Early Ch'ing Legacy of Huang Tsung-hsi: A Reexamination," *Asia Major* 1, no. 1 (1988): 83–122.
29. Some liken Huang to "China's Rousseau" on account of his antistatist position and involvement in a struggle against monarchy. A Taiwanese editor of Huang's *Waiting for the Dawn* (*Mingyi daifang lu*) asserts that his ideas point to the early modern roots of electoral democracy in China; a Mainland editor asserts that Huang was an advocate of land reform and popular democracy, and his work laden with the "battlesome spirit" (*zhandouxing*) celebrated in Party ideology (Huang Zongxi, *Xinyi mingyi daifang lu*, ed. Li Guangbo and Li Zhenxing [Taibei: Sanmin shuju, 2014], 1–5, 10–17, 18, 35–42; Huang Zongxi, *Mingyi daifang lu* [Beijing: Zhonghua shuju, 1981], 1–2).
30. Stephen Platt, *Provincial Patriots: The Hunanese and Modern China* (Cambridge, MA: Harvard University Press, 2007), 16.
31. Huang Zongxi, *Xinyi mingyi daifang lu*, 18–24. Eric T. Schluessel, "The Law and the 'Law': Two Kinds of Legal Space in Late-Qing China," *Extrême-Orient Extrême-Occident* 40 (November 2016): 40–42. Translations from Huang Zongxi, *Waiting for the Dawn*, trans. Wm. Theodore de Bary (New York: Columbia University Press, 1993), 4–5, 97–99.
32. De Bary translates this phrase more freely, but perceptively, as "spirit among men that went beyond the letter of the law."
33. Katanov, "Man'chzhursko-Kitaiskii 'Li,'" 31–34.
34. Young-Oak Kim, "The Philosophy of Wang Fu-chih (1619–1692)" (PhD diss., Harvard University, 1982), 33–55.
35. Kim, "The Philosophy of Wang Fu-chih," 366–67.
36. With all due respect to the scholars concerned, several have relied on chains of mistranslations and slippage between theoretical terminology in order to verify Wang Fuzhi's "nationalism." This concern with individual terms without context is reflected in Prasenjit Duara's *Rescuing History from the Nation* (*Rescuing History from the Nation: Questioning Narratives of Modern China* [Chicago: University of Chicago Press, 2005], 75), which follows Frank Dikötter's *Discourse of Race in Modern China* ([Stanford: Stanford University Press, 1992], 29), who in turn cites Ernstjoachim Vierheller (*Nation und Elite im Denken von Wang Fu-chih, 1619–1692* [Hamburg: Gesellschaft für Natur- und Völkerkunde Ostasiens, 1968], 11–12, 26–27, 30), whose early work on Wang Fuzhi included this original flaw. Vierheller himself worked from an exploratory comment by Étienne Balázs (*Political Theory and Administrative Reality in Traditional China* [London: School of Oriental and African Studies, 1965], 40–49). Peter Perdue's "Nature and Nurture on Imperial China's Frontiers" (*Modern Asian Studies* 43, no. 1 [2009]: 254–55) takes advantage of another scholar's mistranslation of *qi* as "clime" to imply Wang's identity as a biological determinist in the modern European mode. Thus it would seem that several important monographs and articles include a characterization of Wang Fuzhi that is a few steps removed from any primary source. A few scholars have raised objections to this

characterization of Wang as a nationalist or racialist, which can be traced to the "national essence" (*guocui*) thinkers of the turn of the century (Fa-ti Fan, "Nature and Nation in Chinese Political Thought: The National Essence Circle in Early-Twentieth-Century China," in *The Moral Authority of Nature*, ed. Lorraine Daston and Fernando Vidal [Chicago: University of Chicago Press, 2004]), 409–37. A somewhat subtler analysis can be found in Mi-chu Wiens, "Anti-Manchu Thought During the Qing" (Papers on China 22A [1969]), although even Wiens worked in no small part from Derk Bodde, "Harmony and Conflict in Chinese Philosophy" (in *Studies in Chinese Thought*, ed. Arthur F. Wright [Chicago: University of Chicago Press, 1953], 19–80) and Bodde in turn from Ji Wenfu, *Chuanshan zhexue* (Shanghai, 1936). Ji emphasized the metaphysical dimensions of Wang's writings. For Wang Fuzhi's own brief discussion, which has generated so much ink, see the relevant passage of the *Huangshu* reproduced in *Chuanshan quanshu*, 16 vols. (Changsha: Yuelu shushe, 1988), 12:532–37.

37. Bol, *Neo-Confucianism in History*, 241–43.

38. Wang Fuzhi, *Chuanshan quanshu*, 4:657, 1,437–38, 12:467–68, 534.

39. Bol, *Neo-Confucianism in History*, 238–42.

40. On-cho Ng, "A Tension in Ch'ing Thought: 'Historicism' in Seventeenth- and Eighteenth-Century Chinese Thought," *Journal of the History of Ideas* 54, no. 4 (October 1993): 561–83, 572. To quote Wang Fuzhi: "This [the rites] is the norm of Heaven and the propriety of Earth. It is what makes people different from beasts, the Middle Kingdom different from barbarians, and the gentleman different from the savage (*yeren*). It fosters their essence (*qi*) and substance (*ti*). It exerts a subtle influence on vulgar, licentious, and rude essence without them even knowing." Wang Fuzhi, *Chuanshan quanshu*, 4:1, 437–38.

41. Wiens, "Anti-Manchu Thought," 11, 14; Wang Fuzhi, *Chunqiu jiashuo*, in *Chuanshan yishu*, 8 vols. (Beijing: Beijing chubanshe, 1999), *juan* 29, 3:16b, 17; Wang Fuzhi, *Chuanshan quanshu*, 12:501–2.

42. "Peasants into Frenchmen," indicating the fraught process of transforming a vast and variegated population into a putative nation, is detailed in Eugen Weber, *Peasants Into Frenchmen: The Modernization of Rural France, 1870-1914* (Stanford: Stanford University Press, 1976).

43. Mary Clabaugh Wright, *The Last Stand of Chinese Conservatism: The T'ung-chih Restoration, 1862-1874* (Stanford: Stanford University Press, 1962), 1–3.

44. Tobie Meyer-Fong, *What Remains: Coming to Terms with Civil War in Nineteenth-Century China* (Stanford: Stanford University Press, 2013), 23; William T. Rowe, *China's Last Empire: The Great Qing* (Cambridge, MA: Belknap Press of Harvard University Press, 2009), 162–63.

45. Daniel McMahon, "The Yuelu Academy and Hunan's Nineteenth-Century Turn Toward Statecraft," *Late Imperial China* 26, no. 1 (2005): 72–95; Platt, *Provincial Patriots*, 13–15, 20–24; William T. Rowe, "Ancestral Rites and Political Authority in Late Imperial China: Chen Hongmou in Jiangxi," *Modern China* 24, no. 4 (October 1998): 378–82, 397; Rowe, *Saving the World*, 148–51, 424–25.

46. Lanny Fields, "The Importance of Friendships and Quasi-Kinship Relations in Tso Tsung-t'ang's Career," *Journal of Asian History* 10, no. 2 (1976): 172–86; Kuhn, *Rebellion and Its Enemies*, 183–85; Platt, *Provincial Patriots*, 13–24; Wang Jiping, "Lun Xiangjun jituan," *Xiangtan daxue xuebao (zhexue shehui kexue ban)* 1996, no. 6:59–63; Wang Jiping, *Xiangjun jituan yu wan Qing Hunan* (Beijing: Zhongguo shehui kexue chubanshe, 2002), 3–4; Zhao Weixi, *Xiangjun jituan*, 18–19.

47. Kim, "The Philosophy of Wang Fu-chih," 358.

48. This division between North and West on the one hand and South and East on the other is delineated in Nicola Di Cosmo, "Qing Colonial Administration in Inner Asia," *International History Review* 20, no. 2 (June 1998): 287–309, 293–94.

49. Nailene Josephine Chou, "Frontier Studies and Changing Frontier Administration in Late Ch'ing China: The Case of Sinkiang, 1759–1911" (PhD diss., University of Washington, 1976), 84–143; James Millward, *Beyond the Pass: Economy, Ethnicity, and Empire in Qing Central Asia, 1759–1864* (Stanford: Stanford University Press, 1998), 92–96, 106–9, 241–45; L. J. Newby, *The Empire and the Khanate: A Political History of Qing Relations with Khoqand c. 1760–1860* (Boston: Brill, 2005), 111–17. Matthew Mosca illustrates how this transition in knowledge production took place in the case of Qing Mongolia. Mosca, "The Literati Rewriting of China in the Qianlong-Jiaqing Transition," *Late Imperial China* 32, no. 2 (December 2011): 89–132. Zuo Zongtang's specific intellectual genealogy is addressed on pages 120–21.

50. Millward, *Beyond the Pass*, 244.

51. For a poem from 1833 expressing Zuo's stance, see "Guisi Yantai za gan ba shou," in Zuo Zongtang, *Zuo Wenxiang Gong shiji* (Shanghai: Shanghai guji chubanshe, 1995), 2a.

52. Platt, *Provincial Patriots*, 16.

53. Kuhn, *Rebellion and Its Enemies*, 49–62.

54. Meyer-Fong, *What Remains*, 27–29.

55. Alexander, "Virtues of the Vernacular," 18–20; Meyer-Fong, *What Remains*, 23.

56. Yu Zhi, *Deyi lu*, preface.

57. Prasenjit Duara, *Culture, Power, and the State: Rural North China, 1900–1942* (Stanford: Stanford University Press, 1988).

58. Stephen Platt, *Autumn in the Heavenly Kingdom: China, the West, and the Epic Story of the Taiping Civil War* (New York: Knopf, 2012), 24, 357; Wang Jiping, "Lun Xiangjun jituan"; Zhao Weixi, *Xiangjun jituan*, 18–19.

59. Wang Dun, *Xiangjun shi* (Changsha: Yuelu shushe, 2014), 248–49.

60. Wang Dun, 235–71.

61. Chou, "Frontier Studies," 125, 135; Hannah Theaker, "Moving Muslims: The Great Northwestern Rebellion and the Transformation of Chinese Islam, 1860–1896" (PhD diss., University of Oxford, 2018), 94. Zhao Weixi provides one important example of Zuo's defiance (or duplicitousness) toward the court in the resettlement of Muslims in Gansu (*Xiangjun jituan*, 112).

62. Zhao Weixi, *Xiangjun jituan*, 83–89, 203.

63. Recorded in Ai Weijun et al., comps., *Gansu xin tongzhi* (1909), *juan* 35, *shuyuan*.

64. Lu Yao, "Lun Huimin qi," in He Changling, *Jingshi wenbian* (Beijing: Zhonghua shuju, 1992), *juan* 69, 10b–11a.

65. Eric T. Schluessel, "Language and the State in Late Qing Xinjiang," in *Historiography and Nation-Building Among Turkic Populations*, ed. Birgit Schlyter and Mirja Juntunen (Istanbul: Swedish Research Institute in Istanbul, 2014), 145–68, 153.

66. He Rong, "Shi lun Yang Zengxin shiqi Xinjiang xiangyue de tedian," *Xinjiang daxue xuebao (zhexue renwen shehui kexue ban)* 36, no. 3 (May 2008): 67–70; Rowe, *Saving the World*, 390–92; Zhao Weixi, *Xiangjun jituan*, 341–45.

67. Lanny Fields, *Tso Tsung-t'ang and the Muslims: Statecraft in Northwest China, 1868–1880* (Kingston: Limestone, 1978), 81–82. Zhao Weixi (*Xiangjun jituan*, 23) has "200,000"; this is surely an error.

68. TZ 9.7.18 "Shoufu Huimin ancha gengken pian" in Zuo Zongtang, *Zuo Wenxiang gong quanji* (Taipei: Wenhai chubanshe, 1979), *juan* 36, 38a–39b. Wen-djang Chu, *The Moslem Rebellion in Northwest China, 1862–1878* (The Hague: Mouton, 1966), 149–61; Fields,

Tso Tsung-t'ang and the Muslims, 85; Theaker, "Moving Muslims," 93–95, 98, 107; Zhao Weixi, *Xiangjun jituan*, 110–14, 366.

69. Fields, *Tso Tsung-t'ang and the Muslims*, 85.

70. TZ 10.4.8 "Qing jinjue Huimin Xinjiao zhe," in *Zuo Wenxiang Gong quanji*, j. 38, 62a–66a. On the "Old" and "New Teachings" in Qing China, see Jonathan N. Lipman, *Familiar Strangers: A History of Muslims in Northwest China* (Seattle: University of Washington Press, 1991), 91. Theaker ("Moving Muslims," 90–93, 104–8) discusses the logic of resettlement in greater detail.

71. Stevan Harrell, "Introduction: Civilizing Projects and the Reaction to Them," in *Cultural Encounters on China's Ethnic Frontiers*, ed. Stevan Harrell (Seattle: University of Washington Press, 1995), 3–36, 3–8, 27. Harrell himself notes that his conception of the Confucian civilizing project requires further exploration.

72. Edward Said, *Culture and Imperialism* (New York: Knopf, 1994), 9.

73. Osterhammel, *The Transformation of the World*, 828.

74. Homi Bhabha, "Of Mimicry and Man: The Ambivalence of Colonial Discourse," *October* 102 (Spring 1984): 125–33.

75. Millward, *Eurasian Crossroads*, 125–27.

2. Xinjiang as Exception

1. Zhongguo diyi lishi dang'anguan, eds., *Guangxu chao zhupi zouzhe* (Beijing: Zhonghua shuju, 1995–96), 106:260.

2. James Millward, *Beyond the Pass: Economy, Ethnicity, and Empire in Qing Central Asia, 1759–1864* (Stanford: Stanford University Press, 1998), 1–2. On exile in Xinjiang in the Qing, see Joanna Waley-Cohen, *Exile in Mid-Qing China: Banishment to Xinjiang, 1759–1860* (New Haven, CT: Yale University Press, 1991).

3. *Chu jun ying zhi*, reproduced in *Guojia tushuguan cang Qingdai bingshi dianji dangce huilan* (Beijing: Xueyuan chubanshe, 2005), 64:1–110.

4. Until the spring of 1875, Zuo Zongtang's primary responsibility in Gansu had actually been logistics and supplies. Several units of the greater army, mainly led by Manchu generals, had already gone "beyond the Pass" in 1873 to retake the nearer outposts of Qing power and secure supplies lines. Their leaders included Lieutenant General Irgen Gioro Jinshun (1830–86) of the Han Banner Troops, Ningxia general Nahata Mutushan (1823–87), Guangdong commander-in-chief Zhang Yao (1832–91), and Hunan commander-in-chief Song Qing (1820–1902). The latter Han generals commanded much smaller forces. In 1874, Ürümchi lieutenant-general Yanja Jinglian (1823–85) was made military superintendent of Xinjiang, while Jinshun became his deputy, the assistant resident, maintaining the principle of Manchu and Mongol military dominance in Xinjiang. Only after Zuo Zongtang was promoted to military superintendent did the Xiang Army's major movement into Xinjiang begin. Zuo's armies, in Kim's estimation, were successful mainly because of the collapse of Ya'qūb Beg's forces. Hodong Kim, *Holy War in China: The Muslim Rebellion and State in Chinese Central Asia, 1864–1878* (Stanford: Stanford University Press, 2004), 173; Li Enhan, *Zuo Zongtang shoufu Xinjiang* (Singapore: Xinjiapo Guo li da xue Zhong wen xi, 1984), 2–3.

5. Bodleian Library, Aurel Stein papers, MS 216, entry for July 15, 1914, and MS 97, entry for August 3, 1918. I must extend special gratitude to Justin Jacobs for pointing out a number of Western-language sources on Hunanese officials that have greatly enriched this chapter.

6. For a comment on the end of "little Hunan," see Xie Bin, *Xinjiang youji* (Lanzhou: Lanzhou guji shudian, 1990), 99.
7. Giorgio Agamben, *State of Exception* (Chicago: University of Chicago Press, 2005), 2–5; Bonnie Honig, *Emergency Politics: Paradox, Law, Democracy* (Princeton: Princeton University Press, 2009); Achille Mbembe, "Necropolitics," *Public Culture* 15, no. 1 (2003): 11–40; Carl Schmitt, *Political Theology: Four Chapters on the Concept of Sovereignty* (Chicago: University of Chicago Press, 2005), 97–98.
8. FHA 04-01-16-0210-035.
9. Nailene Josephine Chou, "Frontier Studies and Changing Frontier Administration in Late Ch'ing China: The Case of Sinkiang, 1759–1911" (PhD diss., University of Washington, 1976), 258.
10. Zhao Weixi, *Xiangjun jituan yu Xibei Huimin da qiyi zhi shanhou yanjiu: yi Gan-Ning-Qing diqu wei zhongxin* (Shanghai: Shanghai guji chubanshe, 2013), 29.
11. Chou, "Frontier Studies," 229–44, 267; James Millward, *Eurasian Crossroads: A History of Xinjiang* (New York: Columbia University Press, 2007), 131–58.
12. Eric T. Schluessel, "Language and the State in Late Qing Xinjiang," in *Historiography and Nation-Building Among Turkic Populations*, ed. Birgit Schlyter and Mirja Juntunen (Istanbul: Swedish Research Institute in Istanbul, 2014), 145–68, 153.
13. Zhao Weixi, *Xiangjun jituan*, 332.
14. FHA 04-01-16-0209-012; *QXDX* 1: 31–32, 49, 88.
15. GX 7.10.1 Liu Jintang, "Yu ken shou cheng ming ling jian xianneng jieti zhe," in *Liu xiangqin gong zougao* (Taipei: Chengwen chubanshe, 1968), *juan* 3, 1a–3b.
16. GX 8.4.5 Liu Jintang, "Qing gei bing jia yi yue zai ying tiaoli pian," in *Liu xiangqin gong zougao, juan* 3, 34a–34b; GX 8.7.3 Liu Jintang, "Xinjiang ge dao ting zhou xian qing gui Gansu wei yi sheng zhe," in *Liu xiangqin gong zougao, juan* 3, 50a–53b.
17. FHA 04-01-16-0210-035.
18. Certain areas of what became Xinjiang had this system established later on, notably the Ili Valley, where the Russian occupation only ended with the Treaty of St. Petersburg of 1881.
19. Ma Dazheng and Wu Fengpei, comps., *Qingdai Xinjiang xijian zoudu huibian, Tongzhi, Guangxu, Xuantong chao juan (shang)* (Wulumuqi: Xinjiang renmin chubanshe, 1997), 287, 409–10. This was particularly difficult given the delayed establishment of the counties-and-prefectures system in Ili.
20. Ma and Wu, 308–9.
21. This section is based mainly on 336 documents concerning imperial officials examined at the First Historical Archives (FHA) in Beijing and the National Palace Museum (NPM) in Taipei. These documents describe the careers of 610 officials, 381 of whom can be identified by place of origin. They include officeholders from every level of government, within the limits described later. It would be cumbersome to list all of them here. The documents in question cover the years 1872–1912 and include both draft memorials (*lufu zouzhe*) and vermillion-rescripted palace memorials (*zhupi zouzhe*). Most request imperial approval for promotions, transfers, and the granting of honors, while many others request the cashiering (dismissal) of officials for their offenses. Some are lists of civil officials by position. I have corroborated the biographies of many officials with travelers' accounts, local documents from Turpan, and other official sources, including gazetteers (*zhi*) from their places of origin. All of this information was entered into a biographical database in which some officials might be mentioned in dozens of sources, while others have only one mention. Kataoka Kazutada's work on the composition of officialdom in late-Qing Xinjiang largely corroborates my findings (Kataoka, "Shin-matsu shinkyōshō kan'in kō," *Ōsaka kyōiku daigaku kiyō* 11, no. 31

[February 1983]: 119–38). However, Kataoka's work was based entirely on periodic reference guides to officialdom (*jinshen lu*), which I have found by comparison with documents to be incomplete and in places inaccurate. Indeed, my data shows that Hunanese people were even more prominent in Xinjiang's government than Kataoka concludes.

Unfortunately, outside of Turpan, data is only available for officials who held at least the rank of county or prefectural secretary (*jingli*), correspondence secretary (*zhaomo*), subdirector of schools (*xundao*), warden (*limu, dianshi*), or registrar (*zhubu*). Data is only consistently reliable for those holding a magisterial rank, including second-class subprefects (*tongpan*), subdistrict magistrates (*xunjian*), and assistant district magistrates (*xiancheng*). These latter officials, although of a lower rank than a county magistrate (*zhixian*), first-class subprefect (*tongzhi*), department magistrate (*zhizhou*), or prefect (*zhifu*), nevertheless effectively managed the affairs of a prescribed geographical area and those who lived in it with minimal interference from their superiors. We should not ignore other officials who held similar ranks but remained in Dihua on temporary or permanent service at the pleasure of provincial officials. However, data on their activities is extremely difficult to find.

22. Eric T. Schluessel, "Cong chenghuang dao shuzu: Dingxiang Wang zai Xinjiang," *Lishi renleixue xuekan* 15, no. 2 (October 2017): 169–86; Yu Zhi, *Deyi lu* (Baoshan tang, 1885).

23. Yu Zhi, *Deyi lu*. Zhou Han's story deserves more thorough attention than space allows. See Stephen Platt, *Provincial Patriots: The Hunanese and Modern China* (Cambridge, MA: Harvard University Press, 2007), 64–66.

24. FHA 04-01-12-0652-048. Lanny Fields, *Tso Tsung-t'ang and the Muslims: Statecraft in Northwest China, 1868-1880* (Kingston: Limestone, 1978), 81–82; Zhao Weixi, *Xiangjun jituan*, 13–19, 24–25.

25. Fields, *Tso Tsung-t'ang and the Muslims*, 81–82.

26. Zhou Chongfu (1840–1893). FHA 04-01-13-0435-003; FHA 04-01-13-0431-040; FHA 04-01-12-0526-001; FHA 03-5188-017; FHA 03-5281-057; FHA 03-5285-054; FHA 03-5302-118; NPM 408002777.

27. Guangxi-born He Rujin (b. 1840) was granted the position of Suilai magistrate (today's Manas) in 1872, and briefly served in Xinjiang, but left the Northwest in 1877 never to return. FHA 04-01-12-0520-068; FHA 04-01-12-0548-106; FHA 04-01-13-0368-040.

28. NPM 408002907; NPM 408002829; Zhao Weixi, *Xiangjun jituan*, 387.

29. Incidentally, the example of late-Qing Xinjiang leads us to reflect on the significance of degree purchase (*juanna*). Lawrence Zhang has argued that, while historians tend to see the purchaser of a degree as less qualified or worthy than an official who passed the examinations, it in fact had no discernible bearing on an official's performance (Zhang, "Power for a Price: Office Purchase, Elite Families, and Status Maintenance in Qing China" [PhD diss., Harvard University, 2010], 170–71, 268, 275–76). Instead, Zhang argues, degree purchase both sustained a de facto nobility capable of buying status and helped to rationalize a system that, while it was superficially meritocratic, actually reinforced patronage networks. In Xinjiang, degree purchase played many roles: It was an entrance fee—without purchasing a degree, new Hunanese would not be recruited. Later on, purchasing a degree could have been an attempt to escape the system, or to advance within it, without needing to rely on existing patronage networks. It may also have functioned as a simple status symbol, a means for officials in an otherwise ossified system to display relative success.

30. The Gansu Flexibility Plan is quoted almost in its entirety in FHA 04-01-01-0955-001. I have been unable to locate the original memorial in which the plan was proposed.

31. FHA 03-5220-052.

32. FHA 04-01-12-0587-144.

33. FHA 04-01-12-0625-065; FHA 04-01-13-0409-051/FHA 03-5962-048.

34. Mbembe, "Necropolitics." For a parallel case in the Punjab, just over the Pamirs, in the same period, see Robert Nichols, *The Frontier Crimes Regulation: A History in Documents* (Oxford: Oxford University Press, 2013), ix–xxv.

35. Eugene John Gregory III, "Desertion and the Militarization of Qing Legal Culture" (PhD diss., Georgetown University, 2015), explores the extension of military discipline into the legal system that resulted in the use of exceptional punishment into the mid-eighteenth century. Weiting Guo, "The Speed of Justice: Summary Execution and Legal Culture in Qing Dynasty China, 1644–1912" (PhD diss., University of British Columbia, 2016), examines this technique's transformations and the effects of its widespread use on the legal transformation of the Qing in the nineteenth century. For a seminal study, see Zhang Shiming, "Qian-Jia shiqi gong qing wang ming qi pai xian xing chengfa zhi zhi de kuan yan zhang chi," *Nei Menggu shifan daxue xuebao (zhexue shehui kexue ban)* 39, no. 4 (July 2009): 44–58.

36. Chou, "Frontier Studies," 125–27; Lanny Fields, "The Importance of Friendships and Quasi-Kinship Relations in Tso Tsung-t'ang's Career," *Journal of Asian History* 10, no. 2 (1976): 172–86, 179, 181–84; Gregory, "Desertion," 423–24.

37. Lin Zexu, "Shenming yixi xuhuo feifan jiudi zhengfa pian," Bian Baoquan, "Zhuoni qianjie zhongan jiudi zhengfa ge tiao shu," and Liu Jintang, "Renming zhongan ainan jufu jiuzhi shu" in Ge Shijun, comp., *Huangchao jingshi wen xu bian* (Shanghai: Tushu jicheng ju, 1888); Qiu Yuanyou, "Taiping tianguo yu wan Qing 'jiudi zhengfa zhi zhi,'" *Jindai shi yanjiu* 1998, no. 2: 31–50.

38. Gregory, "Desertion," 424–27; Guo, "The Speed of Justice," 238–46; Eric T. Schluessel, "The Law and the 'Law': Two Kinds of Legal Space in Late-Qing China," *Extrême-Orient Extrême-Occident* 40 (November 2016): 42–47.

39. Guo, "The Speed of Justice," 247–86.

40. Schluessel, "The Law and the 'Law,'" 13–14.

41. Schluessel, 47–51. Much of this section is based on a survey of 417 capital cases from late-Qing Xinjiang, 1877–1911. These documents were gathered from metropolitan-level reports of both "execution on the spot" and capital cases that followed routine procedures for reporting and approval. For reasons of space, it is impossible to describe all of the relevant documents here. All cases were collected from the First Historical Archives in Beijing and the National Palace Museum in Taipei, either directly or through published compilations, early in the research for this project. While the data are useful in the aggregate, they are problematic because of the process of editing that produced them, as will be explored later in this book. The relevant documents are FHA 04-01-08-0132-002; 03-7346-064; 03-7247-018; 03-7248-043; 03-7250-007; 04-01-26-0076-006; 03-7250-072; 03-7250-056; 03-7250-056; 03-7309-045; 03-7309-045; 04-01-26-0076-021; 04-01-26-0076-081; 03-7254-041; 04-01-26-0076-036; 04-01-26-0076-039; 04-01-26-0076-043; 04-01-26-0076-060; 04-01-26-0076-058; 04-01-26-0076-059; 04-01-26-0076-057; 04-01-28-0023-073; 04-01-28-0023-072; 03-7256-063; 04-01-26-0077-033; 04-01-26-0077-032; 04-01-26-0077-029; 04-01-26-0077-093; 04-01-26-0077-094; 04-01-26-0077-090; 04-01-26-0077-091; 04-01-26-0077-055; 04-01-26-0077-064; 03-7256-033; 04-01-26-0077-063; 04-01-26-0077-061; 04-01-26-0077-062; 04-01-26-0077-048; 04-01-26-0077-047; 04-01-26-0077-041; 04-01-26-0077-042; 04-01-26-0077-076; 04-01-26-0077-085; 04-01-26-0077-084; 04-01-26-0077-

082; 04-01-26-0077-083; 04-01-26-0077-080; 04-01-26-0077-081; 03-7312-016; 03-7357-032; 03-7369-069; 03-7383-077; 03-7333-012; 03-7584-111; 04-01-26-0096-006; 04-01-26-0096-004; 03-7584-104; 03-7268-024; 03-7321-021; 03-7376-054; 03-7378-103; *Guangxu chao zhupi zouzhe* vol. 106, 260, 272, 306, 309, 310, 311, 312, 326, 343; Guoli gugong bowuyuan Gugong wenxian bianji weiyuan hui, comp., *Gongzhong dang Guangxu chao zouzhe* (Taipei: Guoli gugong buwuyuan, 1973–75), vol. 4, 455–56, 484–85, 499–500, 500–501, 502–4, 574–75, 583–84, 602–3, 603–4, 621–22, 625–26, 687–88, 898–900, 893–94; vol. 5, 72–74, 209–10, 208–9, 243–44, 274–75, 275–76, 483–84, 664–65, 687–88, 711–12, 733–34, 759, 760, 900–901, 902–3, 903–4; vol. 6, 150, 818–19; vol. 7, 34–35, 58–59, 56–57, 57–58, 65–66, 67, 301–2, 261, 307–8, 314–15, 382–83, 403–4, 401–3, 415–16, 414–15, 416–17, 435–36, 431–32, 476–77, 593–94, 239–41, 234–36, 222–23, 219, 613–14, 648–50, 694–95, 699–700, 722–23, 747–49, 749–50, 774–75, 880–81, 882–83, 891–92; vol. 8, 81–82, 82–83, 262, 287–88, 423, 429–30, 466–67, 651, 934–35, 940–41; vol. 11, 402–3, 659–61; NPM 121979; 131093; 131935; 132093; 131459; 408006240; 138093; 139248; 143637; 147755; 157132; 159936; 408010765; 165182; 181983; 125450; 125716.

42. For an overview of dispute resolution, see Ildikó Bellér-Hann, *Community Matters in Xinjiang, 1880–1949: Towards a Historical Anthropology of the Uyghur* (Leiden: Brill, 2008), 179–88.

43. John K. Fairbank and Ssü-yu Têng, *Ch'ing Administration: Three Studies* (Cambridge, MA: Harvard University Press, 1960), 30.

44. These figures are derived from palace memorials examined at the First Historical Archives in Beijing and the National Palace Museum in Taipei, which record the date of the offense, when it was reported, the date of the memorial, and when it received a vermillion rescript (*zhupi*).

45. This case is described in a series of documents in QXDX 65:155, 159, 160, 179, 191–93, 212–13, 219–20. For a more detailed analysis, see Schluessel, "The Law and 'the Law,'" 17–19.

46. These examples are taken from FHA 03-7247-018, 03-7346-064, 03-7312-016, 03-7256-063, 03-7254-041, and 03-7250-072.

47. FHA 03-7584-111.

48. Brian McKnight, *The Quality of Mercy: Amnesties and Traditional Chinese Justice* (Honolulu: University of Hawaii Press, 1981), 1–2.

49. Eric T. Schluessel, *The World as Seen from Yarkand: Ghulām Muḥammad Khān's 1920s Chronicle* Mā Tītayniŋ wāqi'asi (Tokyo: NIHU Program Islamic Area Studies, 2014), 72.

50. Donald S. Sutton, "Violence and Ethnicity on a Qing Colonial Frontier: Customary and Statutory Law in the Eighteenth-Century Miao Pale," *Modern Asian Studies* 37, no. 1 (February 2003): 41–80. *Juan* 86–88 of the *Jingshi wenbian* are dedicated to defense against the Man and Miao.

51. Fu Nai, "Zhi Miao," in He Changling, comp., *Huangchao jingshi wenbian, juan* 88, 7a–8a.

52. Alice Conklin, *A Mission to Civilize: The Republican Idea of Empire in France and West Africa, 1895–1930* (Stanford: Stanford University Press, 1997), 7.

53. Wang Shu'nan et al., comps., *Xinjiang tuzhi* (Taipei: Wenhai chubanshe, 1965), *juan* 29; Zhang Jiangcai, *Tianjin Yangliuqing xiao zhi*, reprinted in *Tianjin fengtu congshu* (1938; Taipei: Jinxue shuju, 1969), 197–214, 202–4, 213–14.

54. *Gongzhong dang Guangxu chao zouzhe*, 6:228–29. Local documents provide a richer picture of the events, but I will only cite a few key documents here: QXDX 59:21; QXDX 58:50; QXDX 59:18; QXDX 59:21; QXDX 59:59; QXDX 59:68. The Shanshan gazetteer records the incident in similar terms. *Shanshan xian xiangtuzhi*, in Ma Dazheng et al., comps., *Xinjiang xiangtuzhi gao* (1904–08; Beijing: Quanguo tushuguan wenxian

suowei fuzhi zhongxin, 2011), 138–39. *Xinjiang xiangtuzhi gao* is henceforth abbreviated *XTZG*.

55. For example, a group of Musulmans in Keriyä conspired to rid themselves of long-standing debts to a Han trader who had sold them cotton at a high markup (*Gongzhong dang Guangxu chao zouzhe*, 5:209–10).

56. *Gongzhong dang Guangxu chao zouzhe*, 7:35–36; *QXDX* 29:438–39; *QXDX* 29:444.

57. Emma Jinhua Teng, "Taiwan as a Living Museum: Tropes of Anachronism in Late-Imperial Chinese Travel Writing," *Harvard Journal of Asiatic Studies* 59, no. 2 (1999): 445–84.

58. Chou, "Frontier Studies," 258–59, 282–85.

59. C. P. Skrine and Pamela Nightingale, *Macartney at Kashgar* (London: Methuen, 1973), 70; Tao Mo, *Tao Qinsu gong zouyi yigao*, reproduced in Zhongguo shaoshu minzu guji jicheng (Hanwen ban), vol. 71 (Chengdu: Sichuan Minzu Chubanshe, 2002), *juan* 1, 19a–20b.

60. Liu Jintang, *Liu Xiangqin gong zougao, juan* 3, 15a–15b.

61. This shift is documented in several classic works, such as William T. Rowe, *Hankow: Commerce and Society in a Chinese City* (Stanford: Stanford University Press, 1984), that point to diminished state capacity in the late Qing as a reason for the devolution of public responsibilities to private interests. For a contrary analysis emphasizing the negotiated nature of this relationship, see Maura Dykstra, "Complicated Matters: Commercial Dispute Resolution in Qing Chongqing from 1750 to 1911" (PhD diss., University of California, Los Angeles, 2014), 228–66. While the province's reliance on merchants in late-Qing Xinjiang was indeed prompted by the difficulty of managing the economy from the provincial capital, it nevertheless appears that lower-level officials, or those beyond Tao's influence, contracted their own complex relationships with merchants.

62. Chou, "Frontier Studies," 260–62.

63. Eric T. Schluessel, "Water, Justice, and Local Government in Turn-of-the-Century Xinjiang," *Journal of the Social and Economic History of the Orient* 62, no. 4 (December 2019): 595–621.

64. Tao Mo, "Xinjiang xunfu Tao fuchen ziqiang daji zhe," in Gan Han, comp., *Huangchao jingshi wen xin bian xu ji, juan* 1, 1a–1b.

65. Yuan Dahua, *Xinjiang Yili luanshi benmo* (Taipei: Wenhai chubanshe, 1979), relates that Chinese merchants in Ili raised this amount very swiftly in order to combat the Brothers and Elders Society.

66. NPM 408002824.

67. Chou, "Frontier Studies," 292–95; Judd Kinzley, *Natural Resources and the New Frontier: Constructing Modern China's Borderlands* (Chicago: University of Chicago Press, 2018), 46–54.

68. FHA 04-01-16-0284-062.

69. *QXDX* 36:245–47.

70. *Gongzhong dang Guangxu chao zouzhe*, 13:398–400.

71. Sutton, "Violence and Ethnicity on a Qing Colonial Frontier," 47–48, 63; *Qingdai Xinjiang xijian zoudu huibian*, 105–6; Zeng Wenwu and Shen Yunlong, *Zhongguo jingying Xiyu shi*, reproduced in Xu Zhisheng et al., comps., *Zhongguo xibu kaifa wenxian* (1936; Beijing: Quanguo Tushuguan Wenxian Suowei Fuzhi Zhongxin, 2004), 364.

72. NPM 177921; *Qing shilu* (Beijing: Zhonghua shuju, 1985–87), entry for GX 31.8.18.

73. Arash Bormanshinov, "Prince Palta," in *Proceedings of the International Conference on China Border Area Studies*, ed. Lin En-shean et al. (Taipei: Guoli zhengzhi daxue, 1985), 1,015–40, 1,024; NPM 159014.

74. Several individuals who fit this description are listed as follows. In order to conserve space, I have provided only the chronologically latest memorials attesting to their careers:

Jiang Yupu (1825–1904) joined the Xiang Army as early as 1853, died in office as the intendant of Aksu (FHA 04-01-16-0280-040). Luo Enshou (1838–1904) served under Zuo, died as the magistrate of Tarbaghatai (FHA 04-01-12-0644-027). Zhu Mianrong (1839–1903) joined Zuo in 1878, died as the prefect of Dihua (FHA 04-01-12-0627-008). Huang Guangda (ca. 1845–1901), served under Zeng Guofan, then Zuo, served as the Kashgar intendant, died on the way to take up a post as Gansu judicial commissioner (FHA 04-01-14-0098-083). Chen Xiluo (1845–1899) served under Zeng Guofan, then Zuo, died as the magistrate of Wensu (FHA 03-5393-023). Huang Yuan (1843–1902) served under Zuo, died as the Yengisar magistrate (FHA 03-5394-056).

75. Yale University, MS 1, Ellsworth Huntington Papers; Gustaf Mannerheim, *Dagbok förd under min resa i Centralasian och Kina 1906-07-08* (Helsingfors: Svenska Litteratursällskapet i Finland, 2010), 308.

76. Wang Shu'nan, *Taolu laoren sui nian lu* (Beijing: Zhonghua Shuju, 2007), 71.

77. Wang Shu'nan, 96–102; Wang Shu'nan, *Xila xue an* (n.d.); Chŏn Pyŏng-hun, *Jingshen zhexue tong bian* (Shanghai, 1920); Wang Shu'nan, "Hanguo Jin Zuitang xiansheng (Bingxun) *Jingshen zhexue xin bian* xu," in *Taolu wenji* (Taipei: Wenhai Chubanshe, 1915), 357–61; Mannerheim, *Dagbok*, 309; NPM 186991.

78. Sally Borthwick, *Education and Social Change in China: The Beginnings of the Modern Era* (Stanford: Stanford University Press, 1983), 73–74; Zhang Jiangcai, *Tianjin Yangliuqing xiao zhi*, 202–4, 213–14.

79. Wang Shu'nan's position corresponds to that of one participant in a "dialogue" recorded in *Xinjiang tuzhi* (*juan* 38, 7b). For Wang's extended explanation of his ideas, see a memorial dated *zhupi* XT 1.4.24, Liankui, reproduced in *Xuebu guanbao* 92 (July 8, 1909).

80. Kinzley, *Natural Resources and the New Frontier*; Skrine and Nightingale, *Macartney at Kashgar*, 153; Zhong Guangsheng and Sun Anfu, *Xinjiang zhi gao* (1928; Taipei: Xuesheng Shuju, 1967), *juan* 2, 51a–52b; National Library of China, *Xinjiang shuiwu ju zongban huiyi pimao gongsi gaiwei guanxing xiang*; Zeng and Shen, *Zhongguo jingying Xiyu shi*, 396.

81. Jürgen Osterhammel, *The Transformation of the World: A Global History of the Nineteenth Century* (Princeton: Princeton University Press, 2014), 323.

82. Lian-kui, memorial dated *zhupi* XT 1.r2.12, reproduced in *Xuebu guanbao* 83 (April 11, 1909).

83. NPM 186991.

84. For an overview of the Xinhai Revolution in Xinjiang, see Millward, *Eurasian Crossroads*, 164–67. The Hunanese presence is discussed in Wei Changhong, ed., *Xinhai geming zai Xinjiang* (Wulumuqi: Xinjiang renmin chubanshe, 1981), and is widely attested in primary documents, including Hunan Provincial Library, Gong Yuanji, *Zhuidao Xinjiang shouyi lieshi jinian pin*, 21b–22a.

85. National Library of China, *Xinjiang gaodeng xunjing xuetang wendu, zhangcheng*.

86. Zeng and Shen, *Zhongguo jingying Xiyu shi*, 364.

87. Justin Jacobs, "Empire Besieged: The Preservation of Chinese Rule in Xinjiang, 1884–1971" (PhD diss., University of California, San Diego, 2011), 136; Justin Jacobs, *Xinjiang and the Modern Chinese State* (Seattle: University of Washington Press, 2016), 53–55. On Yang Zuanxu and the Society, see Millward, *Eurasian Crossroads*, 165–69. Yang's own writings on his time in Xinjiang can be found in Yang Zuanxu, *Xinjiang chuyi*, reproduced in *Xinjiang shizhi*, di 2 bu, vol. 5 (Beijing: Quanguo tushuguan

wenxian suowei fuzhi zhongxin, 2003), 399–492. The British consul at Kashgar frequently reported on the activities of the "Gamblers," by which he indicated the Society (IOR L/P&S/10/330).
88. Jacobs, *Xinjiang and the Modern Chinese State*, 49–50; Kinzley, *Natural Resources and the New Frontier*, 61–68.

3. Frontier Mediation

1. XUAR Archive, M16.004.YJ.2153, M16.004.YJ.2162.
2. The term *tongshi* dates back to at least the Jürchen Jin dynasty (1115–1234) and was used later in Mongolia, where the Mongolized term *tüngshi* indicated an intermediary for Chinese officials or merchants. Christopher Atwood, "Chinese Merchants and Mongolian Independence," in *XX zuuny Mongol: tuux, soyol, geopolitik, gadaad xariltsaany tulgamdsan asuudluud*, ed. S. Chuluun and S. Battulga (Ulaanbaatar: Admon print, 2017), 62–75, 64; Martha Cheung Pui Yiu and Lin Wusun, eds., *An Anthology of Chinese Discourse on Translation*, vol. 1, *From Earliest Times to the Buddhist Project* (Manchester: St. Jerome, 2006), 198–99.
3. David Brophy, "The Junghar Mongol Legacy and the Language of Loyalty in Qing Xinjiang," *Harvard Journal of Asiatic Studies* 73, no. 2 (2013): 246–47.
4. This book project was initially inspired by two works that address local government and its agents in the Qing: Bradley Reed, *Talons and Teeth: County Clerks and Runners in the Qing Dynasty* (Stanford: Stanford University Press, 2000); and Melissa Macauley, *Social Power and Legal Culture: Litigation Masters in Late Imperial China* (Stanford: Stanford University Press, 1998). On the litigation masters, see Macauley, as well as Fuma Susumu, "Litigation Masters and the Litigation System of Ming and Qing China," *International Journal of Asian Studies* 4, no. 1 (January 2007): 79–111.
5. Bruno Latour, *We Have Never Been Modern* (Cambridge, MA: Harvard University Press, 1993), 81.
6. Naoki Sakai, *Translation and Subjectivity: On "Japan" and Cultural Nationalism* (Minneapolis: University of Minnesota Press, 1997), 1–12.
7. Prasenjit Duara, *Culture, Power, and the State: Rural North China, 1900–1942* (Stanford: Stanford University Press, 1988).
8. Karasawa Yasuhiko, "Hanasukoto to kakukoto no hazama de—shindai saiban bunsho ni okeru kyōjutsusho no tekusutosei," *Chūgoku: Shakai to bunka* 10 (1995): 212–50.
9. M. T. Taussig, *Mimesis and Alterity: A Particular History of the Senses* (London: Routledge, 1993), xviii.
10. Li Bianqi, "Huijiang fa wenhua yu Da Qing fa wenhua de chongtu yu zhenghe," *Xizang daxue xuebao* 16, no. 2 (June 2001): 38–42; Ma Xiaojuan, "Qingchao fazhi zai Tulufan diqu de chongjian," *Xinjiang daxue xuebao (zhexue shehui kexue ban)* 40, no. 1 (January 2012): 61–66.
11. The term *ākhūnd* literally meant "teacher," but by the late nineteenth century, it came to be used as a generic title akin to "mister," albeit limited to male members of a community who could both read and write.
12. Nailene Josephine Chou, "Frontier Studies and Changing Frontier Administration in Late Ch'ing China: The Case of Sinkiang, 1759–1911" (PhD diss., University of Washington, 1976), 135; Qi Yunshi, *Xi chui zhu zhici* (Shanghai: Shanghai Guji Chubanshe, 2010), 317.
13. Xiao Xiong, *Xijiang za shu shi* (Suzhou: Zhenxin shushe, 1895–97), 333–34.
14. *QXDX* 51:336, 356, 357a, 357b, 358–59.

15. *QXDX* 51:399–400.
16. Maram Epstein, "Making a Case: Characterizing the Filial Son," in *Writing and Law in Late Imperial China: Crime, Conflict, and Judgment*, ed. Robert Hegel and Katherine Carlitz (Seattle: University of Washington Press, 2007), 27–43.
17. I make a similar argument in Eric T. Schluessel, "Muslims at the Yamen Gate: Translating Justice in Late-Qing Xinjiang," in *Kashgar Revisited: Uyghur Studies in Memory of Gunnar Jarring*, ed. Ildikó Bellér-Hann, Birgit Schlyter, and Jun Sugawara (Leiden: Brill, 2016), 116–38.
18. Staatsbibliothek zu Berlin, Hartmann 44.
19. For example, *QXDX* 28:300, 333, 336–37.
20. *QXDX* 1:118, 139.
21. Hundreds of documents in the Turpan archive's "appointments" section (*li ke*) address these officials' appointments; for examples in the first volume alone, see *QXDX* 1:16, 18–19, 20, 25, 41, 47, 48, 93, 98, 99, 100, 103, 116, 119, and so on. Ildikó Bellér-Hann, *Community Matters in Xinjiang 1880–1949: Towards a Historical Anthropology of the Uyghur* (Leiden: Brill, 2008), 121–22.
22. The title has a long and complex history dating back to the Mongol conquests. It is attested earlier as *dārūgha*, whereas *dorgha* reflects its pronunciation in East Turkestan. Its meanings have varied over time and space, the most obvious one being "governor" or, as in the Mongol administration of this region, "resident." James Millward, *Eurasian Crossroads: A History of Xinjiang* (New York: Columbia University Press, 2007), 62. In the Turpan context, its later meaning of "superintendent" seems most appropriate. Gerhard Doerfer, *Türkische und mongolische Elemente im Neupersischen* (Wiesbaden: F. Steiner, 1963), 1:319–23.
23. David Brophy, *Uyghur Nation: Reform and Revolution on the Russia-China Frontier* (Cambridge, MA: Harvard University Press, 2016), 9–10.
24. On the management of water resources, see L. Wawryzn Golab, "A Study of Irrigation in East Turkestan," *Anthropos* 46 (1951): 187–99; and Eric T. Schluessel, "Water, Justice, and Local Government in Turn-of-the-Century Xinjiang," *Journal of the Social and Economic History of the Orient* 62, no. 4 (December 2019): 595–621.
25. Su Beihai and Jiang Jianhua, *Hami, Tulufan Weiwuer wang lishi* (Wulumuqi: Xinjiang daxue chubanshe, 1993), 224–28.
26. *QXDX* 51:336.
27. *QXDX* 50:385–86, 415–16.
28. *QXDX* 34:119, 141.
29. *QXDX* 58:353, 354, 355, 357.
30. For example, *QXDX* 2:33–35.
31. For example, *QXDX* 88:33–34.
32. The earliest document I have found relating to the Turpan court dates to 1880 (*QXDX* 51:364). Various other documents mention it in passing. Wang Jianxin discusses it in a later era in greater detail (Wang Jianxin, *Uyghur Education and Social Order: The Role of Islamic Leadership in the Turpan Basin* [Tokyo: Institute for the Study of the Languages and Cultures of Asia and Africa, 2004], 40–41). The Kashgar court is evidenced by partial records and manuals held in European and Chinese collections, including a hefty file of divorce cases (Staatsbibliothek Berlin, Hartmann 44) and manuals of jurisprudence (for example, Kashgar Museum 0105, *Majmūʿat al-Masāʾil* and Leiden University Library, Or. 26.684 *Majmūʿat al-Masāʾil*). Courts in towns near Khotan are attested in documents currently held at the Center for Research on Islam in Xinjiang.
33. Wang Shu'nan et al., comps., *Xinjiang tuzhi* (Taipei: Wenhai chubanshe, 1965), *juan* 38, 7b.

34. David Brophy, "The Junghar Mongol Legacy and the Language of Loyalty in Qing Xinjiang," *Harvard Journal of Asiatic Studies* 73, no. 2 (2013): 231–58.

35. For an exploration of Qing language ideology and the centrality of Manchu, see David Porter, "Bannermen as Translators: Manchu Language Education in the Hanjun Banners," *Late Imperial China* 40, no. 2 (December 2019).

36. Erich Haenisch, "Turco-Manjurica aus Turfan," *Oriens* 4, no. 2 (December 1951), 256–72.

37. According to the Manchu and Chaghatay postscripts of the translation Fušan made, he was a Manchu bannerman of the bordered blue banner and the son of the adjutant (*janggin*) of the Ili Solon Camp Mandangga. At the Kashgar circuit intendant's office, he was only one of about eighty functionaries, but only two translators. He held the rank of sixth-rank secretary (*zhongshu*) and was a bachelor of the Department of Study of the National Academy (*shujishi*). Such secretaries were often employed for translation work in border stations. Fušan was known at the British and Russian consulates, as he was also fluent in Russian, having studied in Vernyi (later Almaty). Gustaf Mannerheim, *Dagbok förd under min resa i Centralasian och Kina 1906-07-08* (Helsingfors: Svenska Litteratursällskapet i Finland, 2010), 242–43. Fušan later sent his son to learn Russian there as well. Fušan eventually returned to Ghulja in Ili, where in 1907 Carl Gustaf Emil Mannerheim stayed briefly in his home. Mannerheim refers to Fušan as "Sibe-Solon," the Turki *Exhortations* calls him a "Manchu," and the Manchu afterword to the *Exhortations* notes his presence with the "Solon tribe (*aiman*)." It is sufficient to describe him as a "Manchu-speaker."

38. Guoli gugong bowuyuan Gugong wenxian bianji weiyuan hui, comp., *Gongzhong dang Guangxu chao zouzhe*, 24 vols. (Taipei: Guoli gugong buwuyuan, 1973–75), 7:316–17.

39. On the printing, see Rian Thum, *The Sacred Routes of Uyghur History* (Cambridge, MA: Harvard University Press, 2014), 178–81. For a biography of an official involved in the printing, see National Library of China, Shen Tongfang, *Xinjiang teyong dao Yingjishaer zhili Tongzhi Huang jun zhuan*. There were several printings of the text, with minor variations. For a good example, see Staatsbibliothek zu Berlin, Hartmann Collection, Zu 8390, *Yuzhi quanshan yaoyan*.

40. Johannes Avetaranian, *A Muslim Who Became a Christian: The Story of John Avetaranian, an Autobiography* (London: AuthorsOnline, 2002), 80–82. Avetaranian's own account suggests that the missionary himself played a vital role in Fušan's work, but this is not verified by the other sources.

41. Staatsbibliothek zu Berlin, Zu 8390.

42. For a comprehensive study of these manuals, see J. E. Dağyeli, *"Gott liebt das Handwerk": Moral, Identität und religiöse Legitimierung in der mittelasiatischen Handwerksrisāla* (Wiesbaden: Reichert, 2011).

43. Staatsbibliothek zu Berlin, Zu 8390, 59–60; Thum, *Sacred Routes*, 178–79.

44. National Library of China, *Kechäk terädurghanning bayāni*. The text was originally in English, and then translated into Chaghatay through Chinese. I am grateful to Peter Lavelle for sharing this text with me.

45. Vatican Library, R. G. Oriente IV 395 6-1-3, *Han Hui hebi*, preface; Chen Zongzhen, "Han-Hui hebi yanjiu," *Minzu yuwen* 1989, no. 5. Chen Zongzhen identifies the Ming glossary *Gaochang yiyu* as a likely model. The book was in use in Xinjiang's schools through the first decade of the twentieth century.

46. On translingual practice, see Lydia He Liu, *The Clash of Empires: The Invention of China in Modern World Making* (Cambridge, MA: Harvard University Press, 2004), 11–13.

47. *Luopu xian xiangtuzhi*, in XTZG, 403–7.

48. Eric T. Schluessel, "Language and the State in Late Qing Xinjiang," in *Historiography and Nation-Building Among Turkic Populations*, ed. Birgit Schlyter and Mirja Juntunen (Istanbul: Swedish Research Institute in Istanbul, 2014), 145–68, 153.

49. Jürgen Osterhammel, *The Transformation of the World: A Global History of the Nineteenth Century* (Princeton: Princeton University Press, 2014), 828.

50. Stevan Harrell, "Introduction: Civilizing Project and the Reaction to Them," in *Cultural Encounters on China's Ethnic Frontiers*, ed. Stevan Harrell (Seattle: University of Washington Press, 1995), 3–36, 18–20, 27.

51. Thomas Babington Macauley, "The Minute on Education," in *Sources of Indian Tradition*, vol. 2, ed. Stephen Hay (New York: Columbia University Press, 1988), 69–72. Homi Bhabha provides an enlightening discussion of Macaulay and others like him who deployed the language of liberalism in service of colonial discipline. Homi Bhabha, "Of Mimicry and Man: The Ambivalence of Colonial Discourse," *October* 102 (Spring 1984): 127–28.

52. India Office Records, L/P&S/7/202; Mannerheim, *Dagbok*, 85.

53. This narrative first appears in 1934 in the newspaper *Chīn Turkistān awāzi* (Chinese *Bianduo yue kan*), and later in Alptekin's memoirs. It is reproduced in Hamada Masami, "Jihâd, hijra et 'devoir du sel' dans l'histoire du Turkestan Oriental," *Turcica* 33 (2001): 31; Kataoka, *Shinchō Shinkyō tōji kenkyū* (Tōkyō: Yūzankaku, 1990), 323; James A. Millward and Nabijan Tursun, "Political History and Strategies of Control, 1884–1976," in *Xinjiang: China's Muslim Borderland*, ed. S. Frederick Starr (Armonk, NY: M. E. Sharpe, 2004), 63–98, 66; and Millward, *Eurasian Crossroads*, 142–143. It has become somewhat of a trope of writing on late-Qing Xinjiang, and an emblem of its cultural violence in the absence of other sources.

54. IOR L/P&S/7/202; Mannerheim, *Dagbok*, 85.

55. Chou, "Frontier Studies," 296; Zhao Yuntian, "Qingmo xinzheng qijian Xinjiang wenhua jiaoyu de fazhan," *Xiyu yanjiu* 2002, no. 2:47–55.

56. Li Yan and Wang Xiaohui, "Qingmo Xinjiang shanhou ju chuyi," *Xibei Minzu Daxue xuebao (zhexue shehui kexue ban)* 2005, no. 3:10, 13; Zuo Zongtang, *Zuo Wenxiang gong quanji* (Taipei: Wenhai chubanshe, 1979), 2,254–57.

57. *QXDX* 29:387–91; 30:11–13.

58. Wang Shu'nan et al., *Xinjiang tuzhi, xuexiao*.

59. Quoted in *QXDX* 32:192–95.

60. *QXDX* 29:142.

61. *QXDX* 28:138–39, 142, 159, 196.

62. *QXDX* 28:404.

63. *QXDX* 29:203, 210–11.

64. *QXDX* 36:245–47.

65. *QXDX* 28:373–74.

66. *QXDX* 28:446, 449. Yu Xueshi's age is estimated on the basis of the known ages of some of his classmates.

67. Millward, *Eurasian Crossroads*, 143. (Millward cites XUAR 15-11-309, dated GX 12.9.25. I have been unable to locate this document in the published Turpan archive, and so I suspect that it is from the currently inaccessible provincial-level archive.) *QXDX* 29:391–95, 406–11.

68. *QXDX* 29:217–18; 36:245–47.

69. Hening, *San zhou ji lüe* (Taipei: Chengwen chubanshe, 1968), 213–19.

70. Michael Szonyi, *The Art of Being Governed: Everyday Politics in Late Imperial China* (Princeton: Princeton University Press, 2017), 22.

71. Xiao Xiong, *Xi jiang za shu shi, xu, juan* 3, 1b–2a. Xiao Xiong (d. 1892) probably made these observations on his visit to Xinjiang in 1888.

72. IVR RAN B 779, Abū 'l-Maḥdī, *Ushbu ötkän dhamānada*, 5r–8r.

73. *QXDX* 30:403–4.

74. FHA 04-01-38-0167-025; *QXDX* 29:56–57.

75. School of Oriental and African Studies Archives, PP MS 8, Papers of Professor Sir Edward Denison Ross and Lady Dora Ross, #57.

76. TH/Jarring, 126v.

77. *QXDX* 36:365–68.

78. *QXDX* 28:404–5, 406–7, 408–9.

79. *QXDX* 30:419. Unfortunately, because Sājid seems to have been a very common name in Turpan at the time, it is difficult to determine whether other Sājids in the archive were the same man.

80. *QXDX* 30:282, 282–83, 366.

81. *QXDX* 36:7.

82. *QXDX* 28:226.

83. *Gongzhong dang Guangxu chao zouzhe*, 4:502–4.

84. *QXDX* 2:33–35, 127.

85. *QXDX* 32:156–58; 36:245–47.

86. *QXDX* 31:81–82, 127–29, 395–96; 32:156–58.

87. *QXDX* 32:192–95.

88. *QXDX* 32:156–58, 196, 207–8.

89. *QXDX* 33:412–17.

90. John Törnquist, *Kaschgar: några bilder från innersta Asiens land, folk och mission* (Stockholm: Svenska missionsförbundets förlag, 1926), 231.

91. Yang Zengxin, comp., *Buguozhai wendu* (Taipei: Chengwen chubanshe, 1982), *xinji yi*, 2,518–19.

92. Yang Zengxin, *dingji xia*, 1,072–73; *xinji yi*, 2,484–86; XUAR Archive M16.004.YJ.2214; M16.015.YJ.0274; M16.019.YJ.3826; M16.018.YJ.3396; M16.010.YJ.7691.

93. XUAR Archive M16.004.YJ.2153; M16.004.YJ.2162; M16.004.YJ.2632; M16.005.YJ.3078; M16.005.YJ.3707; M16.006.YJ.4124.

94. For example, Zhang Shicai et al., eds., *Weiwuerzu qiyue wenshu yi zhu* (Wulumuqi: Xinjiang daxue chubanshe, 2015), 772–74.

95. XUAR Archive M16.004.YJ.2807; M16.004.YJ.2806; M16.004.YJ.2807; M16.005.YJ.3407; M16.005.YJ.3665.

96. Daniele Conversi, "Reassessing Current Theories of Nationalism: Nationalism as Boundary Maintenance and Creation," *Nationalism and Ethnic Politics* 1, no. 1 (1995): 73–85.

97. Sidiq Musayup, "'Chala tongchi adäm öltürür' degän sözning kelip chiqish järyani," *Shinjang tarikh materiyalliri* 38:352–55. I am grateful to Aynur Kadir for mentioning this saying.

98. Tailaiti Wubuli and Ailijiang Aisa, "Yijian guanyu Minguo qinian Kuche panluan de xin wenshu—'Mahemude su Ali Hezhuo panluan zhuang' yishi," *Xiyu yanjiu* 2014, no. 3:27–49.

99. I discuss this case in greater detail in Eric T. Schluessel, "Muslims at the *Yamen* Gate: Translating Justice in Late-Qing Xinjiang," in *Kashgar Revisited: Uyghur Studies in Memory of Gunnar Jarring*, ed. Ildikó Bellér-Hann, Birgit Schlyter, and Jun Sugawara (Leiden: Brill, 2016), 116–38.

100. M. M. Bakhtin, *The Dialogic Imagination* (Austin: University of Texas Press, 1981), 299; Miyako Inoue, "Stenography and Ventriloquism in Late Nineteenth Century Japan," *Language and Communication* 31 (2011): 181–90.

101. Janet Theiss, "Explaining the Shrew: Narratives of Spousal Violence and the Critique of Masculinity in Eighteenth-Century Criminal Cases," in *Writing and Law in*

Late Imperial China: Crime, Conflict, and Judgment, ed. Robert Hegel and Katherine Carlitz (Seattle: University of Washington Press, 2007), 44–63, 44.

102. Karasawa, "Hanasukoto to kakukoto no hazama de."
103. Thomas Buoye, "Suddenly Murderous Intent Arose: Bureaucratization and Benevolence in Eighteenth-Century Homicide Reports," *Late Imperial China* 16, no. 2 (1995): 62–97; Jennifer Neighbors, "Criminal Intent and Homicide Law in Qing and Republican China" (PhD diss., University of California, Los Angeles, 2004), 6.
104. *QXDX* 58:104–6, 264–66.
105. Karasawa, "Hanasukoto to kakukoto no hazama de."
106. Schluessel, "Muslims at the *Yamen* Gate," 131.
107. Sally Engle Merry, "Law and Colonialism," *Law and Society Review* 25, no. 4 (1991): 892–93.
108. Karl Menges and N. Th. Katanov, *Volkskundliche Texte aus Ost-Türkistan*, 2 vols. (1933, 1946; Leipzig: Zentralantiquariat der Deutschen Demokratischen Republik, 1976), 1:48–50; 2:38–42.
109. *QXDX* 29:91–92.
110. Jarring Prov. 207, "Butlarning bayāni." ... *wä bā-kassal bolmaydur, shahargä ot almaydur, dep bāṭil khiyāllarni qiladur.*
111. *QXDX* 28:299; XUAR Archive M16.002.YJ.0081.
112. *QXDX* 29:71.

4. Bad Women and Lost Children

1. *QXDX* 58:208, 217.
2. Rogers Brubaker, *Grounds for Difference* (Cambridge, MA: Harvard University Press, 2015), 87–89.
3. On the ethnography of women's lives and sexuality, see Linda Benson, "A Much-Married Woman: Marriage and Divorce in Xinjiang 1850–1950," *Muslim World* 83, nos. 3–4 (July–October 1993): 227–47; Linda Benson, "The Question of Women: Discovering Uyghur Women's History in Northwestern China," *Oriental Archive* 79 (2011): 47–70; Ildikó Bellér-Hann, *Community Matters in Xinjiang, 1880–1949: Towards a Historical Anthropology of the Uyghur* (Leiden: Brill, 2008), 188–201, 235–302, particularly 266–78 on temporary marriage, prostitution, and adultery.
4. Adrienne Davis, "'Don't Let Nobody Bother Yo' Principle': The Sexual Economy of American Slavery," in *Sister Circle: Black Women and Work*, ed. Sharon Harley and the Black Women and Work Collective (New Brunswick, NJ: Rutgers University Press, 2002), 103–27, 118–19.
5. Shahla Haeri, *Law of Desire: Temporary Marriage in Shi'i Iran* (Syracuse: Syracuse University Press, 2014); Matthew Sommer, *Polyandry and Wife-Selling in Qing Dynasty China: Survival Strategies and Judicial Interventions* (Oakland: University of California Press, 2015), 2. For a case study of female bodies as objects of exchange in the creation of male community, see Amy Stanley, *Selling Women: Prostitution, Markets, and the Household in Early Modern Japan* (Berkeley: University of California Press, 2012).
6. Ann Stoler, "Sexual Affronts and Racial Frontiers: European Identities and the Cultural Politics of Exclusion in Colonial Southeast Asia," *Comparative Studies in Society and History* 34, no. 3 (1992): 514–51.
7. My conception and treatment of marriage throughout this chapter are informed by Matthew Sommer's work on sexuality and marriage in imperial China: Sommer, *Sex, Law and Society in Late Imperial China* (Stanford: Stanford University Press, 2000); and Sommer, *Polyandry and Wife-Selling.*

8. For an extended study of the feminization and eroticization of the Miao people in Chinese discourse and representation, see Louisa Schein, *Minority Rules: The Miao and the Feminine in China's Cultural Politics* (Durham, NC: Duke University Press, 2000).
9. Bellér-Hann, *Community Matters*, 266.
10. Bellér-Hann, 256–66; British Library, India Office Records L/P&S/10/976; *Nanjiang nongcun shehui* (Beijing: Minzu chubanshe, 2009), 10; Benson, "A Much-Married Woman."
11. IVR RAN B 779, *Ushbu ötkän dhamānada*.
12. On women's economic life, see Bellér-Hann, *Community Matters*, 196–202.
13. Similar dynamics are documented in Jay Dautcher, *Down a Narrow Road: Identity and Masculinity in a Uyghur Community in Xinjiang China* (Cambridge, MA: Harvard University Asia Center, 2009).
14. QXDX 27:102–9. The tax-paying household, as Qing officials in Turpan assessed it, represented a group of people living in the same house. This number approximates family size.
15. Average household size is calculated from aggregate population data collected in 1877, 1906, 1911, and 1936. Data for 1906 and 1911 distinguish Muslims from Han and provide numbers of individual men and women, as well as numbers of households. Household size in Musulman-majority areas was consistently around five to six members. Wei Guangtao, *Kanding Xinjiang ji* (Harbin: Heilongjiang jiaoyu chubanshe, 2014), *juan* 7, 2r–2v; anonymous, "Xinjiang shexing sheng yi" in *Xiaofanghu zhai yudi congchao*, 2 *zhi*, 2, 117a–18b; Cao Jiguan, *Xinjiang jianzhi zhi*, 1:7b–11b; Wang Shu'nan et al., comps. *Xinjiang tuzhi* (Taipei: Wenhai chubanshe, 1965), *minzheng* 4a–14b; Wu Tiequn, "Qingdai Xinjiang jiansheng qianhou Yili renkou bianqian kao," *Xinjiang difang zhi* 3 (March 2009): 52–56; Zhang Dajun, *Xinjiang fengbao qishi nian* (Taibei: Lanxi chubanshe, 1980), 2,902–6. Tax registers from Turpan confirm that the same was true locally (*QXDX* 27:102–9 and 147–48).
16. Bellér-Hann, *Community Matters*, 266–75. A research report from 1958 from Ghulja appears to describe one instance of temporary marriage (*Weiwuerzu shehui lishi diaocha* [Beijing: Minzu chubanshe, 2009], 90) while the Kashgar report from 1956 comments briefly on such "secret" marriages (*Nanjiang nongcun shehui*, 10). One woman in the Kashgar village who was married thirty-three times may certainly have done so through temporary marriage. India Office records also comment on these issues where they touched on British subjects (India Office Records, L/P&S/10/976).
17. Haeri, *Law of Desire*, 49–51, 60, 66.
18. I have studied the available manuscripts, but there is no room to discuss them at length here. See Leiden University Library Or. 26.684 *Majmūʿat al-Masāʾil*; Kashgar Museum 0105 *Majmūʿat al-Masāʾil*; Leiden University Library Or. 26.667 *Zubdatu ʾl-masāʾil wa ʾl-ʿaqāʾid*.
19. Bellér-Hann, *Community Matters*, 275–78.
20. Bellér-Hann, 274.
21. Xiao Xiong, *Xijiang za shu shi* (Suzhou: Zhenxin shushe, 1895–97), 1a–1b, 8b.
22. Stevan Harrell asserts that "Civilizers of all sorts have seen peripheral peoples as both erotic and promiscuous in their behavior, as being at a lower level of culture where they have not yet learned the proper civilized morals of sexual repression and/or hypocrisy." Stevan Harrell, "Introduction: Civilizing Project and the Reaction to Them," in *Cultural Encounters on China's Ethnic Frontiers*, ed. Stevan Harrell (Seattle: University of Washington Press, 1995), 3–36, 10.
23. Of course, any reasonably well-traveled Chinese literatus would have recognized the great diversity of practices surrounding marriage and sexuality in China

proper. (Sommer, *Polyandry and Wife-Selling*, covers a range of them.) Invoking these tropes of difference reflected a long tradition of essentializing the Other in terms of deviation from elite Confucian familial norms.

24. Gui E, "Jin Hami shiyi shu," in *Mingdai Hami Tulufan ziliao huibian*, ed. Chen Gaohua (Wulumuqi: Xinjiang renmin chubanshe, 1984), 459–65, 460–62.

25. Bellér-Hann, *Community Matters*, 258–66.

26. See passages in *Baicheng xian xiangtuzhi*, 268; *Yanqi fu xiangtuzhi*, 282; *Ruoqiang xian xiangtuzhi*, 309; *Kuche zhilizhou xiangtuzhi*, 320; and *Xinping xian xiangtuzhi*, 289, 293, all in *XTZG*. On the history of Uyghur surnames, see Äsäd Sulayman, "Hybrid Name Culture in Xinjiang: Problems Surrounding Uyghur Name/Surname Practices and Their Reform," in *Situating the Uyghurs Between China and Central Asia*, ed. Ildikó Bellér-Hann, Cristina Cesaro, Rachel Harris, and Joanne Smith Finley (Aldershot, UK: Ashgate, 2007), 109–127, 109, 112.

27. *Wensu xian xiangtuzhi*, 262; *Shaya xian xiangtuzhi*, 328; *Hetian zhilizhou xiangtuzhi*, 386, 397, 399; *Shule fu xiangtuzhi*, 342; *Pishan xian xiangtuzhi*, 377, ad nauseam, in *XTZG*.

28. A story about Musulman sponsorship of tomb maintenance was part of Du Tong's argument that the Musulman possessed a spirit of generosity embodied in their veneration of ancestors. Wang Shu'nan et al., *Xinjiang tuzhi, juan* 38, 7b.

29. *QXDX* 1:229.

30. William C. Jones, trans., *The Great Qing Code* (New York: Oxford University Press, 1994), 133–35; *Da Qing lü li*, 1899 edition, http://lsc.chineselegalculture.org/, statute 125, *chu qi*.

31. Sommer, *Sex, Law, and Society*, 11, 141.

32. NPM 119940. The provincial plan for Hunan established by memorial in 1883 specifically increased punishments for demobilized soldiers who committed crimes. Liu Yanbo, "Wan Qing liang Hu diqu zhouxian 'jiudi zhengfa' shulun," *Jinan xuebao (zhexue shehui kexue ban)* 2012, no. 3:138–42.

33. James Millward, *Eurasian Crossroads: A History of Xinjiang* (New York: Columbia University Press, 2007), 138.

34. Brian Steele, "Thomas Jefferson's Gender Frontier," *Journal of American History* 95, no. 1 (June 2008): 19–23.

35. Wei Guangtao, *Kanding Xinjiang ji, juan* 7, 2r–2v.

36. *QXDX* 28:110. This order is not recorded in metropolitan documents but is found in the Turpan archives.

37. *QXDX* 28:109.

38. Bellér-Hann, *Community Matters*, 271; F. Grenard, *Mission scientifique dans la Haute Asie, 1890–1895*, pt. 2, *Le Turkestan et le Tibet, étude ethnographique et sociologique* (Paris: Ernest Leroux, 1898), 122–23.

39. *QXDX* 28:150–51, 153.

40. GX 7.8.7 "Qinhuo An yi jianjin yijiu fenbie banli zhe," in Liu Jintang, *Liu Xiangqin gong zougao* (Taipei: Chengwen Chubanshe, 1968), *juan* 2, 72a–75a.

41. *QXDX* 28:105.

42. *QXDX* 28:134.

43. *QXDX* 29:89–91. The catalogers appear to have misdated this document to GX 13.r4.28 and misread Wei's surname as Zhao.

44. Scattered stories indicate that Xiang Army elites also engaged in the trade, but perhaps they were better at hiding their activities, or conducting them in seemingly legitimate ways. G. G. Warren, "D'Ollone's Investigation on Chinese Moslems," *New China Review* 2 (1920): 276.

45. Jarring Prov. 117, Ṭālib Ākhūnd, *History of Yaʿqūb Beg*, 115r.

46. *QXDX* 28:218.

47. See, for example, a case from 1877: *QXDX* 28:104.
48. *QXDX* 28:105a, 105b, 106, 106–7.
49. *QXDX* 27:102–9.
50. Guoli gugong bowuyuan Gugong wenxian bianji weiyuan hui, comp., *Gongzhong dang Guangxu chao zouzhe*, 24 vols. (Taipei: Guoli gugong buwuyuan, 1973–75), 7:58–59.
51. Bellér-Hann, *Community Matters*, 246–56.
52. Chaghatay document dated MG 16.10.10, private collection, Ürümchi.
53. In Khazīmah's case, for example, her young husband's inability to provide her with a promised *toyluq* of clothing was one source of friction in their marriage. For an example of a silver *toyluq*, see *QXDX* 29:415.
54. Sommer, *Polyandry and Wife-Selling*.
55. *QXDX* 28:326–27, 327; IOR L/P&S/10/825, L/P&S/10/976, L/P&S/7/203, and L/P&S/7/202.
56. Eric T. Schluessel, "The Law and the 'Law': Two Kinds of Legal Space in Late-Qing China," *Extrême-Orient Extrême-Occident* 40 (November 2016): 12.
57. *Da Qing lüli*, statute 286, *lüe ren lüe mai ren*.
58. *QXDX* 29:178.
59. *QXDX* 28:414, 415, 421, 441, 444. The name "Piyaza" comes from a tradition of naming a child after a common item that is close at hand, in this case "onion," with an added -a to indicate feminine gender.
60. *QXDX* 30:13, 14, 49.
61. *QXDX* 29:251, 258–59, 261–62, 284, 345, 371–72, 378; 58:227.
62. Dautcher, *Down a Narrow Road*, 75–77.
63. Karl Menges and N. Th. Katanov, *Volkskundliche Texte aus Ost-Türkistan*, 2 vols. (1933, 1946; Leipzig: Zentralantiquariat der Deutschen Demokratischen Republik, 1976), 2:38–42.
64. Janet Theiss, *Disgraceful Matters: The Politics of Chastity in Eighteenth-Century China* (Berkeley: University of California Press, 2005), 17–23. The case presented here is similar to the one Theiss narrates in 1792 on the Miao frontier.
65. *QXDX* 56:143, 153, 155, 159, 165, 168, 177, 197, 250, 281.
66. Charles Adolphus Murray, Earl of Dunmore, *The Pamirs: Being a Narrative of a Year's Expedition on Horseback and on Foot Through Kashmir, Western Tibet, Chinese Tartary, and Russian Central Asia*, 2 vols. (London: J. Murray, 1893), 1:328–29.
67. *QXDX* 27:102–9. While the date of this household register is unclear, judging from circumstantial evidence, it was written when this case took place or within a few years after.
68. *QXDX* 56:281.
69. Vivien W. Ng, "Ideology and Sexuality: Rape Laws in Qing China," *Journal of Asian Studies* 46, no. 1 (1987): 57–70; Theiss, *Disgraceful Matters*, 192–209.
70. Menges and Katanov, *Volkskundliche Texte*, 2:38–42.
71. *QXDX* 28:321. "Baiheitang" is probably a transliteration of the name Bakhta Khan, and yet the unique choice of characters to represent those sounds was stable across documents, unlike many transliterations. This suggests that the woman in question was known by this specific name and its characters' meanings.
72. *QXDX* 28:189.
73. Menges and Katanov, *Volkskundliche Texte*, 2:38–42.
74. *QXDX* 64:300, 325–26, 327; 65:21, 23, 37, 50–51.
75. For examples, see Jeff Snyder-Reinke, "Afterlives of the Dead: Uncovering Graves and Mishandling Corpses in Nineteenth-Century China," *Frontiers of History in China* 11, no. 1 (2016): 1–20; Melissa Macauley, *Social Power and Legal Culture: Litigation Masters in Late Imperial China* (Stanford: Stanford University Press, 1998), 197–99.

76. *Gongzhongdang Guangxu chao zouzhe*, 8:81–82.
77. *QXDX* 28:268.
78. Menges and Katanov, *Volkskundliche Texte*, 2:38–42.
79. *QXDX* 28:321.
80. *QXDX* 28:379.
81. *QXDX* 31:90–91.
82. *QXDX* 28:362.
83. *QXDX* 28:326–27, 327.
84. Xiao Xiong, *Xijiang za shu shi, juan* 3, 9a–9b.
85. A similar conception of transgressive mobility, and of "transgressive intimacies," can be found in David Ambaras, *Japan's Imperial Underworlds: Intimate Encounters at the Borders of Empire* (Cambridge: Cambridge University Press, 2018).
86. Michel Foucault, *The History of Sexuality*, vol. 1, *An Introduction* (New York: Vintage, 1990), 103.
87. Ann Stoler, "Rethinking Colonial Categories: European Communities and the Boundaries of Rule," *Comparative Studies in History and Society* 31, no. 1 (January 1989): 143–50; Stoler, *Race and the Education of Desire: Foucault's History of Sexuality and the Colonial Order of Things* (Durham, NC: Duke University Press, 1995), 7–13.
88. *QXDX* 32:187, 188.
89. *QXDX* 51:34; 29: 397.
90. *QXDX* 28:148–49; 51:82, 83.
91. *Da Qing lü li*, statute 87, *shouliu mishi zinü*.

5. Recollecting Bones

1. *QXDX* 51:31–32; *QXDX* 51:86.
2. Rahilä Dawut, *Uyghur mazarliri* (Ürümchi: Shinjang khälq näshriyati, 2001), 201–9; Qurbān ʿAlī Khālidī, *Tārīkh-i jarīda-ye jadīda* (Kazanʾ: Qazān universitetining ṭabʿkhānasi, 1889), 34–40. Sayrāmī discusses the shrine at length and, in a later version of his history, provides a critique of its authenticity from an Islamic reformist perspective (TH/Beijing, 340–81).
3. TH/Beijing, 127. *Thāniyan, Khiṭāylar kelgünchä, yul özrä söngäkläri qurup yattilar.*
4. TH/Beijing, 258.
5. Dominick LaCapra, *Writing History, Writing Trauma* (Baltimore: Johns Hopkins University Press, 2014), xiv–xv.
6. LaCapra, 46, 53–58.
7. Feng Junguang, *Xi xing riji* (Shanghai, 1881 [Guangxu xinsi]), 3b, 12a–14a, 31a–33b, 67b–70a.
8. Feng Junguang, 4a, 73a.
9. Feng Junguang, 1a–2b; 67b–70a, 74a–74b.
10. Feng Junguang refers to Wang Zhengsheng by his style name Xiaocun (*Xi xing riji*, 8a–8b, 21a, 30a, 53b–54a, 55a, 59a).
11. Wang Zhensheng, *Xi zheng riji* (1900), 1a.
12. Wang Zhensheng, 26a–27b.
13. Qi Yunshi's (1751–1815), *Xi chui zhu zhici* (Shanghai: Shanghai Guji Chubanshe, 2010).
14. The word *Fan* has a broad range of meanings, roughly approximating "outsider."
15. Tobie Meyer-Fong, *What Remains: Coming to Terms with Civil War in Nineteenth-Century China* (Stanford: Stanford University Press, 2013), 4.
16. Zhang Daye, *The World of a Tiny Insect: A Memoir of the Taiping Rebellion and Its Aftermath*, trans. Xiaofei Tian (Seattle: University of Washington Press, 2013), 16–21.

17. *Huitu Xiangjun ping ni zhuan* (Shanghai: Shanghai shuju, 1899 [Guangxu *jihai*]); *Huitu Zuo gong ping xi zhuan* (Shanghai: Shanghai shuju, 1899 [Guangxu *jihai*]). Reprintings were made at several printing houses, including the Jinzhang shuju, Guangyi shuju, and Gonghe shuju. Print and microfilm copies are held in the Harvard, Columbia, and Princeton libraries.

18. The novel was apparently rather popular, as it was reprinted, often under the title *Romance of Prince Zuo Wenxiang [Zongtang] Recovering the West* (*Zuo Wenxiang gong zhengxi yanyi*). There is evidence to suggest that these novels themselves were based on a pair of recent plays of the same titles, also published in Shanghai.

19. Nigel C. Hunt, *War, Memory, and Trauma* (Cambridge: Cambridge University Press, 2010), 102–5.

20. TA/Pelliot, 3r; TH/Beijing, 5–7; TH/Jarring, 2r.

21. Yixin et al., comps., *Qinding pingding Shaan Gan Xinjiang Hui fei fanglüe*, in *Qi sheng fanglüe*, vols. 833–1,154, *juan* 305, 3.

22. *Fuping xian zhi* (1891 [Guangxu *xinmao*]), *juan* 8, 6–9. For more such stories, see, for example, Zhou Mingyi, comp., *Qianzhou zhi gao* (Qianying shuyuan, 1884 [Guangxu *jiashen*]), *juan* 4, 13; and Hou Chengxiu and Huang Heqing, comps., *Fenghuang ting xu zhi*, reproduced in *Zhongguo difangzhi jicheng* (1892; Shanghai: Shanghai shuju, 2002), *juan* 15.

23. Matthew Sommer, *Polyandry and Wife-Selling in Qing Dynasty China: Survival Strategies and Judicial Interventions* (Oakland: University of California Press, 2015), 3, demonstrates that unorthodox practices like widow remarriage were much more common than the official historical record would lead us to believe.

24. *Fuping xian zhi* (1891), *juan* 9.

25. Sun Yingke, comp., *Qianhou ershisi xiao tushuo* (Yangzhou: Banwu tang, 1841 [Daoguang *xinchou*]), 4, 17.

26. Meyer-Fong, *What Remains*, 108–9.

27. Hunt, *War, Memory, and Trauma*, 163.

28. See, for example, Tao Mo's argument for establishing Confucian schools and the *baojia* system in NPM 408002835; QXDX 28:370.

29. This is evidenced in a number of gazetteers in XTZG, including those for Dihua county (13), Qitai (37), Changji (48), Hutubi (89), and Turpan (125, 129), just to name a few.

30. Wei Guangtao, *Kanding Xinjiang ji* (Harbin: Heilongjiang jiaoyu chubanshe, 2014), *juan* 7, 2a–3a.

31. Yixin et al., *Qinding pingding Shan-Gan-Xinjiang huifei fanglüe*, *juan* 305, 2–4; *juan* 406, 4–5.

32. *Fuyuan xian xiangtu zhi*, 24, in XTZG.

33. *Qitai xian xiangtu zhi*, 31, in XTZG.

34. Ananya Jahanara Kabir, "Analogy in Translation: Imperial Rome, Medieval England, and British India," in *Postcolonial Approaches to the European Middle Ages: Translating Cultures*, ed. Ananya Jahanara Kabir and Deanne Williams (Cambridge: Cambridge University Press, 2005), 183–204.

35. Wu Aichen, *Lidai Xiyu shi chao* (Wulumuqi: Xinjiang renmin chubanshe, 2001), 219.

36. Nailene Josephine Chou, "Frontier Studies and Changing Frontier Administration in Late Ch'ing China: The Case of Sinkiang, 1759–1911" (PhD diss., University of Washington, 1976), 243–50.

37. Xiao Xiong, *Xijiang za shu shi* (Suzhou: Zhenxin shushe, 1895–97), *juan* 2, 39b–40a, 14a. Wang Shu'nan provides a striking contrast. Wang emphasized the distinctiveness of the Han-Tang legacy for the Chinese but excluded the Musulmans from it. (Wang Shu'nan et al., comps., *Xinjiang tuzhi* [Taipei: Wenhai chubanshe, 1965],

xuexiao 1, 1,387: "The other kind's origins are different from ours. To speak with them about our Han and Tang is like when our people listen to the ancient history of India: It is confusing and alien.") Yet Wang was a prolific antiquarian who produced an entire book of inscriptions found in the region.

38. *Fuyuan xian xiangtuzhi*, 26, in *XTZG*.
39. *Luntai xian xiangtuzhi*, 300, in *XTZG*.
40. *Suilai xian xiangtuzhi*, 80, in *XTZG*.
41. L. J. Newby, "The Chinese Literary Conquest of Xinjiang," *Modern China* 25, no. 4 (October 1999): 451–74; James Millward, "'Coming Onto the Map': 'Western Regions' Geography and Cartographic Nomenclature in the Making of Chinese Empire in Xinjiang," *Late Imperial China* 20, no. 2 (1999): 61–98.
42. For example, Pei Jingfu, *He hai Kunlun lu* (Shanghai: Wenming shuju, 1906 [Guangxu 32]), 182, 262, 360.
43. Piper Gaubatz, *Beyond the Great Wall: Urban Form and Transformation on the Chinese Frontiers* (Stanford: Stanford University Press, 1996), 72–74; Hening, *San zhou jilüe* (Taipei: Chengwen chubanshe, 1968), *juan* 2.
44. Pei Jingfu, *He hai Kunlun lu*, 256; Dai Liangzuo, *Xiyu beiming lu* (Wulumuqi: Xinjiang renmin chubanshe, 2013), 451–53.
45. Prasenjit Duara, "Superscribing Symbols: The Myth of Guandi, Chinese God of War," *Journal of Asian Studies* 47, no. 4 (1988): 778.
46. Eric T. Schluessel, "Cong chenghuang dao shuzu: Dingxiang Wang zai Xinjiang," *Lishi renleixue xuekan* 15, no. 2 (October 2017): 169–86.
47. *Dihua xian xiangtu zhi*, 12, in *XTZG*; Gaubatz, *Beyond the Great Wall*.
48. Khālidī, *Tārīkh-i Jarīda-ye Jadīda*, 4; IVR RAN C 578, Khālidī, *Tārīkh-i Jarīda-ye Jadīda*, 3a–5a.
49. Seyyed Hossein Nasr et al., eds., *The Study Quran: A New Translation and Commentary* (New York: HarperOne, 2015), 25:53.
50. This quotation is from the print version of the book. The manuscript reads, "Other people need a place to live, too! If you don't go to the tomb, there'll be no danger. Therefore, no other land will be given to you."
51. Rian Thum, *The Sacred Routes of Uyghur History* (Cambridge, MA: Harvard University Press, 2014), 159.
52. There is a rich tradition of scholarship on this topic. For one provocative theory on the interconnection of history, ritual, community, and the sacred, see Paul Steven Sangren, *History and Magical Power in a Chinese Community* (Stanford: Stanford University Press, 1987).
53. Meyer-Fong, *What Remains*, 62–63, 99–102, 127. On the idea of mortuary politics, see Vincent Brown, *The Reaper's Garden: Death and Power in the World of Atlantic Slavery* (Cambridge, MA: Harvard University Press, 2008).
54. *QXDX* 50:163, 165, 166, 167a, 170a.
55. *QXDX* 50:164, 167b, 170b.
56. Lee J. Alston, Edwyna Harris, and Bernardo Mueller, "The Development of Property Rights on Frontiers: Endowments, Norms, and Politics," *Journal of Economic History* 72, no. 3:741–70.
57. Liu Jintang, *Liu Xiangqin gong zou gao* (Taipei: Chengwen Chubanshe, 1968), *juan* 2, 72a–75a.
58. *Da Qing lü li*, 1899 edition, http://lsc.chineselegalculture.org/, statute 276, *fa zhong*.
59. *QXDX* 34:58, 60, 65–68, 96, 108–9, 380.
60. *QXDX* 28:325–26.
61. Cao Jiguan, *Xinjiang jianzhi zhi* (Taipei: Xuesheng Shuju, 1963), *juan* 1, 7b–11b; Wang Shu'nan et al., *Xinjiang tuzhi, minzheng* 4–5, 5b–6b.

62. This section is summarized from Eric T. Schluessel, "Exiled Gods: Territory, History, Empire, and a Hunanese Deity in Xinjiang," *Late Imperial China* (forthcoming).

63. Yi Baisha, *Diwang chunqiu* (Shanghai: Shanghai shudian, 1991), 89.

64. Yu Zhi, *Deyi lu* (Baoshan tang, 1885), 2b–4a.

65. Kataoka, *Shinchō Shinkyō*, 290–91. For details, see *XTZG*, 27, 209, 170, 259, 318, 394, and 372; and anonymous, comp., *Shache fu zhi*, in *Zhongguo xibei xijian fangzhi xu ji* (1909; Beijing: Zhonghua quanguo tushuguan wenxian suowei fuzhi zhongxin, 1997 [Xuantong 1]), 10:621–75, 661.

66. Mao Dun, "Xinjiang fengtu za yi," in *Mao Dun wenji* (Beijing: Renmin wenxue chubanshe, 1958–61), 9:408–30, 416–17.

67. Mao Dun, 417; Wang Penghui, "Chongjian fenghua: wan Qing Minguo qianqi Wulumuqi de miaoyu yu shehui ronghe," *Xiyu fazhan yanjiu* 2014:98.

68. E. J. Hobsbawm, *Nations and Nationalism Since 1780: Programme, Myth, Reality* (Cambridge: Cambridge University Press, 2002), 80–82.

69. Rogers Brubaker, *Grounds for Difference* (Cambridge, MA: Harvard University Press, 2015), 87–89.

70. Devin DeWeese, *Islamization and Native Religion in the Golden Horde: Baba Tükles and Conversion to Islam in Historical and Epic Tradition* (University Park: University of Pennsylvania Press, 1994), 50.

6. Historical Estrangement and the End of Empire

1. TA/Pelliot, 57v; TH/Beijing, 105–6, 293–94; TH/Jarring, 44v, 116r, 118v–118r.

2. TA/Pelliot, 3r; TH/Beijing, 5–7; TH/Jarring, 2r.

3. Mulla Musa Sayrami, *Tarikhi Hämidi*, trans. Änwär Baytur (Beyjing: Millätlär Näshriyati, 2008), 1–16; Änwär Baytur, "Mulla Musa Sayrami she'irliridin tallanma," *Bulaq* 15 (1985): 194–227.

4. The title of the *Tārīkh-i Ḥamīdī* is difficult to translate. Mullah Mūsa's history was originally called the *Tārīkh-i Amniyya*, the name of which refers to the patron of a manuscript he composed in 1901. According to one explanation, it reflects the time of peace—*amniyya*—in which he wrote, and so we may call it the "History of Peace." By 1908, according to the same argument, Sayrāmī was disillusioned with Qing and found hope instead in the Ottoman sultan Abdülhamid II. Thus he named the new version of his work, which was greatly expanded, the *Tārīkh-i Ḥamīdī* after him. The *Tārīkh-i Amniyya* was also named for a Musulman official in Aksu named Amīn Beg who had patronized Sayrāmī, but of course the title could have a dual meaning (K. Usmanov, "Molla Musa Sayrami: Ta'rikh-i amniya," in *Materialy po istorii kazakhskikh khanstv XV–XVIII vekov* [Alma Ata: Nauka, 1969], 1–15). Moreover, Amīn Beg is only mentioned as a patron in the earliest known version. In any case, the later *Tārīkh-i Ḥamīdī* contains nearly all of the text of the earlier *Tārīkh-i Amniyya* but also expands upon it significantly. Musa Sayramiy, *Tarikhi Hämidiy: Yengi tärjimä nuskha*, trans. Abdurä'op Polat Täklimakani (Istanbul: Täklimakan Uyghur näshriyati, 2019), 14–15. I therefore find it useful to refer to both as the *Tārīkh-i Ḥamīdī*.

5. Hodong Kim praises Sayrāmī extensively for his accuracy and "sound historical judgment." Kim, *Holy War in China: The Muslim Rebellion and State in Chinese Central Asia, 1864-1878* (Stanford: Stanford University Press, 2004), xvi.

6. The *Shajarah-i Turk*, for example, details the story at length. Abū 'l-Ghāzī Bahadur Khan, *Histoire des Mongols et des Tatares par Aboul-Ghâzi Béhâdour Khân, souverain de Kharezm et historien Djaghataï, 1603-1664 A.D., texte Turc-Oriental, publié d'après le manuscrit du Musée Asiatique de St-Pétersbourg, collationné sur les manuscrits de Göttingue et de Berlin*

et sur l'édition de Kazan, 1825, avec une traduction française, des notes critiques des variants et un index, ed. and trans. Petr I. Desmaisons (Amsterdam: Philo, 1970), 61–63.

7. TH/Beijing, 21–22.

8. Abū 'l-Fażl b. Mubārak, *The History of Akbar*, vol. 1, ed. and trans. Wheeler M. Thackston (Cambridge, MA: Harvard University Press, 2015), 219.

9. Devin DeWeese, *Islamization and Native Religion in the Golden Horde: Baba Tükles and Conversion to Islam in Historical and Epic Tradition* (University Park: University of Pennsylvania Press, 1994), 516–21.

10. The *Tārīkh-i Rashīdī* of Mirza Ḥaydar Dughlat presents the story of Tughluq Temür Khan at length (*Mirza Haydar Dughlat's Tarikh-i Rashidi: A History of the Khans of Moghulistan*, trans. Wheeler M. Thackston [Cambridge, MA: Harvard University, Department of Near Eastern Languages and Civilizations, 1996], 8–11).

11. TH/Beijing, 15–17; TH/Jarring, 5v–6v. The story is adapted closely from the *Shajarah-i Turk*.

12. Kim, *Holy War in China*, 130; TH/Beijing, 48. While the text about Tughlug Temür Khan is adapted from the *Tarikh-i Rashidi*, Sayrāmī apparently felt that it was important also to include the first Islamizer of the Turks, whom the *Tarikh-i Rashidi* does not mention.

13. TH/Beijing, 67; TH/Jarring, 28r.

14. TH/Beijing, 67–70; TH/Jarring 28r–29v; TA/Pelliot 30r.

15. TH/Beijing, 70; TH/Jarring, 29v.

16. This may a joke on Sayrāmī's part or that of his sources about the exchange value of Chinese for Muslims. On the other hand, the number forty is numerologically significant in Uyghur culture and often signifies "many" of something.

17. TH/Beijing has simply *Musulmān boladur*, while TA/Pelliot and TH/Jarring have *maḥfī Musulmān boladur*.

18. Sayrāmī introduces a second narrative of dynastic change in China that would seem to contradict this assertion of unbroken descent. The "Muslim emperor" story is present in the earlier manuscripts of the *Tarikh-i Amniyya*, while this new narrative, from a Chinese source via Qurbān ʿAlī Khalidi's work, was added only in the 1908 *Tarikh-i Hamidi*.

19. Anthony Smith, *The Cultural Foundations of Nations: Hierarchy, Covenant and Republic* (Malden, MA: Blackwell, 2008), 77–78.

20. TH/Beijing, 77–78, 80–81; TH/Jarring, 32v–33r, 34r; TA/Pelliot, 37r–37v.

21. Hamada, "Jihad, Hijra, et 'devoir du sel,'" 54–59.

22. Haiyun Ma, "The Mythology of the Prophet's Ambassadors in China: Histories of Sa'd Waqqas and Gess in Chinese Sources," *Journal of Muslim Minority Affairs* 26, no. 3 (2006): 445–52; Zvi Ben-Dor Benite, "From 'Literati' to 'Ulama': The Origins of Chinese Muslim Nationalist Historiography," *Nationalism and Ethnic Politics* 9, no. 4 (2004): 83–85.

23. Svetlana Rimsky-Korsakoff Dyer, "T'ang T'ai-Tsung's Dream: A Soviet Dungan Version of a Legend on the Origin of the Chinese Muslims," *Monumenta Serica* 35 (1981–83): 545–70.

24. J. E. Dağyeli, *"Gott liebt das Handwerk": Moral, Identität und religiöse Legitimierung in der mittelasiatischen Handwerks-risāla* (Wiesbaden: Reichert, 2011), 88–89; Rian Thum, *The Sacred Routes of Uyghur History* (Cambridge, MA: Harvard University Press, 2014), 99.

25. Staatsbibliothek zu Berlin, Ms. Or. oct. 1670, *Tārīkh-i jarīda-ye jadīda*, 206–26.

26. Thierry Zarcone, "Between Legend and History: About the 'Conversion' to Islam of Two Prominent Lamaists in the Seventeenth-Eighteenth Centuries," in *Islam and Tibet—Interactions Along the Musk Routes*, ed. Anna Akasoy, Charles Burnett, and Ronit Yoeli-Tlalim (New York: Routledge, 2011), 281–95, 285–88.

27. British Library OR 8164, 56b–57a; Jarring Prov. 191; Zayit Akun Pazilbay, *Iskändär-namä*, ed. Qurban Wäli (Beyjing: Millätlär Näshriyati, 1990), 87–102; Staatsbibliothek zu Berlin Ms. Or. quart. 1294, *Volkstümliche Scherzerzählung*; British Library, IO Islamic 4860/Mss Turki 17, *Three Prose Tales*.
28. Mary Louise Pratt, "Arts of the Contact Zone," *Profession* (1991): 33–40.
29. Sidney Griffith, "Christian Lore and the Arabic Quran: The 'Companions of the Cave' in Surat al-Kahf and in Syriac Christian Tradition," in *The Quran in Its Historical Context*, ed. Gabriel Said Reynolds (London: Routledge, 2008), 109–138, 114–16.
30. See, for example, Abū Isḥāq Aḥmad ibn Muḥammad ibn Ibrāhīm al-Thaʿlabī, ʿArāʾis al-majālis fī qiṣaṣ al-anbiyāʾ' or "Lives of the Prophets," trans. William M. Brinner (Leiden: Brill, 2002), 104.
31. Nāṣir al-Dīn b. Burhān al-Dīn al-Rabghūzī, *The Stories of the Prophets: Qiṣaṣ al-Anbiyāʾ,' an Eastern Turkish Version*, ed. H. E. Boeschoten, M. van Damme, and S. Tezcan (Leiden: Brill, 1995). Rabghūzī quotes an earlier writer of "stories of the prophets," Abū Isḥāq al-Nīshābūrī. For an overview of the work and the problems of researching the Rabghūzī text, see Robert Dankoff, "Rabghuzi's Stories of the Prophets," *Journal of the American Oriental Society* 117, no. 1 (January–March 1997): 115–26.
32. Karl Jahn, *Die Chinageschichte des Rašīd ad-Dīn: Übersetzung, Kommentar, Facsimiletafeln* (Vienna: Verlag der Österreichischen Akademie der Wissenschaften, 1971).
33. Karl Jahn, *China in der islamischen Geschichtsschreibung* (Vienna: Hermann Böhlaus Nachf., 1971), 70–71. Other official chronicles that directly related to China also found their way into broader circulation during this period, yet still maintained their generic separation from legendary or sacred history, for example, Ghiyāthuddīn Naqqāsh, "Report to Mirza Baysunghur on the Timurid Legation to the Ming Court at Peking," in *Album Prefaces and Other Documents on the History of Painters and Calligraphers*, ed. Wheeler M. Thackston (Leiden: Brill, 2001), 53–68. This work, under various other titles, became quite popular, being incorporated into a number of Persian- and, later, Turkic-language histories. (Ildikó Bellér-Hann, *A History of Cathay: A Translation and Linguistic Analysis of a Fifteenth-Century Turkic Manuscript* [Bloomington, IN: Research Institute for Inner Asian Studies, 1995], 1–23; David J. Roxburgh, "The 'Journal' of Ghiyath al-Din Naqqash, Timurid Envoy to Khan Balïgh, and Chinese Art and Architecture," in *The Power of Things and the Flow of Cultural Transformations*, ed. Lieselotte E. Saurma-Jeltsch and Anja Eisenbeiß [Berlin: Deutscher Kunstverlag, 2010], 90–113, 109n15.) Some version of the text appeared in Mīrkhwānd's *Rawżat al-safāʿ* (Garden of purity, before 1498), and then the *Ḥabīb al-siyār* of his son Khwāndamīr. Yet it never seems to have influenced other East Turkestani depictions of China, not even the *Tārīkh-i Ḥamīdī*, despite the fact that Sayrāmī cites the *Rawżat* in several places.
34. Schluessel, *The World as Seen from Yarkand: Ghulām Muḥammad Khān's 1920s Chronicle Mā Tīṭayniŋ wāqiʿasi* (Tokyo: NIHU Program Islamic Area Studies, 2014), 11–12. An odd exception appears in the form of British Library OR 5329, which is a Chaghatay translation of an as-yet-unidentified Chinese novel that a beg gave his son as a gift. An enigmatic doodle in the margin signed by one Naqqāsh Niyāz, "Niyāz the Painter," copies an example of a plum blossom apparently from a painting manual, probably Wu Taisu's *Pine Studio Plum Painting Manual* (*Songzhai meipu*, 1351) or one of the many Ming manuals that followed. These efforts suggest a closer engagement with Chinese culture on the part of the elite in pre-uprisings Xinjiang than we would otherwise expect. However, at least within the limits of the available sources, the novel and its single marginalia are isolated cases.
35. Muḥammad Taqī Bahār, ed., *Mujmal al-tāwārīkh w-al-qiṣaṣ* (Tehran: Muʾassasah-i Khāwar, 1939), 420–23.

36. Rashīduddīn Fażlullah, *Jamiʿu ʾl-tawārīkh*, trans. Wheeler M. Thackston (London: I. B. Tauris, 2012), 129, 130, 214.
37. Rashīduddīn Fażlullah, 15–20, 25–27, 56–57.
38. Khwāndamīr, *Ḥabīb al-siyār*, trans. Wheeler M. Thackston (London: I. B. Tauris, 2012), 1–2.
39. There is much about Islamic knowledge of China and East Asia that cannot be addressed here for reasons for space. See especially Hyunhee Park, *Mapping the Chinese and Islamic Worlds: Cross-Cultural Exchange in Pre-Modern Asia* (Cambridge: Cambridge University Press, 2012), 68–71.
40. Abū ʾl-Fażl ibn Mubarak, *The History of Akbar*, 1:191–97.
41. Abū ʾl-Ghāzī Bahadur Khan, *Histoire des Mongols et des Tatares*, 5–18.
42. Thum, *Sacred Routes*, 20–23.
43. Limitations of space preclude the extensive discussion of this text and its variations. See Dankoff, "Rabghuzi's *Stories of the Prophets*"; Jarring, "The Qisas ul-anbiya," *Acta Regiae Societatis Humanorum Litterarum Lundensis* 74 (1980): 15–68; Jarring, *Studien Zu Einer Osttürkischen Lautlehre* (Lund: Borelius, 1933), 20–23; and M. van Damme, "Rabg͟hūzī," in *Encyclopaedia of Islam*, 2nd ed., ed. P. Bearman, Th. Bianquis, C. E. Boswort͟h, E. van Donzel, and W. P. Heinrichs (Brill Online, 2014). Manuscripts and prints consulted include British Library OR 5328; G. W. Hunter, trans., *Mohammedan "Narratives of the Prophets": Covering the Period from Zacharias to Paul, Turki Text with English Translation* (Tifwafu, Sinkiang, 1916); Jarring Prov. 159; Jarring Prov. 242; Jarring Prov. 262; Jarring Prov. 412; Jarring Prov. 431; Jarring Prov. 448; IVR RAN D 45; IVR RAN D 46; and *Qiṣaṣu ʾl-anbiyāʾ*, Tashkent, 1899.
    To be clear, others had suggested Japhetic descent for the Chinese, among them the Persian geographer ibn Khurradādhbih (d. 911) (Nathan Light, "Muslim Histories of China: Historiography Across Boundaries in Central Eurasia," in *Frontiers and Boundaries: Encounters on China's Margins*, ed. Zsombor Rajkai and Ildikó Bellér-Hann [Wiesbaden: Harrassowitz, 2012], 151–76, 154–57). Al-Masʿūdī's *Murūj al-dhahāb* presents the same legend, but only in passing, and his imagined Chinese king contests it.
44. IVR RAN D 45, *Qiṣaṣu ʾl-anbīyāʾ*, 46v–47v; Allen J. Frank, "The Mong͟hōl-Qalmāq Bayānī: A Qing-Era Islamic Ethnography of the Mongols and Tibetans," *Asiatische Studien* 63 (2009): 323–47.
45. Jarring Prov. 242, 54v.
46. TH/Beijing 10–23; TH/Jarring 3r–8v. The story for the most part resembles that advanced in the *Akbarnāma*, and parts of it are nearly word-for-word identical to a partial narrative produced in Turkic in the *Stories of the Strange and Wondrous* (*Qiṣaṣ al-gharāyib wa ʾl-ʿajāyib*), compiled in 1851/52 by Muḥammad Niyāz b. Ghafūr Beg in Khotan (Jarring Prov. 21).
47. TA/Pelliot, 5r; TH/Beijing, 15; TH/Jarring, 5v. TH/Beijing excludes the word *tongchi* but retains the word *tilmach*, "interpreter."
48. TH/Beijing, 15. Tibetans, as sons of Ham, remain an exception to the correspondence of Japhetic descent with Inner Asian identity. Gog and Magog (Jūj and Maʿjūj) are included as well in the TH/Beijing list. The list in TH/Jarring, 5v, is identical save for the exclusion of Daching.
49. Qurbān ʿAlī Khālidī, *Tawārīkh-i khamsa-ye sharqī* (Kazan', n.d.), 749. In Khālidī's text the term is written *Dayching*, reflecting an alternate pronunciation of the Chinese. Sayrāmī clarifies the meaning of "Daching" in his discussion of the descendants of Chinggis Khan (TH/Beijing, 26–29; TH/Jarring, 9v–10v).
50. Gertraude Roth Li, "State Building Before 1644," in *The Cambridge History of China*, vol. 9, pt. 1, *The Ch'ing Empire to 1800*, ed. Willard J. Peterson (Cambridge: Cambridge

University Press, 2002), 9–72, 30–34; Johan Elverskog, *Our Great Qing: The Mongols, Buddhism and the State in Late Imperial China* (Honolulu: University of Hawai'i Press, 2006), 14–27, 85–89.

51. Ruth W. Dunnell and James A. Millward, "Introduction," in *New Qing Imperial History: The Making of Inner Asian Empire at Qing Chengde*, ed. James A. Millward et al. (London: RoutledgeCurzon, 2004), 1–12, 3; James Millward, *Beyond the Pass: Economy, Ethnicity, and Empire in Qing Central Asia, 1759-1864* (Stanford: Stanford University Press, 1998), 200–201. Pamela K. Crossley characterizes the Qing royal house's relationship with its subject communities as one of "simultaneity." Crossley, *A Translucent Mirror: History and Identity in Qing Imperial Ideology* (Berkeley: University of California Press, 1999), 11–12.

52. A. Azfar Moin, *The Millennial Sovereign: Sacred Kingship and Sainthood in Islam* (New York: Columbia University Press, 2012), 1–55; Roy Mottahedeh, *Loyalty and Leadership in an Early Islamic Societ* (London: I. B. Tauris, 1980), 175; John E. Woods, *The Aqquyunlu: Clan, Confederation, Empire: A Study in 15th/9th Century Turko-Iranian Politics* (Chicago: Bibliotheca Islamica, 1976), 4–7. Mottahedeh: "This role of arbiter, distant from the society for which it arbitrated, known to live largely for its own interest and not for any particular interest in society, was the role of the king. The king who fulfilled this role and saw that each interest got its due, but no more than its due, was 'just.'"

53. For an overview of Islamic reimaginings of Chinggis, see Michal Biran, *Chinggis Khan* (Oxford: Oneworld, 2007), 75–108.

54. Michal Biran, "The Islamisation of Hülegü: Imaginary Conversion in the Ilkhanate," *Journal of the Royal Asiatic Society* 26, nos. 1–2 (January 2016): 79–88.

55. Moin, *The Millennial Sovereign*, 23–26; John Woods, "The Rise of Timurid Historiography," *Journal of Near Eastern Studies* 46, no. 2 (1987): 81–108.

56. TH/Beijing, 310–11; Hamada, "Jihad, Hijra, et 'devoir du sel,'" 52–54.

57. TH/Beijing, 300–301; TH/Jarring, 120v–121r; TA/Pelliot, 187v–188r.

58. Kim, *Holy War in China*, 76–89; TH/Beijing, 152; TH/Jarring, 64v.

59. TH/Beijing, 314–15.

60. TH/Beijing, 23–24; TH/Jarring, 9r. Although Chinggis's enemy is named "Altan Khan" in the text, Sayrāmī also makes it clear that "Altan Khan" was the name for the rulers of China.

61. IVR RAN D 106 *Qiṣaṣu 'l-gharāyib*, 22r. Muḥammad Niyāz states that Chinggis Khan's conquests were nearly as deadly as the Flood and included the land of China. Sayrāmī quotes Muḥammad Niyāz extensively but contradicts him on this point. His readers could have known Rashīduddīn's *Jamiʿu 't-tawārīkh*, in which it is clearly stated that Chinggis Khan's fourth wife, *Gūngjū* (< Ch. *gongzhu*, "princess") was the daughter of Altan Khan, ruler of the "Cathaians" or Khitans (*Khiṭāy*); nevertheless, along with the southerly lands of Chīn and Māchīn, Cathay was meant to be "destroyed" under Chinggis. Mirza Ḥaydar Dughlat, *Mirza Haydar Dughlat's Tarikh-i Rashidi: A History of the Khans of Moghulistan*, trans. Wheeler M. Thackston (Cambridge, MA: Harvard University, Department of Near Eastern Languages and Civilizations, 1996), 35, 148, 221.

62. TH/Beijing, 213; TH/Jarring, 86v; TA/Pelliot, 126r.

63. TH/Beijing, 29–33; TH/Jarring, 12r–13r.

64. TH/Beijing 243; TH/Jarring 99v.

65. Khālidī, *Tawārīkh-i khamsa-ye sharqī*, 112–33.

66. Khālidī, 119.

67. Ghulām Muḥammad Khan's "The Story of Commander Ma" (*Mā Tītayning wāqiʿasi*) is only known in one manuscript dating to the early 1930s, Lund University Library Jarring Prov. 163, in which it is attached to an incomplete copy of the *Tarikh-i*

Hamidi, the only known posthumous manuscript of Sayrāmī's work. As I have argued elsewhere, its language, themes, composition, and plot all mark this chronicle as an intentional continuation of the *Tarikh-i Hamidi*. Schluessel, *The World as Seen from Yarkand*, 1–23.

68. Schluessel, *The World as Seen from Yarkand*, 8; TH/Jarring, 125r.
69. TH/Jarring, 125r, 130r–131r.
70. Äbdullah Poskami, *Kitabi Äbdullah* (Ürümchi: Shinjang Khälq Näshriyati, 2004), 154–55, facsimile 284.
71. "Oh, Master!" (*Yā pīrim!*) refers to a Sufi recitation, also used in craft guilds, in which a disciple praises a spiritual master and predecessor.
72. "Order" (*ṭarīqat*) has a double meaning here. It means both a Sufi order and a way of doing things. In the Sufi sense, it also indicates one who has taken the second step in the journey toward knowledge, *ṭarīqat*, but not the first step, *shariat*.
73. Ṗoskāmī refers to a man's obligation to do ablutions after having sex, presumably only once he is married.
74. Alternatively, we could translate this line as "They get (or learn) their Muslim-ness from their Chantou-ness."
75. Poskami, *Kitabi Äbdullah*, 150.
76. On bringing petitions to the Chinese authorities, see Poskami, 153, facsimile 282; 160.
77. "Biz Türkmu? Yā Chanto?" in *Sharqī Turkistān Ḥayāti*, no. 11.
78. Menges and Katanov, *Volkskundliche Texte*, 1:48–50, 2:38–42. On Chantou, "local," and "Muslim," see also David Brophy, "Tending to Unite: The Origins of Uyghur Nationalism" (PhD diss., Harvard University, 2011), 30–34, 376–77.
79. David Brophy, *Uyghur Nation: Reform and Revolution on the Russia-China Frontier* (Cambridge, MA: Harvard University Press, 2016), 239, 245; David Brophy, "The Qumul Rebels' Appeal to Outer Mongolia," *Turcica* 42 (2010): 329–41.
80. Sally Engle Merry, "Law and Colonialism," *Law and Society Review* 25, no. 4 (1991): 889–922, 892–93.
81. Khālidī, *Tārīkh-i jarīda-i jadīda*, 4.
82. IVR RAN C 579, *Risāla-ye Khāqān ichidä Tūngānlāri qilghan ishi*; Lund University Library, Jarring Prov. 117, Ṭālib Ākhūnd, *History of Yaʿqūb Beg*, 128r.
83. National Library of China, *Kechäk terädurghanning bayāni*, 22v.
84. Jarring Prov. 207, I.49, "Ölüm jazālarining qasmlari."
85. Gustaf Raquette, *Eastern Turki Grammar: Practical and Theoretical with Vocabulary*, vol. 1 (Berlin: Reichsdruckerei, 1912), 1:24.
86. Riksarkivet, Stockholm, SE/RA/730284/6/130, file of Rachel O. Wingate.
87. Justin Jacobs makes this argument at length: Jacobs, *Xinjiang and the Modern Chinese State* (Seattle: University of Washington Press, 2016).
88. Matthew King, *Ocean of Milk, Ocean of Blood: A Mongolian Monk in the Ruins of the Qing Empire* (New York: Columbia University Press, 2019), 91, 102–3, 123–36, 204.
89. Henrietta Harrison, *The Man Awakened from Dreams: One Man's Life in a North China Village, 1857–1942* (Stanford: Stanford University Press, 2005), 7–9, 95–104.

Conclusion

1. Macartney, "Eastern Turkestan: The Chinese as Rulers Over an Alien Race," *Proceedings of the Central Asian Society*, 1909.
2. Dipesh Chakrabarty, "Postcoloniality and the Artifice of History: Who Speaks for 'Indian' Pasts?," *Representations* 37 (1992): 1–26.

3. Quoted in Paul R. Katz, *Divine Justice: Religion and the Development of Chinese Legal Culture* (New York: Routledge, 2009), 3.

4. Jürgen Osterhammel, *Colonialism: A Theoretical Overview* (Princeton: Markus Wiener, 2005), 4; Frederick Cooper, *Colonialism in Question: Theory, Knowledge, History* (Berkeley: University of California Press, 2005), 17, 23–26.

5. Emma Jinhua Teng, *Taiwan's Imagined Geography: Chinese Colonial Travel Writing and Pictures, 1683-1895* (Cambridge, MA: Harvard University Asia Center, 2004), 8–12, 256–58.

6. Albert Memmi, *The Colonizer and the Colonized* (Boston: Beacon, 1965), 10–14. Multiple accounts of the Tianjinese merchant networks that dominated late-Qing trade have been produced in Chinese, the most thorough being a chapter in Zhou Hong, *Quntuan yu quanceng—Yangliuqing: shenshang yu shenshen de shehui* (Shanghai: Shanghai renmin chubanshe, 2008), 312–413. Nevertheless, little work has been done on the smaller merchant houses and their activities outside of short articles.

7. Robert Crews, *For Prophet and Tsar: Islam and Empire in Russia and Central Asia* (Cambridge, MA: Harvard University Press, 2006), 31–91.

8. Alexander Morrison, *Russian Rule in Samarkand, 1868-1910: A Comparison with British India* (Oxford: Oxford University Press, 2008), 55–73, 247–85.

9. Mark Allee, *Law and Local Society in Late Imperial China: Northern Taiwan in the Nineteenth Century* (Stanford: Stanford University Press, 1994), 256–58; John Shepherd, *Statecraft and Political Economy on the Taiwan Frontier, 1600-1800* (Stanford: Stanford University Press, 1993).

10. Donald S. Sutton, "Violence and Ethnicity on a Qing Colonial Frontier: Customary and Statutory Law in the Eighteenth-Century Miao Pale," *Modern Asian Studies* 37, no. 1 (February 2003): 41–80.

11. Knight Biggerstaff, *The Earliest Modern Government Schools in China* (Ithaca, NY: Cornell University Press, 1961), 7–8.

12. P. Kerim Friedman, "Entering the Mountains to Rule the Aborigines: Taiwanese Aborigine Education and the Colonial Encounter," in *Becoming Taiwan: From Colonialism to Democracy*, ed. Ann Heylen and Scott Summers (Wiesbaden: Harrassowitz, 2010), 19–32, 20; Stevan Harrell, "From Xiedou to Yijun, the Decline of Ethnicity in Northern Taiwan, 1885-1895," *Late Imperial China* 11, no. 1 (1990): 99–127.

13. Ssü-yu Teng, *The Nien Army and Their Guerilla Warfare, 1851-1868* (Paris: Mouton, 1961), 185.

14. For a much more complete study than I can offer here, see Tonio Andrade, *How Taiwan Became Chinese: Dutch, Spanish, and Han Colonization in the Seventeenth Century* (New York: Columbia University Press, 2008).

15. Shepherd, *Statecraft and Political Economy*, 257.

16. Lauren Benton, *Law and Colonial Cultures: Legal Regimes in World History, 1400-1900* (Cambridge: Cambridge University Press, 2002), 11.

17. Stephen Platt makes this argument in *Provincial Patriots*, but the distinct Hunanese contribution has been clear for as long as scholars have studied *jingshi*. Platt, *Provincial Patriots: The Hunanese and Modern China* (Cambridge, MA: Harvard University Press, 2007). See, for example, Mary Clabaugh Wright, *The Last Stand of Chinese Conservatism: The T'ung-chih Restoration, 1862-1874* (Stanford: Stanford University Press, 1962).

18. Achille Mbembe, "Necropolitics," *Public Culture* 15, no. 1 (2003): 11–40.

19. Weiting Guo, "The Speed of Justice: Summary Execution and Legal Culture in Qing Dynasty China, 1644-1912" (PhD diss., University of British Columbia, 2016), 361.

20. Partha Chatterjee, *The Nation and Its Fragments: Colonial and Postcolonial Histories* (Princeton: Princeton University Press, 1993); Prasenjit Duara, *Rescuing History from*

the Nation: Questioning Narratives of Modern China (Chicago: University of Chicago Press, 2005).

21. Rogers Brubaker, *Grounds for Difference* (Cambridge, MA: Harvard University Press, 2015), 87–89.

22. Reinhart Koselleck, *The Practice of Conceptual History: Timing History, Spacing Concepts* (Stanford: Stanford University Press, 2002), 227.

23. Chatterjee, *The Nation and Its Fragments*, 76–97.

24. Achille Mbembe, *Critique of Black Reason*, trans. Laurent Dubois (Durham, NC: Duke University Press, 2017), 38–77.

25. David Brophy, *Uyghur Nation: Reform and Revolution on the Russia-China Frontier* (Cambridge, MA: Harvard University Press, 2016); L. J. Newby, "'Us and Them' in Eighteenth and Nineteenth Century Xinjiang," in *Situating the Uyghurs Between China and Central Asia*, ed. Ildikó Bellér-Hann, Cristina Cesaro, Rachel Harris, and Joanne Smith Finley (Aldershot, UK: Ashgate, 2007), 15–30; Rian Thum, *The Sacred Routes of Uyghur History* (Cambridge, MA: Harvard University Press, 2014).

26. Media reports on the situation have multiplied as of the time of writing, leading to an unprecedented level of news coverage of East Turkestan in the Western press. In the spirit of this book, I refer the reader to a true account of detention from the summer of 2017 (Special Correspondent, "A Summer Vacation in China's Muslim Gulag," *Foreign Policy*, February 28, 2018) and to original documents leaked from the Chinese government: Bethany Allen-Ebrahimian, "Exposed: China's Operating Manuals for Mass Internment and Arrest by Algorithm," *International Consortium of Investigative Journalists*, November 24, 2019, www.icij.org/investigations/china-cables/exposed-chinas-operating-manuals-for-mass-internment-and-arrest-by-algorithm/; Austin Ramzy and Chris Buckley, "'Absolutely No Mercy': Leaked Files Expose How China Organized Mass Detentions of Muslims," *New York Times*, November 16, 2019, www.nytimes.com/interactive/2019/11/16/world/asia/china-xinjiang-documents.html.

27. Amy Anderson, "A Death Sentence for a Life of Service," *Living Otherwise*, January 22, 2019, https://livingotherwise.com/2019/01/22/death-sentence-life-service/.

28. David Brophy, "Little Apples in Xinjiang," *China Story*, February 16, 2015, www.thechinastory.org/2015/02/little-apples-in-xinjiang/.

29. See in particular Darren Byler, "The Future of Uyghur Cultural—and Halal—Life in the Year of the Pig," *Living Otherwise*, March 9, 2019, https://livingotherwise.com/2019/03/09/future-uyghur-cultural-halal-life-year-pig/; and Darren Byler, "Images in Red: Han Culture, Uyghur Performers, Chinese New Year," *Living Otherwise*, February 23, 2018, https://livingotherwise.com/2018/02/23/images-red-han-culture-uyghur-performers-chinese-new-year/.

30. Mobashra Tazamal, "Chinese Islamophobia Was Made in the West," *Al Jazeera*, January 21, 2019, www.aljazeera.com/indepth/opinion/chinese-islamophobia-west-190121131831245.html.

31. Sean R. Roberts, "The Biopolitics of China's 'War on Terror' and the Exclusion of the Uyghurs," *Critical Asian Studies* 50, no. 2 (2018): 232–58.

Bibliography

Abbreviations

FHA: First Historical Archives of China
IOR: British Library, India Office Records
IVR RAN: Institute of Oriental Manuscripts, Russian Academy of Sciences
NPM: National Palace Museum
QXDX: *Qingdai Xinjiang dang'an xuanji*
XTZG: Ma Dazheng et al., comps., *Xinjiang xiangtuzhi gao*
XUAR Archives: Xinjiang Uyghur Autonomous Region Archives

Archives

British Library, India Office Records
First Historical Archives of China, Beijing
National Palace Museum, Taipei
Xinjiang Uyghur Autonomous Region Archives, accessed through Zhongguo dang'an.
    http://archives.gov.cn/

Archival Manuscripts and Rare Books

British Library
    IO Islamic 4860/Mss Turki 17, *Three Prose Tales*. Catalogued 1896.
    OR 5328, *Qiṣaṣu 'l-anbīyā'*, eighteenth-nineteenth century.
    OR 5329, translated Chinese novel.
    OR 8164, A history of Alexander the Great, XVIII–XIXth century.
Hunan Provincial Library, Rare Books (*guji*): Gong Yuanji. *Zhuidao Xinjiang shouyi lieshi jinian pin.*

Institute of Oriental Manuscripts, Russian Academy of Sciences (IVR RAN)
  B 779, Abū 'l-Maḥdī, *Ushbu ötkän dhamānida Mullā Abū 'l-Maḥdī degän bir ādamning beshidin ötkän ishning bayānidurlar.*
  C 578, Qurbān ʿAlī Khālidī, *Tārīkh-i jarīda-ye jadīda.*
  C 579, *Risāla-ye Khāqān ichidä Tūngānlāri qilghan ishi,* copied 1316/1897–98.
  C 759, ʿAshūr Ākhūnd b. Ismāʾīl b. Muḥammad Ghāribī, *Amīr-i ʿālī.*
  D 45, *Qiṣaṣu 'l-anbīyā',* copied on Jumada al-awwal 15, 1165/April 1, 1752, by Mullā ʿAbdalshukūr at the ʿAbdallaṭīf Khwāja Madrasa.
  D 46, *Qiṣaṣu 'l-anbīyā'.*
  D 106, Muḥammad Niyāz, *Qiṣaṣu 'l-gharāyib.*
  D 124, Ḥājjī Yūsuf, *Jamīʿ al-tawārīkh.*
Kashgar Museum: 0105, *Majmūʿat al-Masāʾil.*
Leiden University Library
  Or. 26.667 *Zubdatu 'l-masāʾil wa 'l-ʿaqāʾid.*
  Or. 26.684 *Majmūʿat al-Masāʾil.*
Lund University Library
  Jarring Prov. 21, Muḥammad Niyāz b. Ghafūr Beg, *Qiṣaṣ al-gharāyib wa 'l-ʿajāyib,* 1851/52.
  Jarring Prov. 117, Ṭālib Ākhūnd, *History of Yaʿqūb Beg,* 1317/1899.
  Jarring Prov. 159, *Qiṣaṣu 'l-anbīyā',* 1331/1912–13.
  Jarring Prov. 191, Story of Alexander the Great.
  Jarring Prov. 207, Muḥammad ʿAlī Dāmullā and Waḥīd Ākhūnd, *A Collection of Essays on Life in East Turkestan.*
  Jarring Prov. 242, *Qiṣaṣu 'l-anbīyā',* eighteenth century.
  Jarring Prov. 262, *Qiṣaṣu 'l-anbīyā',* circa 1933.
  Jarring Prov. 412, *Qiṣaṣu 'l-anbīyā',* late nineteenth century.
  Jarring Prov. 431, *Qiṣaṣu 'l-anbīyā',* early nineteenth century.
  Jarring Prov. 448. *Qiṣaṣu 'l-anbīyā',* 1208/1793–94.
National Library of China, Ordinary Rare Books (*putong guji*)
  Kechäk terädurghanning bayāni.
  Shen Tongfang. *Xinjiang teyong dao Yingjishaer zhili Tongzhi Huang jun zhuan.* Manuscript. 1910.
  Xinjiang gaodeng xunjing xuetang wendu, zhangcheng. Manuscript.
  Xinjiang shuiwu ju zongban huiyi pimao gongsi gaiwei guanxing xiang. Manuscript. 1907 (GX 33).
Riksarkivet, Stockholm: SE/RA/730284/6/130, file of Rachel O. Wingate.
School of Oriental and African Studies Archives: PP MS 8, Papers of Professor Sir Edward Denison Ross and Lady Dora Ross.
Staatsbibliothek zu Berlin
  Hartmann Collection 44, *Protokollbuch eines Kašgarer Gerichts, 1892.*
  Ms. Or. oct. 1670, Qurbān ʿAlī Khālidī, *Tārīkh-i jarīda-ye jadīda.*
  Ms. Or. quart. 1294, *Volkstümliche Scherzerzählung.*
  Zu 8390, *Yuzhi quanshan yaoyan.*
University of Oxford, Bodleian Library: Aurel Stein papers.
Vatican Library: R. G. Oriente IV 395 6-1-3, *Han Hui hebi.*
Yale University: MS 1, Ellsworth Huntington papers.

Manuscripts and Prints of Mullah Mūsa b. Mullah ʿĪsa Sayrāmī, Tārīkh-i Amniyya and Tārīkh-i Ḥamīdī, Consulted for This Book

TA/Jarring: Lund University Library, Jarring Prov. 478, *Tārīkh-i Amniyya*. Copied in 1912/13.

TA/Pantusov: Pantusov, N. N., ed. *Taarikh-i emenie, istoriia vladetelei Kashgarii*. Kazan': Tabkhana-ye madrasa-ye ʿulum, 1905.

TA/Pelliot: Bibliothèque Nationale, Paris, Collection Pelliot B 1740. *Tārīkh-i Amniyya*. Copied in 1325/1907–08.

TA/StP: IVR RAN C 335, *Tārīkh-i Amniyya*. Copied 1328/1910 by Mullā Muḥammad Tīmūr Qamūlī b. ʿUmar b. Nūr Mullā Tokhta Niyāz Qamūlī.

TH/Beijing: *Tārīkh-i Ḥamīdī*. Copied 1329/1911. Reproduced in Miao Pusheng, ed., *Xibei shaoshu minzu wenzi wenxian*. Beijing: Xianzhuang shuju, 2006. According to Tākli-makani (*Tarikhi Hämidiy*). This manuscript is held in the library of Minzu University in Beijing. Page numbers cited are as indicated in the published photoreproduction. (The manuscript is foliated, but the folio numbers are not visible in the published version.)

TH/Jarring: Lund University Library, Jarring Prov. 163, *Tārīkh-i Ḥamīdī*. Copied not prior to 1927. http://laurentius.ub.lu.se/jarring/volumes/163.html.

Printed Collections of Archival Sources

Guoli gugong bowuyuan Gugong wenxian bianji weiyuan hui, comp. *Gongzhong dang Guangxu chao zouzhe*. 24 vols. Taipei: Guoli gugong buwuyuan, 1973–75.

Liu Jintang. *Liu Xiangqin gong zougao*. Taipei: Chengwen Chubanshe, 1968.

Ma Dazheng et al., comps. *Xinjiang xiangtuzhi gao*. 1904–08; Beijing: Quanguo tushuguan wenxian suowei fuzhi zhongxin, 2011.

Ma Dazheng and Wu Fengpei, comps. *Qingdai Xinjiang xijian zoudu huibian, Tongzhi, Guangxu, Xuantong chao juan*. 3 vols. Wulumuqi: Xinjiang renmin chubanshe, 1997.

Qingdai Xinjiang dangʾan xuanji. 91 vols. Guilin: Guangxi Shifan Daxue Chubanshe, 2012.

Tao Mo. *Tao Qinsu gong zouyi yigao*. Reproduced in Zhongguo shaoshu minzu guji jicheng (Hanwen ban), vol. 71. Chengdu: Sichuan Minzu Chubanshe, 2002.

Xuebu guanbao. Taipei: Guoli gugong bowuyuan, 1980.

Yang Zengxin, comp. *Buguozhai wendu*. Taipei: Chengwen chubanshe, 1982.

Zhang Shicai et al., eds. *Weiwuerzu qiyue wenshu yi zhu*. Wulumuqi: Xinjiang daxue chubanshe, 2015.

Zhongguo diyi lishi dangʾanguan. *Guangxu chao zhupi zouzhe*. Beijing: Zhonghua shuju, 1995–96.

——. *Zuo Wenxiang gong quanji*. Taipei: Wenhai chubanshe, 1979.

Zuo Zongtang. *Zuo Wenxiang Gong shiji*. Shanghai: Shanghai guji chubanshe, 1995.

Other Sources

Abū Isḥāq Aḥmad ibn Muḥammad ibn Ibrāhīm al-Thaʿlabī. *ʿArāʾis al-majālis fī qiṣaṣ al-anbiyāʾ or "Lives of the Prophets."* Translated by William M. Brinner. Leiden: Brill, 2002.

Abū 'l-Fażl b. Mubārak. *The History of Akbar*, vol. 1. Edited and translated by Wheeler M. Thackston. Cambridge, MA: Harvard University Press, 2015.

Abū 'l-Ghāzī Bahadur Khan. *Histoire des Mongols et des Tatares par Aboul-Ghâzi Béhâdour Khân, souverain de Kharezm et historien Djaghataï, 1603-1664 A.D., texte Turc-Oriental, publié d'après le manuscrit du Musée Asiatique de St-Pétersbourg, collationné sur les manuscrits de Göttingue et de Berlin et sur l'édition de Kazan, 1825, avec une traduction française, des notes critiques des variants et un index*. Edited and translated by Petr I. Desmaisons. Amsterdam: Philo, 1970.

Adas, Michael. "Imperialism and Colonialism in Comparative Perspective." *International History Review* 20, no. 2 (June 1998): 371–88.

Agamben, Giorgio. *State of Exception*. Chicago: University of Chicago Press, 2005.

Ai Weijun et al., comps. *Gansu xin tongzhi*. 80 juan. 1909.

Alexander, Katherine Laura Bos. "Virtues of the Vernacular: Moral Reconstruction in Late Qing Jiangnan and the Revitalization of Baojuan." PhD diss., University of Chicago, 2016.

Allee, Mark. *Law and Local Society in Late Imperial China: Northern Taiwan in the Nineteenth Century*. Stanford: Stanford University Press, 1994.

Allen-Ebrahimian, Bethany. "Exposed: China's Operating Manuals For Mass Internment and Arrest by Algorithm." *International Consortium of Investigative Journalists*, November 24, 2019. www.icij.org/investigations/china-cables/exposed-chinas-operating-manuals-for-mass-internment-and-arrest-by-algorithm/.

Alston, Lee J., Edwyna Harris, and Bernardo Mueller. "The Development of Property Rights on Frontiers: Endowments, Norms, and Politics." *Journal of Economic History* 72, no. 3:741–70.

Ambaras, David. *Japan's Imperial Underworlds: Intimate Encounters at the Borders of Empire*. Cambridge: Cambridge University Press, 2018.

Anderson, Amy. "A Death Sentence for a Life of Service." *Living Otherwise*, January 22, 2019. https://livingotherwise.com/2019/01/22/death-sentence-life-service/.

Anderson, Benedict. *Imagined Communities: Reflections on the Origin and Spread of Nationalism*. London: Verso, 2006.

Andrade, Tonio. *How Taiwan Became Chinese: Dutch, Spanish, and Han Colonization in the Seventeenth Century*. New York: Columbia University Press, 2008.

Anonymous, comp. *Shache fu zhi*. Xuantong 1 (1909). In *Zhongguo xibei xijian fangzhi xu ji*, 10:621–75. Beijing: Zhonghua quanguo tushuguan wenxian suowei fuzhi zhongxin, 1997.

Anonymous. "Xinjiang shexing sheng yi." In *Xiaofanghu zhai yudi congchao*, 2 zhi, 2, 117a–18b.

Atwill, David G. *The Chinese Sultanate: Islam, Ethnicity, and the Panthay Rebellion in Southwest China, 1856-1873*. Stanford: Stanford University Press, 2005.

Atwood, Christopher. "Chinese Merchants and Mongolian Independence." In *XX zuuny Mongol: tuux, soyol, geopolitik, gadaad xariltsaany tulgamdsan asuudluud*, edited by S. Chuluun and S. Battulga, 62–75. Ulaanbaatar: Admon print, 2017.

Avetaranian, Johannes. *A Muslim Who Became a Christian: The Story of John Avetaranian, an Autobiography*. London: AuthorsOnline, 2002.

Bai Zhensheng et al., eds. *Xinjiang xiandai zhengzhi shehui shilüe*. Beijing: Zhongguo shehui kexue chubanshe, 1992.

Bakhtin, M. M. *The Dialogic Imagination*. Austin: University of Texas Press, 1981.

Balázs, Étienne. *Political Theory and Administrative Reality in Traditional China*. London: School of Oriental and African Studies, 1965.

Banerjee, Sukanya. *Becoming Imperial Citizens: Indians in the Late-Victorian Empire*. Durham, NC: Duke University Press, 2010.

Baytur, Änwär. "Mulla Musa Sayrami she'irliridin tallanma." *Bulaq* 15 (1985): 194–227.

Bellér-Hann, Ildikó. *Community Matters in Xinjiang 1880–1949: Towards a Historical Anthropology of the Uyghur.* Leiden: Brill, 2008.

——. *A History of Cathay: A Translation and Linguistic Analysis of a Fifteenth-Century Turkic Manuscript.* Bloomington, IN: Research Institute for Inner Asian Studies, 1995.

Ben-Dor Benite, Zvi. "From 'Literati' to 'Ulama': The Origins of Chinese Muslim Nationalist Historiography." *Nationalism and Ethnic Politics* 9, no. 4 (2004): 83–109.

Benson, Linda. "A Much-Married Woman: Marriage and Divorce in Xinjiang 1850–1950." *Muslim World* 83, nos. 3–4 (July–October 1993): 227–47.

——. "The Question of Women: Discovering Uyghur Women's History in Northwestern China." *Oriental Archive* 79 (2011): 47–70.

Benton, Lauren. *Law and Colonial Cultures: Legal Regimes in World History, 1400–1900.* Cambridge: Cambridge University Press, 2002.

Bhabha, Homi. "Of Mimicry and Man: The Ambivalence of Colonial Discourse." *October* 102 (Spring 1984): 125–33.

Biggerstaff, Knight. *The Earliest Modern Government Schools in China.* Ithaca, NY: Cornell University Press, 1961.

Biran, Michal. *Chinggis Khan.* Oxford: Oneworld, 2007.

——. "The Islamisation of Hülegü: Imaginary Conversion in the Ilkhanate." *Journal of the Royal Asiatic Society* 26, nos. 1–2 (January 2016): 79–88.

Bodde, Derk. "Harmony and Conflict in Chinese Philosophy." In *Studies in Chinese Thought*, edited by Arthur F. Wright, 19–80. Chicago: University of Chicago Press, 1953.

Bol, Peter. *Neo-Confucianism in History.* Cambridge, MA: Harvard University Asia Center, 2008.

Bormanshinov, Arash. "Prince Palta." In *Proceedings of the International Conference on China Border Area Studies*, edited by Lin En-shean et al., 1,015–40. Taipei: Guoli zhengzhi daxue, 1985.

Borthwick, Sally. *Education and Social Change in China: The Beginnings of the Modern Era.* Stanford: Stanford University Press, 1983.

Bovingdon, Gardner. "The History of the History of Xinjiang." *Twentieth-Century China* 26, no. 2 (April 2001): 95–139.

——. *The Uyghurs: Strangers in their Own Land.* New York: Columbia University Press, 2010.

Brook, Timothy, Michael van Walt van Praaf, and Miek Boltjes, eds. *Sacred Mandates: Asian International Relations Since Chinggis Khan.* Chicago: University of Chicago Press, 2018.

Brophy, David. "He Causes a Ruckus Wherever He Goes: Saʿid Muḥammad al-ʿAsali as a Missionary of Modernism in North-West China." *Modern Asian Studies* 2009:1–33.

——. "The Junghar Mongol Legacy and the Language of Loyalty in Qing Xinjiang." *Harvard Journal of Asiatic Studies* 73, no. 2 (2013): 231–58.

——. "Little Apples in Xinjiang." *China Story*, February 16, 2015. www.thechinastory.org/2015/02/little-apples-in-xinjiang/.

——. "The Qumul Rebels' Appeal to Outer Mongolia." *Turcica* 42 (2010): 329–41.

——. "Tending to Unite: The Origins of Uyghur Nationalism." PhD diss., Harvard University, 2011.

——. *Uyghur Nation: Reform and Revolution on the Russia-China Frontier.* Cambridge, MA: Harvard University Press, 2016.

Brown, Vincent. *The Reaper's Garden: Death and Power in the World of Atlantic Slavery.* Cambridge, MA: Harvard University Press, 2008.

Brubaker, Rogers. *Ethnicity Without Groups.* Cambridge, MA: Harvard University Press, 2004.

——. *Grounds for Difference*. Cambridge, MA: Harvard University Press, 2015.

Brunnert, H. S., and V. V. Hagelstrom. *Present Day Political Organization of China*. Translated by A. Beltchenko and E. E. Moran. Shanghai: Kelly and Walsh, 1912.

Buoye, Thomas. "Suddenly Murderous Intent Arose: Bureaucratization and Benevolence in Eighteenth-Century Homicide Reports." *Late Imperial China* 16, no. 2 (1995): 62–97.

Burak, Guy. "The Second Formation of Islamic Law: The Post-Mongol Context of the Ottoman Adoption of a School of Law." *Comparative Studies in Society and History* 55, no. 3 (July 2013): 579–602.

Byler, Darren. "The Future of Uyghur Cultural—and Halal—Life in the Year of the Pig." *Living Otherwise*, March 9, 2019. https://livingotherwise.com/2019/03/09/future-uyghur-cultural-halal-life-year-pig/.

——. "Images in Red: Han Culture, Uyghur Performers, Chinese New Year." *Living Otherwise*, February 23, 2018. https://livingotherwise.com/2018/02/23/images-red-han-culture-uyghur-performers-chinese-new-year/.

Cao Jiguan. *Xinjiang jianzhi zhi*. Taipei: Xuesheng Shuju, 1963.

Chakrabarty, Dipesh. "Postcoloniality and the Artifice of History: Who Speaks for 'Indian' Pasts?" *Representations* 37 (1992): 1–26.

Chang Hao. "On the *Ching-shih* Ideal in Neo-Confucianism." *Ch'ing-shih wen-t'i* 3, no. 1 (November 1974): 36–61.

Chang, Wejen. *In Search of the Way: Legal Philosophy of the Classic Chinese Thinkers*. Edinburgh: Edinburgh University Press, 2016.

Chatterjee, Partha. *The Nation and Its Fragments: Colonial and Postcolonial Histories*. Princeton: Princeton University Press, 1993.

Chen, Gideon. *Tso Tsung T'ang, Pioneer Promoter of the Modern Dockyard and the Woollen Mill in China*. Peiping: Yenching University, 1938.

Chen Zongzhen. "*Han-Hui hebi* yanjiu." *Minzu yuwen* 1989, no. 5:49–72.

CHGIS, Version: 6. (c) Fairbank Center for Chinese Studies of Harvard University and the Center for Historical Geographical Studies at Fudan University, 2016.

Chŏn Pyŏng-hun. *Jingshen zhexue tong bian*. Shanghai, 1920.

Chou, Nailene Josephine. "Frontier Studies and Changing Frontier Administration in Late Ch'ing China: The Case of Sinkiang, 1759-1911." PhD diss., University of Washington, 1976.

Chu jun ying zhi. Reproduced in *Guojia tushuguan cang Qingdai bingshi dianji dangce huilan*, 64:1–110. Beijing: Xueyuan chubanshe, 2005.

Chu, Wen-djang. *The Moslem Rebellion in Northwest China, 1862-1878*. The Hague: Mouton, 1966.

Confucius. *Analects*. Translated by Edward Slingerland. Indianapolis: Hackett, 2003.

Conklin, Alice. *A Mission to Civilize: The Republican Idea of Empire in France and West Africa, 1895-1930*. Stanford: Stanford University Press, 1997.

Conversi, Daniele. "Reassessing Current Theories of Nationalism: Nationalism as Boundary Maintenance and Creation." *Nationalism and Ethnic Politics* 1, no. 1 (1995): 73–85.

Cooper, Frederick. *Colonialism in Question: Theory, Knowledge, History*. Berkeley: University of California Press, 2005.

Crews, Robert. *For Prophet and Tsar: Islam and Empire in Russia and Central Asia*. Cambridge, MA: Harvard University Press, 2006.

Crossley, Pamela K. *A Translucent Mirror: History and Identity in Qing Imperial Ideology*. Berkeley: University of California Press, 1999.

Dağyeli, J. E. *"Gott liebt das Handwerk": Moral, Identität und religiöse Legitimierung in der mittelasiatischen Handwerks-risāla*. Wiesbaden: Reichert, 2011.

Dai Liangzuo. *Xiyu beiming lu*. Wulumuqi: Xinjiang renmin chubanshe, 2013.

Dankoff, Robert. "Rabghuzi's Stories of the Prophets." *Journal of the American Oriental Society* 117, no. 1 (January–March 1997): 115–26.

Da Qing lü li. 1899 edition. http://lsc.chineselegalculture.org/.

Dautcher, Jay. *Down a Narrow Road: Identity and Masculinity in a Uyghur Community in Xinjiang China*. Cambridge, MA: Harvard University Asia Center, 2009.

Davis, Adrienne. "'Don't Let Nobody Bother Yo'Principle': The Sexual Economy of American Slavery." In *Sister Circle: Black Women and Work*, edited by Sharon Harley and the Black Women and Work Collective, 103–27. New Brunswick, NJ: Rutgers University Press, 2002.

Dawut, Rahilä. *Uyghur mazarliri*. Ürümchi: Shinjang khälq näshriyati, 2001.

DeWeese, Devin. *Islamization and Native Religion in the Golden Horde: Baba Tükles and Conversion to Islam in Historical and Epic Tradition*. University Park: University of Pennsylvania Press, 1994.

Di Cosmo, Nicola. "The Qing and Inner Asia: 1636–1800." In *The Cambridge History of Inner Asia*, edited by Nicola Di Cosmo, Allen J. Frank, and Peter B. Golden, 333–62. Cambridge: Cambridge University Press, 2009.

——. "Qing Colonial Administration in Inner Asia." *International History Review* 20, no. 2 (June 1998): 287–309.

Dikötter, Frank. *The Discourse of Race in Modern China*. Stanford: Stanford University Press, 1992.

Doerfer, Gerhard. *Türkische und mongolische Elemente im Neupersischen*. Wiesbaden: F. Steiner, 1963.

Duara, Prasenjit. *Culture, Power, and the State: Rural North China, 1900-1942*. Stanford: Stanford University Press, 1988.

——. *Rescuing History from the Nation: Questioning Narratives of Modern China*. Chicago: University of Chicago Press, 2005.

——. "Superscribing Symbols: The Myth of Guandi, Chinese God of War." *Journal of Asian Studies* 47, no. 4 (1988): 778–95.

Dunmore, Charles Adolphus Murray, Earl of. *The Pamirs: Being a Narrative of a Year's Expedition on Horseback and on Foot Through Kashmir, Western Tibet, Chinese Tartary, and Russian Central Asia*. 2 vols. London: J. Murray, 1893.

Dunnell, Ruth W., and James A. Millward. "Introduction." In *New Qing Imperial History: The Making of Inner Asian Empire at Qing Chengde*, edited by James A. Millward et al., 1–12. London: RoutledgeCurzon, 2004.

Dyer, Svetlana Rimsky-Korsakoff. "T'ang T'ai-Tsung's Dream: A Soviet Dungan Version of a Legend on the Origin of the Chinese Muslims." *Monumenta Serica* 35 (1981–83): 545–70.

Dykstra, Maura. "Complicated Matters: Commercial Dispute Resolution in Qing Chongqing from 1750 to 1911." PhD diss., University of California, Los Angeles, 2014.

Elliott, Mark C. "The Limits of Tartary: Manchuria in Imperial and National Geographies." *Journal of Asian Studies* 59, no. 3 (August 2000): 603–46.

——. *The Manchu Way: The Eight Banners and Ethnic Identity in Late Imperial China*. Stanford: Stanford University Press, 2001.

Elman, Benjamin A. *From Philosophy to Philology: Intellectual and Social Aspects of Change in Late Imperial China*. Los Angeles: UCLA Asian Pacific Monograph Series, 2001.

Elverskog, Johan. *Our Great Qing: The Mongols, Buddhism and the State in Late Imperial China*. Honolulu: University of Hawai'i Press, 2006.

Epstein, Maram. "Making a Case: Characterizing the Filial Son." In *Writing and Law in Late Imperial China: Crime, Conflict, and Judgment*, edited by Robert Hegel and Katherine Carlitz, 27–43. Seattle: University of Washington Press, 2007.

Fairbank, John K., and Ssü-yu Têng. *Ch'ing Administration: Three Studies*. Cambridge, MA: Harvard University Press, 1960.

Fan, Fa-ti. "Nature and Nation in Chinese Political Thought: The National Essence Circle in Early-Twentieth-Century China." In *The Moral Authority of Nature*, edited by Lorraine Daston and Fernando Vidal, 409–37. Chicago: University of Chicago Press, 2004.

Faust, Drew Gilpin. *This Republic of Suffering: Death and the American Civil War*. New York: Knopf, 2008.

Feng Junguang. *Xi xing riji*. Shanghai, 1881 (Guangxu *xinsi*).

Fields, Lanny. "The Importance of Friendships and Quasi-Kinship Relations in Tso Tsung-t'ang's Career." *Journal of Asian History* 10, no. 2 (1976): 172–86.

——. *Tso Tsung-t'ang and the Muslims: Statecraft in Northwest China, 1868–1880*. Kingston: Limestone, 1978.

Fletcher, Joseph. "The Heyday of the Ch'ing Order in Mongolia, Sinkiang, and Tibet." In *The Cambridge History of China*, vol. 10, *Late Ch'ing, 1800–1911*, pt. 1, edited by John K. Fairbank, 351–408. Cambridge: Cambridge University Press, 1978.

Fogel, Joshua A. *Politics and Sinology: The Case of Naitō Konan, 1866–1934*. Cambridge, MA: Harvard University Press, 1984.

Foucault, Michel. *The History of Sexuality*, vol. 1, *An Introduction*. New York: Vintage, 1990.

Frank, Allen J. "The Monghōl-Qalmāq Bayānī: a Qing-Era Islamic Ethnography of the Mongols and Tibetans." *Asiatische Studien* 63 (2009): 323–47.

Friedman, P. Kerim. "Entering the Mountains to Rule the Aborigines: Taiwanese Aborigine Education and the Colonial Encounter." In *Becoming Taiwan: From Colonialism to Democracy*, edited by Ann Heylen and Scott Summers, 19–32. Wiesbaden: Harrassowitz, 2010.

Fuping xian zhi. 1891 (Guangxu *xinmao*).

Gan Han, comp. *Huangchao jingshi wen xin bian xu ji*. Shangyi xuezhai shuju, 1897.

Gaubatz, Piper. *Beyond the Great Wall: Urban Form and Transformation on the Chinese Frontiers*. Stanford: Stanford University Press, 1996.

Gellner, Ernest. *Nations and Nationalism*. Ithaca, NY: Cornell University Press, 1983.

Ge Shijun, comp. *Huangchao jingshi wen xu bian*. 120 juan. Shanghai: Tushu jicheng ju, 1888.

Ghiyāthuddīn Naqqāsh. "Report to Mirza Baysunghur on the Timurid Legation to the Ming Court at Peking." In *Album Prefaces and Other Documents on the History of Painters and Calligraphers*, edited by Wheeler M. Thackston, 53–68. Leiden: Brill, 2001.

Golab, L. Wawryzn. "A Study of Irrigation in East Turkestan." *Anthropos* 46 (1951): 187–99.

Gregory, Eugene John, III. "Desertion and the Militarization of Qing Legal Culture." PhD diss., Georgetown University, 2015.

Grenard, F. *Mission scientifique dans la Haute Asie, 1890–1895*, pt. 2, *Le Turkestan et le Tibet, étude ethnographique et sociologique*. Paris: Ernest Leroux, 1898.

Griffith, Sidney. "Christian Lore and the Arabic Quran: The 'Companions of the Cave' in Surat al-Kahf and in Syriac Christian Tradition." In *The Quran in Its Historical Context*, edited by Gabriel Said Reynolds, 109–38. London: Routledge, 2008.

Gui E. "Jin Hami shiyi shu." In *Mingdai Hami Tulufan ziliao huibian*, edited by Chen Gaohua, 459–65. Wulumuqi: Xinjiang renmin chubanshe, 1984.

Guo, Weiting. "The Speed of Justice: Summary Execution and Legal Culture in Qing Dynasty China, 1644–1912." PhD diss., University of British Columbia, 2016.

Haenisch, Erich. "Turco-Manjurica aus Turfan." *Oriens* 4, no. 2 (December 1951): 256–72.

Haeri, Shahla. *Law of Desire: Temporary Marriage in Shi'i Iran*. Syracuse: Syracuse University Press, 2014.

Hallaq, Wael B. *Sharīʿa: Theory, Practice, Transformations*. Cambridge: Cambridge University Press, 2009.

Hamada Masami. "*L'Histoire de Hotan* de Muḥammad Aʿlam (I), commentaires avec deux appendices." *Zinbun* 15 (1979): 1–45.

——. "*L'Histoire de Hotan* de Muḥammad Aʿlam (III), texte turque oriental édité, avec une introduction." *Zinbun* 18 (1982): 65–93.

——. "Jihâd, hijra et 'devoir du sel' dans l'histoire du Turkestan Oriental." *Turcica* 33 (2001): 35–61.

Harrell, Stevan. "From Xiedou to Yijun, the Decline of Ethnicity in Northern Taiwan, 1885–1895." *Late Imperial China* 11, no. 1 (1990): 99–127.

——. "Introduction: Civilizing Project and the Reaction to Them." In *Cultural Encounters on China's Ethnic Frontiers*, edited by Stevan Harrell, 3–36. Seattle: University of Washington Press, 1995.

Harrison, Henrietta. *The Man Awakened from Dreams: One Man's Life in a North China Village, 1857–1942*. Stanford: Stanford University Press, 2005.

He Changling, comp. *Jingshi wenbian*. Beijing: Zhonghua shuju, 1992.

Hening. *San zhou ji lüe*. Taipei: Chengwen chubanshe, 1968.

He Rong. "Shi lun Yang Zengxin shiqi Xinjiang xiangyue de tedian." *Xinjiang daxue xuebao (zhexue renwen shehui kexue ban)* 36, no. 3 (May 2008): 67–70.

Hobsbawm, E. J. *Nations and Nationalism Since 1780: Programme, Myth, Reality*. Cambridge: Cambridge University Press, 2002.

Hofman, H. F. *Turkish Literature: A Bio-Bibliographical Survey*. Section 3, *Moslim Central Asian Turkish Literature*. Utrecht: Library of the University of Utrecht, 1969.

Honig, Bonnie. *Emergency Politics: Paradox, Law, Democracy*. Princeton: Princeton University Press, 2009.

Hou Chengxiu and Huang Heqing, comps. *Fenghuang ting xu zhi*. Reproduced in *Zhongguo difangzhi jicheng*. 1892; Shanghai: Shanghai shuju, 2002.

Huang Zongxi. *Mingyi daifang lu*. Beijing: Zhonghua shuju, 1981.

——. *Waiting for the Dawn*. Translated by Wm. Theodore de Bary. New York: Columbia University Press, 1993.

——. *Xinyi mingyi daifang lu*. Edited by Li Guangbo and Li Zhenxing. Taibei: Sanmin shuju, 2014.

Huitu Xiangjun ping ni zhuan. Shanghai: Shanghai shuju, 1899 (Guangxu jihai).

Huitu Zuo gong ping xi zhuan. Shanghai: Shanghai shuju, 1899 (Guangxu jihai).

Hunt, Nigel C. *War, Memory, and Trauma*. Cambridge: Cambridge University Press, 2010.

Hunter, G. W., trans. *Mohammedan "Narratives of the Prophets," Covering the Period from Zacharias to Paul, Turki Text with English Translation*. Tifwafu, Sinkiang, 1916.

Huntington, Ellsworth. "The Depression of Turfan." *Geographical Journal* 30 (July–December 1907): 254–73.

Hutchinson, John, and Anthony D. Smith, eds. *Ethnicity*. Oxford: Oxford University Press, 1996.

Inoue, Miyako. "Stenography and Ventriloquism in Late Nineteenth Century Japan." *Language and Communication* 31 (2011): 181–90.

Jacobs, Justin. "Empire Besieged: The Preservation of Chinese Rule in Xinjiang, 1884–1971." PhD diss., University of California, San Diego, 2011.

——. *Xinjiang and the Modern Chinese State*. Seattle: University of Washington Press, 2016.

Jahn, Karl. *Die Chinageschichte des Rašīd ad-Dīn: Übersetzung, Kommentar, Facsimiletafeln*. Vienna: Verlag der Österreichischen Akademie der Wissenschaften, 1971.

——. *China in der islamischen Geschichtsschreibung*. Vienna: Hermann Böhlaus Nachf., 1971.

Jarring, Gunnar. "The Qisas ul-anbiya." *Acta Regiae Societatis Humanorum Litterarum Lundensis* 74 (1980): 15–68.

——. *Studien Zu Einer Osttürkischen Lautlehre.* Lund: Borelius, 1933.

Jia Jianfei. *Qing Qian-Jia-Dao shiqi Xinjiang de neidi yimin shehui.* Beijing: Shehui kexue wenxian chubanshe, 2012.

Ji Wenfu. *Chuanshan zhexue.* Shanghai, 1936.

Jones, William C., trans. *The Great Qing Code.* New York: Oxford University Press, 1994.

Kabir, Ananya Jahanara. "Analogy in Translation: Imperial Rome, Medieval England, and British India." In *Postcolonial Approaches to the European Middle Ages: Translating Cultures,* edited by Ananya Jahanara Kabir and Deanne Williams, 183–204. Cambridge: Cambridge University Press, 2005.

Karasawa Yasuhiko. "Hanasukoto to kakukoto no hazama de—shindai saiban bunsho ni okeru kyōjutsusho no tekusutosei." *Chūgoku: Shakai to bunka* 10 (1995): 212–50.

Katanov, Nikolai. "Man'chzhursko-Kitaiskii 'li' na narechii Tiurkov Kitaiskogo Turkestana." *Zapiski vostochnogo otdeleniia imperatorskogo Russkogo arkheologicheskogo obshchestva* 14 (1901): 31–75.

Kataoka Kazutada. *Shinchō Shinkyō tōji kenkyū.* Tōkyō: Yūzankaku, 1990.

——. "Shin-matsu shinkyōshō kan'in kō." *Ōsaka kyōiku daigaku kiyō* 11, no. 31 (February 1983): 119–38.

Katz, Paul R. *Divine Justice: Religion and the Development of Chinese Legal Culture.* New York: Routledge, 2009.

Kerkvliet, Benedict J. *Everyday Politics in the Philippines: Class and Status Relations in a Central Luzon Village.* Berkeley: University of California Press, 1990.

Khālidī, Qurbān ʿAlī. *Tārīkh-i jarīda-ye jadīda.* Kazanʾ: Qazān universitetining ṭabʿkhānasi, 1889.

——. *Tawārīkh-i Khamsa-ye Sharqī.* Kazanʾ, n.d.

Khwāndamīr. *Ḥabīb al-siyār.* Translated by Wheeler M. Thackston. London: I. B. Tauris, 2012.

Kim, Hodong. *Holy War in China: The Muslim Rebellion and State in Chinese Central Asia, 1864–1878.* Stanford: Stanford University Press, 2004.

Kim, Young-Oak. "The Philosophy of Wang Fu-chih (1619–1692)." PhD diss., Harvard University, 1982.

King, Matthew. *Ocean of Milk, Ocean of Blood: A Mongolian Monk in the Ruins of the Qing Empire.* New York: Columbia University Press, 2019.

Kinzley, Judd. *Natural Resources and the New Frontier: Constructing Modern China's Borderlands.* Chicago: University of Chicago Press, 2018.

Koselleck, Reinhart. *The Practice of Conceptual History: Timing History, Spacing Concepts.* Stanford: Stanford University Press, 2002.

Kuhn, Philip A. *Rebellion and Its Enemies in Late Imperial China: Militarization and Social Structure, 1796–1864.* Cambridge, MA: Harvard University Press, 1970.

——. "The Taiping Rebellion." In *The Cambridge History of China,* vol. 10, *Late Ch'ing 1800–1911,* pt. 1, edited by John K. Fairbank, 264–317. Cambridge: Cambridge University Press, 1978.

LaCapra, Dominick. *Writing History, Writing Trauma.* Baltimore: Johns Hopkins University Press, 2014.

Latour, Bruno. *We Have Never Been Modern.* Cambridge, MA: Harvard University Press, 1993.

Lavelle, Peter. "Cultivating Empire: Zuo Zongtang's Agriculture, Environment, and Reconstruction in the Late Qing." In *China on the Margins,* edited by Sherman Cochran and Paul G. Pickowicz, 43–64. Ithaca: Cornell University East Asia Series, 2010.

Li Bianqi. "Huijiang fa wenhua yu Da Qing fa wenhua de chongtu yu zhenghe." *Xizang daxue xuebao* 16, no. 2 (June 2001): 38–42.

Li Enhan. *Zuo Zongtang shoufu Xinjiang*. Singapore: Xinjiapo Guo li da xue Zhong wen xi, 1984.

Light, Nathan. "Muslim Histories of China: Historiography Across Boundaries in Central Eurasia." In *Frontiers and Boundaries: Encounters on China's Margins*, edited by Zsombor Rajkai and Ildikó Bellér-Hann, 151–76. Wiesbaden: Harrassowitz, 2012.

Lipman, Jonathan N. *Familiar Strangers: A History of Muslims in Northwest China*. Seattle: University of Washington Press, 1991.

Liu, Lydia He. *The Clash of Empires: The Invention of China in Modern World Making*. Cambridge, MA: Harvard University Press, 2004.

Liu Yanbo. "Wan Qing liang Hu diqu zhouxian 'jiudi zhengfa' shulun." *Jinan xuebao (zhexue shehui kexue ban)* 2012, no. 3:138–42.

Li Yan and Wang Xiaohui. "Qingmo Xinjiang shanhou ju chuyi." *Xibei Minzu Daxue xuebao (zhexue shehui kexue ban)* 2005, no. 3:9–14.

Macartney, George. "Eastern Turkestan: the Chinese as Rulers Over an Alien Race." *Proceedings of the Central Asian Society*, 1909.

Macauley, Melissa. *Social Power and Legal Culture: Litigation Masters in Late Imperial China*. Stanford: Stanford University Press, 1998.

Macauley, Thomas Babington. "The Minute on Education." In *Sources of Indian Tradition*, vol. 2, edited by Stephen Hay, 69–72. New York: Columbia University Press, 1988.

Ma, Haiyun. "The Mythology of the Prophet's Ambassadors in China: Histories of Sa'd Waqqas and Gess in Chinese Sources." *Journal of Muslim Minority Affairs* 26, no. 3 (2006): 445–52.

Maier, Charles. *Among Empires: American Ascendancy and Its Predecessors*. Cambridge, MA: Harvard University Press, 2006.

Mannerheim, Gustaf. *Dagbok förd under min resa i Centralasian och Kina 1906-07-08*. Helsingfors: Svenska Litteratursällskapet i Finland, 2010.

Mao Dun. *Mao dun wenji*. 9 vols. Beijing: Renmin wenxue chubanshe, 1958–61.

Ma Xiaojuan. "Qingchao fazhi zai Tulufan diqu de chongjian." *Xinjiang daxue xuebao (zhexue shehui kexue ban)* 40, no. 1 (January 2012): 61–66.

Mbembe, Achille. *Critique of Black Reason*. Translated by Laurent Dubois. Durham, NC: Duke University Press, 2017.

——. "Necropolitics." *Public Culture* 15, no. 1 (2003): 11–40.

McKnight, Brian. *The Quality of Mercy: Amnesties and Traditional Chinese Justice*. Honolulu: University of Hawaii Press, 1981.

McMahon, Daniel. "The Yuelu Academy and Hunan's Nineteenth-Century Turn Toward Statecraft." *Late Imperial China* 26, no. 1 (2005): 72–109.

Memmi, Albert. *The Colonizer and the Colonized*. Boston: Beacon, 1965.

Menges, Karl, and N. Th. Katanov. *Volkskundliche Texte aus Ost-Türkistan*. 2 vols. 1933, 1946; Leipzig: Zentralantiquariat der Deutschen Demokratischen Republik, 1976.

Merry, Sally Engle. "Law and Colonialism." *Law and Society Review* 25, no. 4 (1991): 889–922.

Meyer-Fong, Tobie. *What Remains: Coming to Terms with Civil War in Nineteenth-Century China*. Stanford: Stanford University Press, 2013.

Millward, James. *Beyond the Pass: Economy, Ethnicity, and Empire in Qing Central Asia, 1759-1864*. Stanford: Stanford University Press, 1998.

——. "'Coming Onto the Map': 'Western Regions' Geography and Cartographic Nomenclature in the Making of Chinese Empire in Xinjiang." *Late Imperial China* 20, no. 2 (1999): 61–98.

——. "Eastern Central Asia (Xinjiang), 1300–1800." In *The Cambridge History of Inner Asia*, edited by Nicola Di Cosmo, Allen J. Frank, and Peter B. Golden, 260–76. Cambridge: Cambridge University Press, 2009.

——. *Eurasian Crossroads: A History of Xinjiang*. New York: Columbia University Press, 2007.

Millward, James A., and Nabijan Tursun. "Political History and Strategies of Control, 1884–1976." In *Xinjiang: China's Muslim Borderland*, edited by S. Frederick Starr, 63–98. Armonk, NY: M. E. Sharpe, 2004.

Mirza Ḥaydar Dughlat. *Mirza Haydar Dughlat's Tarikh-i Rashidi: A History of the Khans of Moghulistan*. Translated by Wheeler M. Thackston. Cambridge, MA: Harvard University, Department of Near Eastern Languages and Civilizations, 1996.

Moin, A. Azfar. *The Millennial Sovereign: Sacred Kingship and Sainthood in Islam*. New York: Columbia University Press, 2012.

Morrison, Alexander. *Russian Rule in Samarkand, 1868–1910: A Comparison with British India*. Oxford: Oxford University Press, 2008.

Mosca, Matthew. "The Literati Rewriting of China in the Qianlong-Jiaqing Transition." *Late Imperial China* 32, no. 2 (December 2011): 89–132.

Mottahedeh, Roy. *Loyalty and Leadership in an Early Islamic Society*. London: I. B. Tauris, 1980.

Muhammad Gherib Shahyari, "Ishtiyaqnamä," edited by Yasin Imin. *Bulaq* 17 (1985): 217–312.

Muḥammad Taqī Bahār, ed. *Mujmal al-tāwārīkh w-al-qiṣaṣ*. Tehran: Muʾassasah-i Khāwar, 1939.

Mulla Musa Sayrami. *Tarikhi hämidi*. Translated by Änwär Baytur. Beyjing: Millätlär Näshriyati, 2008.

Musa Sayramiy. *Tarikhi Hämidiy: Yengi tärjimä nuskha*. Translated by Abdurä'op Polat Täklimakani. Istanbul: Täklimakan Uyghur näshriyati, 2019.

Musayup, Sidiq. "'Chala tongchi adäm öltürür' degän sözning kelip chiqish järyani." *Shinjang tarikh materiyalliri* 38:352–55.

Nanjiang nongcun shehui. Beijing: Minzu chubanshe, 2009.

Nāṣir al-Dīn b. Burhān al-Dīn al-Rabghūzī. *The Stories of the Prophets: Qiṣaṣ al-Anbiyā', an Eastern Turkish Version*. Edited by H. E. Boeschoten, M. van Damme, and S. Tezcan. Leiden: Brill, 1995.

Nasr, Seyyed Hossein, et al., eds. *The Study Quran: A New Translation and Commentary*. New York: HarperOne, 2015.

Neighbors, Jennifer. "Criminal Intent and Homicide Law in Qing and Republican China." PhD diss., University of California, Los Angeles, 2004.

Newby, L. J. "The Chinese Literary Conquest of Xinjiang." *Modern China* 25, no. 4 (October 1999): 451–74.

——. *The Empire and the Khanate: A Political History of Qing Relations with Khoqand c. 1760–1860*. Boston: Brill, 2005.

——. "'Us and Them' in Eighteenth and Nineteenth Century Xinjiang." In *Situating the Uyghurs Between China and Central Asia*, edited by Ildikó Bellér-Hann, Cristina Cesaro, Rachel Harris, and Joanne Smith Finley, 15–30. Aldershot, UK: Ashgate, 2007.

Ng, On-cho. "A Tension in Ch'ing Thought: 'Historicism' in Seventeenth- and Eighteenth-Century Chinese Thought." *Journal of the History of Ideas* 54, No. 4 (October 1993): 561–83.

Ng, Vivien W. "Ideology and Sexuality: Rape Laws in Qing China." *Journal of Asian Studies* 46, no. 1 (1987): 57–70.

Nichols, Robert. *The Frontier Crimes Regulation: A History in Documents*. Oxford: Oxford University Press, 2013.

Oidtmann, Max. *Forging the Golden Urn: The Qing Empire and the Politics of Reincarnation in Tibet*. New York: Columbia University Press, 2018.

Osterhammel, Jürgen. *Colonialism: A Theoretical Overview*. Princeton: Markus Wiener, 2005.

——. *The Transformation of the World: A Global History of the Nineteenth Century.* Princeton: Princeton University Press, 2014.

Park, Hyunhee. *Mapping the Chinese and Islamic Worlds: Cross-Cultural Exchange in Pre-Modern Asia.* Cambridge: Cambridge University Press, 2012.

Pazilbay, Zayit Akhun. *Iskändärnamä.* Edited by Qurban Wäli. Beyjing: Millätlär Näshriyati, 1990.

Pei Jingfu. *He hai Kunlun lu.* Shanghai: Wenming shuju, 1906 (Guangxu 32).

Perdue, Peter C. "Comparing Empires: Manchu Colonialism." *International History Review* 20, no. 2 (June 1998): 255–62.

——. "Nature and Nurture on Imperial China's Frontiers." *Modern Asian Studies* 43, no. 1 (2009): 245–67.

Pirie, Fernanda. *The Anthropology of Law.* Oxford: Oxford University Press, 2013.

Platt, Stephen. *Autumn in the Heavenly Kingdom: China, the West, and the Epic Story of the Taiping Civil War.* New York: Knopf, 2012.

——. *Provincial Patriots: The Hunanese and Modern China.* Cambridge, MA: Harvard University Press, 2007.

Porter, David. "Bannermen as Translators: Manchu Language Education in the Hanjun Banners." *Late Imperial China* 40, no. 2 (December 2019).

Poskami, Äbdullah. *Kitabi Äbdullah.* Ürümchi: Shinjang Khälq Näshriyati, 2004.

Potanin, G. N. *Ocherki severo-zapadnoi Mongolii.* St. Petersburg: Tipografiia V. Kirshbauma, 1881.

Pratt, Mary Louise. "Arts of the Contact Zone." *Profession* (1991): 33–40.

Qing shilu. Beijing: Zhonghua shuju, 1985–87.

Qiṣaṣu 'l-anbiyāʾ. Tashkent, 1899.

Qiu Yuanyou. "Taiping tianguo yu wan Qing 'jiudi zhengfa zhi zhi.'" *Jindai shi yanjiu* 1998, no. 2:31–50.

Qi Yunshi. *Xi chui zhu zhici.* Shanghai: Shanghai Guji Chubanshe, 2010.

Ramzy, Austin and Chris Buckley. "'Absolutely No Mercy': Leaked Files Expose How China Organized Mass Detentions of Muslims." *New York Times*, November 16, 2019. www.nytimes.com/interactive/2019/11/16/world/asia/china-xinjiang-documents.html.

Raquette, Gustaf. *Eastern Turki Grammar: Practical and Theoretical with Vocabulary*, vol. 1. Berlin: Reichsdruckerei, 1912.

Rashīduddīn Fażlullah. *Jamiʿu 'l-tawārīkh.* Translated by Wheeler M. Thackston. London: I. B. Tauris, 2012.

Rawski, Evelyn S. *The Last Emperors: A Social History of Qing Imperial Institutions.* Berkeley: University of California Press, 1998.

Reed, Bradley. *Talons and Teeth: County Clerks and Runners in the Qing Dynasty.* Stanford: Stanford University Press, 2000.

Rippa, Alessandro. "Re-Writing Mythology in Xinjiang: The Case of the Queen Mother of the West, King Mu and the Kunlun." *China Journal* 71 (January 2014): 43–64.

Roberts, Sean R. "The Biopolitics of China's 'War on Terror' and the Exclusion of the Uyghurs." *Critical Asian Studies* 50, no. 2 (2018): 232–58.

Roth Li, Gertraude. "State Building Before 1644." In *The Cambridge History of China*, vol. 9, pt. 1, *The Ch'ing Empire to 1800*, edited by Willard J. Peterson, 9–72. Cambridge: Cambridge University Press, 2002.

Rowe, William T. "Ancestral Rites and Political Authority in Late Imperial China: Chen Hongmou in Jiangxi." *Modern China* 24, no. 4 (October 1998): 378–407.

——. *China's Last Empire: The Great Qing.* Cambridge, MA: Belknap Press of Harvard University Press, 2009.

——. *Hankow: Commerce and Society in a Chinese City.* Stanford: Stanford University Press, 1984.

——. *Saving the World: Chen Hongmou and Elite Consciousness in Eighteenth-Century China.* Stanford: Stanford University Press, 2001.

Roxburgh, David J. "The 'Journal' of Ghiyath al-Din Naqqash, Timurid Envoy to Khan Balïgh, and Chinese Art and Architecture." In *The Power of Things and the Flow of Cultural Transformations*, edited by Lieselotte E. Saurma-Jeltsch and Anja Eisenbeiß, 90–113. Berlin: Deutscher Kunstverlag, 2010.

Said, Edward. *Culture and Imperialism.* New York: Knopf, 1994.

Sakai, Naoki. *Translation and Subjectivity: On "Japan" and Cultural Nationalism.* Minneapolis: University of Minnesota Press, 1997.

Sangren, Paul Steven. *History and Magical Power in a Chinese Community.* Stanford: Stanford University Press, 1987.

Schein, Louisa. *Minority Rules: The Miao and the Feminine in China's Cultural Politics.* Durham, NC: Duke University Press, 2000.

Schluessel, Eric T. "Cong chenghuang dao shuzu: Dingxiang Wang zai Xinjiang." *Lishi renleixue xuekan* 15, no. 2 (October 2017): 169–86.

——. "Exiled Gods: Territory, History, Empire, and a Hunanese Deity in Xinjiang." *Late Imperial China.* Forthcoming.

——. "Hiding and Revealing Pious Endowments in Late-Qing Xinjiang." *Muslim World* 108, no. 4 (December 2018): 613–29.

——. "Language and the State in Late Qing Xinjiang." In *Historiography and Nation-Building Among Turkic Populations*, edited by Birgit Schlyter and Mirja Juntunen, 145–68. Istanbul: Swedish Research Institute in Istanbul, 2014.

——. "The Law and the 'Law': Two Kinds of Legal Space in Late-Qing China." *Extrême-Orient Extrême-Occident* 40 (November 2016): 39–58.

——. "Muslims at the Yamen Gate: Translating Justice in Late-Qing Xinjiang." In *Kashgar Revisited: Uyghur Studies in Memory of Gunnar Jarring*, edited by Ildikó Bellér-Hann, Birgit Schlyter, and Jun Sugawara, 116–38. Leiden: Brill, 2016.

——. "Water, Justice, and Local Government in Turn-of-the-Century Xinjiang." *Journal of the Social and Economic History of the Orient* 62, no. 4 (December 2019): 595–621.

——. *The World as Seen from Yarkand: Ghulām Muḥammad Khān's 1920s Chronicle* Mā Tītaynïŋ wāqiʿasi. Tokyo: NIHU Program Islamic Area Studies, 2014.

Schmitt, Carl. *Political Theology: Four Chapters on the Concept of Sovereignty.* Chicago: University of Chicago Press, 2005.

Schorkowitz, Dittmar, and Ning Chia, eds. *Managing Frontiers in China: The Lifanyuan and Libu Revisited.* Leiden: Brill, 2017.

Sharqī Turkistān Ḥayāti. Kashgar, 1933–34.

Shepherd, John. *Statecraft and Political Economy on the Taiwan Frontier, 1600-1800.* Stanford: Stanford University Press, 1993.

Skrine, C. P., and Pamela Nightingale. *Macartney at Kashgar.* London: Methuen, 1973.

Smith, Anthony. *The Cultural Foundations of Nations: Hierarchy, Covenant and Republic.* Malden, MA: Blackwell, 2008.

Snyder-Reinke, Jeff. "Afterlives of the Dead: Uncovering Graves and Mishandling Corpses in Nineteenth-Century China." *Frontiers of History in China* 11, no. 1 (2016): 1–20.

Sommer, Matthew. *Polyandry and Wife-Selling in Qing Dynasty China: Survival Strategies and Judicial Interventions.* Oakland: University of California Press, 2015.

——. *Sex, Law and Society in Late Imperial China.* Stanford: Stanford University Press, 2000.

Special Correspondent. "A Summer Vacation in China's Muslim Gulag." *Foreign Policy*, February 28, 2018.

Stanley, Amy. *Selling Women: Prostitution, Markets, and the Household in Early Modern Japan.* Berkeley: University of California Press, 2012.

Steele, Brian. "Thomas Jefferson's Gender Frontier." *Journal of American History* 95, no. 1 (June 2008): 17–42.

Stoler, Ann. *Along the Archival Grain: Epistemic Anxieties and Colonial Common Sense*. Princeton: Princeton University Press, 2009.

——. *Race and the Education of Desire: Foucault's History of Sexuality and the Colonial Order of Things*. Durham, NC: Duke University Press, 1995.

——. "Rethinking Colonial Categories: European Communities and the Boundaries of Rule." *Comparative Studies in History and Society* 31, no. 1 (January 1989): 134–61.

——. "Sexual Affronts and Racial Frontiers: European Identities and the Cultural Politics of Exclusion in Colonial Southeast Asia." *Comparative Studies in Society and History* 34, no. 3 (1992): 514–51.

Struve, Lynn A. "The Early Ch'ing Legacy of Huang Tsung-hsi: A Reexamination." *Asia Major* 1, no. 1 (1988): 83–122.

——. "Huang Zongxi in Context: A Reappraisal of His Major Writings." *Journal of Asian Studies* 47, no. 3 (1988): 474–502.

Su Beihai and Jiang Jianhua. *Hami, Tulufan Weiwuer wang lishi*. Wulumuqi: Xinjiang daxue chubanshe, 1993.

Sulayman, Äsäd. "Hybrid Name Culture in Xinjiang: Problems Surrounding Uyghur Name/Surname Practices and Their Reform." In *Situating the Uyghurs Between China and Central Asia*, edited by Ildikó Bellér-Hann, Cristina Cesaro, Rachel Harris, and Joanne Smith Finley, 109–127. Aldershot, UK: Ashgate, 2007.

Sun Yingke, comp. *Qianhou ershisi xiao tushuo*. Yangzhou: Banwu tang, 1841 (Daoguang xinchou).

Susumu, Fuma. "Litigation Masters and the Litigation System of Ming and Qing China." *International Journal of Asian Studies* 4, no. 1 (January 2007): 79–111.

Sutton, Donald S. "Violence and Ethnicity on a Qing Colonial Frontier: Customary and Statutory Law in the Eighteenth-Century Miao Pale." *Modern Asian Studies* 37, no. 1 (February 2003): 41–80.

Szonyi, Michael. *The Art of Being Governed: Everyday Politics in Late Imperial China*. Princeton: Princeton University Press, 2017.

Taussig, M. T. *Mimesis and Alterity: A Particular History of the Senses*. London: Routledge, 1993.

Tazamal, Mobashra. "Chinese Islamophobia Was Made in the West." *Al Jazeera*, January 21, 2019. www.aljazeera.com/indepth/opinion/chinese-islamophobia-west -190121131831245.html.

Teng, Emma Jinhua. "Taiwan as a Living Museum: Tropes of Anachronism in Late-Imperial Chinese Travel Writing." *Harvard Journal of Asiatic Studies* 59, no. 2 (1999): 445–84.

——. *Taiwan's Imagined Geography: Chinese Colonial Travel Writing and Pictures, 1683-1895*. Cambridge, MA: Harvard University Asia Center, 2004.

Teng, Ssü-yu. *The Nien Army and Their Guerilla Warfare, 1851-1868*. Paris: Mouton, 1961.

Theaker, Hannah. "Moving Muslims: The Great Northwestern Rebellion and the Transformation of Chinese Islam, 1860–1896." PhD diss., University of Oxford, 2018.

Theiss, Janet. *Disgraceful Matters: The Politics of Chastity in Eighteenth-Century China*. Berkeley: University of California Press, 2005.

——. "Explaining the Shrew: Narratives of Spousal Violence and the Critique of Masculinity in Eighteenth-Century Criminal Cases." In *Writing and Law in Late Imperial China: Crime, Conflict, and Judgment*, edited by Robert Hegel and Katherine Carlitz, 44–63. Seattle: University of Washington Press, 2007.

Thum, Rian. "China in Islam: Turki Views from the Nineteenth and Twentieth Centuries." *Cross-Currents: East Asian History and Culture Review* 3, no. 2 (November 2014): 573–600.

———. "Modular History: Identity Maintenance Before Uyghur Nationalism." *Journal of Asian Studies* 71, no. 3 (August 2012): 627–53.

———. *The Sacred Routes of Uyghur History.* Cambridge, MA: Harvard University Press, 2014.

Törnquist, John. *Kaschgar: några bilder från innersta Asiens land, folk och mission.* Stockholm: Svenska missionsförbundets förlag, 1926.

Usmanov, K. "Molla Musa Sayrami: Ta'rikh-i amniya." In *Materialy po istorii kazakhskikh khanstv XV–XVIII vekov,* 1–15. Alma Ata: Nauka, 1969.

van Damme, M. "Rabg̲h̲ūzī." In *Encyclopaedia of Islam,* 2nd ed., edited by P. Bearman, Th. Bianquis, C. E. Bosworth, E. van Donzel, and W. P. Heinrichs. Brill Online, 2014.

Vierheller, Ernstjoachim. *Nation und Elite im Denken von Wang Fu-chih, 1619-1692.* Hamburg: Gesellschaft für Natur- und Völkerkunde Ostasiens, 1968.

von le Coq, Albert, ed. "Das Lî-Kitâbî." *Kőrösi Csoma Archivum* 1, no. 6 (1925): 439–80.

———. *Sprichwörter und Lieder aus der Gegend von Turfan mit einer dort aufgenommen Wörterliste.* Leipzig: Druck und Verlag von B. G. Teubner, 1911.

Waley-Cohen, Joanna. *Exile in Mid-Qing China: Banishment to Xinjiang, 1759-1860.* New Haven, CT: Yale University Press, 1991.

———. "The New Qing History." *Radical History Review* 88 (Winter 2004): 193–206.

Wang Dingan. *Xiangjun ji.* Jiangnan shuju, Guangxu 15 (1889).

Wang Dun. *Xiangjun shi.* Changsha: Yuelu shushe, 2014.

Wang Fuzhi. *Chuanshan quanshu.* 16 vols. Changsha: Yuelu shushe, 1988.

———. *Chuanshan yishu.* 8 vols. Beijing: Beijing chubanshe, 1999.

Wang Jianxin. *Uyghur Education and Social Order: The Role of Islamic Leadership in the Turpan Basin.* Tokyo: Institute for the Study of the Languages and Cultures of Asia and Africa, 2004.

Wang Jiping. "Lun Xiangjun jituan." *Xiangtan daxue xuebao (zhexue shehui kexue ban)* 1996, no. 6:59–63.

———. *Xiangjun jituan yu wan Qing Hunan.* Beijing: Zhongguo shehui kexue chubanshe, 2002.

Wang Penghui. "Chongjian fenghua: wan Qing Minguo qianqi Wulumuqi de miaoyu yu shehui ronghe." *Xiyu fazhan yanjiu* 2014:85–101.

Wang Shu'nan. *Taolu laoren sui nian lu.* Beijing: Zhonghua Shuju, 2007.

———. *Taolu wenji.* Taipei: Wenhai Chubanshe, 1915.

———. *Xila xue an.* n.d.

Wang Shu'nan et al., comps. *Xinjiang tuzhi.* Taipei: Wenhai chubanshe, 1965.

Wang Zhensheng. *Xi zheng riji.* 1900 (Guangxu 26).

Warren, G. G. "D'Ollone's Investigation on Chinese Moslems." *New China Review* 2 (1920): 267–86 and 398–414.

Weber, Eugen. *Peasants Into Frenchmen: The Modernization of Rural France, 1870-1914.* Stanford: Stanford University Press, 1976.

Wei Changhong, ed. *Xinhai Geming zai Xinjiang.* Wulumuqi: Xinjiang renmin chubanshe, 1981.

Wei Guangtao, *Kanding Xinjiang ji.* Harbin: Heilongjiang jiaoyu chubanshe, 2014.

Weinstein, Jodi. *Empire and Identity in Guizhou: Local Resistance to Qing Expansion.* Seattle: University of Washington Press, 2013.

Weiwuerzu shehui lishi diaocha. Beijing: Minzu chubanshe, 2009.

Wiens, Mi-Chu. "Anti-Manchu Thought During the Qing." *Papers on China* 22A (1969).

Woods, John E. *The Aqquyunlu: Clan, Confederation, Empire: A Study in 15th/9th Century Turko-Iranian Politics.* Chicago: Bibliotheca Islamica, 1976.

———. "The Rise of Timurid Historiography." *Journal of Near Eastern Studies* 46, no. 2 (1987): 81–108.

Wright, Mary Clabaugh. *The Last Stand of Chinese Conservatism: The T'ung-chih Restoration, 1862-1874.* Stanford: Stanford University Press, 1962.

Wu Aichen. *Lidai Xiyu shi chao.* Wulumuqi: Xinjiang renmin chubanshe, 2001.

Wubuli, Tailaiti, and Ailijiang Aisa, "Yijian guanyu Minguo qinian Kuche panluan de xin wenshu—'Mahemude su Ali Hezhuo panluan zhuang' yishi." *Xiyu yanjiu* 2014, no. 3, 27–49.

Wu Chucai, comp. *Gangjian yi zhi lu.* Taipei: Chengwen, 1964.

Wu Tiequn. "Qingdai Xinjiang jiansheng qianhou Yili renkou bianqian kao." *Xinjiang difang zhi* 3 (March 2009): 52–56.

Xiao Xiong. *Xijiang za shu shi.* Suzhou: Zhenxin shushe, 1895–97.

Xie Bin. *Xinjiang youji.* Lanzhou: Lanzhou guji shudian, 1990.

Xin Xia. *Shengyu shiliutiao fu lü yijie.* Reproduced in *Zhongguo lüxue wenxian, di si ji,* edited by Zhang Yifan. Beijing: Shehui kexue wenxian chubanshe, 2007.

Yang Shengxin. *Qingmo Shaan-Gan gaikuang.* Xi'an: San Qin chubanshe, 1997.

Yang Zuanxu. *Xinjiang chuyi.* Reproduced in *Xinjiang shizhi,* di 2 bu, 5:399–492. Beijing: Quanguo tushuguan wenxian suowei fuzhi zhongxin, 2003.

Yi Baisha. *Diwang chunqiu.* Shanghai: Shanghai shudian, 1991.

Yiu, Martha Cheung Pui, and Lin Wusun, eds. *An Anthology of Chinese Discourse on Translation,* vol. 1, *From Earliest Times to the Buddhist Project.* Manchester: St. Jerome, 2006.

Yixin et al., comps. *Qinding pingding Shaan Gan Xinjiang Hui fei fanglüe.* In *Qi sheng fanglüe,* vols. 833–1,154. Guangxu reign.

Yuan Dahua. *Xinjiang Yili luanshi benmo.* Taipei: Wenhai chubanshe, 1979.

Yu Zhi. *Deyi lu.* Baoshan tang, 1885.

Zarcone, Thierry. "Between Legend and History: About the 'Conversion' to Islam of Two Prominent Lamaists in the Seventeenth-Eighteenth Centuries." In *Islam and Tibet—Interactions Along the Musk Routes,* edited by Anna Akasoy, Charles Burnett, and Ronit Yoeli-Tlalim, 281–95. New York: Routledge, 2011.

Zeng Wenwu and Shen Yunlong. *Zhongguo jingying Xiyu shi.* Reproduced in Xu Zhisheng et al., comps., *Zhongguo xibu kaifa wenxian.* 1936; Beijing: Quanguo Tushuguan Wenxian Suowei Fuzhi Zhongxin, 2004.

Zhang Dajun. *Xinjiang fengbao qishi nian.* 12 vols. Taibei: Lanxi chubanshe, 1980.

Zhang Daye. *The World of a Tiny Insect: A Memoir of the Taiping Rebellion and Its Aftermath.* Translated by Xiaofei Tian. Seattle: University of Washington Press, 2013.

Zhang Jiangcai. *Tianjin Yangliuqing xiao zhi.* Reprinted in *Tianjin fengtu congshu,* 197–214. 1938; Taipei: Jinxue shuju, 1969.

Zhang, Lawrence. "Power for a Price: Office Purchase, Elite Families, and Status Maintenance in Qing China." PhD diss., Harvard University, 2010.

Zhang Shiming. "Qian-Jia shiqi gong qing wang ming qi pai xian xing chengfa zhi zhi de kuan yan zhang chi." *Nei Menggu shifan daxue xuebao (zhexue shehui kexue ban)* 39, no. 4 (July 2009): 44–58.

Zhao Weixi. *Xiangjun jituan yu Xibei Huimin da qiyi zhi shanhou yanjiu: yi Gan-Ning-Qing diqu wei zhongxin.* Shanghai: Shanghai guji chubanshe, 2013.

Zhao Yuntian. "Qingmo xinzheng qijian Xinjiang wenhua jiaoyu de fazhan." *Xiyu yanjiu* 2002, no. 2:47–55.

Zhong Guangsheng and Sun Anfu. *Xinjiang zhi gao.* 1928; Taipei: Xuesheng Shuju, 1967.

Zhou Hong. *Quntuan yu quanceng—Yangliuqing: shenshang yu shenshen de shehui.* Shanghai: Shanghai renmin chubanshe, 2008.

Zhou Mingyi, comp. *Qianzhou zhi gao.* Qianying shuyuan, 1884 (Guangxu *jiashen*).

Zito, Angela. *Of Body and Brush: Grand Sacrifice as Text/Performance in 18th-Century China.* Chicago: University of Chicago Press, 1997.

Index